Setting in Order

Setting in Order

Pastoral Praxis in Titus

T. PATRICK JENSEN

Foreword by Charles Fritts

WIPF & STOCK · Eugene, Oregon

SETTING IN ORDER
Pastoral Praxis in Titus

Copyright © 2025 T. Patrick Jensen. All rights reserved. Except for brief quotations in critical publications or reviews, no part of this book may be reproduced in any manner without prior written permission from the publisher. Write: Permissions, Wipf and Stock Publishers, 199 W. 8th Ave., Suite 3, Eugene, OR 97401.

Wipf & Stock
An Imprint of Wipf and Stock Publishers
199 W. 8th Ave., Suite 3
Eugene, OR 97401

www.wipfandstock.com

PAPERBACK ISBN: 979-8-3852-4428-7
HARDCOVER ISBN: 979-8-3852-4429-4
EBOOK ISBN: 979-8-3852-4430-0

07/28/25

Scripture quotations are taken from the New Revised Standard Version Updated Edition. Copyright © 2021 National Council of Churches of Christ in the United States of America. Used by permission. All rights reserved worldwide.

To pastors everywhere, who serve with humility and lead courageously, setting the church in order. To my wife, who, with loving affection, attunes our household/*Haustafel* to the sacred. To my children, who are to be righteous seed upon the earth interceding for the kingdom to come to earth. To future Jensens, who may take up this book and read and who, I hope, will be strangely warmed by the breath of the Holy Spirit. To my Lord and Savior, Christ, who is all in all, I dedicate this work.

Contents

Figures and Tables | ix
Foreword by Charles Fritts | xi
Acknowledgments | xiii
Introduction | 1

Chapter 1   Setting Sonship in Order | 9
Chapter 2   Setting Fatherhood in Order | 19
Chapter 3   Setting Church Roles in Order | 27
Chapter 4   Setting the Soul in Order | 38
Chapter 5   Setting in Order the Temptation for Adulation | 50
Chapter 6   Setting Elders in Order I | 62
Chapter 7   Setting Elders in Order II | 71
Chapter 8   Setting in Order Through Admonition | 84
Chapter 9   Setting in Order and Luther's Three Orders | 95
Chapter 10 Setting in Order and Trinitarian Emulation | 104
Chapter 11 Setting in Order and a New Paterfamilias | 112
Chapter 12 Setting in Order: The Wife and the Haustafel | 120
Chapter 13 Setting in Order: The Father and the Haustafel | 127
Chapter 14 Setting in Order: The Mother and the Haustafel | 134
Chapter 15 Setting in Order: The Child and the Haustafel | 146
Chapter 16 Setting in Order: The Servant and the Haustafel | 170
Chapter 17 Setting in Order: The Master and the Haustafel | 189
Chapter 18 Setting in Order: The Elderly Men and the Haustafel | 208

CONTENTS

Chapter 19 Setting in Order: The Elderly Women and the Haustafel | 218

Chapter 20 Setting in Order: The Young Women and the Haustafel | 230

Chapter 21 Setting in Order: The Young Men and the Haustafel | 266

Chapter 22 Setting in Order and Submission | 286

Chapter 23 Setting in Order and Heresy | 305

Chapter 24 Setting in Order and the Pastor's Winter | 318

Appendix A: Spiritual Dynamics Inventory | 325

Appendix B: Mark Driscoll Resignation Letter | 327

Appendix C: Liturgy for the Ordination of Elders | 329

Appendix D: Church Discipline, Restoration, and Reconciliation | 334

Appendix E: A Polity for Local Church Elders | 342

Appendix F: Martin Luther's Table of Duties | 346

Appendix G: My Genogram | 350

Appendix H: Erik Erikson's Stages of Psychosocial Development | 351

Appendix I: The Haustafel: Covenantal Relating in the Church | 352

Bibliography | 361

Scripture Index | 369

Figures and Tables

Figure 1. Titus Family Tree | 7
Figure 2. Single-Parent Homes on the Rise | 24
Figure 3. Mother-Only Households | 25
Figure 4. Disqualifications for the Priesthood | 40
Figure 5. Andrei Rublev's *The Trinity* | 107
Figure 6. Gotcha Day | 143
Figure 7. The Grasp | 144
Figure 10. My Genogram—Appendix G | 350

Table 1. Church Governance | 37
Table 2. Elder Attributes and Behavioral Correlates | 83
Table 3. Haustafel Pathos and Praxis | 111
Table 5. The Genesis-1 Peter Parallels | 259
Table 6. Theological-Emotive Potentials of Laughter | 261
Table 7. Human Dignity | 283

Foreword

WHEN I FIRST MET Patrick I was immediately impressed with his passion for Jesus and his love for the people of God. That passion and zeal have fueled his ministry both as a physician and a pastor. As I have labored together with him in the context of a local church, I have seen these same character traits motivate his ministry to the people he serves. He leads, as do all followers of Christ, by example. If he never preached a sermon or taught a lesson, his life would still be showing the way for others to follow. That same passion and zeal has motivated him to cast an even wider net by sharing his heart through his writing, including what follows in this book.

Setting things in order that are lacking within the context of a local church is no easy task. It was not easy for Paul and Titus in the first Century, and it is not easy for those called to that ministry in the twenty-first Century. We live in a broken world filled with broken people. Although there are two thousand years between where I sit today and where Titus sat when he received his letter from the apostle Paul; although we are in a different culture, on different continents, speaking different languages; although so much has changed in the world that surrounds us, the human heart remains the same. The same basic needs have not changed at all.

Having served as a lead or senior pastor for over thirty-six years, I have wrestled with the issues and questions that Patrick lifts up in this book. I know what it is to be sent by the Lord to a church that is hurting, broken, and disordered with a mandate to restore, renew, and revive, and I have witnessed the manifold grace of God at work as he brings healing and life to that which was dying or already dead. But that work of restoration and renewal is never really completed. Servant leaders move on, sent by the Lord to other hurting and broken people and places. What has been set in order can and does fall back into disorder very quickly. People are frail—all of us, including pastors and leaders, are prone to wander.

FOREWORD

There is a very real enemy that never sleeps and never stops trying to steal and kill and destroy. No wonder so many pastors and leaders deal with discouragement and disillusionment.

The Japanese have a brilliant philosophy called wabi-sabi. It centers on the transience and imperfection of art, but it is true of all of life. It has three basic tenets: Nothing lasts. Nothing is finished. Nothing is perfect. You may see this as a dismal worldview, but I see it as an honest attempt to embrace life as it really is, not as we want it to be. Jesus understood this paradoxical complexity when he walked this earth. He was able to move in the power of God to do miracles and signs and wonders and yet at the same time know that the Roman Empire hovered over him in lethal power. Yes—nothing lasts in this world, nothing is ever finished in this world, and nothing is perfect in this world. But our hope is not found in this world. Our hope is in God and his word.

That is why Patrick's work here is so important. His aim is to better equip the men and women of God who have been called to face these challenging times, challenging places, and challenging people, those who are sent to make the crooked straight. He cries out for elders, spiritual fathers and mothers, who are desperately needed for this process. He calls for troublemakers like Elijah to confront the systems that bring disorder. He reminds us that every spiritual father needs a son in the faith, and every son in the faith needs a spiritual father. He warns with words of grace to guard our own hearts with integrity before God. The broken are used by God to mend the broken.

He attempts to present this reflection on Paul's Letter to Titus with faithful scholarship toward the scriptural text and real-world application for the pastor of a local church in our modern world. In my view, he succeeds in being both prophetic and practical, which is evidence of the Holy Spirit at work. My prayer is that the Lord will use this work to raise up a mighty army of fathers and mothers, sons and daughters, willing to face the hopelessness that surrounds them with hope. "Those from among you shall build the old waste places; you shall raise up the foundations of many generations; and you shall be called the Repairer of the Breach, the Restorer of Streets to Dwell In" (Isa 58:12 NKJV).

Charles Fritts
Senior Pastor
Sixth Avenue Church of God

Acknowledgments

THIS WORK WOULD NOT be possible without the many faithful friends and acquaintances who have labored on its behalf. I want to thank Jesus for our early morning meetings contemplating theological notions and motifs. I would like to thank Pastor Charles Fritts for contributing the foreword. I want to thank pastors everywhere, who I am convinced have one of the most difficult tasks among society. I want to thank all the editing staff at Wipf & Stock, who painstakingly reviewed each word, punctuation mark, footnote, jot, and tittle to ensure a scholarly presentation. I would like to thank my family, who teach me every day that God's household begins with our immediate family; it is the rich laboratory where God's grace transforms our souls. Finally, I would like to thank you, readers, for taking seriously the task of setting the church in order.

Introduction

PASTOR AS PUBLIC NUISANCE

TITUS, A GENTILE CALLED to pastor and journey with Paul, the Jew. He was likely a Macedonian who may have been led to Christ by Paul himself (see Gal 2:3 and Titus 1:4). What if his conversion was the result of Paul's obedience to the Macedonian vision (see Acts 16:6–10)? Paul was forbidden to preach the gospel by the Holy Spirit in places where he sought to do that very thing. It was the Holy Spirit who had a particular location for Paul to preach. Could this still be in operation today? Is the Holy Spirit forbidding pastors to preach in some places so that they will be in a posture to receive a vision of another? Is it possible that a Titus awaits those who need to hear the gospel and thus be forever changed? Titus would not only find Christ but become a trusted and sought-out companion among Paul's missionary and solitary journeys. Titus would come to pastor some of the hardest soil when coming to Crete. Titus would receive a letter that has been included in the canon of Scripture that is an aid to pastors of all generations. However, it may have begun with a closed door.

Pastors, where there are closed doors, there is a vision awaiting. Where there are divine stops, there is a voice calling for you to come and preach. Where you are hedged in, it is for the purpose of a Titus that needs an encounter in the word that God will enable you to utter. Let us, therefore, envisage closed doors as an open vision, being forbidden as divine opportunity for a place and a person appointed for revelation.

Apparently, Paul had grown in his own audacity to shake the yoke of criticism that undoubtedly would come from the Jewish proselytes and literalists who would demand Titus's circumcision upon conversion.

Where Paul encouraged Timothy to undergo circumcision to prevent such backlash from the Jewish community, he forbade Titus the act of circumcision. Perhaps this was the very opportunity the Spirit of the Lord would take in formulating a type and kind of spiritual circumcision of the heart. Paul would go on to write on the juxtaposition of a lawful circumcision without true freedom, contrasted with an inner circumcision that begets true freedom. He refuses to conform as Titus becomes a prophetic symbol of the freedom of Christ in and through the Holy Spirit (see Gal 2:1–5).

The cross had leveled all disparities. There were no inferior races, no second-class citizens, no Greek, no slave, no male, no female, no distinction of persons, no marginalized, no oppressed, no haves and have nots, no privileged, no lacking. Indeed, the person and work of Jesus Christ has secured access to the Father regardless of circumcision. Rather, it is circumcision of the heart, namely altogether utter faith that propels one into the divine community.

Paul had grown. And the pastor grows as one who may be desperately longing to fit into his own congregation, tempted to conform to a type of circumcision. But rather, with great audacity from the Spirit, he gathers the sheep to go deeper into Christ, deeper into freedom, deeper into intimacy, and deeper into joy! The codifying of behavior is insufficient, the outward marks of belonging will not stand the test of time. No, the sheep require the circumcision of the heart, the cutting away with the knife of God the idols that bemoan of captivity. The pastor must take the church out of Egypt, through the wilderness, into the promised land of Canaan, into the Sabbath rest of God and the realm of faith (see Heb 3:19)!

A few with influence from the church attempted to dissuade Pastor Scott from the type of preaching that burned like a fire in his bones. He was tempted to conform to these calls of preference from those who would then go on to mischaracterize his words. During a business meeting, a board member stated that Pastor Scott sought the church's destruction and quoted one of his sermons as cause to believe the same. The board member made mention of a quote from A. B. Simpson on the sense that God annihilates for the purpose of redeeming and charged Pastor Scott with proof that he wanted the church destroyed.

Further explication is thus warranted here. A. B. Simpson was giving his testimony on seminal moments in his life that compelled him deeper into Christ and further into the work of the kingdom. These were experiences of sanctification and also some crisis moments of spiritual awakening. Simpson was amid one such spiritual crisis when he communed with an old friend who provided a provocative response to Simpson's cry for guidance and comfort. His reply was, "All you need in order to bring you into the blessing you are seeking, and to make your life a power for God, is to be annihilated."[1]

Shocking as it was, it would hold a prophetic significance for Simpson, who would go on in his ministry to call people to this kind of self-annihilation in his preaching on holiness. The glory of the resurrection indeed follows the fellowship of suffering and the bearing of a cross (see Phil 3:10). Pastor Scott's intent was to call the people to the same—a life of cross bearing to be a vessel of resurrection glory and power. However, like many provocative statements, they can be misconstrued, which was the lamentable case here. Indeed, Jesus was accused of destroying the temple as well when referring to his own body (see John 2:19).

But prophetic literature almost necessitates misunderstandings from those with a religious preponderance and the vehicle of such misunderstandings must also be subjected to criticisms. For it is the inevitable role that provides momentum to the message. As A. G. Gardiner has rightly asserted,

> When a prophet is deified, his message is lost. The prophet is only useful so long as he is stoned as a public nuisance, calling us to repentance, disturbing our comfortable routines, breaking our respectable idols, shattering our sacred conventions.[2]

Indeed, this is what Paul is doing in resisting the perceived solitary method of circumcision. He espouses a wholly different mechanism of circumcision, that of the heart. He has witnessed the transformation in his spiritual son, Titus, and thus sees no need for the perfunctory measure of outward conformation. Indeed, Titus becomes an illustration for Paul to begin prophesying that Jesus has come to mark a person in a way that circumcision could never muster. His Epistle to the Galatians becomes a homily and polemic that this respectable practice is now redeemed by our Christ, who is now the only author of true circumcision vis-à-vis the Holy Spirit. Where Paul became concerned with criticism concerning Timothy, he no longer fears being a public nuisance and thus will not compel Titus to be circumcised. If Timothy was circumcised as a

---

1. Simpson, "A Personal Testimony," 11.
2. A. G. Gardiner is cited in Wallis, *In the Day of Thy Power*, 92.

pastor who longs to be accepted, Titus was not as a prophet and seer who can envision a wholly different way for the sheep to follow. As reiterated by Ravenhill for emphasis, the prophet is

> ordained by God but disdained by men. The degree of his effectiveness is determined by his measure of unpopularity. Compromise is not known to him. He marches to a different drummer! He is a seer who comes to lead the blind. He is a scourge to the nation before He is scourged by the nation.[3]

For the prophet pastor, the tenure may not be long until the religious of the congregation begin to throw stones and ask for his or her departure. The message of repentance and the smashing of idols is palatable for only so long. For the pastor who operates in such a way, he must prepare for criticism. One should not be surprised when accusations, coups, angry mobs, or riotous acts emerge in the context of preaching repentance.

So, Pastor Scott must own that God has called him to a ministry of John the Baptist—to preach repentance in the wilderness. He is a preacher on a mission to speak of repentance, conviction of sin, holiness, and genuine revival birthed upon the altars of our own tears. This is in preparation for the second parousia of Jesus Christ whose appearance draws near. But where there are John the Baptists, there are certainly Herods that will also rise to confront these prophets and even imprison their message if possible.

Pastor Scott was asked by one of his board members to change his messages. He was asked to do more to make comfortable those who allegedly were departing because of his messages. Of course, this could not be confirmed, but the weight of this criticism would shackle his heart and consign him to the depth of insecurity for a time. My charge to you as pastors, do not change your message if God is burning it within your soul, rather speak more fervently. If you are cast away from the shores of a congregation, know that Jesus was as well. With each stone cast your way, greater audacity is the fruit. Paul grows in the prophetic from Timothy to Titus, such can be the case for prophet-pastor as well.

---

3. Leonard Ravenhill is cited in Brown, *Real Kosher Jesus*, 46.

INTRODUCTION

SETTING A FAMILY IN ORDER

From Paul we turn to Titus, the semblance and prophetic picture of upending the convention. Titus met considerable resistance when attempting to organize the churches in Crete. Titus had been with Paul during the evangelistic efforts in Crete. He doubtless witnessed countless come to Christ in supernatural fashion. Many now belonged to Christ, but without any true leader or shepherd. Paul was unable to stay, for other missions compelled him away. However, Titus would remain as the shepherd to bring order, clarity, and teaching to the fledgling churches in Crete. To understand Titus's formidable task, listen to Paul's description: "There are also many rebellious people, idle talkers and deceivers, especially those of the circumcision" (Titus 1:10).

And there remain many today who despise authority and actively undermine godly leadership in the name of independence. Notice that it is those of the circumcision who may have been the Judaizers of the day, yoking a religious code to the fledgling congregations. Those who oppose pastors are often religious. There are those who gossip, deceive, falsely accuse, and go to any extent to disparage the character of the pastor and shepherd appointed for organization. As any shepherd can convey, once boundaries are placed on the sheep, there will no doubt be some pushing back on these boundaries. The Epistle to Titus is Paul's encouragement to face head on the confrontation arising within the Jewish sect of these congregations. Titus must persist in organizing the church with bodies of elders for church governance. Again, Titus is instructed to appoint elders, there was no instruction to hold elections. Pastors, let this be another sign of confirmation that God has given you authority to appoint elders in your local congregation. God will guide you and enable you to inspect the fruit of the sheep. Paul would also instruct Titus to be selective in what battles to fight. Titus was not to engage in every conflict that would come to him but would discern the imperative ones and thus invest his time and spiritual wisdom in those disputations (see Titus 3:9).

We cannot overlook Paul's request to Timothy that he come to him at Nicopolis, for Paul is determined to winter there (see Titus 3:12). It is that Paul desires company. He does not want to winter there alone. When winter comes seek out a Titus to visit with you. Winter can be a lonely season, but also a beautiful one. Titus can reveal beauty even in a Roman prison, or the honor of a pending martyrdom (in Paul's case), or the comfort of an understanding heart and kindred spirit. The cup of

Setting in Order

cold water is still as refreshing in the winter as it is in the summer (Matt 10:42).

Indeed, it is possible that Paul is writing this letter to Titus while at Nicapolis sometime between his first and second imprisonments in Rome (see Titus 3:12). I have chosen the theme of setting in order as the tone for the letter as Paul's first charge (Titus 1:5). Titus is to set in order through sound doctrine, the appointment of elders, honoring and obedience to authority, and committing to good works. The outline below may be helpful for us as we proceed with this journey of setting in order.

A. Setting in Order by Installing a Son (1:1–4)

B. Setting in Order by Appointing Elders (1:5–16)

    i. Qualifications for Elders (1:5–9)

    ii. Function of Elders to Rebuke (1:10–16)

C. Setting in Order in the *Haustafel* (2:1–15)

    i. Ordering the Elderly Men (2:1–2)

    ii. Ordering the Elderly Women (2:3)

    iii. Ordering the Young Women (2:4–5)

    iv. Ordering the Young Men (2:6–8)

    v. Ordering the Servant (2:9–10)

    vi. Ordering All (2:11–15)

D. Setting in Order by Submission to Authority (3:1–11)

    i. Submission from Mercy (3:1–7)

    ii. Submission Through Good Works (3:8–11)

E. Setting in Order and A Pastor's Winter and Invitation to a Son (3:12–15)

And so, we begin Paul's Letter to Titus and instructions for Titus to order the household of faith. As you can see, for Titus to speak into the *Haustafel*,[4] he must first embed himself in one. The inclusion that marks

---

4. The term *Haustafel* is attributed to Martin Luther and rendered as "house table." Luther would codify house rules with this term, asserting that each family member had a certain code of ethics whereby behaviors are determined, and this was known as a House Code. See Lovik, "Look at the Ancient House Codes," 49–50.

the book is one that illustrates Paul as father and Titus as son. Indeed, I do wonder if Titus was able to set the church in order in part because he had the endorsement of his spiritual father. The churches in Crete may have been more amenable to instruction with this kind of transactional authority. Whenever pastors go to a church and either the previous pastor or the regional/state overseer or supervisor do not provide a hearty endorsement, there begins an opposition that may be difficult to quell. The structure of Titus speaks to the nature and necessity of having a father in the faith to aid the pastor in setting the Haustafel in order and subsequently the church in order. May we learn the lessons it speaks so that we may emulate its pattern and as pastors or church leaders contribute to the godly ordering of our own household of faith.

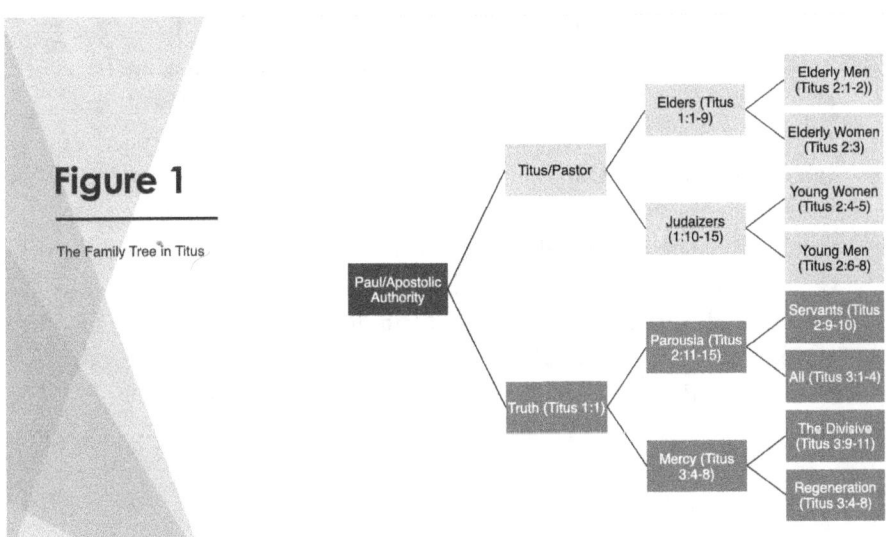

Figure 1. Titus Family Tree

A helpful schematic in figure 1 illustrates for us a kind of family tree inherent in Titus's task. This would be a more novel structure for Titus where we see the apostolic founder of the church commissioned by Christ (see Titus 1:1-3) and his spiritual progeny Titus, a son (Titus 1:4). Titus inherits relationships that he is to steward within the church including elders (Titus 1:5-9), elderly men (Titus 2:1-2), young men (Titus 2:6-8), elderly women (Titus 2:3), young women (Titus 2:4-5), and servants (Titus 2:9-10). Paul is keen to include those who are disruptive as well. The Judaizers are to be rebuked and silenced although Paul falls short in calling for their expulsion (see Titus 1:10–16). However, he does call for the rejection of divisive people which may imply an early kind of admonition leading to disfellowship (see Titus 3:10–11).

We should also note that there are spiritual dynamics that Paul seeks for Titus to integrate into the relational dynamics of the churches of Crete. These include truth (Titus 1:1), admonition (Titus 1:11,13), grace (Titus 2:11), righteousness (Titus 2:12), parousia (Titus 2:13), mercy (Titus 3:5), regeneration (Titus 3:5), and rejection (Titus 3:10). These are the inherent spiritual dynamics, the intangible way of relating that Paul calls to be present in and among the church. Indeed, a pastor can take an inventory and ask himself, Are these spiritual dynamics present in the church right now? Do we see the fruit of each dynamic in how we relate to one another? Please see appendix A where an inventory has been constructed for this kind of spiritual reflection. Chances are, in our current culture, admonition and rejection are likely diminished as we have moved away from church discipline because of how emotionally difficult it can be. However, one may also find that, if honest, some aspects of righteousness and an emphasis on the parousia of Christ have also been neglected in the body.

Thus, we now begin a journey where we will envision the Letter to Titus as a treatise to a pastor navigating a family tree. We will engage with thinkers both ancient and contemporary in this journey and hope to understand our own families of origin as we faithfully attempt to undertake the task of leading these families toward the celestial family.

Chapter 1

Setting Sonship in Order

> To Titus, my true child in the faith we share: Grace and peace from God the Father and Christ Jesus our Savior.
>
> Titus 1:4

PAUL INTRODUCES HIMSELF TO Titus with a typical greeting. He describes himself as a servant and apostle of Jesus Christ. This will be important as Titus will be an extension of apostolic authority for the churches in Crete. The apostolic ordination was through election in truth. Paul uses the word ἐκλεκτός (ek-lek-tos') which is to be chosen or elected. It intimates a preference or a choice among many.[1] The word is given greater nuance in Matthew's Gospel where Christ creates a distinction between the called and chosen when he says, "So the last will be first, and the first will be last. For many are called, but few chosen" (Matt 20:16).[2]

ELECTION

The nuance of ἐκλεκτός here is a distinction between the contract workers and the noncontract workers. It is a distinction between the last and first. The chosen are the ones who accept by faith from the hand of God without requiring a certain contract before laboring. The chosen are the

---

1. Zodhiates and Baker, *Hebrew-Greek Key Word*, 1712.
2. Of note, the latter half of this verse is in the footnotes of the NRSVUE with the inscription that some ancient manuscripts include it.

ones who are last. The call is issued out for all, but those who become last, who become the appointed ones do not require anything but God's decree. And so it is with Paul. He has already described himself as a servant. He has not required that God give him certain terms for his labor or a contract that guarantees his security. In this way, he is the ἐκλεκτός, chosen by God to be an apostle. And rather than being esteemed, this is a work that condescends. Paul has come at the eleventh hour, much later than the previous apostles and yet his reward is the same. He has the promise of eternal life and believes God is and will do right by him as a laborer in the vineyard. He was in the marketplace, standing without true kingdom work. He encountered Christ on his way to Damascus and was enlisted as a worker in the kingdom without terms of agreement. He was appointed of God, not of any institution or man. It was not the synagogue or the fledging church that conferred the office of apostle, but God himself. The ἐκλεκτός provide a trusting yes to God's call. The hired servants seek conditions for their work.

We find our Lord employing this term again in Luke's Gospel when he says, "And will not God grant justice to his chosen ones who cry to him day and night? Will he delay long in helping them?" (Luke 18:7).

And here the context is a parable of an importunate widow. She is the elect by virtue of her consistency in prayer and belief in the efficacy of her appeal. The ἐκλεκτός here are characterized by constant appeal to God. There is also a suggestion that the ἐκλεκτός are to be people of faith as the inquiry is extended from the promise. This inquiry is whether the Son of Man will find faith upon the earth with the advent of the second parousia. Thus, the ἐκλεκτός are importunate in prayer and full of faith in Christ. Prayer and faithfulness are illustrated by the ἐκλεκτός who endure great pains because of God's great mercy upon the earth.

Paul writes with the hope of eternal life as a backdrop (Titus 1:2). Indeed, if he does not have this hope, he is a man most miserable. It is the hope that enables him to endure abject persecution, imprisonments, stripes, and rejection. Eternal life is the energizing sentiment that compels him to write, to preach, and to travel. He is currently at liberty to travel, implying that he has not yet been imprisoned. This is implied as he can winter in Nicopolis and asks that Titus join him there (see Titus 3:12). Thus, the tone of Titus may be somewhat distinct from the tone in his Epistles to Timothy. He writes from a platform of freedom to Titus, and imprisonment and pending death to Timothy. His authority was under suspicion at Ephesus, but less so at Crete.

Nonetheless, he establishes his authority as an apostle early in his introduction to Titus. His authority, persistence, and ministry hinges upon his hope of eternal life. Pastors, when setting in order a church venturing from the way, return to your own hope of eternal life. It just might be the necessitating disposition that will aid in your setting in order recalcitrant communities who are "unruly, vain talkers, and deceivers" (Titus 1:10). And although much more can be said of hope, this is not our aim. Rather, I would like to emphasize Paul's claim upon Titus as his "own son."

TITUS AS PAUL'S SPIRITUAL SON

Paul has asserted that preaching has been "revealed" to him—that is, the word of God is being channeled through Paul. The object of his preaching in this context is Crete. This assertion of apostleship and the manifestation of preaching he now hopes to confer to Titus as his own extension of ministry at Crete. By establishing a father-son relationship he has created a context of intimacy, yes, but also of authority. It is an emulation of the Father-Son dyad of heaven where the Father sends the Son to rescue humanity. The Father confers all authority to the Son. In this instance, Paul is recapitulating this dyadic relationship and establishing for Crete that Titus is his spiritual son and that his preaching and authority are being conferred to Titus for the purpose of setting in order the churches of Crete. Prior to charging Titus with the command to set in order, Paul is intentional to establish his own credentials and authority and then create a context for transferability. That is, Titus has this authority because he is Paul's son. He is loved by Paul, he is trusted by Paul, he has been chosen by Paul. By creating a context of intimacy, authority is born. By drawing Titus close, he can be sent. By publicly affirming his status as son, Titus can now begin to lead in the name of Christ, the one who Paul preaches.

Indeed, Titus begins with establishing this father-son dyad, but also ends with a reference to this relationship completing an *inclusio* in Titus. Where the charge is explicated in the context of intimacy at the outset, the invitation to commune with Paul is then rendered to complete the epistle. It is as if Paul longs to spend time with Titus to affirm his work and to affirm his relational status once more.

And so, who was Titus, and how did such an intimate relationship form between the two? We find a reference to Titus in Paul's Epistle to the Corinthians: "But my mind could not rest because I did not find my brother Titus there. So I said farewell to them and went on to Macedonia" (2 Cor 2:13).

Paul had come to Troas to preach Christ because of an open door. However, he was restless without peace of mind. He could not settle into his ministry at Troas because he could not find Titus. He longed for Titus to accompany him in the preaching of the gospel. In some way, unexplained by Paul, Titus provided a type of anchor or rest that may have satisfied a longing and brought Paul emotional rest to remain in Troas. But without Titus, he departed to Macedonia.

Now trouble seemed to follow Paul, for he comments later in 2 Cor 7 that he had no rest while in Macedonia as well. Perhaps he would have left there as well if not for Titus. Perhaps Paul would have been restless whether by fears or disappointment, departing yet again for a place that would receive him. But we have a comment by Paul regarding Titus as an advocate and comfort. Indeed, he comes with a message of affirmation—an often-forgotten sentiment. Listen to Paul's description here:

> For even when we came into Macedonia, our flesh had no rest, but we were afflicted in every way—disputes without and fears within. But God, who consoles the downcast, consoled us by the arrival of Titus, and not only by his arrival but also by the consolation with which he was consoled about you, as he told us of your longing, your mourning, your zeal for me, so that I rejoiced still more. (2 Cor 7:5-7)

Paul describes the trouble as outward conflicts and inward fears. Both components serve as a recipe for restlessness. Many a minister is chased away by these two forces. The visible conflict is often beyond the control of a minister—it is an inevitable component of preaching. The external conflict pummels the pastor like waves that beat down the residue of a cliff. The inner fear is perhaps fear of rejection, fear of life or limb, fear that posterity is being threatened, fear of a destroyed reputation, fear of failing the Lord or the community of faith. Fear commingled with conflict are two vices that can create context for restlessness. And yet, it is as if a rescue has been hatched. In this case, the rescue is God bringing comfort through Titus to Paul. The comfort began when the Macedonians received and comforted Titus. Titus acts as a herald to communicate that Paul's ministry was not without fruit. Indeed, many in Macedonia weep for Paul, love him dearly, and long for his communion. This report may have settled Paul so that he would remain for a little while longer to preach the gospel and make disciples. Who knows if Paul would have stayed in Macedonia without Titus. Could it be, then, that the son in the father-son dyad brings a sense of comfort to the aged spiritual father whose cup, filled with criticism and rejection, can find consolation in the affirmation of his son? Titus was a son who brought consolation and who may have acted as a catalyst for Paul to the Corinthian churches.

Moreover, Titus is mentioned once again in the same chapter concerning the way he was received by the Macedonians:

> In this we have found consolation. In addition to our own consolation, we rejoiced still more at the joy of Titus, because his mind has been set at rest by all of you. For if I have been somewhat boastful about you to him, I was not put to shame, but just as everything we said to you was true, so our boasting to Titus has proved true as well. And his heart goes out all the more to you, as he remembers the obedience of all of you and how you welcomed him with fear and trembling. I rejoice because I have complete confidence in you. (2 Cor 7:13–16)

Titus was not only received by the Macedonians but refreshed by being with them in Christ. This reception confirms Paul's confidence in the Corinthians church to obey, receive, love, and refresh those who come in the name of Christ. This welcoming reception is a kind of outcome that the gospel is taking hold in Macedonia and that Paul's spiritual son is taking up the mantle Paul is passing. Paul rejoices that his son was received, that his son was accepted and refreshed. His boasts of the church are in direct correlation to their treatment of Titus. The father longs for his son to be received and to carry the legacy of the work. Perhaps this also deposited a seed in Paul to later trust Titus with the work in Crete.

Perhaps this was Titus's first ministry post, for Paul also describes a work begun by Titus that he longed to be complete in grace (see 2 Cor 8:6). Paul would go on to affirm Titus's earnest desire to be with the Macedonians and minister among them (see 2 Cor 8:16). He was exhorted and requested to come to the Corinthians, but also expressed a sincere longing to come as well. Paul notes the following: "But thanks be to God, who put in the heart of Titus the same eagerness for you that I myself have" (2 Cor 8:16).

Paul finishes chapter 8 of 2 Corinthians with a declaration of Titus's status: "As for Titus, he is my partner and coworker in your service" (v. 23). Just as the Macedonians received Paul, he urges that they receive Titus. Titus and Paul are equivalent in this regard as this is emphasized by dual adjectives—partner and coworker. The spiritual father advocates on behalf of the son providing a status and place that is equivalent to his own. The son is a son but also a partner. He is a worker that joins the father in completing the work of the Lord.

This is also emphasized in Titus when Paul describes the faith as "common" (Titus 1:4). Both Titus and Paul have access to this faith and gospel. This therefore begs the question, Do we have spiritual fathers in the church today? Do we have spiritual fathers commending their sons to the church? Do we have spiritual fathers working side by side with their sons in the work of the ministry? Do we have spiritual fathers who send and exhort their sons to mission posts? Do we have spiritual fathers sending letters to ministry posts exercising authority that these ministry posts would receive and accept the ministry of their son as they would if he were present?

I would argue that we have largely created a culture of commerce in the church where CEOs preside over organizational plans and are largely threatened by spiritual sons and daughters. I would argue that there is very little intentionality to invest in a spiritual son or daughter and commend him or her to ministry by advocating for them and bringing them close to the side of the father who is laboring. I would argue that we have created a Hezekiah generation where the shortsighted comments resound even today: "At least it will be fine during my tenure." There is no weeping for the pain of the next generation, no passing of the baton unless necessary and, even in this, without the intentionality of investment. Now, with this being said, I know these statements cannot be generalized as there are exceptions with some churches sincerely investing in spiritual sons and daughters and commending them to certain works alongside the fathers of the faith and abroad.

WHERE ARE THE SPIRITUAL FATHERS?

Pastor Preston was taking his first ministry post after serving the church in various capacities for several years. The prior pastor had resigned abruptly, sending shock waves throughout the church. The previous pastor had commended Pastor Preston some two years earlier by sharing his plan to hire Pastor Preston as an associate pastor and then retire so that Pastor Preston could inherit the work and pastor the church.

However, Pastor Preston was unable to accept the hire at the time as he was required to work out of state. After two years and an announcement of the pastor's retirement, Pastor Preston was encouraged to apply by some prior laborers at the church. Once Pastor Preston arrived, he hoped to establish a father-son relationship with the previous pastor. However, after a few meetings with the previous pastor, he left these meetings feeling shame. The shame was after recurrent comments that the church was not doing enough to evangelize the community and that the church would die if personal witnessing did not become the main thrust of its mission. Although he agreed that the church needed a missional zeal, Pastor Preston had questions about the staff, church discipline, navigating those who would undermine authority, and so on. The answers never came as, each time Pastor Preston met with the previous pastor, he left feeling ashamed by his own personal lack of apparent zeal for personal witnessing.

Moreover, the previous pastor did not publicly commend Pastor Preston to the congregation as Paul does for both Timothy and Titus. There was likely disappointment in Pastor Preston when attempts were made to enable others to participate with greater responsibility in the mission trips abroad. Perhaps this was perceived as attempts to take away the role the previous pastor was playing in these mission trips. There was no mantle transferred to Pastor Preston, no verbal affirmation, no commendation, and no call for the congregation to honor and follow Pastor Preston as a shepherd.

Pastors who are retiring would do well to have a mantle service where the mantle of pastor is transferred to the new pastor with public commendation. Elijah was a father to Elisha and throws his mantle over Elisha essentially commending him as the prophet for the next generation. We have so few spiritual fathers commending their successors in the faith. O how we need this in congregational life as many sheep become convinced by wolves to defy the new shepherd! The prior pastor's commendation may act as a tool to mitigate such defiance by prayerful affirmation. This prophetic act could also encourage the new pastor to endure hardship as the spiritual father advocates for his son or daughter.

There are two high profile churches that have, in recent years, filled the pastoral occupancy. These two churches have had vacancies under disparate circumstances. Willow Creek Church had navigated a scandal where the previous pastor Bill Hybels was accused of sexual impropriety and thus was unable to commend the new pastor as a vacuum of leadership was left in the wake of his resignation. The previous pastor of Moody Church retired and is filling what appears to be a pastor emeritus position. I wonder if Erwin Lutzer, previous pastor of Moody Church, is commending in a public forum the new pastor, and I wonder how the new pastor of Willow Creek is navigating leadership where there is no public commendation from the previous pastor. We have some evidence that Pastor Lutzer is commending and advocating for Pastor Miller as Moody has released the following statement from pastor Lutzer:

> Let me be among the first to congratulate Philip Miller on being called as the new Senior Pastor of The Moody Church!
>
> I am pleased that after years of prayer and waiting, God has brought him to us. When he and I met some time ago, I sensed that he was the man of God we had been waiting for. He has my complete support and blessing and I look forward to doing all that I can to make his ministry at The Moody Church successful!
>
> Rebecca joins me in celebrating this important moment. We are excited as The Moody Church embarks on a new future.[3]

We also receive a glimpse of Pastor Miller's gracious experience with spiritual fatherhood when he comments on his previous pastorate in the following manner: "While we made mistakes along the way, the strength of the transition came down to the personal relationship between Pastor Lee and myself."[4]

In contrast, I was unable to find a statement from Willow Creek, either from senior leaders or the church board/elders affirming the new pastor. This does not mean that it did not exist but certainly remains inconspicuous. Both men will have the task of ordering the church, and perhaps with a new vision from the Lord. However, I wonder how both experiences will compare with one another. I also wonder if a father-son relationship creates a path in the wilderness where setting the church in order is more feasible without the loneliness implied when the arrows start flying.

Titus was a son to Paul who walked in the same spirit and in the same steps (see 2 Cor 12:18). Paul commends Titus to Corinth with this affirmation that stipulates that the father-son dyad is one of spiritual

---

3. Moody Church, "Meet Our Senior Pastor," paras. 3–5.
4. Moody Church, "Meet Our Senior Pastor," para. 19.

alignment. Titus can set in order because he represents Paul and, more importantly, he represents the Christ of Paul. Paul did not require circumcision of Titus, defending Titus has he became a tangible illustration of the gospel's power to circumcise the heart (see Gal 2:3). The father defends the son or daughter and protects him or her from oppressive codes that legitimize human anxiety for control. Titus will set in order not as one who requires oppressive regimes, but as one who has been freed from them.

We have already explored the use of τέκνον (tek'-non), for Paul has also referred to Timothy with this term of endearment.[5] It does bear remembering that this term denotes a kind of birth or begetting.[6] The relationship is earthy, one that intimates a child in reference to his or her mother or father. It is quite distinct from the *Huios* designation given to Christ, who is the only begotten of the Father and who is distinctly the Son of God (see Matt 1:21, 23, 25; Luke 1:31; 2:7).

The child of God and, in terms of our assertion here, the child of spiritual fathers or mothers is given the more corporeal designation τέκνον. Paul uses an adjective to describe his fatherhood of Timothy when he says γνήσιος τέκνῳ, which confers a sense that Timothy was genuine, true, and legitimate. Paul's identity as father to Timothy is a spiritual jurisdiction over his biological lineage. That is, Jewish law would exclude Timothy from Jewish community secondary to his gentile father. But Paul's claim over Timothy as father brings a sense of genuine inclusion, overcoming this biological propensity. Spiritual lineage overcomes biological lineage.[7]

Paul would employ a term of endearment for Timothy in the second Epistle to him where he describes Timothy as ἀγαπητό τέκνῳ, which is to say, "my beloved son" (2 Tim 1:2). Paul would also employ the term γνήσιος for Titus which co-opts him from his gentile lineage and brings him into a spiritual lineage of the faith. Indeed, Paul would clarify this kind of grafting when he adds the caveat, "in the faith we share" (Titus 1:4). The term γνήσιος is Paul's signature of legitimacy. Timothy and Titus are not illegitimate sons as Jewish code may imply, but genuine sons of the faith in Christ who become the ones who will carry the legacy of

---

5. A discussion on τέκνον can be found in my book *Legacy: Pastoral Praxis of 2 Timothy*, published by Wipf and Stock in January of 2024.

6. Zodhiates and Baker, *Hebrew-Greek Key Word*, 1761.

7. Rogers and Rogers, *New Linguistic and Exegetical Key*, 487.

the gospel in the authority of Paul who has received an apostolic charge from Christ himself.

Thus, I would like to explore the need for spiritual fathers in a modern era where there is great paucity of these father-son dyads. Therefore, I am calling for a reemergence of this relational phenomenon in the church as a prescription to preserve the posterity of the community and the extension of holy authority and call. I would like to furthermore explore the homilies of John Chrysostom to explicate further the import of spiritual fatherhood and motherhood in the church. These homilies direct us to a certain ordering of the soul that is required before taking up either the mantle of spiritual father or son.

Chapter 2

Setting Fatherhood in Order

To Titus, my true child in the faith.

TITUS 1:4

LET US BEGIN WITH Chrysostom's story, which is a tale of initial tragedy that became quite formative. John's father, Secundus, was a military officer, likely an unbeliever, who died when John was merely an infant. Thus, John would grow up without a father. It is ironic that we would turn to a fatherless child to explore the depth of spiritual fatherhood. And yet this tragedy would provide the context for his formation under the tutelage of his mother, Anthusa.

Anthusa repeatedly and consistently turned down offers of remarriage after becoming a widow at the age of twenty. She devoted her entire life to the upbringing of her daughter and son. She trained them in the paideia of the Lord. Indeed, she gained such admiration from the community at Antioch that the prevailing advocate of heathenism, Libanius, once exclaimed, "Bless me! what wonderful women there are among the Christians."[1]

Chrysostom was born in Antioch, the famous city where Paul preached. It was also Antioch where Jews greatly opposed the work to the extent that Paul and Barnabus were expelled from the city (see Acts 13:50). Chrysostom would inherit the legacy of the published word of

---

1. Schaff, "Prolegomena," 11.

the Lord (see Acts 13:49) and become a herald, to be given the name Chrysostom by his contemporaries, which means "the golden mouth."[2]

I do wonder, however, in what way Chrysostom's fatherlessness colored his view of spiritual fatherhood. I wonder if he draws from the depth of his own experience and integrates a high view of motherhood given the constant attention and training he himself received. I wonder if we will see glimpses of this in his work on the priesthood. Perhaps we see in Chrysostom a life with an *inclusio*. He begins without a father, rises to the pinnacle of oration, and then finds himself exiled and alone. What a story arc to explore as we investigate the nuances of spiritual fatherhood through his homilies.

CHRYSOSTOM'S BEGINNINGS

John Chrysostom began his career as a lawyer and was quite a rhetorician. However, at his conversion he gave up law, fearing that he was taking wages from Satan.[3] He was quite eager to join the monastic life but was convinced otherwise when his mother pleaded with him:

> My son, my only comfort in the midst of the miseries of this earthly life is to see thee constantly, and to behold in thy features the faithful image of my beloved husband who is no more. This comfort commenced with your infancy before you could speak. I ask only one favor from you: do not make me a widow a second time; wait at least till I die; perhaps I shall soon leave this world. When you have buried me and joined my ashes with those of your father, nothing will then prevent you from retiring into monastic life. But as long as I breathe, support me by your presence, and do not draw down upon you the wrath of God by bringing such evils upon me who have given you no offense.[4]

Chrysostom relented and remained with his mother, although he adopted many ascetic practices, including silence. Being the only semblance of his father must have evoked compassion for his mother. Is it possible that even this tender exchange colored his view of the priesthood or his view of spiritual fatherhood?

---

2. Schaff, "Prolegomena," 11.
3. Schaff, "Prolegomena," 7.
4. Schaff, "Prolegomena," 8.

Libanius may have been Chrysostom's first father figure but was by no means a spiritual father. Indeed, Libanius was a popular sophist who often wrote in opposition to Christianity and promotion of paganism. Chrysostom came under his tutelage and began what may have been an illustrious journey of success and recognition for rhetoric and political influence. Indeed, Libanius speaks of Chrysostom in the following manner during his own death, when asked who his successor would be: "It would have been John," he replied, "if the Christians had not stolen him from us."[5]

Chrysostom would depart from this first father figure as changes were occurring within his heart and mind. He found the work he was doing repugnant and sought the piety of Christianity as a worthy cause for which to spend his life efforts. He left the law profession and sought a life in the monastic tradition, heavily influenced by his good friend and contemporary Basil. Chrysostom would create his homilies on the priesthood quite before he himself was given an episcopal post. His reflections came early in his devoted consecration as he was contemplating during his monastic excursion.[6]

It is likely that Bishop Meletius, appointed as bishop of Antioch in 361, had become Chrysostom's father figure as Meletius gave Chrysostom his first appointment as reader in the church. Meletius also baptized Chrysostom after his conversion, no doubt a monumental and formative encounter for Chrysostom as this entailed for many at the time a consummate consecration to Christ and devotion to his gospel.[7]

For all the rich contributions of Chrysostom to the body of Christian literature, there is one stain of treachery that he himself writes about in his first book on the priesthood, although it could be argued that Chrysostom did not view such an act as nefarious or injurious. He rather framed it a "pious fraud" in an effort to advance his good friend Basil to an episcopal position as he deemed Basil quite worthy of the position, and himself quite unworthy.[8]

Both Chrysostom and Basil had bound themselves together, not so unlike Jonathan and David. They had formed what appeared to be an intimate bond of friendship and desired that their fates would be the same. They would either both allow their "capture," as many a bishop was

---

5. Schaff, "Prolegomena," 12.
6. Schaff, "Prolegomena," 16.
7. Schaff, "Prolegomena," 13.
8. Schaff, "Prolegomena," 15–16.

ordained and swiftly caught away to their post, even against their will, or evade such capture to commit their lives to prayer and meditation of Scripture. However, Chrysostom betrays Basil as he evades the ordination ritual while Basil is led to believe that Chrysostom accepted such a post and thus acquiesces to become a bishop.[9]

PERILOUS FATHERHOOD

Chrysostom writes about their exchange after Basil learns of Chrysostom's evasion and laments this kind of grievous treatment of their friendship. It is noteworthy that Basil's description of their own society and the perils of the priesthood that follow can serve as our first example of spiritual fatherhood—it can be and most likely will be quite perilous. Listen to Basil admonish Chrysostom in the following manner:

> And I never ceased reminding you of these things: saying the age is a cruel one, and designing men are many, genuine love is no more, and the deadly pest of envy has crept into its place: we walk in the midst of snares, and on the edge of battlements; those who are ready to rejoice in our misfortunes, if any should befall us, are many and beset us from many quarters: whereas there is no one to console with us, or at least the number of such may be easily counted.[10]

The irony of spiritual fatherhood is that our first lesson is from the intimate friend of Chrysostom. It is Basil who laments his installment as a bishop. He lives in a cruel age; lawlessness is on the ascent and love wanes. Men design evil schemes for self-elevation and prodigal living. Envy lurks around every corner and if a position, title, or designation is threatened, great lengths are employed to destroy the character of another for its preservation.

Snares and battles rage all around the servant who delivers the word of God. There are many who rejoice when the servant is pierced, beat down, and left for dead. Once left with wounds, there are far less who seek to console the pastor who is bleeding. Spiritual fatherhood therefore is perilous work. There are Absaloms who seek your authority and who raise an army of accusations against you. Not to mention there are emissaries of religion, oppressive regimes, and other powers who are

---

9. Schaff, "Prolegomena," 15–17.
10. Chrysostom, "Treatise," 55.

threatened by a message of repentance and who are ready to banish the servant to a prison. There are many a Herodian who will decapitate the prophet and end the father/mother legacy being established. Spiritual fatherhood is not for the faint of heart, for there are those who seek to undermine any authority God has bestowed. Fathers are ones who go into the battlefield of the Lord. They ought not be surprised by constant attacks, accusations, slander, and actions to remove any mantle of authority. And if you find yourself in exile, alone, poor in heart, humiliated, questioning, and doubting every step across the sand, look around and find manna for your journey. Look around and find water from the rock to console the loneliness. When your name is never mentioned and every memory of your work is erased, God has a memorial stone for you with a name Ebenezer. It is also a new name to be written upon a white stone.

FATHERHOOD BEGINS IN THE HOME

But it must be that fatherhood begins in the home. This is necessary before it can be translated to the church. But do we not have homes where there is a dearth of faithful fatherhood? We live in a culture and society with the following hallmarks:

- An estimated 20 percent of all US children live in a one parent home.[11]
- An estimated 57.6 percent of black children, 31.2 percent of Hispanic children, and 20.7 percent of white children are living absent their biological fathers.[12]
- According to the National Center for Fathering fatherlessness is the most significant family or social problem facing America.[13]
- In 1970, mother-only households consisted of about 11 percent of the US population. By 2023, approximately 23 percent of all US households were mother-only households. The fatherless epidemic doubled over fifty years.[14]

---

11. United States Census Bureau, "Parents' Living Arrangements," table 1.
12. Vespa et al., "America's Families," 2.
13. National Center for Fathering, "Extent of Fatherlessness," para. 8.
14. United States Census Bureau, "Parent/Child Family Groups," figure 1.

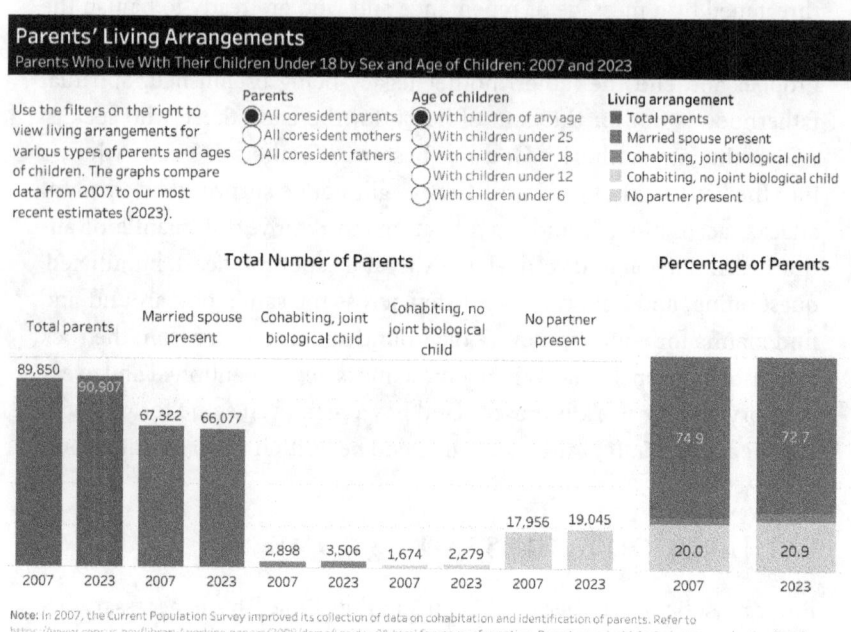

Figure 2. Single-Parent Families on the Rise. According to the US Census data of 2023, nearly 20 percent of children are being raised in single-parent households.

No wonder that we know very little about how to be a spiritual father or mother. We remain casual in our relationships and superficial—with a common objective that brings us together. But, if you remove this objective, there is no depth to the relationship. Where is the father who will listen to our story? With a church culture bent on performance through attendance, revenue, and buildings, knowing a heart is a rare exchange.

What Chrysostom does not know in the moment, but would find out, is that Basil's words here have a prophetic semblance as Chrysostom would face one peril after another as he fulfills his ministry to preach against the luxury of the priesthood, the vice of the society, and call one and all to repentance. Persecution will come to all who take a risk and preach repentance. I dare say that persecution will also come to the one who assumes the post of a spiritual father or mother.

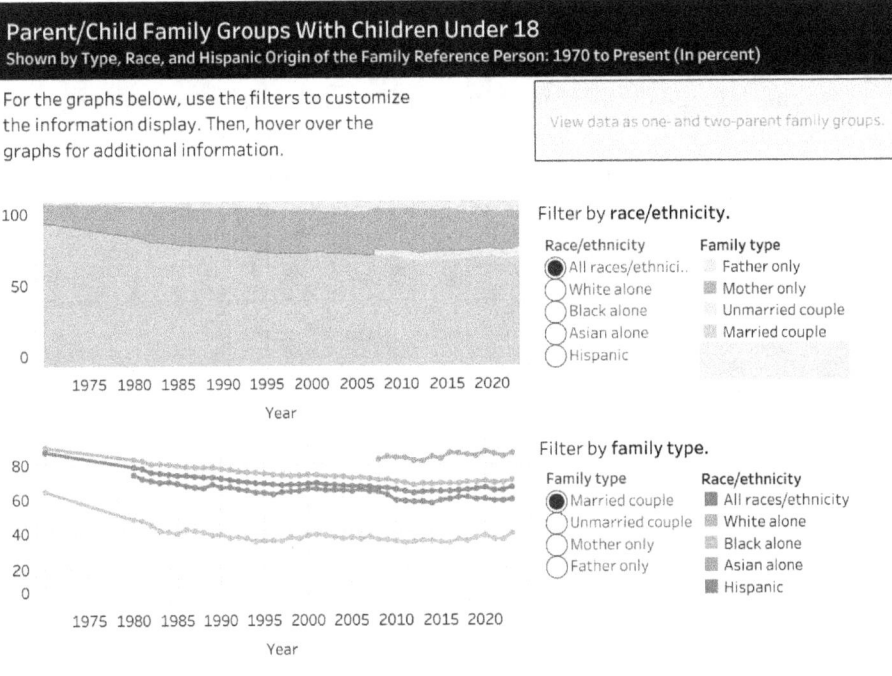

Figure 3. Mother-Only Households. Note the doubling of mother-only households from 1970 to 2020.

Chrysostom will later recapitulate Basil's commentary on the priesthood when he says,

> Moreover, in the case of the shepherd of irrational creatures, those who wish to destroy the flock, when they see the guardian take to flight, cease making war upon him, and are contented with the seizure of the cattle: but in this case, even should they capture the whole flock, they do not leave the shepherd unmolested, but attack him all the more, and wax bolder, ceasing not until they have either overthrown him, or have themselves been vanquished.[15]

15. Chrysostom, "Treatise," 66.

Setting in Order

Chrysostom has lifted up the notion that the shepherd loves the flock. He references the restoration of Peter with the three love inquiries as an example. He then proceeds to comment on the tumults of shepherding because of the enemy's constant warfare against the shepherd, and I would also say in opposition to spiritual fatherhood. The enemy has chosen the cornerstone of society, the family institution itself, to remove the legacy of fatherhood. Without the father in the home, we are left without spiritual fathers in the church.

Chapter 3

Setting Church Roles in Order

I left you behind in Crete for this reason, so that you should put in order what remained to be done.

TITUS 1:5

THE ROLE OF CONTEMPT

Now we move from the perilous activity and mission of spiritual fatherhood to the navigation of contempt. Chrysostom oscillates between shepherd and physician metaphors when explicating priesthood. In the following case, he has underscored the use of a physician's remedy that has no authority to heal when the patient has no willingness to receive such treatment:

> For if any one when he is bound becomes restive (which it is in his power to be), he makes the mischief worse; and if he should pay no heed to the words which cut like steel, he inflicts another wound by means of this contempt, and the intention to heal only becomes the occasion of a worse disorder. For it is not possible for anyone to cure a man by compulsion against his will.[1]

I would like to reflect on the notion of contempt when navigating spiritual fatherhood. Perhaps, we can all relate as either the perpetrator

---

1. Chrysostom, "Treatise," 67.

or victim of such contempt in our own families. How often have we rejected the counsel of our own fathers and how often have we likewise lamented the prescription rejected by our own sons and daughters and thus could foresee a pending calamity?

Chrysostom is keen to identify two wounds in this interchange. The first wound was incurred with the initial transgression that led to a sickness of the soul. The patient then visits his or her physician, in this case the priest or spiritual father, who renders a prescription which is discourse that "cut[s] like steel." This implies a kind of upbraiding and likely encapsulates a charge to repent. It reminds me of the kind of fathering Christ displays when leaving a final charge to his disciples just before his ascension.

The Gospel of Mark gives us a window into such a scene when Christ first upbraids his disciples. That is, Christ ὀνειδίζω (on-i-did'-zo); the Greek can be harsh wherein it indicates a strong rebuke or insult. It has also come to encapsulate a railing or chiding. The word has a type of illustration which would be understood by the cultural euphemism of casting reproach to one's teeth. We might better understand this in our culture when we proverbially remark that what someone said or did was a "slap in the face."[2]

And yet, this is part and parcel of being a spiritual father. The father must learn the art of rebuke and must courageously dispense the rebuke with such vigor that it cuts the gangrenous lesion from the soul, awakens the soul asleep to his or her sickness, and cauterizes a wound from hemorrhaging. Christ identifies the source for his rebuke in the two aspects of unbelief and hardness of heart, both of which can exacerbate the other. It appears that Christ sought to shake the disciples from such a hardness that influenced and consumed Pharaoh so that he rejected the word of God. If Christ was to work signs through his disciples, an obstinate or hard heart would not do. Indeed, it must be ravaged and undone so that a soft, malleable, and believing heart could be the result. If they were to preach a convincing gospel, they must themselves first believe it.

The disciples had first doubted the reports of Christ's resurrection, which was the object of Christ's harsh rebuke here. Christ's prescription was to cut them with the kind of words that would jolt them from erroneous dependence on rationality over faith. The gospel depends on the resurrection and must be believed, preached, and illustrated by those

---

2. See Zodhiates and Baker, *Hebrew-Greek Key Word*, 52, and Rogers and Rogers, *New Linguistic and Exegetical Key*, 104, for these nuanced definitions of ὀνειδίζω.

who would endeavor to live in and for Christ. If Christ be not raised, how do we therefore anticipate our own resurrection? How can we hope for something that we do not yet believe in?

Spiritual fatherhood is as much about admonition as it is about giving a charge. The commission Christ provides to his disciples begins first with a stinging rebuke. Spiritual fathers must determine to incorporate this into their disposition even if it runs contrary to a type of default temperament. Spiritual fathers cannot relinquish the task of rebuke with the excuse that "I simply do not have the temperament for this." They cannot relinquish this task in the name of a feigned love or compassion that has eradicated forms of correction. The spiritual father has authority from Christ who lays it upon his disciples and shepherds with a charge to go and make disciples (see Matt 28:18).

When Pastor Preston was asked to resign by his church board, it was a small cohort who had convinced the entire board to proceed in this manner. When the state director facilitated further conversations and, in the course of time and with further reflection, the board reversed their determination, those who were adamant about his resignation continued to slander Pastor Preston until he would be vanquished. O how relentless attacks can be when one is a father! It is as if a wholly different impetus has consumed the enemies of fathers to seek their demise with a delusion that it is a just cause. Perhaps this sense of righteousness, no matter how feigned, motivates the assailants to perpetuate the attacks which only accomplish the wounding and perhaps destruction of the sheep.

Pastor Preston was in a precarious position. Should he correct and rebuke the board members bent on his destruction? Was he able to do so being the object of such scorn and thus be an altogether objective source of correction? In this case, the state director was the objective adjudicator, and Pastor Preston had to submit to the verdict arrived at by his state director. Pastor Preston was unable to relieve the board members of their position as this would obviously be construed as retaliatory.

Consequently, two instigating board members resigned while the other one remained to continue opposing Pastor Preston. In the end, Pastor Preston had to accept this as the will of God for him and seek to father his children in a manner that wholly protected them from the slander that continued to escalate. To protect his children, he resigned. But woe unto the church who does not mend their ways in how they deal with the shepherds and spiritual fathers who God sends to them!

At once, Chrysostom notes the dilemma of spiritual fathers and explicates further, drawing on the metaphor of a surgeon. If the surgeon cuts more gently, there remains some of the cancer that can again proliferate to the total consumption and destruction of the victim. But, if the surgeon cuts unsparingly, he may create context where the patient wholly rejects the remedy, throwing off the bonds that are actively mending the soul. Listen to his description of the pastoral dilemma:

> For if you deal too gently with him who needs a severe application of the knife, and do not strike deep into one who requires such treatment, you remove one part of the sore but leave the other: and if on the other hand you make the requisite incision unsparingly, the patient, driven to desperation by his sufferings, will often fling everything away at once, both the remedy and the bandage, and throw himself down headlong, "breaking the yoke and bursting the band."[3]

The surgical metaphor is rightly correlated to discipline and correction. The spiritual father is a spiritual surgeon. In surgical oncology, the goal for removal of a tumor or mass is to have clean margins. That is, the tissue adjacent to the incision must be free of all cancer cells for it to be considered a successful removal. The sample is sent to pathology to confirm clean margins so that the team can either rejoice over having taken the full metastatic mass from plaguing the body or plan yet another surgery to ensure that one has clean margins.

And so it is with the doctor of the soul, the rebuke must be enough to have clean margins but not so severe that healthy tissue is eradicated. For if the knife penetrates too deep, one may also injure the health of the soul when attempting to remove the cancer from the soul. The spiritual father or pastor must exercise great discernment, sometimes restraint, but not too much restraint that one avoids the art of rebuke altogether.

The reference to the prophet Jeremiah is an interesting one as the prophet recounts the injurious sins of Jerusalem and Judah. The remedy here is a visitation from the Lord, who will enact a calamity in judgment. The prophet brings a stark contrast in Jer 5:5 between the "great men" and those who break the yoke of holiness and healing and burst the bonds of the balm sent by God for the reformation of the soul.

The great men have God "into them." The possession of God in these men is predicated on them having known the way of the Lord. The

---

3. Chrysostom, "Treatise," 67.

way of the Lord is instrumental in God inhabiting a soul who is ever bent on knowing the path of God and sojourning this way with him. The great man knows and abides by the judgment of God. In contrast, the one not inhabited by God is rather visited by God. But this visitation is for the purpose of judgment.

When God offers a yoke, he intends that one binds the self to him as two oxen would be bound together to plow a certain field. When God offers a bond, it is to heal the soul from the way of transgressions. Those who reject the yoke will also and eventually reject the bonds. Perhaps this reference from Jeremiah can be taken further in application to spiritual fatherhood in priesthood. That is, a father yokes his son or daughter to him. This yoke is for a kind of apprenticeship where the son follows the father wherever he goes in the journey of ministry. The son or daughter is there when trial or discipline is warranted and is present when joy and triumph have accompanied this pilgrimage.

Thus, I would like to assert that we need a revival of spiritual fatherhood where the yoke of togetherness is applied to the sons and daughters in the form of an apprenticeship. We cannot hope to train the next generation of spiritual fathers by simply lecturing them in a classroom. They must put their hands in the dirt of the garden for a flower to grow. The yoke requires a tandem journey where one is face to face with the dying and sick, the poor and homeless, the imprisoned and marginalized, the orphan and widow. As Elisha was known by the entire community as Elijah's spiritual son, the entire community is a witness and confesses that a father has chosen a son, a mother has chosen a daughter, and their journey is thus the same. It ought to be obvious to the community. Thus, the seminary journey from the outset could begin to seek out such fathers who would take sons and daughters and incorporate this kind of apprenticeship not for one or two months, but throughout the entire journey of seminary. The yoke must be applied for a father and mother to be born.

Second, the yoke is required for the bonds to be applied. The father or mother is close enough to identify the wounds of the son and daughter when in a close relationship vis-à-vis the yoke. The yoke creates a context for proximity and thus breeds the kind of diagnosis that can only come with proximity. During the seminary journey, the wound is either confessed or identified, the father or mother exercises his or her role as physician and applies the anointing and thereafter dresses the wound. This dressing is not so much a concrete solution for the ailing son or daughter, but rather it is embedded in the attuning ear of the father and the healing is implicit within the relationship itself. Relationships are the medicine for the soul. I do not seek to undermine speech that can heal but would like to underscore that it is the emphasis on the yoke that provides pretext for the healing. Are we not called to yoke ourselves to Christ? Is it not that his yoke is light and as such unshackles the soul from the burden of wounds and cancers that consume the soul (see Matt 11:29–30)? Was it not Christ who yoked himself with the twelve disciples for three years, sojourning with them, preparing them to be spiritual fathers, providing a template for future discipleship? We would do well to emulate his example.

THE ROLE OF NEGLIGENCE

The irony of Chrysostom is that he writes a detailed account of the priesthood while at the same time declining to become one. He considers himself unworthy of carrying out the very charges he espouses. He again states the dilemma for the pastor when he says the following:

> For as many are uplifted to pride, and then sink into despair of their salvation, from inability to endure severe remedies, so are there some, who from paying no penalty equivalent to their sins, fall into negligence, and become far worse, and are impelled to greater sins.[4]

Pastor Preston was conducting a church business meeting with the church board. When discussing the prospective budget, a board member lamented that he had been called by a staff member who verbally assailed him and threatened him, saying that he ought to advocate for a reversal of the already-approved portion of the budget. Pastor Preston, already broken by stinging remarks from board members, did not have the wherewithal to investigate further. This staff member was not identified, and a thorough inquiry was not made. As a result, no penalty was meted out and no church discipline was applied to this staff member, which created a context for negligence.

It is negligence on the part of the pastor to not investigate such injurious acts, and no doubt from a staff member who ought to conduct him- or herself with great temperance. If Pastor Preston could have this moment back, he would have interviewed the board member to discover the identity of the staff member and then confront such a staff member

4. Chrysostom, "Treatise," 68.

with disciplinary consequences for interfering with board business, when this body is designed to be independent from staff influences. However, when a pastor is negligent either from woundedness or from a kind of feigned graciousness, the perpetrator is emboldened to greater impropriety. The church body becomes ill, and a great sickness invades the leadership. Church discipline must restrain itself from such an austere discipline that it ruins a reputation or sows a seed of despair, but must be consequential enough to mitigate further grievous sins of the soul.

Without church discipline, the entire flock is diseased. And as an aside, the pastor or father of the flock ought to consider casting away a church member—whether staff or not—who works aggressively to transgress in his or her ways. Perhaps the delivering over to Satan will exact repentance (see 1 Tim 1:20).

THE ROLE OF DIVINE APPOINTMENT

We learn another great lesson concerning spiritual fatherhood in Chrysostom's treatise—it is a decree and ordination brought from a divine origin, the Holy Spirit himself:

> For the priestly office is indeed discharged on earth, but it ranks amongst heavenly ordinances; and very naturally so: for neither man, nor angel, nor archangel, nor any other created power, but the Paraclete Himself, instituted this vocation, and persuaded men while still abiding in the flesh to represent the ministry of angels.[5]

Thus we find an office not brought about by men, but by Christ through the Holy Spirit. Christ himself appointed Peter to tend his sheep, choosing Peter to do so in the context of confessional love (see John 21:17). And so the question emerges: If the shepherd and pastor is appointed by Christ in the Holy Spirit, who then has the authority to remove a pastor from such a vocation? That is, does the pastor not need someone to whom he or she is accountable? Would it be his own spiritual father—the pastor of the pastor? And do we have such a semblance of spiritual fatherhood in the church that faithfully discharges this kind of spiritual fatherhood to pastors?

Chrysostom will go on to assert that, with this ordination by Christ himself, there comes a heavenly authority that far surpasses that of our

---

5. Chrysostom, "Treatise," 77.

earthly authorities, for the outcome of such authority bears eternal and soteriological significance. Listen to Chrysostom's reflections on priestly authority:

> For it has not been said to them, "Whatsoever ye shall bind on earth shall be bound in Heaven, and whatsoever ye shall loose on earth shall be loosed in Heaven." They who rule on earth have indeed authority to bind, but only the body: whereas this binding lays hold of the soul and penetrates the heavens; and what priests do here below God ratifies above, and the Master confirms the sentence of his servants. For indeed what is it but all manner of heavenly authority which He has given them when He says, "Whose sins ye remit they are remitted, and whose sins ye retain they are retained?" What authority could be greater than this? "The Father hath committed all judgment to the Son?" But I see it all put into the hands of these men by the Son. For they have been conducted to this dignity as if they were already translated to Heaven, and had transcended human nature, and were released from the passions to which we are liable.[6]

I would imagine that some of what Chrysostom asserts here is difficult for the modern ear to render for application. Chrysostom is concretely applying Matt 18:18, John 20:23, and John 5:22 in a kind of collective substantiation of pastoral authority. He speaks of this kind of authority as being transferred from Christ himself to the priest who then renders or perhaps participates in the grace of forgiveness and the judgment of consequence. In Chrysostom's mind, this kind of heavenly honor and responsibility also entails a translation of human nature. They are not simply given a charge but are thoroughly equipped through means of regeneration in the Spirit to transcend human passions and trifle temptations that attempt to ensnare. I would further argue that spiritual fathers also provide a transfer of authority to spiritual sons and daughters who become pastors with the task of setting churches in order.

Moreover, Chrysostom will make a direct comparison in his treatise on the priesthood between one's natural parents and the priests as parents. He notes that there is a corporeal begetting entrusted to our parents, but a spiritual begetting entrusted to the priesthood. The tools of such begetting Chrysostom notes as instruction, admonition, and prayer. He states that often a priest will beget such children into the kingdom through teaching of the gospel, correcting one from sin, and praying with one in

---

6. Chrysostom, "Treatise," 79.

faith. This direct comparison accentuates a type of spiritual parenting as a role of ministry and one that carries the weight of one's soul.[7]

This then creates a type of conflict between the Reformation's notion of the priesthood of all believers. On one hand, the idea liberates all believers to access a call to ministry and to speak on behalf of Christ; on the other hand, it has the potential to abolish a spiritual parenting in the body of Christ and perhaps injure a certain begetting that can occur in the church. If all are priests, who renders authority? It would be intuitive to then answer that it is Christ who renders authority. What then if a conflict arises? Who renders judgment? Did the apostle Paul not render judgment upon the church at Corinth, while at a distance (see 1 Cor 5:3)?

Was it because he was commissioned as an ambassador to the gentiles by Christ himself that he was able to render such authority? Could the gentile elders reject his judgment and authority for yet another rendering? If we take the Pastoral Epistles as a microcosm of ecclesiological practice, they illustrate Paul as a spiritual father to the church at Ephesus and those at Crete. He advocates for Timothy and Titus to render judgment on his behalf, correcting erroneous heresies and creating governing structures in the church through appointment. Thus, Timothy and, in our case here, Titus become the priests who render the authority that began in Paul through Christ. Paul begins this context of appointing Titus by noting their relationship as father and son. This relationship, in my mind, is critical in the transfer of such authority. Without such a transfer, without a spiritual father, the son or daughter who takes up the mantle of pastor is often left to fight off the wild beasts at Ephesus alone and thus heighten the odds that he or she will be thoroughly wounded, disoriented, and left for dead by those who have sought to strip the pastor of any dignity.

Moreover, the apostle Paul also takes up the subject of spiritual parenting when he notes that the people of Corinth are his children, and as his children, Paul asserts that he ought to provide relief for his children rather than the reverse. The irony here is that Paul notices that the more he loves his children, the less he is loved:

7. Chrysostom, "Treatise," 79–80, where he asserts the following: "For our natural parents generate us unto this life only, but the others unto that which is to come. And the former would not be able to avert death from their offspring, or to repel the assaults of disease; but these others have often saved a sick soul, or one which was on the point of perishing, procuring for some a milder chastisement, and preventing others from falling altogether, not only by instruction and admonition, but also by the assistance wrought through prayers."

> Here I am, ready to come to you this third time, and I will not be a burden because I do not want what is yours but you, for children ought not to save up for their parents but parents for their children. I will most gladly spend and be spent for you. If I love you more, am I to be loved less? (2 Cor 12:14–15)

Paul not only laments but seems to anticipate there to be both a filial relationship with his flock, while at the same time a rejection of this filial relationship. It is as if the children seek to cast off the authority of their spiritual father. Now, one at first may be confused as to Paul's identification of the entire church at Corinth as his children. I believe Paul is making the same distinction as our heavenly Father makes in how he distinguishes Christ as *Huios*, or son, and the body of Christ as *teknon*, or children. Timothy and Titus hold a special office as sons whereas the church members in general are children. In this distinction, the sons, Titus and Timothy, are given governing authority in the churches where the children are given inheritance as fruit of the labors of their spiritual fathers and mothers. (Please see table 1 below for a summary of church roles and governance.)

If we continue to reflect on this dyadic dynamic, we might also envision a modification of the Reformation's priesthood of all believers. Every believer is a priest in terms of his or her access to the Father directly through Christ. As such, this gives every believer the rite of communion, fellowship, intercession, and mission. However, not every believer is called to govern or tend to the sheep (please see table 1 below). These sons or daughters are appointed by spiritual fathers or mothers who have gone before them and affirmed this ecclesiastical appointment upon them through the Spirit of God.

This then necessitates a charge to such spiritual fathers and mothers—the weight of your authority must be deposited with the appointment. That is, the spiritual father and mother would need to install, defend, and advocate for the appointment when contested by some in the body. For we live in a contesting culture, seeking one's own authority so that it is only a matter of time when the pastor's authority becomes questioned. As Paul defended and advocated for Titus with the weight of a personal letter to be publicly read in the hearing of the churches at Crete, so ought spiritual fathers to do likewise for those appointed to the pastorate of a flock. A public letter or treatise ought to be written and declared in the hearing of the church—this would be wind in the sails of a wounded pastor and would stamp out the wolves of envy who seek to ravage the body.

Identity	Role	Governance	Accountable
Teknon Children (members)	Submission	Advisory only	To the elders
Huios Sons (pastors)	Local authority	Presiding elder	To the apostle
Apostolos Fathers	Regional authority	Instruct and defend the sons (pastors).	Christ/other apostles
Episkopos Elders	Spiritual and financial direction	Lead with the pastor	To the pastor
Diakonos Deacons	Service and hospitality	Serve under the church leadership	To the elders
Priesthood of all believers	All serve	Not all govern	To the elders

Table 1. Church Governance

Chapter 4

Setting the Soul in Order

For a bishop, as God's steward, must be blameless.
Titus 1:7

THE SOUL AND KENOSIS

Now Chrysostom will move to yet another attribute of priesthood and, for our discussion, spiritual fatherhood. He will press the need that the priest, pastor, and father be kenotic. I have written elsewhere on this subject,[1] but it comes to bear here as well. He cites Rom 9:3 where Paul would gladly consider himself cursed if his brothers could be saved. This is like Moses's plea that he be blotted out for the sake of Israel (see Exod 32:32). Listen to Chrysostom's depiction of this attribute:

> If, then, he who went beyond the ordinances of God, and nowhere sought his own advantage, but that of those whom he governed, was always so full of fear when he considered the greatness of his government, what shall our condition be who in many ways seek our own, who not only fail to go beyond the commandments of Christ, but for the most part transgress them?[2]

---

1. Jensen, *Coming Winter*.
2. Chrysostom, "Treatise," 81.

The spiritual father is always seeking the advantage of his sons and daughters, even at the expense of his own. The spiritual mother enters the appointment with fear and trembling, aware of her weaknesses and giving glory to God when those weaknesses are on display. The spiritual father enters the appointment after weighing and accepting the destiny of lifelong kenosis, constantly seeking the promotion of others and condescension of the self. The way of leadership is not to ascend but rather descend into greater depths of humility and contrition. The life of a spiritual father and mother is one of being poured out day after day on behalf of another (see Phil 2:17). Chrysostom himself is making an elaborate defense of his unworthiness to obtain this office. He finds that his disposition is not yet ready to illustrate the temperament and characteristics necessary to be a spiritual father. And yet, as his defense proceeds, he ironically substantiates his qualifications given his humility and exposition of the Scriptures. His friend Basil sees what Chrysostom is blind to in himself.

Furthermore, Chrysostom provides a stark warning to anyone who would enter the ministry as a pastor or spiritual father. The following citation ought to be given to anyone considering the call to be a shepherd, praying and fasting if any of these temptations are indeed a snare to the soul. And if the answer is yes, one ought to seek the advantage of confession and accountability prior to assuming the office of a spiritual father to prevent the ruin of the soul by means of vanity.

> Do you ask what those wild beasts are? They are wrath, despondency, envy, strife, slanders, accusations, falsehood, hypocrisy, intrigues, anger against those who have done no harm, pleasure at the indecorous acts of fellow ministers, sorrow at their prosperity, love of praise, desire of honor (which indeed most of all drives the human soul headlong to perdition), doctrines devised to please, servile flatteries, ignoble fawning, contempt of the poor, paying court to the rich, senseless and mischievous honors, favors attended with danger both to those who offer and those who accept them, sordid fear suited only to the basest of slaves, the abolition of plain speaking, a great affectation of humility, but banishment of truth, the suppression of convictions and reproofs, or rather the excessive use of them against the poor, while against those who are invested with power no one dare open his lips.[3]

---

3. Chrysostom, "Treatise," 82–83.

Setting in Order

This self-assessment from Chrysostom is so important for any considering the pastorate/priesthood, I have chosen to include his reproofs in an infographic for emphasis (please see figure 4 below). Any ministerial student or seminarian would do well to heed Chrysostom's words and ask him- or herself what obstacles remain in the soul and are necessary to purge before embarking on such a perilous journey.

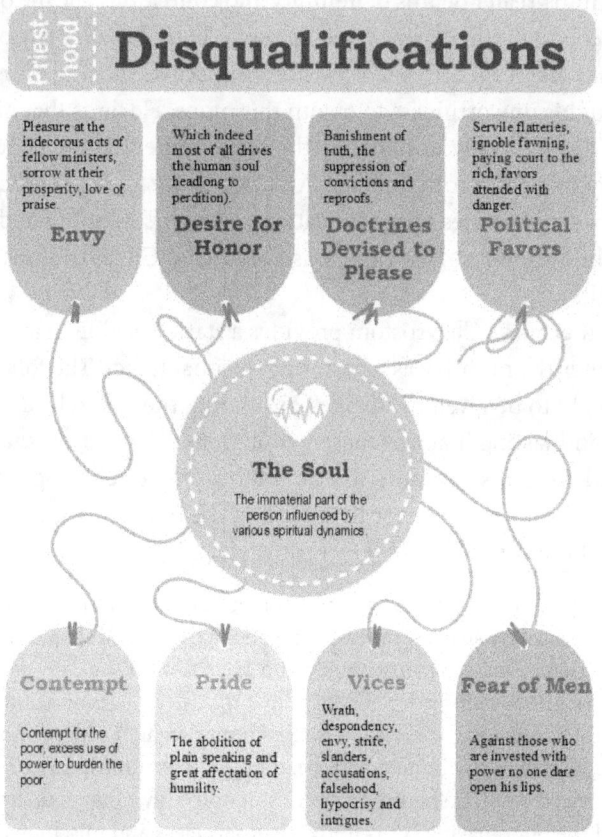

Figure 4. Disqualifications for the Priesthood

I would like to underscore envy, as this has plagued so many a pastor who finds him- or herself ensnared by the constant comparison to another. Chrysostom sees in himself this potential and is citing such an attribute that should disqualify him from priesthood. And yet, if we truly search deeply into our own soul, how often have we secretly enjoyed the fall of a fellow minister? Perhaps it was a local minister who needed to resign no matter the cause and we secretly hoped and anticipated that we would inherit his or her members so that our empire could thus grow. Or perhaps we have secretly been sorrowed at the success of a fellow minister, lamenting that the harvest is being won at the expense of our own following. Perhaps we envy the programs, charisma, Facebook likes, Twitter/X followers, number of views on their livestream, or a host of other successes because we ourselves do not have such a following.

Then Chrysostom hits on a subject that every minister ought to deeply reflect on—the love of or desire for honor and praise. Is it possible that pastors, ministers, or even spiritual fathers or mothers have a primary motive for entering such an office because it meets a felt need of honor and affirmation? Perhaps we have a deep need to be recognized, and we carry this emotional need into the ministry. When this emotional need is unmet or—worse—further exacerbated by ridicule and insult, when one's dignity is assaulted, as is often the case in ministry, then one may enter a state of despair, finding it challenging to endure, and attempting to find a different context where this emotional need can be met. All the while, it is the person and fellowship with Christ that meets this need.

This desire for honor appears to be the greatest vice in Chrysostom's litany of temptations for a minister or spiritual father. It is the one snare that throws one headlong into perdition. Perhaps because it catches the minister unaware. Perhaps because it coaxes the minister into a false security that he or she is responsible for the honor or praise, rather than Christ. Of course, this would not be what we consciously utter but it may be how we act and behave as ministers. Perhaps it is honor that ensnares a minister by way of redirecting his or her attention away from more sinister schemes operating covertly, even by those who may have once honored the minister. Honor itself is not the vexing vice, for we are called by Paul to give double honor to our elders. Rather, it is the receiving of honor in a way that self-adulates. If one receives an honor and does not respond with condescension, or if one seeks to honor others for greater influence and power, then illness of the soul ensues.

Chrysostom is keenly aware of human nature as he continues to reveal insincere motives that may compel one to leadership. He cites the courting of favors, the oppression of the poor, the fawning over the rich, and banishment of the truth. He identifies a system of human relating that remains fallen, and he fears that he would be unable to resist the sirens of this fallen way of relating and thus shipwreck the church.

Setting in Order

Not too long ago I was talking with a good friend. He is good, as he is honest to raise inquiries that provoke greater contemplation on my part. He is of course patient to listen to my recurrent lamentations about past hurts and wounds along with deep longings for ministry. I speak to him of desires to preach, teach, and pastor. He asked a question that at once provoked me to examine myself. He asked what my motives were for such deep longings. As I underwent an honest assessment of my soul, I was compelled to conclude that there was a commingling of motivations. On one hand, there were primary motivations of loving God and loving neighbor. However, there were also influences from some secondary motivations such as a need for affirmation, a desire to be recognized, and a love to lead. These secondary motivations may not be as strong as the primary motivations, but if I am honest with myself, they are present to some degree.

Indeed, it makes no difference to me whether I am identified as a physician or recognized in a public gathering for this accomplishment. But to be called a pastor or minister seems to bring a level of affirmation that substantiates a sense of worth to my soul. Perhaps it is because I devalue the practice of medicine as a role that is not fit for the Master's use. Perhaps it is because my ministry has been rejected by others, and I seek yet another source of affirmation as a type of vindication. Perhaps it is because I seek affirmation from others that I did not quite receive from my own parents. Perhaps it is because I have no spiritual father and as such, I long for this kind of dyadic relationship within the context of the church. Perhaps my age confers a kind of in-between state of departing as a son and becoming a spiritual father myself, and I find myself navigating the waters of a confused identity. Perhaps my need for affirmation has become more than an emotional need, broaching the precipice of idolatry. Perhaps I have elevated human affirmation in esteem within the ranks of my soul. Perhaps I also long to carry a legacy that has involved previous generations—that is, to carry the legacy of ministry that I have inherited from my family of origin. Whatever the source, I must find a way to crucify these human passions and give space to the searchlight of heaven to uncover every hidden place in the heart. Every minister would do well to investigate his or her soul on these matters before attempting to set a church in order. For our souls must be set in order if we hope to set God's church in order.

O how Chrysostom cuts the heart of improper aspiration, noting that the one vice above all that can plague a minister or spiritual father is the lust for the dignity of the office of pastor, leader, father, or priest. When the office is attained it may fan the flame of this lust, perpetuating impropriety in the basest way to hold onto the office. O God forgive us all for this undignified lust that invites the wrath of God upon the body of Christ! And how gentle he is to show us our hearts that we may repent to avoid such calamity upon the church. Anyone who speaks out is now thrust in leadership without scrutiny of one's fruit, call, ambition, and motivation. If one shows a smidgeon of charisma, he or she is put in front of people as a pastor. How are we examining pastors today? How is their marriage, their children, their motive, their interaction with others? What drives them? O how we need to restore such a discerning rod to the church, to prevent both the sorrow of the soul who enters the office with erroneous ambitions and the stain of the church.

Listen to Chrysostom substantiate his own evasion of the office as he confesses that some of this desire for dignity was also within himself:

> For there are very many other qualities, Basil, besides those already mentioned, which the priest ought to have, but which I do not possess; and, above all, this one:—his soul ought to be thoroughly purged from any lust after the office: for if he happens to have a natural inclination for this dignity, as soon as he attains it a stronger flame is kindled, and the man being taken completely captive will endure innumerable evils in order to keep a secure hold upon it, even to the extent of using flattery, or submitting to something base and ignoble, or expending large sums of money.[4]

How does one thoroughly purge oneself from the lust of the office? Is it through prayer and fasting or confession and contrition? Is it by working tireless to evade the office and thus if one is compelled to the office one accepts this as from the hand of God? Is it venturing into a monastic quality of life vis-à-vis simplicity, silence, and surrender?

Although I cannot be sure myself how one purges the self of a lust for dignity, office, recognition, power, and authority, I do wonder if this lust has infiltrated many in the church. I must also wonder if some of this lust is within my own soul, in need of the launderer's soap of heaven. Any spiritual father must ask himself, To what extent will I traverse to hold to the office of spiritual guide, leader, or father? Any spiritual mother must ask, What sort of compromise am I willing to undertake to hold to the

---

4. Chrysostom, "Treatise," 84.

dignity of my position? If tempted to commit an ignoble act of impropriety, will you resign? If tempted to destroy those dear to you, will you grasp the title of authority? If tempted to bow to the will of the politically savvy and wealthy, will you abase yourself with flattery to secure your office?

THE SOUL AND TEMPERANCE

Next, Chrysostom speaks of temperance as a necessary aspect of priesthood and spiritual fatherhood. Those who are carried away with anger will certainly succumb to it when insults are hurled, or authority is undermined. The flock will likely bite at the shepherd and some of these assaults will feel personal and provoke either sorrow or anger or both. Chrysostom invokes Christ's words that to call a brother fool in one's anger is to be in the very danger of hell itself (see Matt 5:22). Therefore, he asserts that temperance is a necessary attribute of any priest and, by virtue of our discussion, any father. The apostle Paul admonishes familial fathers to prevent the provocation of children by stoking one's anger toward them. How much more ought a spiritual father or mother to have such temperance when modelling calm in the storm of vitriolic attacks? Chrysostom's words are worth noting here:

> As then the lover of vainglory, when he takes upon him the government of numbers, supplies additional fuel to the fire, so he who by himself, or in the company of a few, is unable to control his anger, but readily carried away by it, should he be entrusted with the direction of a whole multitude, like some wild beast goaded on all sides by countless tormentors, would never be able to live in tranquility himself, and would cause incalculable mischief to those who have been committed to his charge.[5]

Mark Driscoll had founded a church, Mars Hill, that he subsequently pastored for nearly twenty years. Perhaps it was fame and fortune, or pressure and busyness, or perhaps it was wound after wound that would pressure Pastor Driscoll into becoming a more domineering leader. Whatever the cause, Pastor Driscoll found that he would need to resign for the sake of his family and the church. He cites the following reasons that led to his conclusion:

> There are many things I have confessed and repented of, privately and publicly, as you are well aware. Specifically, I have

---

5. Chrysostom, "Treatise," 87.

confessed to past pride, anger and a domineering spirit. As I shared with our church in August, "God has broken me many times in recent years by showing me where I have fallen short, and while my journey, at age 43, is far from over, I believe He has brought me a long way from some days I am not very proud of and is making me more like Him every day."[6]

Driscoll confesses to pride, anger, and a domineering spirit. And although he is grateful that the conclusion of the board of elders was not to disqualify him from ministry for these attributes, Driscoll resigns himself, perhaps noting that there was more personal work to be done before assuming leadership once more. He seeks to safeguard the church, hoping to alleviate the divisiveness which he may have personally caused. He states the following:

> Other issues, such as aspects of my personality and leadership style, have proven to be divisive within the Mars Hill context, and I do not want to be the source of anything that might detract from our church's mission to lead people to a personal and growing relationship with Jesus Christ.[7]

What is it that brings pastors to a place of domineering leadership styles, anger outbursts, or pride? Is it possible that pastors are caught up in a celebrity Christian culture which creates, reinforces, and enflames these attributes in their leaders? Is it possible that pastors inherit this culture unawares and find that over a few years that they must accomplish an online presence, book sales, conference speaking engagements, and anything else that nurtures the ache for significance that appears lacking if these things are not listed on one's resume? Is it possible that this drive for significance or recognition becomes an idol—subtly, secretly, and unconsciously?

I would argue that our Christian subculture creates the context where we prop up a charismatic figure with such a notoriety that can only lead to their potential destruction. And when destruction does come, the result is further wounding in the form of a harsh criticism that becomes an emotional exile. I also wonder as to the part church staff and an elder or church board contributes to any ensuing conflict. For example, although we publish resignation letters as above and pounce on exiting pastors, there does not appear to be the same scrutiny upon church staff

---

6. Bailey, "Exclusive: Mark Driscoll's Resignation," para. 4.
7. Bailey, "Exclusive: Mark Driscoll's Resignation," para. 5.

or boards who may have a share in grievous sins of slander and character disparagement in the wake of conflict. We speak of the need for accountability for the pastor, but who keeps the church board or elders accountable? Is it the church members? Is it a regional bishop or pastoral supervisor? It appears to me that more can be done with ecclesiastical infrastructure to assist churches when navigating conflict.

The words of Chrysostom several centuries earlier still resonate today. Have we as pastors committed ourselves to an examination of our temperament? And I would like to assert that this goes beyond the MMPI (Minnesota Multiphasic Personality Inventory), Myers-Briggs, and Disc profiles. These psychological tools have become so popular that churches are eager to perform them with an expectation that these assessments will be a source of great revelation concerning a person's leadership style and temperament, while providing reductionistic solutions to entrenched interpersonal dynamics. I do not seek to disparage such tools but implore that we do not invest so much emotional stock and confidence in them as answers to wounds of childhood, the loss of a child, the slander of character, or the attack on one's integrity. These are heavily nuanced experiences and carry with them several months of contemplation, prayer, and outside wisdom to bring an accurate hermeneutic.

Chrysostom rightly asserts the correlation of vainglory with anger. He goes beyond the personality inventory and asks the question that every pastoral candidate, pastor, and spiritual father should ask: Do I seek my own glory? We may not like the answer to this question but ask we must. For if this is the case, then an anger outburst and unbridled tongue is lurking somewhere in the future. Moreover, perhaps a barrage of intemperance awaits the pastor seeking fame. Our Christian culture has created a monster in that a radio or television program is the aspiration of every pastor. Conference-style churches are the teleological dreams of many a pastor. The means to this end are not always measured. But what if we, as a Christian culture, decided to do away with media altogether? Would this not be a radical, albeit reforming posture for the church? What if we once again relied on personal relationships and interpersonal transactions of sharing the gospel and teaching the flock without the ensnaring temptations of an online following? What would the church look like? It may once again be people sharing their stories around a dinner table, coming together for simple and yet profound worship of our Lord without the need to perform a production with a Hollywood veneer to please the senses. And yet again, I am torn. So many can be reached using media; at the same time, we create all kinds of snares for the celebrity pastors we prop up before a camera. This is a dilemma indeed, without a simple solution.

Chrysostom also notes that the pastor who is prone to be carried away with his or her anger is like a wild beast goaded by tormentors. And perhaps he is keenly aware of the many who will poke and prod the pastor with allegations, accusations, painful attacks, and all kinds of animosity if the pastor illustrates any type of angry disposition. The church has refined its ability to torment its own shepherds for the slightest misstep.

Chrysostom will go on to explicate the unraveling nature of anger to the soul and ministry of the priest/pastor. Commenting on Prov 15:1, he says the following: "For nothing clouds the purity of the reason, and the perspicuity of the mental vision so much as undisciplined wrath, rushing along with violent impetuosity. 'For wrath,' says one, 'destroys even the prudent.'"[8]

Perhaps it is anger at being opposed, attacked, undermined, or slandered. Whatever the medium, anger is at the door of the pastor to provoke an outburst that further alienates those who support his or her vision. Perhaps this was the case for James MacDonald, former pastor of Harvest Bible Church, who comments further with some level of vulnerability concerning his tenure as pastor:

> I confess to all who have followed my ministry, a regression into sinful patterns of fleshly anger and self-pity that wounded co-workers and others. These sin issues had been points of growth and victory as expressed through my preaching and writing, but I fell back beginning in late 2016 and have only myself to blame. I wrestled with the stress I felt, the injustice I endured, etc. Yet, over time I have come to see only myself and my own relational failing in the mirror, and with grief and sorrow I ask your forgiveness.[9]

Anger was the seed that dissolved relational ties that further entrenched sides that were taken in a community of faith that was splintering at the level of leadership. Macdonald is not specific but does cite injustices and stress that became the seedbed for his anger to be provoked. And isn't this the case? Can an attack on one's integrity, dignity of call, and identity provoke within what one may have rendered crucified?

---

8. Chrysostom, "Treatise," 87.
9. MacDonald, "Pastor James' Statements of Repentance," para. 9.

Is it justifiable to become angry when an injustice has been rendered? Is wrath sinful anger when provoked in the context of an injustice? This is the dilemma of human nature and interaction.

Certainly anger can wound a relationship, certainly anger can dissolve even the strongest of bonds. But is anger sinful when it is the response to an injustice? Not knowing the specific instances in the mind of MacDonald, we must take his confession as a true recognition that his anger was out of proportion to the cause of insult or injury, which is why he sorrows. However, I do wonder if this reveals a larger issue for the church to grapple with—the nuance of anger. When and in what way is anger appropriate and how can it be on display with the right measure in response to a grievous context? For example, one could make the claim that Jesus's anger in the temple showed no restraint. It bordered on aggression when he constructed a whip to drive out the money changers. Of course, we do not call this sinful anger. We have rightly asserted that this was righteous zeal that had consumed our Lord. However, when this zeal is displayed by pastors or spiritual fathers, it can be immediately construed as sinful and out of touch.

Does the body of Christ have room in the modern church for holy anger? How would the church in our modern era respond to a prophet, priest, or spiritual father who displays such anger at injustice? Moreover, are there other contexts where anger is appropriate? How does the church discern between sinful and holy anger? What is the hermeneutic? Human relations are far too nuanced for a simple rod of discernment. For example, if one reacts with anger when accused of manipulating and deceit—is this appropriate? I have written on other occasions where temperance is a key virtue for a pastor and a pastoral vignette where a pastor displayed a sense of anger when confronted with an accusation from his staff member that he was manipulative and deceitful. Instinctively the pastor became angry, as this was misleading and an assault on his integrity. Was it virtuous to be angry, or did the pastor further wound the relationship by his anger? Was temperance or holy anger the right reaction to such a situation? Both are virtues, and yet both seem opposed to one another. For example, would Christ be asked to resign as pastor if he displayed the kind of anger when he drove the market changers out of the temple? Would he be accused of having an anger-management problem? I suppose we need great insight to know when each is needed in any particular moment.

Chrysostom will go somewhat deeper with anger when he correlates wrath with pleasure and pleasure as a seed of arrogance when he says the following:

> For the fire of wrath is a kind of pleasure, and tyrannizes over the soul more harshly than pleasure, completely upsetting its healthy organization. For it easily impels men to arrogance, and unseasonable enmities, and unreasonable hatred, and it continually makes them ready to commit wanton and vain offences; and forces them to say and do many other things of that kind, the soul being swept along by the rush of passion and having nothing on which to fasten its strength and resist so great an impulse.[10]

The rendering of punishment in wrath can become pleasurable to the soul, a pleasure that is more powerful in its influence than the pleasure of gentle reciprocity. Or at least, this is what Chrysostom asserts. Chrysostom also correlates an existential relationship between the pleasure of wrath and pride. This raises the question, If punitive measures or church discipline are delivered with wrath and there is a communal affirmation, does this then lead one headlong into greater arrogance and thus succumb to a tyranny of wrath? Certainly we cannot stereotype all churches, but it seems to me that the current temptation of the modern church is to avoid church discipline altogether in the name of grace rather than the temptation of unbridled wrath when discipline is warranted. And yet, we do have the contemporary examples above where anger appeared to create a stumbling block for Driscoll and MacDonald. This then leads us to inquire, has the pastor or spiritual father first ordered their own souls before they begin the task of ordering the church? Has the pastor weighed the gravity of the call and office with perils that he or she is sure to face? Has there been a thorough examination not only by the self but by spiritual fathers and mothers who are not afraid to raise objections concerning the soul seeking the office of spiritual father?

---

10. Chrysostom, "Treatise," 87.

Chapter 5

Setting in Order the Temptation for Adulation

He must not be arrogant ... or greedy for gain.
TITUS 1:7

SLANDER

JOHN CHRYSOSTOM, AS A spiritual father, rejects the position of being father, asserting a type of self-awareness that precludes him from the office. He also predicts the snares ahead and envisions that his offense would be great, because what may be a small defect in nature when secluded can become an immense failure when one's life becomes a public spectacle. Chrysostom warns all who would become pastors with the following:

> And apart from these things, the faults of insignificant men, even if they are exposed, inflict no injury worth speaking of upon anyone: but they who occupy the highest seat of honor are in the first place plainly visible to all, and if they err in the smallest matters these trifles seem great to others: for all men measure the sin, not by the magnitude of the offence, but by the rank of the offender. Thus, the priest ought to be protected on all sides by a kind of adamantine armour, by intense earnestness, and perpetual watchfulness concerning his manner of life, lest someone discovering an exposed and neglected spot should

inflict a deadly wound: for all who surround him are ready to smite and overthrow him: not enemies only and adversaries, but many even of those who profess friendship.[1]

Chrysostom illuminates a human way of measuring and interrelating that I now desire I would have been made aware of prior to my own tenure as pastor. He looks not at the measure of the offense, but rather the rank of the offender. Would a congregation truly throw stones at their pastor for the same offense that they would give grace and mercy for to others? The short answer is yes: if a pastor despairs, then this is egregious and must be dealt with in the harshest of manners, even his or her expulsion. If a pastor must make difficult decisions in the context of a budget cut, then he is the reason for the shortfall and his preaching must change or rather an altogether new preacher is needed to draw the crowds and ensuing revenue. If a pastor confronts the idols of a congregation, then he himself is practicing idolatry. The accusations can escalate to epic proportions—not necessarily because a mistake was made here or an oversight there, but because of his or her position as shepherd, leader, father, or mother. Chrysostom envisions the level of scrutiny he would have to endure and confesses to his friend that he is neither prepared for nor does he feel qualified to stand in the face of such a tedious examination.

But what makes Chrysostom's remarks all the more painful is when he realizes the ruthless condition of the human heart, particularly those who call themselves friends. Here is the most painful of all realizations that a pastor must face. True friendship is a rare gem in the body of Christ. Those ready to expose a minor blemish take pleasure in the fact that they can inflict a deadly wound to the pastor, one that may be nearly beyond recovery. It is not altogether uncommon for a pastor to find him- or herself surrounded by "friends" who seek his or her overthrow.

It is like the child who begins to push against parental authority as she begins adolescence—seeking to posture herself with more independence. This dynamic can be more striking if a pastor inherits a dynamic where the spiritual father before him exited because of a lack of following. Take for example, Pastor Bennett: it was this dynamic he inherited from a church leadership who were composed mostly of those who were old enough to be his father or mother. Pastor Bennett thought he would win over those in leadership by constant love and devotion to God and

---

1. Chrysostom, "Treatise," 89.

to neighbor. In contrast, what he experienced was a role reversal that eventually came to an impasse.

Pastor Bennett found early on that many of the staff and church board members attempted to lead him. They would provide counsel or advice that was sometimes in direct contradistinction to the vision he was attempting to communicate. In some attempts, the conversations were covert or packaged in spiritual language, and others were not so covert when feelings were expressed that Pastor Bennett reminded these individuals of their own son. However, when it was time to release some of the staff members because of financial difficulty, these staff members gained a following to undermine Pastor Bennett's authority. That is, they were able to recall instances where Pastor Bennett may have performed in a way that was construed as a weakness. They amassed grievances and made a case that Pastor Bennett was unfit for continued ministry. Those who made attempts to reverse the roles achieved a measure of success as the church board would eventually turn on Pastor Bennett and his friends would make no public appeal to the contrary.

If we are all honest with ourselves, there is a part of us that states that we can lead better than the one who is leading us. We convince ourselves that we have a greater measure of virtue, skill, charisma, and experience to be a spiritual father or mother and then use this assessment of ourselves to either covertly or overtly overthrow our own father or mother. Pastor Bennett's age became a liability, and he was asked to resign and did so for the sake of his family before a greater wound might be inflicted. His role as a bivocational pastor and his age were both liabilities for the church board and staff for envisioning him as a spiritual father. Roles were reversed and he was asked to leave. Incidentally, the pastor who would come after him was quite a bit older—perhaps an intentional effort to recruit a pastor who could also be envisioned as a spiritual father.

ENVY

We should also note that a spiritual father and mother can discern and confront envy. To ascend to the nature of a mother, one must descend into the valley of contentment, shirking off envy with every step. Indeed, envy is so notorious in the church that we find it to be the etiological center of the politics thus displayed in the lobbying for status and position. Listen to Chrysostom's lament here:

SETTING IN ORDER THE TEMPTATION FOR ADULATION

> And if you would know the causes of this dreadful evil, you will find that they are similar to those which were mentioned before; for they have one root and mother, so to say—namely, envy; but this is manifested in several different forms. For one we are told is to be struck out of the list of candidates, because he is young; another because he does not know how to flatter; a third because he has offended such and such a person; a fourth lest such and such a man should be pained at seeing one whom he has presented rejected, and this man elected; a fifth because he is kind and gentle; a sixth because he is formidable to the sinful; a seventh for some other like reason; for they are at no loss to find as many pretexts as they want, and can even make the abundance of a man's wealth an objection when they have no other.[2]

Every pastor should prepare for objections to his character and calling. Every pastor should expect resistance to his leadership and guidance. Envy compels one to disqualify the prophetic, run afoul of the shepherd's admonitions, and muster a contingency for murmuring. One envies his position, her preaching, his gifts, his family, his approach, his praise, and her affirmation. It appears to be a travesty in the church that those who, out of envy, work the hardest to gain recognition are rewarded with becoming a spiritual father or mother. But what if these who become fathers did not themselves have a father? What if these who become mothers did not themselves have a mother? Does Chrysostom resist his own election because he is fatherless? Does he not know the epistemology of fatherhood because he never witnessed the model up close, intimate, and personal?

I believe the truth, which is painfully acknowledged, is that most of us who desire to be spiritual fathers have not had spiritual fathers ourselves. So, we grope about in the darkness, not really knowing the existential manner of spiritual fatherhood, and stumble through interpersonal dynamics appealing to the inner father without really knowing how this is realized. There is a dearth of spiritual fathers and mothers in the church. However, we should all examine ourselves; it is good to navigate the fire of refining before taking on such a role, which can be treacherous indeed.

Chrysostom puts forth some qualities of spiritual fatherhood when he states the following:

---

2. Chrysostom, "Treatise," 93.

> Consider, then, what kind of man he ought to be who is to hold out against such a tempest, and to manage skillfully such great hindrances to the common welfare; for he ought to be dignified yet free from arrogance, formidable yet kind, apt to command yet sociable, impartial yet courteous, humble yet not servile, strong yet gentle, in order that he may contend successfully against all these difficulties.[3]

So, as these qualities are often intangible, how does one create a discerning rod for those who may be developing such character, who then may be fit as a spiritual mother, who then can pass on such qualities to spiritual daughters? Moreover, how does a church create the kind of discipling that cultivates these qualities as a rod that will act as a restraining force to prevent the stubble and hay from ascending to a place where he or she may be burned as chaff?

It is prevention, but it is also protection for the soul who may be severely wounded without deep character traits to withstand the fiery darts of the evil one. I would suggest a kind of prolonged apprenticeship, perhaps, a three-year commission where a son or daughter who aspires to be a pastor follows in immersion the steps of a father or mother in the work of the ministry. Throughout the year, fruit is highly inspected, an investigative inquiry is made of both the candidate and spouse. The candidate also experiences the rigors of ministry, the withstanding of fiery darts of slander, the arguments over money, the lobbying for power, the carnality that creeps into the church hidden under spiritual language. Seminaries would do well to pair their students with one who has fought the battle of Jericho and marched until the walls have fallen, or the pastor who has made a careful search to discover the sin in the camp in the aftermath of the defeat at Ai. The apprentice must not only witness, but immerse him- or herself in the process as a kind of fiery baptism and ask the difficult question: Can I withstand what will inevitably come to destroy me?

Pastoring is public work. Public work will draw the ire of many who envy the recognition of this public work. Six-month apprenticeships are simply not enough to identify candidates who are acquiring the kind of fortitude necessary to navigate the tempest of shepherding a flock. And the tempest will surely come when you are not only setting your own soul in order but setting God's church in order.

---

3. Chrysostom, "Treatise," 94.

ADULATION

Furthermore, a pastoral candidate must free themselves of the adulation of their congregation. Many a pastor will claim freedom from such imprisonment but will often preach or interact with their congregation in a way that reveals their bondage. Chrysostom has noted that a preacher would do well to incorporate two elements in his or her pattern of ministry: indifference to the praise of men, and the power of preaching well. Indeed, Chrysostom would draw great applause from the congregation when delivering his sermons only to severely reprimand the congregation for such adulation. He desired no applause from the people he pastored; he was careful to seek the praise of God and to preach repentance of sins.[4]

Chrysostom further notes the following: "And if on the other hand he is successful as a preacher, and is overcome by the thought of applause, harm is equally done in turn, both to himself and the multitude, because in his desire for praise he is careful to speak rather with a view to please than to profit."[5]

To please will often miss the mark of the preacher's aim to profit the soul. For in pleasing the soul, there is no admonition, no call for godly sorrow over sins, no redirecting the church to the holiness of God. A church member would like to see such a wall decorated, such an element incorporated in the service, such a manner in performing the sacraments, such a freedom here and such a rule there, a separate room for hospitality, a gift bag at the guest table or bulletin, or rather not a bulletin at all, a greeter, a parking lot attendant, a certain manner in discipling the children, and so on. A pastor would buckle under the pressure of pleasing all who came with a suggestion.

And so Chrysostom suggests pastors ought to be indifferent to praise—seek rather to profit the soul and expect that it might mean your call for resignation. But this call is far richer and better than the tumult of acclamation. For in ever pressing for greater praise from a congregation, the pastor inherits a storm that cannot be calmed in the culture he or she has created. It is a culture that amasses certain expectations upon the back of one—namely, the preacher—to effect the change for the entire church necessary to draw the large crowds. When this does not happen, the praise transforms into curses. The church has wrongly defined success by

---

4. Schaff, "Prolegomena," 38.
5. Chrysostom, "Treatise," 122.

crowds, revenue, and buildings. We have idolized metrics and have thus sacrificed true discipline on the altar of our own empires. We build an empire as a contrast to the kingdom. The juxtaposition is obvious except for those steeped within its culture. There is no covenant relationship, no apprenticing discipleship, a paucity of father-son dyads, a dearth of mother-daughter interactions. We go our separate ways, looking for a following, and find that we are lonelier in the end than when we started.

But this is not all; Chrysostom asserts that the pastor be indifferent to that which opposes affirmation—slander and envy. The pastor ought to shield his soul from both that which puffs up and that which tears down. For indeed, he or she will undeniably experience both in the tenure of ministry and when setting the soul and church in order. This then leads to the existential statement: Perhaps one is unable to be indifferent to the slander of men if one is not also indifferent to the praise of men.

Chrysostom asserts that slander be dealt with immediately and publicly when he states,

> Unseasonable evil speaking, however (for of course the Bishop undergoes some groundless censure), it is well that he should neither fear nor tremble at excessively, nor entirely pass over; but we ought, though it happen to be false, or to be brought against us by the common herd, to try and extinguish it immediately.[6]

He goes on to liken the church to an undisciplined mob who repeats a report without an inquiry into its veracity. Thus, the falsehood is magnified and disseminated indiscriminately. And, which is often the case, a report about the pastor will be proliferated throughout the congregation without a single person confirming its truth. Often there is a perversion of the truth as the report passes through the ears of the church, for in the report itself there is likely an agenda to either thwart or, worse, destroy the pastor. Thus, Chrysostom urges pastors to immediately and with great effort, "Omit nothing which is able to dispel an ill-favored report."[7]

Otherwise, the report will likely be believed by the hearer, who will concoct vain imaginations concerning the pastor who does not oppose and reject such reports through a careful examination of the word and bold admonitions for the congregation.

What, therefore, may be the consequence of neglecting to confront the evil report? Chrysostom's human insight is again quite probing: "For

---

6. Chrysostom, "Treatise," 123.
7. Chrysostom, "Treatise," 123.

despondency and constant cares are mighty for destroying the powers of the mind, and for reducing it to extreme weakness."[8]

Worries of all sorts consume the heart of the pastor. Sadness, sorrow, and depression hang over the soul of the pastor until he or she is broken without a fight to push back against the powers that rage around them. The weighty words, which push back the forces of hell that slander and take captive congregants with envy, cease from the lips of the broken man or woman who omits confronting the evil reports.

I, of course, fell into this snare. To protect the reputation of those who slandered my character, reputation, and integrity, I became quite despondent, consumed by the cares of those who severely dealt such a blow. I now see that what was an attempt to protect the reputation of those scheming my destruction was a glaring disfavor in that I did not confront the sin of their wickedness with public discipline so that the entire church would fear the Lord. I was not quick to publicly discredit the words that were at the very heart of my despondency. I incorrectly estimated that I ought to be the scapegoat and assume the blame for a difficult situation and be content with my place in the wilderness, cut off from the camp because I was a failure in the minds of a few. When our souls are contingent on the praise of men, then our souls will likely be vulnerable to the curses of men. The pastor must be indifferent to both—seeking, holding to, clinging to God for all worth and purpose.

Chrysostom goes on to explicate a kind of corruption that grief can inflict on the soul when he asserts the following:

> For thus are many constantly springing up against him, in a vain and senseless spirit, and having no fault to find with him, but that he is generally approved of, hate him; and he must bear their bitter malice nobly, for as they are not able to hide this cursed hatred, which they so unreasonably entertain, they both revile, and censure, and slander in private, and defame in public, and the mind which has begun to be pained and exasperated, on every one of these occasions, will not escape being corrupted by grief.[9]

Thus, I am convinced that a pastor must be indifferent to the praise of men, for there will also be an onslaught of reviling and animosity. The indifference will act as a shield to the soul for the pastor. For the aim of

---

8. Chrysostom, "Treatise," 123.
9. Chrysostom, "Treatise," 125.

the pastor is not the pleasing of human opinion, not the political appeal of a congregation's comfort, but the pleasing of God. A pastor is a watchman as was Ezekiel, who charges and warns the sheep of danger and pending judgment as sin continues to be at the door of the heart (see Ezek 33:1–7). If one is unable to disentangle the soul from a need of affirmation, then one may very well experience the grief of slander.

One must consider then, as we read Chrysostom, does grief have a corrupting influence on the soul? I differ from Chrysostom on this as he is not specific about the kind of grief that corrupts the soul. Grief itself is a reaction to loss and can be a healthy expression. Indeed, lamentation is as common a human expression as laughter, joy, or pleasure. We are to weep with others and rejoice with others; Paul would use both juxtaposing emotional displays as an example of common human expression. I would argue that the grief at the loss of popularity, political appeal, and human affirmation is a grief that can potentially corrupt the human soul and the pastor along with his or her family. For in losing human affirmation, one is unable to take pleasure in divine affirmation for having been persecuted for the sake of the Lord's call. If one is contingent on human affirmation for the call of ministry to be perpetuated, then one is highly vulnerable to that call being threatened by human slander and vitriol. This is a kind of grief that perpetuates despair, winnowing out the hope that a pastor is called to convey to the sheep.

My confession is relevant to Chrysostom's warning. For I was at the mercy of human affirmation if I am honest with my feelings. Without affirmation from my father, I sought it out in other people, such as mentoring figures. I was also unaware of this emotional need, which became more obvious after the church I pastored began to dwindle in attendance and revenue. I was quick to cast the blame inward, assuming the scapegoat status, which was perpetuated by personal slander. If affirmation was missing, I quickly assumed that my calling was at stake. This is where the pastor errs, in placing stock in human affirmation rather than obedience to God. This is the kind of grief that is corrupting, for its fruit is hopelessness, despair, and misery. It is a disposition of shame that becomes a heavy fall of rain when there is no shelter in which to take refuge. Unless one can redirect the need of affirmation heavenward, despair is quick to consume a soul. I would argue that the more indifferent a pastor becomes to the affirmation, opinion, and envy of men, the more he or she is able to mitigate the kind of grief that corrupts the soul.

SETTING IN ORDER THE TEMPTATION FOR ADULATION

And yet, we omit a nuance of the kind of grief that remains outside one's personal reaction to human slander; we must ask about one's spouse and children. What if slander, envy, and animosity are directed to the ones the pastor loves? What if they experience the grief of broken relationships, public defamation, and dishonest conversations meant to destroy the reputation of a family member? Very few pastors can watch a family member suffer from such hostilities without escaping the clutches of such a stranglehold on one's family.

Pastor Cory wept before his bishop as he handed his resignation to him in the context of his wife's suffering. Her suffering became his own. Her weeping became his own. Her grief became his own. He could not perpetuate such grief when he had the opportunity to bring a balm through deliverance and an escape from the fowler's snare (see Ps 124). There are few pastors who will witness a family member suffering from public slander within his or her own church and remain within this bondage when he or she is able to provide a reprieve by taking yet another job.

Finally, Chrysostom will bring an anthropomorphic attribute to public praise, likening it to a monster with many heads. This may or may not be an allusion to the mythic creature Hydra, who had many heads and was difficult to kill; when one head was cut off, two more would grow. I'm also reminded of the creature Medusa, who was able with one glance to transform a once valiant hero to stone. Perhaps one can extrapolate this metaphor to conjure up a similar existential reality—that is, the beholding of public praise and appeal as the means to a hardened heart. On one hand, the praise becomes the constant outcome that delineates the efforts of a pastor to the ruin of his or her own soul. For if taken to its logical end, it may involve the belittling or even destruction of another who may be redirecting such public adulation away from the pastor. On the other hand, when curses replace the praise, the pastor who has made public praise such an idol will turn to despair and hopelessness and as such cut short his or her call to a congregation out of self-pity. Beware of both hardenings. Though different in display, both can come from the one source, the monster capable of turning the heart to stone through either vainglory or despair.

Of course, Chrysostom also illustrates this with his own potent description as follows:

> If then there be any man so constituted as to be able to subdue this wild beast, so difficult to capture, so unconquerable, so fierce; that is to say, public fame, and to cut off its many heads,

Setting in Order

or rather to forbid their growth altogether; he will easily be able to repel these many violent assaults, and to enjoy a kind of quiet haven of rest. But he who has not freed himself from this monster, involves his soul in struggles of various kinds, and perpetual agitation, and the burden both of despondency and of other passions.[10]

Greek mythology purports the slaying of Medusa by the sword of Perseus. In like manner, the sword of the Spirit wielded by a resolute soul of contentment in all things and obedience to God can slay the monster of public adulation and slander. A pastor must set him- or herself in order with a heart that has a single aim—to please God. This may be the blade sharp enough to slay such a monster, which in turn provides the fruit of peace when the human assault comes. And no pastor should think of him- or herself as being immune from such assaults. It is not *if* but *when* this might occur.

Therefore, to conclude the previous several chapters, we need a father-son/mother-daughter dyad in all forms of ministry. It is an apprenticeship that aids in the ordering of the soul so that the ordering of the church may be its fruit. This kind of personal exchange takes time and is a journey involving a type of yoking together in all forms of pastoral service whether it be visitation, baby dedication, marriage, funerals, budget meetings, or conflict. The father takes the son into the fray of battle. The father fiercely defends the son from attack and publicly stands with the son in the chaos of arrows that fly from within. The pastor who seeks to be a shepherd must order his or her own soul in temperance and with a kind of resolve that puts to death the love of human praise and thus the despair that comes from human vitriol. The spiritual father is kenotic, pouring him- or herself out on behalf of others. The spiritual father resists negligence in the name of feigned protection of any vainglory of another. The spiritual father navigates the waters of contempt by seeking the profit of the soul through obedience over and above the appeasement of human preference. The spiritual father does not fear the dwindling of numbers in the face of preaching repentance. The spiritual father will emphasize the sacraments over social media, intimacy over the i-culture, the ancient landmarks of Christian discipline over the accolades of popularity, and radical obedience over the riches of superficial metrics.

10. Chrysostom, "Treatise," 128.

The father takes upon himself sons to sojourn together while defending them publicly when overthrow rumbles around the sons and daughters. And this is where the spiritual journey culminates, a transformation from son to father and daughter to mother. I would like to conclude with yet another Catholic writer, writing much later but with a similar emphasis on the need for spiritual fathers. Henri Nouwen comments on Rembrandt's painting of the prodigal son and comes to the following conclusion:

> But Rembrandt who showed me the Father in utmost vulnerability, made me come to the awareness that my final vocation is indeed to become like the Father and to live out his divine compassion in my daily life. Though I am both the younger son and the elder son, I am not to remain them, but to become the Father. No father or mother ever became father or mother without having been son or daughter, but every son and daughter has to consciously choose to step beyond their childhood and become father and mother for others. It is a hard and lonely step to take—especially in a period of history in which parenthood is so hard to live well—but it is a step that is essential for the fulfilment of the spiritual journey.[11]

---

11. Nouwen, *Return of the Prodigal Son*, 140.

Chapter 6

Setting Elders in Order I

I left you behind in Crete for this reason, so that you should put in order what remained to be done and should appoint elders in every town, as I directed you.

Titus 1:5

The task of the presiding elder or local pastor is setting in order a church that is either first forming or careening out of order. After greeting Titus, Paul's first imperative is for Titus to set in order the churches that formed from their mission to Crete. The Greek ἐπιδιορθόω (*epidiorthoo*), denoting "to correct from above," is also used to refer to amending or restoring an organization or institution.[1] This word is used only here in Titus 1:5 and so we must extrapolate from other uses during the same era for greater clarity. The closest intimation of this concept in the New Testament is found in Hebrews: "But deal only with food and drink and various baptisms, regulations for the body imposed until the time comes to set things right" (Heb 9:10).

The word for "reformation" originated in ἐπιδιορθόω and so warrants that we consider reformation as a sense of the imperative given to Titus from Paul. This will make greater sense as we proceed with the text and find Paul describing the attributes of those who oppose Titus's work. Reformation is the task of the pastor. Every pastor can reform what he or she inherits. Every pastor can reform the congregation no matter the age

---

1. Zodhiates and Baker, *Hebrew-Greek Key Word*, 1715.

or how seemingly pristine the infrastructure. If it is human, it has flaws, and the church as an organic, human entity has human frailties in need of reformation.

Titus—and every pastor—is sent to a church to reform it. Setting it in order is one piece of the reformation process. Are there elders? Are they appointed or elected? Who is leading the church? Is it a pastor-led and elder-accountable church or elder-led and thus a pastor who becomes the spokesperson for the elders? Are there qualifications specified for being an elder? Are there job descriptions for the elders, the staff, the deacons, etc.? Are there any formal deacons? How is the church treating authority? Are there covert groups undermining authority? Is there heretical teaching? Are there groups lobbying for the landscape on "prophetic" authority? If so, a pastor must reform these groups by providing structure, form, and purpose along with formally setting elders to teach these groups, or dismissing the leaders who may not qualify as elders. Each group's leader must be interviewed and the fruit inspected to discern whether the minister is bearing good or bad fruit.

Where there is no discipline or accountability, the human default is toward independence, breaking from the vision of the local pastor and, at times, harming the church. Every leader ought to be in harmony and in collaboration with the local pastor's direction for the church. Setting in order is reforming, dismantling the sacred cows, moving the church from unfreedom to freedom, completing what was left undone. Independence is not necessarily freedom and can be unfreedom if couched in the apparatus of rebellion from God's appointed pastor. It is the role of a pastor to set in order and he or she must anticipate resistance in the process.

I was reflecting one day with a friend who is a pastor, and he asked a question that may be pertinent to all who pastor. Can the pastor outlast the critics? It is not a question whether a pastor will be criticized, this is inevitable. But can the pastor outlast his or her critics to make meaningful reforms in the church? Constant criticism can be like waves constantly crashing against a rock and chipping away fragments one breaker at a time.

ORDINATION

One of the first tasks of reform is to ordain elders in a church where there are none and inspect the current elders of an established church. I have written extensively in *The Coming Winter* on the notion of appointments vs. elections regarding establishing a body of elders. Paul is clear to Titus, as he was to Timothy, that elders are to be appointed by the presiding elder or the church pastor. A pastor can expedite reforms in the church if he has a body of elders to help him in governing the church. However, elders must meet the qualifications and be committed to the function of an elder. For a review of such qualifications and job description of elders, please see *The Coming Winter*. However, it may suffice to provide yet another emphasis as Paul is not timid in reiterating how an elder board is chosen.

Elders are ordained. In the Greek, καθίστημι is employed to illustrate one who is being set into an office.[2] For a better understanding of this theological term, we turn to yet another use by Paul when expositing the work of redemption. "For just as through the one man's disobedience the many were made sinners, so through the one man's obedience the many will be made righteous" (Rom 5:19).

Adam is the figurehead of all transgression, the federal head that inaugurates the fall and curse sustained by the globe, infecting all who are human. His disobedience καθίστημι (made) one a sinner. That is, we were appointed or ordained to be a sinner secondary to our head being a sinner and thus have inherited his sinful nature as one inherits DNA from a father. Adam is our sinful father, and we are also made sinners through progeny. However, there is a remedy that acts as a messenger RNA (if you will, holding to the genetic metaphor) to splice out of the genetic code, the preponderance to sin, and translate it into the construct of imputed righteousness. The obedience of Christ καθίστημι (makes) one righteous. Just as we were appointed to be sinners, Christ reappoints us to be righteous. Just as we were ordained to miss the mark, the faithful are transformed into righteousness by the blood of Jesus.

Another way of saying this is that we were declared sinners by God because of the disobedience of Adam and subsequently declared righteous by the blood and obedience of Jesus. In the same way, a pastor declares who are elders, ordaining and appointing them into the office based on their qualification and their call to submit to the role, work, and function of the elder. This ought to become one of the more serious undertakings of a pastor to the extent that a service is dedicated to the ordination of elders for the congregation to declare in the witness of all,

---

2. Zodhiates and Baker, *Hebrew-Greek Key Word*, 1725.

"Amen! Let it be thus." (Please see appendix C for a sample liturgy for the ordination of elders.)

We are given some liturgical elements of such a service when Paul returns to the place where he was persecuted. Despite being expelled from Lystra, Antioch, and Iconium, converts had come to Christ through the ministry of Paul. He returns for the purpose of establishing governing bodies in the local churches through the καθίστημι of elders. "And after they had appointed elders for them in each church, with prayer and fasting they entrusted them to the Lord in whom they had come to believe" (Acts 14:23).

Paul includes fasting as a substantive liturgical element of the ordination proceedings. And why fast? Perhaps it is due to the notion that fasting is a consecrating act of discipleship. It is a voluntary suppression of satiation for the purpose of crucifying the flesh. It is a measure of submitting the primal will to the divine will of God. It is an act of intercessory charge, fueling the appeal from a frail vessel that God would indeed deposit his treasure there. Fasting reveals our true heart, motives, and intentions in serving. Fasting can distinguish the weeds from wheat, the tares from grain, the goats from the sheep, and the wolves from the shepherds. Fasting quiets the inner voices that drive us toward carnal success and attunes our ears to the inner and contemplative life of hearing the Spirit. Therefore, fasting is to consecrate, submit, surrender, crucify, discern, and bend to the will of God in becoming an elder in God's economy.

The Church of God in Christ has suggested the following: Those who "are ordained may come that we, after prayer and fasting, may lay hands on them, that they may be fully set apart for the work of the ministry."[3] Thus, we find in early Pentecostalism a symbiotic relationship between ordination and fasting for the sake of sealing the elder as one consecrated for the work ahead.

This is certainly emphasized in G. W. Batman's comments:

> I fasted and prayed for about three days and during that time I put off the old man Adam in the form of inbred sin and God came in and destroyed the devil's workshop by casting his tools on the outside. Praise God I got real evidence that I was

---

3. The Whole Truth was founded by C. H. Mason, leader of the Church of God in Christ. Mason, "Whole Truth," 3. See also Martin, *Fasting*, 131.

sanctified, and the Blood applied. After that, I received the baptism with the Holy Ghost and fire.[4]

Fasting provides not only a praxis for preparation, but a theological framework for deep prayer leading to a surrender to the call of God. Fasting prayer provided a spiritual wrecking ball abolishing the old man apparatus. In early Pentecostalism, and even today, fasting prayer demolishes not only the work of the devil but the very institution of the devil to stall, oppress, or oppose the believer. Early holiness believers would seek entire sanctification and thus fasting prayer became a normative medium by which this appeal to the Lord was conducted. Fasting prayer prepares the elder for the somber weight of maturing a body of believers in the faith. Fasting can be revelatory, not merely disclosing the Lord but also our true motives. As Richard Foster has insightfully noted,

> More than any other discipline, fasting reveals the things that control us.... At first we will rationalize that our anger is due to our hunger; then we will realize that we are angry because the spirit of anger is within us.[5]

In this way, fasting prayer provides a divine opportunity for repentance with the fruit of such humility being greater consecration and greater destruction of the sin nature. This begs that the consecration of the elders of a church undertake a time of fasting prayer in preparation of their ordination by the local church pastor. The elder candidate is to submit to the combing of the Holy Spirit for any need of repentance, seek for entire sanctification, and ready the soul for the consecration of service as an elder of the church. Pastors, it is incumbent upon you to restore this practice to the church.

THE PRESBYTERY AS JUDGES

Paul employs a different word here to describe an elder than he did when writing to Timothy. When instructing Timothy, he employed the term ἐπισκοπῆς (*episkipos*). For more on this term and its use in the Epistles to Timothy, please see *The Coming Winter*. However, here in Titus, the term πρεσβύτερος (*presbuteros*) is used to convey the office of an elder. It is likely that Paul intends to use these terms interchangeably as he does

---

4. See Martin, *Fasting*, 132.
5. Foster, *Celebration of Discipline*, 55.

use ἐπισκοπῆς in Titus 1:7 when discussing the qualifications of an elder. However, the synonym πρεσβύτερος may give us more clarity concerning the role and office of an elder.[6]

The term πρεσβύτερος resonates with the New Testament literature as one who is an ambassador, and quite literally "one who is older" and thus an elder. It is used in Matt 15:2 to convey ancestry or predecessors. In the Septuagint, we find the use of the word to describe the leaders of Joseph's house in Egypt (see Gen 50:7). In essence, these elders or πρεσβύτερος enjoyed a natural dignity that was then associated with age. Age was honored in this culture and wisdom was intuited as an attribute of age. We would do well as a culture in the church to restore honor to the elderly as men and women who God has graced with a certain dignity because of their age.

Elders or πρεσβύτερος accompanied Moses when declaring the oracle of God to Pharaoh and the imperative that he ought to let them go (see Exod 3:16–18). The πρεσβύτερος were tribal heads and may have enjoyed the filial rite as the firstborn, which was an esteemed role in Judaist culture, as it was the firstborn that received an authoritative blessing from the patriarch (see 1 Kgs 8:1–3). Moses chose seventy πρεσβύτερος who bear with Moses the burden of adjudicating certain cases of disputations among the people to render a verdict (see Num 11:17). This was the first case where the πρεσβύτερος were being appointed by a presiding elder, namely Moses. This was a landmark transition in governance as, prior to this, tribes would choose their representative πρεσβύτερος in some way who was then sent as a tribal ambassador. However, Moses transitions to a wholly different system of governance when he appoints the πρεσβύτερος and then grants them authority to render judgment among the people.[7]

This practice of seventy elders would continue in the assembling of the Sanhedrin during the era of Jesus's ministry (see Luke 22:66–71). By this time, the Sanhedrin had become more elaborate as a bureaucracy, for they had developed a system of assistants. In every city there were elders or ambassadors, but these were non-Sanhedrin members. It is possible that a system had evolved to choose these elders from among the people (see Matt 26:3). Thus, the Sanhedrin represented the chief priests and adjudicators of all major debates or disputations among the people.

---

6. Please note that the terms elder, bishop, and overseer are used interchangeably, as is the case with Paul.

7. Zodhiates and Baker, *Hebrew-Greek Key Word*, 1751.

The assistant-elders were ones who judged smaller and local matters of conflict. It is unclear whether they reported to the Sanhedrin but may have had some method by which they could escalate a case that required further deliberation.[8]

The πρεσβύτερος can also be used as a verb in the form of *proistemi* which provides greater clarity to the office as well. In this manner, *proistemi* is rendered as one who stands before or maintains rule over. In the New Testament governance, the πρεσβύτερος were then appointed and ordained as agents of authority over every local church (see Acts 14:23, 1 Tim 5:17, and Titus 1:5). The πρεσβύτερος received offerings and determined the allocation of these offerings (see Acts 11:30; 12:25). Thus, the πρεσβύτερος were the stewards of financial donations and, in contemporary terms, developed and maintained a church budget. The appointing of deacons in Acts 6 provides the intimation that the first twelves disciples or apostles were also the first body of πρεσβύτερος.[9]

Therefore, a system of governance arises in the early church that comprises three bodies of authority: first, the apostles, chosen by Jesus, who represent the first line of authority as the πρεσβύτερος. The apostles, acting as πρεσβύτερος also exhorted the second body of authority, the local elders, to keep sound doctrine and resist the devil (see 1 Pet 5:1 and Acts 20:17). The apostolic πρεσβύτερος appointed local church elders as is the case in our narrative where both Timothy and Titus are appointed by Paul. The apostolic πρεσβύτερος were commissioned by Jesus and the local πρεσβύτερος were appointed by the apostles. The deacons were first appointed by the apostolic πρεσβύτερος, but later it is implied that local elders such as Timothy were instructed to appoint deacons (see 1 Tim 3:8–16). Thus, it appears that this authority was later conferred to local presiding elders of churches—namely, the church pastor.[10]

Finally, in our excursus on πρεσβύτερος, I would like to conclude with a discussion on the heavenly πρεσβύτερος, and in such manner develop a polemic that our local πρεσβύτερος ought to pattern themselves after the heavenly court. Are not our churches, our gatherings, our church governance, our liturgy, our worship, and work merely a pattern or shadow of the heavenly institution? Are we not to adhere to this pattern in true fidelity and veracity? Are we not to emulate the governance displayed in the heavenly court?

8. Zodhiates and Baker, *Hebrew-Greek Key Word*, 1751.
9. Zodhiates and Baker, *Hebrew-Greek Key Word*, 1751.
10. Zodhiates and Baker, *Hebrew-Greek Key Word*, 1751.

ELDERS AND THE TESTIMONY OF JESUS

The πρεσβύτερος of heaven are given seats that encircle the throne, seats that are paradigmatic for exercising judgment and authority. The thrones being a corollary for judgment is known to hearers later when John sees the thrones, and those who sit upon the thrones are given the rite to exercise judgment (see Rev 20:4). Although we do not have an explicit reference to twenty-four elders envisioned here in the millennial reign of Christ, the implicit notion that those sitting upon the thrones are elders is verified as the only previous description we have of numerous thrones are the ones occupied by the redeemed elders.

Indeed, as Clarence Larkin has noted, elders figuratively represent cities, families, tribes, or nations. Perhaps, as the first Adam is the federal head of fallen humanity and as the second Adam, Christ is the representative of rescued humanity, the twenty-four elders are representatives of redeemed humanity. The fusion of Old and New Testament humanity in the number of the twenty-four elders is an all-encompassing body of humanity, having been redeemed by Christ himself in all human ages and epochs.[11]

It is quite possible that John sees what Daniel has already seen. The difference, however, is that Daniel saw unoccupied thrones where John sees the thrones occupied by the twenty-four elders. Listen to Daniel's description of a plurality of thrones presided over by the Ancient of Days: "As I watched, thrones were set in place, and an Ancient One took his throne; his clothing was white as snow and the hair of his head like pure wool; his throne was fiery flames, and its wheels were burning fire" (Dan 7:9).

Moreover, it is quite possible that those hearing John would recall that just a mere chapter earlier, Jesus had stated that he would grant to those who overcome, the gift to sit with him on his throne (see Rev 3:21). This would then indicate that the elders who occupy the thrones are also those who overcome the world by holding to the testimony of Jesus Christ. And this is important as eldership reflects judgment and judgment must have a moral framework that adheres to the testimony of Christ. Elders who exercise a moral framework based upon any other thesis or foundation of philosophical underpinnings exercise another kind of judgment, not the judgment of Christ. This seems to me why Paul is often pleading with the churches not to entertain another gospel than the one he was preaching, for he was preaching Christ. The πρεσβύτερος

---

11. Larkin, *Book of Revelation*, 40.

must forever refer to the testimony of Christ when a critical decision is called for, when one is formulating the stewardship plan for the church, when one is exercising church discipline with a sinner, when one is rooting out corruption and reforming the church, and when one is leading in worship. It seems obvious to me that the phrase "the testimony of Jesus Christ" is used throughout the Apocalypse to reorient to the centrality of Christ as the culminating figure in the metanarrative of God.

In Rev 1:2 John states that his entire account will be, as it were, a testimony from Jesus Christ both in the words he hears and the visions he sees. Indeed, John will reiterate in 1:9 that he is exiled as a direct result of keeping the testimony of Jesus Christ. In Rev 12:17, it is the dragon who wages war on the seed of the women, the very remnant who keeps the testimony of Jesus Christ. And the final and fourth use of the phrase is found in Rev 19:10, where John's false worship is redirected to the fountainhead of worship, Jesus Christ, and whose testimony is the spirit of prophecy. Those who hold to the testimony of Jesus Christ have overcome the world and its constant refrain to construct one's life on yet another foundation. The elders of the heavenly court are ones who have overcome the world by keeping Christ's testimony and their thrones are a fruit of this overcoming disposition. In the same way, elders in the church must keep to the testimony of Jesus Christ—it is the way of exercising sound judgment in the body of Christ. And indeed, this is one of their functions—to provide sound judgment amid deliberation in the church.

Chapter 7

Setting Elders in Order II

> Holding tightly to the trustworthy word of the teaching, so that he may be able both to exhort with sound instruction and to refute those who contradict it.
>
> TITUS 1:9

ELDERS AS PRIESTS

JOHN'S VISION OF THE throne in heaven includes a description of the πρεσβύτερος. Our first vision of them is simply their number (twenty-four), their location (around the throne of God), and their clothing—wearing white robes with each donning a crown of gold (Rev 4:4). Therefore, we find that the πρεσβύτερος are ones who, like the faithful in Sardis, refused to defile their clothing through idol worship. They "will walk with me in white, for they are worthy," says the Lord (Rev 3:4).

The number would also likely prompt the hearer to discern a possible commingling of the representatives from the twelve tribes of Israel and the twelve apostles. The elders are distinctly mentioned later in Rev 7:11 and are linguistically distinct from the great multitude in v. 9 as ones who may have come out of the multitude but who are marked by appointed seats and proximity to the throne in the heavenly court. The angels encircle the throne and the elders, falling before God to worship him (see Rev 7:11).[1]

We also have a distinguishing remark as one of the elders inquires of John the identity of the multitude in v. 9. Of course, John defers to the elder's knowledge and is informed that this multitude are those "who have come out of the great tribulation; they have washed their robes and made them white in the blood of the Lamb" (Rev 7:14).

The identity of the twenty-four elders is also intimated by the very construct of the new Jerusalem where there are twelve gates named for the twelve tribes of Israel and twelve foundations named for the twelve apostles (see Rev 21:12–14). Certainly, there is a special role for the tribes of Israel and the apostles in the heavenly court.

The πρεσβύτερος are to pattern their lives with utmost fidelity to Christ. They are to forsake all idolatry and walk circumspectly with holiness as their garment and sanctification as their cry and appeal. They are to overcome the world, the domain of Satan, and the temptations of his emissaries, for "he that overcomes, the same will be clothed in white garments" (Rev 3:5). The πρεσβύτερος are overcomers who give direction for the sheep to overcome. They wear white robes as this is a sign of their disposition, the righteousness of Christ in them, their deep desire for holiness, and their allegiance to Jesus.

Clarence Larkin notes that the white robes of the elders do not typify the normative dress of royalty, but rather the garment of a priestly collective. That is, though crowns and thrones are offered as we will see later, the robes are not necessarily a sign of authority or judgment, but rather holiness, redemption, and sanctification.[2]

This priestly role is further exemplified by the fact that the elders have in their possession golden vials full of odors or incense which are the accumulated prayers of saints past and present (see Rev 5:8).

Furthermore, we are given additional clues of what their white raiment typifies when one of the elders inquires of John as to the identity of the congregation in heaven with white robes. Of course, John is unable to provide an adequate answer and so the elder divulges that these are "they

---

1. See Thomas, *Apocalypse*, 207, for more discussion on the identity of the elders in the Apocalypse. He asserts that "the division of the priesthood into twenty-four courses would be common knowledge (1 Chronicles 24:4–6)." Indeed, the reference to Chronicles is important here as David is the first to divide the priesthood into twenty-four priestly representatives.

2. Larkin, *Book of Revelation*, 40.

which came out of the great tribulation, and have washed their robes, and made them white in the blood of the Lamb" (Rev 7:14). The elders are indeed redeemed and sanctified humanity who are chosen as ones who have overcome the world and who have washed themselves in the blood of the Lamb. One cannot serve as priest without first having been bathed in the blood of the Lamb! Redemption is a necessary prerequisite to eldership. Prevailing over the world of tribulation with all its trappings and snares identifies the elder, which is clearly seen by the court of heaven. Deference to the power and authority of Christ is in one who remains under the fountain of the Lamb's blood.

The white robes and priestly function would have made further sense to the hearers of John's Apocalypse when he describes what he sees next, that the ones washed in the blood of the Lamb "serve him day and night in his temple" (Rev 7:15). This is yet another function of the priests, serving the Lord in the collection of prayers (perhaps typified by joining the prayers of the flock) and leading in worship (given the harps the elders carry, see Rev 5:8). Thomas will further assert that this service, and more particularly their white robes, is a sign that "one has an intimate association with Jesus."[3] The one who serves the Lord as priest day and night accumulates a kind of relational intimacy by virtue of continual proximity to Christ.

The harps and vials therefore become the tools of the priests. As priests, they function as vessels of perpetual worship and epistles of memory. That is, they recall to God the prayers of the people. Thomas reminds us that it was the elders who possessed the harps in 5:8, as "the masculine phrase 'each having one,' clearly goes with the elders, which appear in the masculine gender in the Greek text as well."[4]

The harps were utilized in the new song that only the 144,000 could learn (see Rev 14:2). The harps were employed with recapitulation of the song of Moses, who himself was a priest who sang to God and over the nation of Israel (see Rev 15:2). Indeed, it was after the song of Moses that the temple was open, which implies that worship can function to open aspects of God's imminent work upon the earth. Moreover, the πρεσβύτερος as elders must model this worship for the congregation.

The psalmist reminds us that prayers are akin to incense and sacrifice in the heavenly temple (see Ps 141:2). The psalmist also reminds

---

3. Thomas, *Apocalypse*, 208.
4. Thomas, *Apocalypse*, 229.

us of the collection of prayerful tears in God's economy (see Ps 56:8). We find the author of Hebrews also recalling this heavenly transaction when he affirms that praise is the spiritual sacrifice unto the Lord and is offered through speech (see Heb 13:15). And we will find, a few chapters later, John describing the golden vial, now in the hands of an angel (see Rev 8:3).

The prayers were deposited upon the heavenly altar, which ascended to the Lord. Now that the vial was emptied, it could be filled with yet another phenomenon, the fire from the altar. It is as if the prayers contributed, in part, to the fire that was engendered upon the heavenly altar, which resulted in an inbreaking of heaven to earth. When the fire, the prayers of the saints, is cast to the earth, the earth responds with "voices, and thundering, and lightning, and an earthquake" (Rev 8:5).

Thomas observes that "the fire that is cast down from the altar is fueled by the prayers of the saints."[5] This is a remarkable phenomenon as it reminds the reader that prayers are collected in heaven, effectual for an appointed time, and will have tangible and eschatological manifestations. The πρεσβύτερος must be continually offering and encouraging the church to offer such prayers for consumption upon the heavenly altar. The white robes, harps, and golden vials are the signs that the πρεσβύτερος are to be priests and as priests, they are to continually serve the Lord vis-à-vis righteous and victorious living in Christ, worship, and prayers.

The white robes in the heavenly court also represent a mantle of sorts. It is a sign of remaining faithful to Jesus even if it may create the context for martyrdom. For white robes were "given to each of them; and it was said to them that they should rest a little while longer, until both *the number of* their fellow servants and their brethren, who would be killed as they *were*, was completed" (Rev 6:11). Thus, the heavenly πρεσβύτερος are also the priests, the priests are the ones who wear the mantle of victory, having passed through a type of death and thus prevailing over the world in Christ. The Apocalypse no doubt here is quite literal, it is the martyrs who receive white robes of victory. These martyrs held to the testimony of Christ at the expense of their very lives (see Rev 6:9). Now, as the language of πρεσβύτερος is not used to describe these martyrs, it should not be assumed that every elder must undergo martyrdom, but that the raiment of the martyrs and the elders are similar and connote a type of prevailing victory. The victory is the Christian paradox

---

5. Thomas, *Apocalypse*, 283.

of death. The πρεσβύτερος must die to personal, earthly, vain, and sinful ambition. The πρεσβύτερος must die to the royal robe that is so often concomitant with overt strength and intelligence and surrender to the Lamb's washing.

I can recall a time when I entered an auditorium filled with family and friends of all those who had come to witness the mark of the physician's robe. The students who were now entering medical school had prevailed over the rigors of academic testing, sacrificed a great deal to withstand the curriculum, standardized tests, and all other deterrents, to arrive finally at the donning of a white coat, which is the sign and symbol of a physician. It is the robe that signifies a type of testing, if you will, in which each candidate had overcome, and which illustrates the passing of one test to enter yet another test. The trial of medical school would be an immense challenge, and one would hope that the call, compassion, and determination of the candidate would aid in the overcoming of yet more trials to come.

It was often fathers, mothers, or mentors who placed the white coat on the medical student in ceremonial fashion. I recall feeling the weight of this robe, a weight of expectation, a donning of immense responsibility. Would I pass the tests to come? Would I come through the fire intact? Would I serve the Lord as a healer? Would I surrender my life and my pride to receive the aid of the Lord and the assistance of my fellow students? These questions would linger throughout medical school. I recall one incident when I nearly withdrew from medical school while I floundered under the weight of academic rigor. As I cried out to the Lord, he was gracious to remind me that failure is not always viewed correctly. Failure may be a victory if in the Lord's economy it reveals human frailty so that God's glory could be manifested. The Lord reminded me that weakness is strength in God's economy.

Pastor Cory would receive in his ministry another type of raiment, a prayer shawl from the prayer team of the church he was pastoring. Pastor Cory was facing multiple challenges as his church was declining in attendance, revenue was shrinking, and critical decisions had to be made to remain financially solvent. These decisions were agreed upon by his council of the church, but as word got out, certain staff members who painfully had to be let go influenced council members to reverse the decision and some council members were so adamant about this that if the decision was not reversed then pastor Cory would need to resign.

Setting in Order

Moreover, Pastor Cory was facing a sexual abuse scandal within the preschool of the church. A preschool employee had been accused of sexually abusing a child, which made local news. Others had written to his state supervisor that his wife was unfit for ministry and thus a replacement was suggested. Thus, Pastor Cory was facing a sexual scandal, a budgetary crisis, a challenge to his leadership, and a spouse who had been severely wounded by those within the church. It was with this weight that he came to speak to the prayer ministry of the church, and it was here that a prayer shawl was ceremonially presented to him and placed upon his shoulders.

Perhaps this became a sign of his role and function as priest—one who carries prayers to God? Perhaps it would later come to mean so much more to Cory—a sign of prevailing by keeping the testimony of Jesus Christ despite the tribulation that sought to undermine his very faith? Pastor Cory would later hear from a prayer team member that he would need to pass the test that had come to him. But what does passing the test really look like? Pastor Cory wrestled with this definition. Surely, a typical way of defining this victory would be to prevail over one's persecutors by remaining and overcoming the ones who rejected and slandered him.

Pastor Cory, however, considered the unintended targets and casualties over prevailing in this way—his spouse and children. His spouse had already been humiliated and undermined by a parishioner of the church. And it seemed that one of his sons was becoming the next target as some level of disgruntlement was being expressed concerning his behavior. What if prevailing for Pastor Cory was prevailing for his wife and children—keeping the testimony of Christ by serving, protecting, loving, and surrendering a dream on their behalf? Perhaps the prayer shawl was given to Pastor Cory as a sign that he was to wrap his family in it through intercession and loving protection that came from the very people who were to love him and his family. Pastor Cory longed for his children to preserve a love for Christ, an endearment that would persist and not be deterred in the infancy of their discipleship by the animosity of those who were actively attempting to destroy him and his family. Prevailing in this sense is keeping the testimony of Christ regardless of context or persecution. Pastor Cory keeps the testimony of Christ; he surrenders his dream of being a pastor, and embraces his dream of being a husband and father. The death of one dream allows greater access to envision an altogether different dream, with the constant refrain of keeping the testimony of Christ.

Pastor Cory will sometimes unearth the prayer shawl in his prayer closet and remind himself that victory takes on different perspectives. What one will call victory, others define as defeat. But as Pastor Cory wraps his head in the prayer shawl and calls upon the living God, he is reminded that sometimes the more meaningful victories are the ones that others simply cannot understand. It is true that God will use the base of this world to confound the wise.

THE ELDERS AS KENOTIC VICTORS

Now we consider a crown given to the elders as a token and gift to memorialize victory. Clarence Larkin has noted that the twenty-four elders are "redeemed mankind."[6] That is, in the heavenly court, they are not angels, they are not the four living creatures, they are not fallen humanity. The elders are ones who have overcome the world, are ones purchased by the blood of Christ, and who now have a seat of authority and access to the throne room and heavenly court of God. Larkin notes that it is only redeemed humanity who are promised thrones and crowns (see Matt 19:28; 2 Tim 4:8; 1 Pet 5:2–4; Rev 2:10; 3:21; 20:4).[7]

If we were to extrapolate further here in a temporal sense, elders are necessarily redeemed. That is, they have exchanged the crown of worldly elevation for a crown of righteousness. The crown's substance is interesting here, for it is a precious metal, that of gold, and is pregnant with meaning. Larkin is keen to note Peter's description of an elder's crown as glory.[8] That is, when the "chief Shepherd appears, those faithful elders will receive the crown of glory that does not fade away" (1 Pet 5:2–4).

Thus, πρεσβύτερος are given a crown of glory and authority from the Lord but are also the ones who continually give it away to the Lord Jesus Christ. The πρεσβύτερος are forever deferring authority to Christ. An elder is always deflecting praise to the Lord Jesus Christ. An elder is never seeking his own glory, fame, recognition, or power. An elder who does seek his own glory is not an elder at all. An elder who is stirring strife in the body, slandering his or her way to recognition, or grasping

---

6. Larkin, *Book of Revelation*, 38.
7. Larkin, *Book of Revelation*, 38.
8. Larkin, *Book of Revelation*, 39.

Setting in Order

for a crown of power is not an elder. The heavenly court is a pattern that instructs us in the discernment and inspection of an elder. The heavenly court is the example par excellence of how our churches ought to be governed as well.

Some of the πρεσβύτερος are included with the "souls of them slain for the word of God and for the testimony"(Rev 6:9). These also are given "white robes . . . and it was said to them that they should rest for a season until their fellow servants . . . should be killed" (Rev 6:11). Martyrdom is a sign of having overcome the world. This is the final and consummate sign of a life completely consecrated to the Lord despite the threat of death and amid passing from this life to the next. There is no greater love on display than for one to lay down his or her life for another (see John 15:13).

Could this also be yet another illustration or qualification for the πρεσβύτερος? That is, has the elder passed the fiery trial of temptation in the wilderness and prevailed in Christ? Has the πρεσβύτερος been crucified with Christ so they no longer live, but Christ in them? Has the πρεσβύτερος passed through the waters of persecution and remained faithful? Has the πρεσβύτερος surrendered his or her life to Christ, forsaken the pursuits of the world, and become prepared to die for the Lord? When we consider this, any man or woman should approach the notion of becoming an elder with much fear and trembling. The overcoming nature of an elder is that of overcoming the fear of death, marginalization, oppression, exile, and persecution from unbelievers and the religious alike. The overcoming here is not necessarily the removal of the fiery trial, but fidelity in the midst of the trial.

To know fully the significance of the white robe upon the πρεσβύτερος, we need turn no further than to inquire of the πρεσβύτερος and await a reply. One such elder volunteered an explanation to John:

> Then one of the elders addressed me, saying, "Who are these, robed in white, and where have they come from?" I said to him, "Sir, you are the one who knows." Then he said to me, "These are they who have come out of the great ordeal; they have washed their robes and made them white in the blood of the Lamb." (Rev 7:13–14)

The elders wear white robes for they have endured a great tribulation. They have remained true to their confession and affection for their Savior and King. They have washed their robes in the blood of Jesus and found this blood to be a launderer's soap (see Mal 3:2). The crimson stain of Christ is for the cleansing of the soul, the washing away of sins, the regeneration of the inner nature, and the strength to endure the mockery of the world. The πρεσβύτερος are intentional to come under the fountain of Christ and hasten to the refrain,

> There is a fountain filled with blood
> Drawn from Immanuel's veins,
> And sinners plunged beneath that flood
> Lose all their guilty stains.[9]

The white robe is also the military garb of heaven. It is the suit of armor that accompanies the entourage who follows Christ into battle. It is the army fatigue of a soldier who is ready to deploy at a moment's notice in reply to the general's command (see Rev 19:14). The πρεσβύτερος are, with every believer, recruited into a heavenly army and yet are the ones to typify this behavior for other believers in the congregation. To follow Christ in battle, our robes must be dipped in his blood; it is the only way to be "white and clean" (Rev 19:14). If the πρεσβύτερος are not following Christ into battle, encouraging others to order and ready themselves for battle, and thus mounting their horses, then are they truly qualified to be πρεσβύτερος? Pastors ought to look at those who have a sense of abandon and intercessory zeal, who go to battle with clean hearts, true motives, and genuine intent. The true mark of a πρεσβύτερος who is *ad victorium* is the contrition of a soul baptized headlong in the blood of Christ.

The crown of gold is a sign that these πρεσβύτερος have been given authority in the kingdom. However, the wonderful irony here is that this authority is immediately relinquished. The πρεσβύτερος "fall before the one who is seated on the throne and worship the one who lives forever and ever; they cast their crowns before the throne, singing" (Rev 4:10). The πρεσβύτερος must therefore pattern their lives of radical generosity by daily giving their authority to Christ and pouring their lives out as a drink offering for the sheep. What is received must be given away. The authority must be relinquished, and this is performed through a posture of extravagant worship of the King. The πρεσβύτερος are forever echoing the following:

> You are worthy, our Lord and God,
> to receive glory and honor and power,
> for you created all things,
> and by your will they existed and were created.
> (Rev 4:13)

---

9. Cowper, "There Is a Fountain," 257.

So, the πρεσβύτερος do not flex authority by lording over others, but are always leading a life of kenosis, a self-emptying of the will and a giving of authority to Christ. This is a life of taking up the towel. In the kingdom's economy, as authority is given away more authority is thus deposited. "Those who try to make their life secure will lose it, but those who lose their life will keep it" (Luke 17:33).

The πρεσβύτερος also assist the grieving to transition from weeping to healing. The elder can substantiate the "weep not" with the appeal to the "Lion of the tribe of Judah, the Root of David, has prevailed" (Rev 5:5). The πρεσβύτερος comes alongside those disoriented by the loss of a loved one, job, identity, or self to reorient them to Christ. This kind of recasting of a vision to see Jesus is to stir the soul to hope again. For the one looking upon Christ is the one looking upon the Victor and thus able to apprehend the potential that he or she can also prevail during grief. And so, the πρεσβύτερος must always bring Christ before the congregation, casting the mission, person, and future of Christ in the cosmos and in the individual soul.

Finally, the πρεσβύτερος live a life of worship. If the πρεσβύτερος are not ever praising the Savior, uttering his glory, and pointing to the One who saves us, then one should prayerfully consider whether a candidate for the πρεσβύτερος is thus qualified to serve. We find that the πρεσβύτερος fall on their faces to worship God and sing,

> We give you thanks, Lord God Almighty,
> who are and who were,
> for you have taken your great power
> and begun to reign.
> The nations raged,
> but your wrath has come,
> and the time for judging the dead,
> for rewarding your servants, the prophets
> and saints and all who fear your name,
> both small and great,
> and for destroying those who destroy the earth.
> (Rev 11:17–18)

The life of the πρεσβύτερος is one of lifted hands without malice or anger (see 1 Tim 2:8), one of continual *eucharisteo* (giving thanks), one of perpetual awakening to the authority of Christ, and one in which there is a redirecting of all attention to the Lamb of God. The πρεσβύτερος emphasize the authority of Christ as the *ultima auctoritate*, pronounce judgment upon the pride of nations, decree judgments in worship upon the wickedness of the nations. The πρεσβύτερος enjoy and proclaim the rewards of the righteous, encourage the faithful, remember the prophets, eulogize the saints, and disseminate the existential premise that to fear the Lord is to begin the trek of wisdom (see Prov 9:10).

Pastor Wil had just completed orienting the church board with the expectations enumerated in a covenant that each one would sign in committing to the qualifications and roles of serving in this capacity. Once he had completed this orientation, some council members explained that they could not commit to attending midweek service or that he came across too strongly in urging the council to abide by these covenantal tenets. The urging was birthed out of the observation over the past years that, although the majority of council members would meet to weigh in on budget decisions, there was a paucity of attendance to midweek services and called prayer meetings. In addition, there were only a few council members that served the congregation in a leadership capacity such as a small group leader or engaging in a teaching role within the congregation. Therefore, he began to emphasize the importance of a council member in acting as an elder to have a spiritual gift of teaching and administration if they were to accept a nomination to serve on the board. He also emphasized the need to be present and engaged within the congregation and not merely a de facto board of governors making financial decisions for a church that they may have had only a superficial knowledge of.

He became more urgent in his appeal to these council members as he found less and less adherence to the very covenants they were signing. It was not long afterward that the same council member who thought he had been too strong in urging that this covenant be taken seriously would undermine pastoral authority. This council member made a concerted effort to preside over a council meeting, derailing the agenda by inserting his own agenda item—namely, Pastor Wil's resignation. In retrospect, this member disqualified himself to serve as an elder by refusing to cooperate with the pastor who was chair of all business meetings, slandering the pastor in a display of unbecoming conduct in a public business meeting, and calling for a resignation, which was outside the bounds of the role of a church board member. Moreover, he did not adhere to the covenant that he signed. That is, he did not attend midweek service, serve in a small group, or attend called prayer meetings. This council member merited immediate dismissal based on the grounds of his behavior and subsequent disqualifications. In retrospect, Pastor Wil would have consulted with his own pastor, the state director, and received his approval to pursue immediate disciplinary action with this council member. But the shock of Pastor Wil's salvation coming into question created a context of paralysis and grief. It would become a chasm too vast to cross and he retreated inwardly to reflect on the alleged criticisms and was therefore tempted by despair.

What does Pastor Wil do in such an instance? He is called to be pastor or elder of a church and is confronted by an "elder" with unbecoming conduct, slander, and inappropriate usurping of authority. It is important to note here that, although there is a theological alignment in the Apocalypse with the doctrine that purports the priesthood of all believers, there is also a special function set apart for certain elders in the kingdom of heaven.[10]

Hollis Gause asserts the fulfillment of the nation of priests in the following manner:

> One of the particularities of this new nation is that all its citizens are priests of God. They all have access to God for worship and service. No citizen in this Kingdom can become the "gateway" to God for another. Consequently, no citizen can bar another from the presence of God. At the same time, every citizen is an intercessor for those who do not know God (Acts 8:20–24; 2 Timothy 2:25) and for fellow citizens in burden bearing (Gal 6:1–3; James 5:16).[11]

Therefore, we must live in the tension of the priesthood of all believers with the appointment of certain elders having a certain unique jurisdiction. For example, the twenty-four elders comprise the priesthood of all nations herein described in Rev 5:10. However, we find that their identity may be somewhat distinct in that they comprise a certain number, having distinct thrones, and perform certain priestly functions that set them apart from the citizenship of priests described in the Apocalypse. Therefore, I would argue that there must be a system of accountability whereby certain priests are admonished by an appointment of priests who stand in pastoral authority to discipline. Every church governance has some way of exercising church discipline in this manner. For Pastor Wil, it was his state director that intervened and arbitrated this conflict.

---

10. See Rev 5:9–10 where people from every tongue, tribe, people, and nation flow into God's kingdom and act as kings and priests.

11. Gause, *Revelation*, 99–100.

He stood as a presiding elder in this case, exercising a priestly duty of judgment at the level of the local church.

In summary, our excursion has brought us to envision a body of elders akin to the elders of heaven who are ordained as judges and priests with a victorious witness. This vision would then call churches to discern the candidacy of elders as ones who have navigated the rigors of ordination as each polity would dictate. This journey will assist the local pastor in discerning the true motivation for an elder candidate while at the same time providing a discipling rubric for the elder candidate to grow in his faith.

The elders, therefore, are also ordained ministers in the church, and this becomes a necessary qualification. The elders operate as priests within priests in a dialectic. They both affirm the priesthood of all believers while at the same time modelling and leading in worship, sacraments, preaching, and teaching of the Scriptures. The elders are judges and must render verdicts concerning heresy, controversy, conflict, heterodoxy, sinful behavior, and unbecoming conduct. The elders also model and provide a victorious witness, not as a display of might but rather meekness and kenosis. The victory of the elders is martyrdom. That is, the elder enters an existential crucifixion of the flesh, an emptying of the will, a taking up of the towel, a condescension to serve, and thus one who emulates the kenotic Christ as a living epistle for the congregation. Perhaps this model of elders will assist any local pastor in setting a church in order. Below is a table summarizing the characteristics of the heavenly elders for contemplation and appropriation into the local church setting.

Elder Attributes	Citation	Behavioral Correlate
Ordination	Titus 1, Acts 14	Church credentials, prayer, fasting
Judges	Titus 1, Acts 14	Arbitrate disputes, church governance/authority, oversee church budget
Adherent to Christ	Rev 1	A student of the Scriptures, refers to the testimony of Christ in all deliberations
Kenotic victors	Rev 7, 11	Self-sacrificing, victory through service, giving Christ all authority

Table 2. Elder Attributes and Behavioral Correlates

Chapter 8

Setting in Order Through Admonition

That testimony is true. For this reason rebuke them sharply, so that they may become sound in the faith.

TITUS 1:13

WE HAVE ALREADY ADDRESSED the setting in order of local parishes through the means of the pastor's authority to ordain elders and what distinguishes an elder as qualified to serve. Paul addresses these qualifications in the first chapter of Titus, which was further reviewed in *The Coming Winter*. And rather than reiterating these qualifications, I chose rather to propose that these qualifications also be complimented by the attributes of the heavenly elders as foreseen by the apostle John. Pastors must realize that one of their primary tasks in setting a church in order is to ordain elders.

Second, and with the assistance of the elders, the pastor must stop the chatter (Titus 1:10–11). The pastor's medium by which he stops the mouths of those who speak in an unruly and vain manner is the rhetorical element of rebuke. We begin with the impetus to stop the subversive tongue from proliferating. "There are also many rebellious people, idle talkers and deceivers, especially those of the circumcision" (Titus 1:10).

Within the walls of every congregation remains a contingency of those who either intentionally or unintentionally speak in a way to cause unrest and dissent. Paul describes them first as unruly. That is, they are not subject to godly authority. They seek to undermine this authority through disobedience and subsequently promulgate dissent within the church vis-à-vis disorderly conduct. When church wanes in respect of godly authority, it wanes in its reputation in the community. The unruly church member seeks authority for the purpose of disrupting established authority. He or she mischaracterizes the current authority to bring his or her own authority into light. The tragedy of Absalom is an illustration of this principle. Absalom undermined his own father, sought to win the hearts of the people by brandishing his own authority, and thus propagated dissent that would eventually be his own demise.

Paul also describes this contingency as vain talkers, speaking that which is useless to the soul. Rather, this kind of talk is tantalizing to the carnal nature and may have a form of godliness without any true power. This speech smacks of irrationality. There is no epicenter of reason, it is emotional chatter, birthed out of discontentment. It bemoans the church's current situation as grievous and scapegoats another to promote the self. The idle talk draws attention away from eternal speech, edifying utterances, and comes forth from a life with little to no fruit of faithfulness.

John Calvin, the reformer, comments on this passage as a polemic against the papal orders of the day, but also brings to light some of the nuances of Paul's language here:

> Instead of disobedient . . . Erasmus translates it incorrigible. He means those who cannot endure to be brought to obey, and who throw off the yoke of subjection. He gives the appellation of vain talkers, not only to the authors of false doctrines, but to those who, addicted to ambitious display, occupy themselves with nothing but useless subtleties. Vain talking is contrasted with useful and solid doctrines, and therefore includes all trivial and frivolous speculations, which contain nothing but empty bombast, because they contribute nothing to piety and the fear of God.[1]

As there was in Paul's day certain members of the body who could not endure submission to godly authority, there was the same in Calvin's day, and there remains the same today. Calvin associates the vain talkers with those who have ambition. Thus, the correlation is therefore that the ambition will interface with the market of subtle speculations so that ambition may pounce at the right moment when the speculations have culminated in full deceit in the slander of another. In the end, the

---

1. Calvin, *Commentaries*, 297.

speculations are empty, without teeth, without truth, vanities, and thus cannot stand in the light of truth. Therefore, pastors ought not to fear the exposure of boasting vanities, for their rhetorical opposition cannot muster the strength to stand where truth is concerned. As the counsel of Ahithophel was frustrated by divine immanence, so will the counsel of mere ambition (see 2 Sam 15:31).

It is not surprising that this contingency comes from the circumcised, a Jewish cohort raising the religious yoke only to oppress the one he or she has fashioned it for (see Titus 1:10). With every word of deception they whittle each curve of the yoke, prescribing a burden for entire households to carry and thus subverting the truth. Deceptions are both believed and preached. "If we have a different pastor, if we did not plant that church, if we focus more on ourselves . . ." and on it goes until the chatter becomes a cacophony of confusion beyond reach.

Titus is instructed clearly here. "Their mouths must be stopped." Do not wait until entire households are subverted. Do not wait until the gossip penetrates your core leadership. Do not wait until those easily influenced are deceived. Do not wait until an army can be consolidated. Do not wait for the deception to gain dishonest traction in the community of faith. Set it in order by the divine tool God has given you, the tool of admonition, the sword of a ready rebuke, the courage to face the foe and discipline him or her sharply. "For this reason rebuke them sharply, so that they may become sound in the faith" (Titus 1:13).

The tool of admonition is one wielded in decreasing frequency in the modern church. It is no wonder why we find many pastors being undermined in the name of doing the Lord a service. Every pastor will eventually need to exercise with discernment the medium of rebuke and admonition, and in some cases a sharp rebuke. Paul spoke of the sharpness of his admonition when writing to the Corinthian church: "So I write these things while I am away from you, so that when I come, I may not have to be severe in using the authority that the Lord has given me for building up and not for tearing down" (2 Cor 13:10).

He gave an ample warning to the church that they ought to correct their course by taking to heart the epistle written in his absence, so that when present he would not need to provide a more austere admonition. Often, the pastor's use of the admonition is impaired by insecurity. A pastor should be relieved with the assent that it is a proper use of authority to provide a sharp rebuke when necessary. The Lord has granted the pastor authority as is illustrated in Paul's instructions to the church at

Corinth and his charge to Titus. Without rebuke, the church will not be set in order. Without admonition, the church will languish in disarray. Without a pastor wielding the rod of discipline, the factions will work to fragment the congregation.

Indeed, as Witherington has noted, it was the very people who claimed to be citizens of the household of faith who were upending the proper roles and authority in the home. That is, as they claimed to be members, they undermined the house dynamics, claiming to believe something they honestly disdained (see Titus 1:16).[2] There is one intervention for these, who exist in every congregation—they must be admonished and silenced (see Titus 1:11).

We are reminded of a similar charge to Timothy and it is the *universae crimen* (universal charge) to all pastors of all generations, one that should color the commissioning services of all being credentialed for the possibility of pastoring a church: "Proclaim the message; be persistent whether the time is favorable or unfavorable; convince, rebuke, and encourage with the utmost patience in teaching" (2 Tim 4:2).

The charge is given to Timothy as it is to Titus and as it is ubiquitously to those who respond to the call to pastor, for every context will, at some juncture in time, require that a pastor reprove and rebuke with longsuffering! Pastors, this is your God-given task, and we can no longer delegate this out or close our eyes, hoping that "this too shall pass." It will not without rebuke that must come from your mouth for the ordering of the body of Christ! Pastors must begin envisioning their call as one who also sets in order the body of Christ in the power of the Holy Spirit with the medium of admonition. Is it possible that the measure by which a pastor reproves is the very measure by which a church is ordered? The religious whose consciences may be seared unto reprobate works will be exposed by the rod of admonition (see Titus 1:16). The abominable and disobedient members of the church will not tolerate the authority of God through the pastor, erupting in tantrums that will need to be removed from the body unless repentance is born (see Titus 1:16).

For the malleable, teachable, meek, and correctable, the gentle nudge of redirection may be all that is required. For the stubborn, obstinate, unruly, unbridled ambitious, and "evil beasts," a sharp resolve and rebuke is required. Although John Calvin may not have coined this term, he employs a metaphor in his commentary which may serve pastors who

---

2. See Witherington, *Letters and Homilies*, 122.

are insecure with the tool of admonition. *À un mauvais noeud il faut un mauvais coin*, which is translated, "for a bad knot there must be a bad wedge."[3] Pastoral ministry is to navigate the knots of life: some are easily untangled and others have been tightened with vice and ignominy. These knots disallow the forward momentum and unity creating a tangled chaos that bends and sways the rope into a garbled mess rather than a linear tool for the rescue of sinners. Pastors, your wedge is the word, your tool is admonition, your task is to reprove when necessary. We need a generation of pastors who are no longer frightened, but with great courage and humility exercise admonition.

This can be a lonely task and feel like the chill of winter. The whistling wind can nip at you and beat upon you so that the very feeling of frostbite seems to overtake your members. But God holds you in the winter. And as God has directed Moses through the wilderness into Jethro's family for a season of training and preparation to encounter God for a destiny-defining moment, God is navigating you through the winter in training for war.

THE EPIMENIDES ILLUSTRATION

As a means of exploring this further, I would like to reflect on the illustration of Epimenides to substantiate the use of admonition. Epimenides, himself a Cretan, makes an assertion about his own people (who are cited in Titus 2:12): "Cretans are always liars, evil beasts, lazy gluttons."[4] This is a poetic device known as the dactylic hexameter, pregnant with meaning and one that has the potential to invoke a strong reaction.

Some have used the statement to argue that Paul is not the author of Titus on the grounds of a redacted insertion outside the usual literary forms that Paul typically utilizes. However, Paul was not unfamiliar with the literature of his day or other cultures. He appears to be widely read as he has invoked other poets and writings before. One of the most notable allusions was his use of an Athenian poet in the famous discourse on Mars Hill: "For 'In him we live and move and have our being'; as even some of your own poets have said, 'For we, too, are his offspring'" (Acts 17:28).

---

3. Calvin, *Commentaries*, 303.

4. Faber, "Evil Beasts, Lazy Gluttons," 135. Faber notes that the early church fathers Clement and Jerome ascribed this statement to Epimenides.

He utilizes the Athenian notion of being an offspring of God to make a polemic that one cannot therefore worship images made of stone, gold, or wood. We cannot rationally worship a god of stone as we are not offspring of such materials. Thus, Paul is not shy to incorporate truth claims of other cultures where it is consistent with the gospel. Thus, I would argue he is doing the same here in Titus.

Moreover, if we explore the culture of Crete at the time of Paul, we will conclude that this euphemism concerning Crete has a history. Homer includes a scene that is quite illustrious concerning the people of Crete. In his Odyssey, Homer describes Odysseus deceiving people on no less than four occasions, and even his own wife, by claiming to be a man of Crete. The Odyssey also depicts Athena's amusement at Odysseus's lies, thus celebrating the feat in irony. Listen to her remarks:

> He would be a sly and cunning rogue who best you in any kind of trick, even though a god face you. Wilful man, nimble-witted, insatiate of tricks, were you not capable, then, not even though you were in your homeland, of ceasing from deceits and lying tales, which are dear to you from the bottom of your heart?[5]

Moreover, it was Aristotle who asserted that "Homer above all has taught the others how to lie."[6] And so by claiming to be a man from Crete, Odysseus weaves a tale with some elements of truth so to convince his hearers of some semblance of veracity. And yet, by lying in this great epic, the cultural phenomenon of cunning deceit becomes substantiated euphemistically as a Cretan mode of ad hominem (personalized attack) heuristic, celebrated as a means of exacting vengeance.

Paul introduces what has become known in antiquity as the Liar Paradox in citing Epimenides. Patrick Gray has explained this paradox in the following manner:

> If Cretans are always liars, and if the speaker—usually identified as Epimenides—is a Cretan, then he must be a liar. And if he is a liar, then his "testimony" cannot be true. On the other hand, if it is true that Cretans are always liars, then his testimony corresponds to the facts of the case and he is not lying. But this would mean that not all Cretans are lying all the time, which would mean that the beginning premise was false. So if he is lying, then he is telling the truth (when he says that Cretans

---

5. Trahman, "Odysseus' Lies," 36.
6. Trahman, "Odysseus' Lies," 34.

are always liars); and if he is telling the truth, then he must be lying (since he himself disproves the stated rule that Cretans are always liars).[7]

Thus, the conundrum may be an intentional one as Paul cites a Cretan who makes a sweeping claim. If he lies, then this proves the statement true. If he tells the truth, then he cannot verify such a generalization as he embodies the proof against such a statement and therefore he lies, nonetheless. It is a double lie, a rhetorical snare, and the listeners thus are held within the grasp of a paradox, unable to refuse or endorse such a statement.

But is it the aim of Paul to entrap the listener? Or is Paul's intent to cite the Liar Paradox as an example of what he has described before? Gray hints at this when he notes that Paul has just warned Titus of "vain talkers" and "deceivers" in Titus 1:10. Perhaps Paul cites the Liar Paradox to underscore the absurdity of such speech. Perhaps he is illustrating the futility of such discourse and cuts through the dilemma through immediate affirmation of the statement but with a sharp denouncing of those who endlessly foster a culture of riddles and circular logic. He utilizes the Liar Paradox not to add to the philosophical discourse on rhetorical logic but to substantiate the need for repeated admonition. And as Gray has also noted,

> Verbal profession of faith unaccompanied by virtuous behavior is detestable (1:16). Propriety in speech is thus a primary concern of the passage in which the author, by dabbling in paradox, plays fast and loose with words.[8]

It appears also that Paul is setting up a strong contrast between God, who cannot lie (Titus 1:2), and the Cretan/Hellenistic Jews who cannot help but lie. The contrast is also illustrated through Paul's exhortation to Titus, that he be of sound speech and doctrine (Titus 2:1). Titus is to model virtuous behavior and speech while admonishing all sorts of ages and classes in both the first and second chapters of Titus. There are no discriminating factors to exempt one from being admonished. And the warning then is the same today, as Gray aptly sums up: "Beware of teachers who put on dazzling dialectical displays while leading their students astray."[9]

7. Gray, "Liar Paradox," 303.
8. Gray, "Liar Paradox," 310.
9. Gray, "Liar Paradox," 313.

RAVENOUS BEASTS

But deceit is not the only indictment Paul confronts by invoking the dactylic hexameter. The Cretans, or rather those Cretans of the circumcision, are also ravenous beasts. That is, they destroy and take advantage of entire households by teaching for monetary gain (see Titus 1:11). Paul had already utilized the ravenous beast metaphor when describing the condition at Ephesus to the Corinthian church (see 1 Cor 15:32). Therefore, ravenous beasts are ubiquitous and, I would argue, stem from the seed of religious oppression and an elitist caste system that aims to castigate the naïve by subverting sound doctrine for dishonest gain. The religion of static triumphalism[10] is a beckoning from lesser gods of the past, the bondage of Egypt that seems to rear its ugly head whenever the institution of the church seeks profit and power over and against sound doctrine. Indeed, it was Polybius who asserted that Cretans are the "only people in the world in whose eyes no gain is disgraceful."[11]

Moreover, the dactylic hexameter seems to encapsulate a microcosm of Paul's broader metanarrative for the Letter to Titus. That is, we have an emphasis on both sound doctrine and ethical behavior. This wedding of the two constructs aligns with the ethical behavioral considerations of elders in chapter 1:1–9 and the emphasis on sound doctrine in 1:10–16. Moreover, the pericope known as the *Haustafel* underscores a kind of behavioral codification for the spiritual household in 2:1–10 with a theological discourse on sound doctrine in 2:11–15.[12]

Thus, we find the themes of doctrine and virtue elaborated after the Epimenides citation to further substantiate that orthodoxy and orthopraxy are necessarily aligned. I would further argue that orthopathy wedded to orthodoxy is required for orthopraxy. Paul will thematically return to the theme of sound doctrine being a precursor for sound living. In contrast, false doctrine precipitated immoral conduct and unbecoming behavior.

---

10. This is a term coined by Walter Brueggemann, who further asserts that "Moses dismantled the religion of static triumphalism by exposing the gods and showing that in fact they had no power and were not gods. Thus, the mythical legitimacy of Pharaoh's social world is destroyed, for it is shown that such a regime appeals to sanctions that in fact do not exist." See Brueggemann, *Prophetic Imagination*, 6.

11. Faber, "Evil Beasts, Lazy Gluttons," 139.

12. See Gombis, "Radically New Humanity," 317, where he provides the following origin: "The German term *Haustafel* ("house table") was first used by Martin Luther and is a common convention used with reference to the household codes in the NT."

Could Paul have this in mind when he replicates the citation from Epimenides? And to what purpose does Paul bring this allusion to bear on the Cretan church? Why does he cause Titus to reflect on this cultural context in which he pastors? Perhaps it is to offer the bedrock by which the pastoral tool of admonition must be applied. If deceit is celebrated and if the more cunning the lie, the greater the hero, then the truth must come with a sense of sound rebuke to foster a whole different culture of celebration—that of truth telling. To abhor one aspect of culture, one must introduce the contrast as producing freedom. However, corrupting cultural influence does not fade by mere fancy of wishing it away. Therefore, Paul states that Titus must "rebuke them sharply, that they may be sound in the faith" (Titus 1:13).

Paul leaves open the possibility of a sharp rebuke to the Corinthian church if indeed he is to visit in person. He is clear to note that the sharp quality of the rebuke is "according to the power which the Lord has given me" (2 Cor 13:10). Moreover, the function of the rhetorical device is for edification, not destruction. The words may sting but are meant to abruptly awaken a sinner out of slumber and to excise the cancer of corruption breeding in their souls.

The intended outcome of the admonition is "sound faith." This is again emphasized by Paul in Titus 2:2 when he describes the attributes of the elder men. The elder men are also to be "sound in the faith." Perhaps, this is the outcome of age secondary to the accumulation of one correction after another. The admonitions accumulate to create a disposition of sobriety, temperance, and sound doctrine. If sound doctrine is the outcome of upbraiding admonition, why are pastors reticent to execute such a pastoral tool? Perhaps we fear the religious who will no doubt become offended. Perhaps the human desire to be liked, to belong, to be accepted overwhelms the divine impulse to admonish. Perhaps pastors have become so wounded and weary that the strength to admonish has been nearly extinguished. And yet, we must recognize that the power to admonish is of divine origin.

A CONTEMPORARY PASTORAL ILLUSTRATION

Pastor Rick had agreed to meet with a church board member and his wife. The board member had already called for his resignation and questioned Pastor Rick's salvation. Moreover, to add insult to injury, he and his wife now sought to meet with Pastor Rick to scrutinize the annual vision statement. However, it was the board member's wife that spoke during the entirety of the meeting. Indeed, the church board member deferred to his wife on theological matters concerning the annual vision. He heartily agreed with his wife when she brought up dispensational thought, using it to cast aspersions upon characters of the Old Testament as being qualitatively inferior to New Testament Christians because we live in the age of grace.

The argument was that we simply have more revelation than Old Testament figures and thus should not attempt to learn from these figures to pattern our lives in any way, shape, or form. Rather, the implication was a misapplication of the new covenant as translating one into a spiritually gnostic and revelatory elitist class that has no need for old covenant admonition.

Looking back, Pastor Rick now wonders, "Is it possible that this church board member did not engage in theological study, but rather, being swayed by his wife, ascribed to himself a superior status in rank in terms of discerning the will of God as an extension of aggressive dispensationalism?" Perhaps this was why he so confidently questioned Pastor Rick's salvation, for surely Pastor Rick may not be saved if he preaches from the old covenant. Surely Pastor Rick's soul was in jeopardy if he ever took a text from the Old Testament as a word of admonition. Of course, the statements are tongue and cheek, but they illustrate quite conspicuously the direct correlation between false doctrine and improper conduct. Moreover, it makes much more sense how certain dispensational members of the church board had reacted when Pastor Rick admonished the church board from Num 12. In expositing the text as a corrective word that brothers and sisters should refrain from personal slander, certain members accused pastor Rick of endorsing a curse upon the church board. This was a gross misinterpretation of the exposition provided by Pastor Rick, who simply warned of the dangers of slandering the servants of the Lord. But, if there is a highly dispensational thinker who devalues the Old Testament, then this would only confirm his or her suspicion that Pastor Rick is inferior in nature and revelation by citing the dusty book of Numbers.

In conclusion, not long after Pastor Rick resigned from what became an untenable situation concerning his family, a veteran pastor of the state called him up. He said something that Pastor Rick still ponders with great admiration. It would come to encourage him for months to follow and is still reaping joy to this day. He said, "Son, you now have earned your combat boots." That is, his time was preparation for a greater war to come. Pastor Rick's timidity, fear, insecurity, and intimidation are that much less because of having navigated the minefield of spiritual snares. Now may the Lord help him wear these combat boots, marching into the fray of battle, and may they be the shoes of peace heralding to all who are broken in this life to find healing in the person of Christ. And may you, O beloved pastor, shod with the combat boots that both are a herald of peace for the humble and admonition for the proud, have the courage to set the church in order. You are called and appointed to set the church in order!

Chapter 9

Setting in Order and Luther's Three Orders

But as for you, teach what is consistent with sound instruction.

TITUS 2:1

SOUND DOCTRINE

PAUL WILL NOW MOVE from the tool of admonition to the tool of instruction for doing the same. The emphasis in Titus 2:1–10 is that of doctrine or faith being sound. Paul will use the Greek construct ὑγιαίνω (hoog-ee-ah'-ee-no) as an intimation of the kind of doctrine that must be disseminated. Perhaps it is not so ironic that there are medical undertones to this Greek word conveying a kind of health that can be a sign of a body which practices such ὑγιαίνω doctrine. Indeed, Rogers has asserted that "correct doctrine should produce correct relationships."[13]

The healing of the withered man's hand in Mark 3:5 was described using ὑγιαίνω as the term to convey his healing. It was restored whole or made healthy once more. When Peter was emphatic that the lame man rise and walk, he was later brought before the scribes and Jewish rulers (see Acts 3:6, 4:7); it was during this examination that Peter used ὑγιαίνω to describe the healing event of the lame man. Thus, could it be that Paul is

---

13. Rogers and Rogers, *New Linguistic and Exegetical Key*, 509.

employing a term with healing intention? Is he providing a type of medicine to an ailing community? It is sound doctrine that has the potential to heal the withered hand of a community that has been deceived by wolves. It is sound doctrine that can bring a church paralyzed with confusion into alignment with God's purposes. Heresy can be virulent in nature, exponentially multiplying unless quelled by the antibodies of truth.

Indeed, ὑγιαίνω is used to describe the healthy faith of the aged men who receive the ὑγιαίνω doctrine which Titus will teach (Titus 2:2). Indeed, Paul had already charged that Titus would rebuke the Cretan liars so that "they would be sound in the faith" (Titus 1:13).

Moreover, doctrine is repeated with the exhortation to young men as a means of dispelling corruption and living with great sobriety and sincerity (see Titus 2:7). And ὑγιαίνω speech is again used to encourage the youth to watch their words—such words that will immediately condemn the adversary whose slander stands in direct juxtaposition of the young man's piety and restraint. The irony here is that the youth are to serve as an example to the community and this of course was reiterated to Timothy when Paul charged him not to let anyone despise his youth (see 1 Tim 4:12).

Finally, the servant is said to adorn the doctrine of God vis-à-vis fidelity (see Titus 2:10). Indeed, this concept of adorning doctrine could be considered a type of glory, light, or luminosity. Paul, writing to the Philippian church, asserts a similar charge when he says the following: "So that you may be blameless and innocent, children of God without blemish in the midst of a crooked and perverse generation, in which you shine like stars in the world" (Phil 2:15).

Thus, we have an ethical praxis in how sound doctrine is illustrated in specific age-related domains. The ethical considerations for the elderly men include temperance, sobriety, benevolence, love, and patience. These embody the virtuous dispositions for this aspect of the Haustafel. The ethical considerations for the elderly women include holiness, a restrained tongue, resisting self-medication with wine, being teachers of the young women, discreet, chaste, keepers of the home, and obedient. The ethical considerations of young men also include sobriety, which appears to be a ubiquitous dispositional virtue across the lifespan. Young men are to engage in good works, labor in doctrine, be sincere and grave. They are to issue sound and pure speech, which is the line of defense against those who are so quick to slander and oppose. The ethical considerations of servants include obedience and resisting the temptation to embezzle the master's estate.

BELONGING

And so, the question must be asked: What if, in going forward, one must go back? If health is intimated by a restoration of what was lost through age, illness, plague, or disease, isn't healing the return of a state that was once lost? The withered man's hand in the Gospel of Mark, returned to a former state of wholeness. The lame man's ability to walk again was a remembrance of his prior state. Sound doctrine thus is healthy doctrine as it has examined the precepts of the past and, with sincere examination, has integrated its metanarrative in the community who looks ahead to the coming Christ! We must look back to the Eucharist to look forward to the Marriage Supper of the Lamb! We must recover the ancient landmarks to recover health for our relationships (see Prov 22:28).

I would like to argue that Paul is asking that we recover the notion of the Haustafel, the family dynamic, ethical virtues, and the design that God has intended for his family as a means of practicing sound doctrine. So, I would like to investigate further the idea of what Martin Luther would later call the *Haustafel* (house table).[14] That is, Paul provides a litany of household dynamics concerning filial relationships. Thus, we ask the question, Does Paul mean for the body of Christ to act as a family? I would like to argue that Titus 2:1–10 does just that—it instructs the various members of the Haustafel how to behave toward one another, always evoking sound doctrine as the rubric for such behavior. Setting in order thus becomes a setting in order of a particular home with ethical codes of behaviors to govern the organic dynamism of the family of God.

Oswald Bayer takes up the subject of Luther's theology on the three orders of society. These orders include the home, the church, and the government. Bayer begins an outline of Luther's theology with a provocative statement:

> Every human being as a human being belongs—and this defines him or her as a human being—to the ecclesial order of creation, which is, it is true, corrupted by human ingratitude, that is, by sin.[15]

---

14. The term *Haustafel* is attributed to Martin Luther and rendered as "house table." Luther would codify house rules with this term, asserting that each family member had a certain code of ethics whereby behaviors are determined, and this was known as a House Code. See Lovik, "Look at the Ancient House Codes," 49–50.

15. Bayer, "Nature and Institution," 128.

The Haustafel therefore originates rather cosmically from a place of belonging. That is, we belong to the human race, which Bayer would assert here is an ecclesial order of creation. That is, God creates a people for himself that can be thought of as an ecclesial body. However, the belonging appears to become disrupted by sin, and in particular ingratitude for the address given by God to humanity. If the Haustafel begins with belonging, then why do so many feel estranged, as scapegoats, on the outside, marginalized, and persecuted by their very own?

I read this potential source of being human and so many emotions are stirred at once. First, I long for the very belonging that Bayer asserts is the definition of humanity. However, I cannot say that I experience belonging, at least not in an existential sense where the true nature of brother, sister, father, and mother are keenly felt. Rather, I feel very much like a resource, an economic vestige to be called upon when there is a specific need. I feel commodified, expendable, and objectified. What if we have made the Haustafel a commerce of service transactions without authentic relatedness? Perhaps, in our obsession to market a brand or build an objective, we have lost how to relate and belong to one another. I would argue that radical belonging is a strange, albeit powerful epistemology lost on the altars of commercially institutionalized ecclesiastical empires. O how elusive belonging is for us who grasp at something we may have never truly known. And yet, if this is true, and Haustafel begins with belonging, how do we recover from an entrenched and pervasive alienation?

And yet, church visions are replete with "belonging" statements. We see a trending vision statement that has some formulation of "Belong, Believe, and Become." The order has some semblance of meaning and has come under some criticism. For example, does one belong prior to believing? Is believing a necessary inclusion factor to become a member of the church or Haustafel? Bayer's assertion is that God's Haustafel is humanity and that one belongs to the human race by virtue of being created, not as necessarily believing in the Creator. Therefore, to be human is to belong, as we are made in the *imago Dei* for community and to relate to the other. To belong to humanity involves alienation as sin has brought estrangement from the human self and thus sin dehumanizes as it strips belonging away.

Thus, is it possible to ever find belonging in our broken world? Perhaps it is possible, but only as a shadow, as a figure of something more fulminant in our future. Or is Paul intending to be more specific in Christian belonging? Does he define Christian belonging by home dynamics? That is, my sons and daughters belong to the Jensen household by virtue of being progeny or by virtue of adoption. Indeed, perhaps adoption is the clearest way to describe Christian belonging as we all were estranged from God because of our inheriting the legacy of the first Adam. But God adopts us with grace and faith perhaps as the ratification of the adoption mechanism.

Pastor Scott recalls first feeling as if he did not belong when the assault on his identity and spouse began to infiltrate the church leadership where he pastored. His bivocational status became a liability in the narrative that was brewing among those he called brother and sister. Then the avalanche came, his call to preach was questioned and was envisioned by his own church board as any other vocation, one that can simply be the product of a choice. The divine apparatus that called him to preach and to pastor was not an object that could be sponged away by the whim of a disgruntled church leader. And yet, the words were enough that he felt that he was no longer understood, his intentions misconstrued, and his belonging disintegrated. He was no longer a part of the very group of people he had loved. His dignity, reputation, and character were repeatedly assaulted until he was the scapegoat cast out into the wilderness.

THE THREE ORDERS

Martin Luther identified three orders or institutions that he claimed were the sanctified institutions of God. Indeed, he would disavow much of the other institutions as outside the economy of God and rather formulated by human imagination. The three orders were the priest (or church), marriage (or family), and civil government (as it relates to human labor).[16] Now, I would assert that there is a dialectic between church and family. That is, there is both a confluence and distinction between the two orders. The organization of the family, however, in its purest form is to influence the order of the church. That is, the very ethics espoused in the family ought to also be demonstrated in the church.

Luther would bring nuance to the orders by also describing them as *de tribus hierarchii*, or the three hierarchies, bringing a sense of systemic authority as an interpersonal dynamic.[17] Moreover, the Haustafel would

---

16. Bayer, "Nature and Institution," 132.
17. Bayer, "Nature and Institution," 133.

also become known as table orders or table codes—implying that the ethical considerations be determined within the confines of the communal meal. I would like to propose that the church could once again glean from the recovery of the agape feasts that have faded into a place of irrelevance. Perhaps it is the agape feasts that create the context for governmental order by creating a constant memorial that love is the bedrock and context of all government and order. The ethos of the table begins with the love of communion. The praxis of the church is formed around a table where Eucharist (both a remembering of Christ, but also a gratitude for his church) is recovered from the ashes of autonomy and policies created in board rooms. I would argue that we must once again lay aside the CEO infiltration of shepherd and restore the table of ethics by sharing the ethos of the church at the table of orders. Let the Eucharist once again become an agape feast, and let the feast be the context for sharing governance from an ethical platform where love of God and neighbor are the ultimate concern rather than revenue and attendance (secondary concerns).

Bayer also brings to light a dialectic that Luther both preached and practiced, and this was a dialectic of continuity and contradiction. On one hand, he argued for the continuity of the three orders of authority (family, church, and government) while at the same time setting a contradiction polemic that was the backdrop of the reformation and albeit revolution he called for. That is, there remains a constant need for reformation for all three orders, but without the dismantling and destruction of the order itself. Luther did not call for the eradication of the church and its identified abuses, but a reformation of the church. This dialectic of continuity and contradiction was emphasized by Christian liberty. That is, a Christian was free to marry or to not marry to the preservation of one's soteriology. Moreover, a Christian remains free and thus voluntarily submits to the service of others in the name of this freedom.[18]

Bayer then goes on to assert a special emphasis of Luther's thought on the three orders in the following manner: "This is to be found in the indissoluble bonding of the ethics of the table of duties and the ethics of discipleship and having them guard one another."[19] That is, the table of duties or ethical considerations must be wedded to the ethics of discipleship. Without discipleship, without a love clinging to Jesus, without a

---

18. Bayer, "Nature and Institution," 139.
19. Bayer, "Nature and Institution," 139.

following of his ways and word, there is no moral center for judgment and living. Morality becomes arbitrary. A code of ethics is founded on another framework outside of divine revelation. There is a dance between discipleship and ethics wherein each informs and guards one another.

It is like what a former staff member said some years ago when I was pastoring: "I do not know what he [another staff member] likes on his hotdog." This statement calls for a restoration of table ethics and duties. That is, the intimate knowledge of another and the intuitive exchange of knowledge that springs from the heart of relationship is the platform for developing ethical codes or praxis. And this is done in the context of the Eucharistic table. That is, we consider ethics of gratitude, suffering, alignment in Christ, and feasting in love. The Haustafel begs consideration be given to restore the banquet of surrender. We surrender to Christ and surrender to others. We formulate maxims that have the regard of a first love in God and a second love in the other. We are intentional in the breaking of bread. The Eucharistic communion is contextualized by rightly dividing the word amid the agape feast that becomes the doorway for ethical praxis. If I do not know what my brother likes on his hotdog, then perhaps I do not know my brother well enough to formulate a code of ethics that will significantly impact my brother.

Every ethical consideration and obedience thereof as a Christian is contingent upon the virtue and motivation of love. That is, in *talibus ordinationibus exercere caritatem*—in such ordinances we should exercise love.[20] Filial relationships, therefore, become the tangible expressions of love. Love and its behavioral applications first take place within a family. Experiments of love find expression through relational dynamics in the home.

Luther would then contend for a synthesis of discipleship ethos with table-of-duties ethos. That is, the radical adherence to the way of Christ in love has as its behavioral counterpart with the table of duties as an ethical paradigm. Bayer would sum it up in this way:

> The "table of duties" directs our attention to forms of existence which fulfill basic needs and the applications of which are in a

---

20. See Bayer, "Nature and Institution," 140, where he cites the Augsburg Confession. Of note, the same confession provides space for dissent from civil authorities with the same premise of love, or rather a correct prioritization of loves. This is the ethical consideration in the final line of the Catechism: "Christians, therefore, must necessarily obey their magistrates and laws, save only when he command any sin; for then they must rather obey God than men (Acts 5:29)." Krauth, *Augsburg Confession*, 59.

constant process of renewal; the material content of these concerns Christians and non-Christians alike.[21]

It would seem then that the Haustafel is in constant need of reform with an aim to where radical love and discipleship are the primers for ethics. The way we treat ourselves at home becomes the object of critical reflection and the very template for how we treat each other in church. For the home can become the house of God, and the ethical considerations take on a broader application when we truly envision our fellow Christian as a brother, sister, mother, father, son, and daughter.

Aristotle also envisioned a society that reflects its most basic component, the family, when he asserted:

> Now that it is clear what are the component parts of the state, we have first of all to discuss household management; for every state is composed of households. Household management falls into departments corresponding to the parts of which the household in its turn is composed; and the household in its perfect form consists of slaves and freemen. The investigation of everything should begin with its smallest parts, and the primary and smallest parts of the household are master and slave, husband and wife, father and children; we ought therefore to examine the proper constitution and character of each of these three relationships, I mean that of mastership, that of marriage, . . . and thirdly the progenitive relationship.[22]

It is as if societal governance begins with filial dynamics. Gombis certainly asserts that Paul writes of the Haustafel as a means of illustrating the new vs. old humanity as the predominant theme in the Epistle to the Ephesians. The new humanity is a church engendered by Christ through the gospel and sustained in and through the Holy Spirit and speaks specifically to a new ontological way of relating to one another. In many ways, Paul's Haustafel in Ephesians stands in direct contrast to the Haustafel codes of the ancient world. The head of the household is not a status of comfort but one of sacrifice. The head lives in a cruciform manner to the benefit of the other members in the home.[23] In summary, the three orders, as purported by Luther, are God-designed institutions and begin with the family, the fundamental unit of any society. As the

---

21. Bayer, "Nature and Institution," 149.
22. Gombis, "Radically New Humanity," 320, where he also cites Aristotle.
23. Gombis, "Radically New Humanity," 319–20.

family goes, so goes society. The church, therefore, is a cadre of families and as such reflects the code of ethics being practiced in the home. If the home dynamics remain toxic, the church can likewise become toxic; the inverse is also true. The same reflection occurs with the third order, namely government. Thus, it is the family that becomes the focus for healthy relationships and the church would do well to invest its energies in healthy relationships within the family. Rather than inflatables, rather than slick musical events, rather than trendy clothes and optics, relationships in the home become a missional core for the church—imagine how healthy the church could become in this kind of investment.

Chapter 10

Setting in Order and Trinitarian Emulation

Let each his lesson learn with care,
And all the household well shall fare.[1]

MARTIN LUTHER

Now LET US LOOK at the order of Luther's Table of Duties in his shorter catechism in comparison to the pericope in Titus 2:1–10 (see appendix F for the entire Table of Duties). The ordering also seems to provide an embedded message in the weight of the three orders (ecclesiastical, civil government, and family). Luther will begin with the duties of the preacher, bishop, or priest. That is, he begins with the ecclesial authorities and their appointed tasks, citing 1 Tim 3:2 and Titus 1:6.

In a similar manner, Paul addressed Titus first with his primary duty to instill sound doctrine. Again, sound doctrine is an overarching metanarrative for the Pastoral Epistles and some permutation of this is repeated also in the periscope of Titus 2:1–10. The aged men are to be "sound in the faith" (Titus 2:2). The aged women are to be "teachers of good things" (Titus 2:3), "that the word of God be not blasphemed" (Titus 2:5). The young men are to show themselves "a pattern of good works in doctrine" (Titus 2:7). And finally, the servants are to "adorn the doctrine of God our Savior in all things" (Titus 2:10).

---

1. Book of Concord, "Table of Duties," para. 15.

SETTING IN ORDER AND TRINITARIAN EMULATION

Thus, the table duty of the pastor or bishop is primarily to teach sound doctrine. No pastor, bishop, or elder can be exempt from this primary obligation to the body of Christ and must execute such a privilege across the lifespan and across socioeconomic classes. The pastor must work to instill a culture of sound doctrine, laboring incessantly to this end. In doing so, the pastor is a progenitor of sorts, laying seed in the ground for the generation of sound doctrine within the entire community. Moreover, sound doctrine is included in the Haustafel for the pastor in Luther's citation of 1 Tim 3:2 and Titus 1:6 as the very qualification for the bishop or elder that "he may be able by sound doctrine both to exhort and to convince the gainsayers."[2]

If we allow ourselves to inspect the other Haustafel discourses in the New Testament, we can find various orders of address. For example, the Haustafel in Ephesians begins with mutual submission (see Eph 5:21). This then begs the question as to whether the Haustafel is an exercise in mutual submission with every member submitting in a nuanced fashion for the healthy exchange of interpersonal dynamics. The notion of submission or ὑποτάσσω (hoop-ot-as'-so) is to order one under someone or something else. It is a message conveying voluntary subordination.[3]

Thus, submission or subordination is voluntary as it is engendered from the motive of love. But is there any compulsory nature to the Haustafel in Ephesians? Is it only voluntary or is there also dutiful nuance in the language as Paul employs the present imperative sense when writing to the church at Ephesus? The present imperative is a command oriented to the future with continuous or repeated iterations.[4]

And how is this kind of continuous voluntary subordination possible? Gombis is keen to note that the imperative "submit yourself one to another" is predicated on the existential genesis of a new humanity that is "filled with the Spirit."[5] It was the Spirit who drove Jesus into the wilderness to which he voluntary submitted (see Mark 1:12). It is the Holy Spirit that was able to mark a new humanity with a new language (see Acts 2). It is the seal of the Spirit that acts as a guarantee for the

2. Book of Concord, "Table of Duties," para. 2.
3. Zodhiates and Baker, *Hebrew-Greek Key Word*, 1765.
4. See Zodhiates and Baker, *Hebrew-Greek Key Word*, 1587, for a definition of the present imperative tense.
5. See Gombis, "Radically New Humanity," 323, where he asserts the following: "The Haustafel must also be read as an extension or elaboration of the command in Eph 5:18–21 to 'be filled by the Spirit'—which is a call to embody and actualize the identity of the New Humanity as the dwelling place of God in Christ."

consummation of a new humanity in a new kingdom (see Eph 1:13). And it is the Spirit that produces both fruit and charismata as tangible expressions of the new humanity in Christ (see Gal 5:22–23).

Moreover, we find that mutual subordination carried a differential nuance contingent upon gender and office. The husband submits to his wife by subordinating himself to Christ and sacrificing himself on her behalf. The wife submits to her husband by obedience and honor of his leadership in the home. The children honor their parents by obedience. The father submits to his children by nurture and admonition. The servants subordinate themselves to a master with singleness of heart and doing what is right behind closed doors. The mutual submission is therefore expressed with an ethical praxis that is explicated by gender, office, filial relationship, and created design.

It is in this light that we can now assert that one of the guiding principles of the Haustafel is voluntary subordination vis-à-vis being filled with the Spirit (see Eph 5:18). The members of the Haustafel cannot function without subordination, and voluntary subordination is altogether lacking if members are not filled with the Spirit. Any table of duties must have both the code of ethics and also the principles by which the code is realized.

This brings me to a certain reflection on a Russian Orthodox icon by the painter Andrei Rublev titled *The Trinity*. I was first exposed to this icon when leading a Bible study on the family where this was introduced as an illustration of submission or subordination within the perichoretic relationship of the Trinity. I thought of the icon as I began reflecting on the Haustafel for this chapter and thus inquire, What if voluntary subordination is also situated in the way the persons of the Trinity interact with one another? That is, submission is rooted in the very nature of God and therefore any Haustafel praxis must also operate within a framework of volitional subordination to emulate the perichoresis of the Trinity.

Russian Orthodox iconography was akin to a theological discourse, and in the case of Rublev, the assertion appears to be the Trinity as the God of hospitality, presence, and habitation. Rublev's painting is the re-creation of the three "angels" who visit Abraham in Gen 18 and the hospitality of Abraham toward his visitors. However, the angels are certainly envisaged as the Trinity, extrapolated from Abraham's worship of the three persons and as the Lord is identified as the one who speaks with Abraham (see Gen18:2, 13).

Rublev's subject is thus the *mysterium Trinitatis* and, as Daniel Louw will assert, is an exercise in providing an *infinition* rather than a definition of the Triune God with a paradigm of perichoretic inhabitation rather than ontological substance.⁶ Louw will introduce us to a differing way of viewing the Trinity, not merely as three persons with one essence, but as persons who inhabit his people in the context of festivity within a pneumatological framework.

Figure 5. Andrei Rublev, *The Trinity*

6. See Louw, "Infiniscience of the Hospitable God," 4, where he describes understanding the Trinity with verb tenses (infination) rather than noun tenses (definition). He sums up his thinking in the following manner: "The notion of 'Father' (perspective of procreator and provider), 'Son' (perspective of incarnation) and Holy Spirit (perspective of inhabitation). The challenge in theological reflection will be to move from definitions of God to 'infinitions of God'. Perhaps, this is the reason why Hebrew thinking did not want to apply personal or substance categories but think in terms of 'to-be-categories' (JHVH-categories) within the paradigmatic framework of promises regarding the 'faithfulness of God': The promise: I will be your God; I am the Exodus God. Therefore, the further promise: Wherever you are, I will be there—the accompanying, pitiful God (God-with-you)."

Setting in Order

This paradigm of the Trinity works well with the Haustafel where the principle of love, voluntary subordination, and being filled with the Spirit are operationalized in how the household of God relates to one another. The context is the festivity of the agape feast and the behavioral duties around the table of manifestations within a pneumatological community who celebrates Pentecost (harvest) with Eucharist (gratitude) and whose purpose is to express love through volitional submission.[7]

Louw goes on to explicate the painting in understanding Trinitarian presence. That is, he notes that all three members have a blue raiment and the same face to illustrate the unity and agreement of the Trinity. Moreover, he notes the circle of fellowship as also alluding to the circle of inhabitation that God has with his humanity. The centrality of the chalice is noteworthy as it points to the theopaschistic (the God who suffers) nature of the Trinity. That is, the Trinity celebrates the chalice even as he (that is, Christ) will suffer to ensure enduring communion. The three persons of the Godhead are seen with Abraham's tent as a backdrop to envisage the sojourning of God with humanity. That is, God will tabernacle with his people. He is on the move in an infinitive manner. That is, he is "to be with" his people.[8]

The Haustafel recapitulates the hospitality of God by encircling themselves around the chalice of Eucharist. The Paschal Lamb unifies the body, and the Holy Spirit inhabits the fellowship. The people of God are dressed in robes of sanctification and covenant to perpetuate voluntary and mutual submission to one another. The perichoresis of the Trinity then is mysteriously evident in the community of faith with love, submission, gratitude, and pneumatological inhabitation as the context of the Haustafel.

If one looks closely at the chalice, one will identify a portion of the sacrificed calf intended to be consumed. The gathering is to emphasize and celebrate the sacrifice, and it is to this sacrifice that the Haustafel gathers to both celebrate and partake in the body of Christ. Each member of the Trinity also handles a staff, likely to indicate the shepherding

---

7. See Louw, "Infiniscience of the Hospitable God," 4, where he situates the Rublev painting within the Russian Orthodox celebration of Pentecost. He cites the following way Russian Orthodox praxis employed the icon: "Bunge (2007:79) pointed out that the very famous Russian icon by Rublev was used as a festival icon related to Pentecost (as result of, amongst other things, the legacy of Sergii of Radoneh). In the Russian tradition, Pentecost became the feast of the Holy Trinity as an indication of a time of the fulfilment of hope; a kind of pneumatological festivity of relationships."

8. Louw, "Infiniscience of the Hospitable God," 5.

SETTING IN ORDER AND TRINITARIAN EMULATION

nature of God.[9] Each member of the Godhead has a bowed head, which appears to be directed to the Father but also toward the chalice. It is as if there is an illustration of a mutual submission to the redemption of humanity. The Father will submit to the giving of his only begotten Son, the Son will submit to the incarnation, the Holy Spirit will submit to perpetual inhabitation of humanity.

Finally, I would like to reproduce Louw's summary of the depiction of Rublev's painting and its theological contribution to Trinitarian thought. Louw gives us an immanent and hospitable Trinity in the following manner:

- The composition, namely, Trinity as an encircling event focused around the chalice: The establishment of reconciliation and forgiveness.
- The Trinity functions within the dynamics of liturgy and not as an abstract dogmatic formulation.
- The paradigmatic framework is Abraham's hospitality: Inviting strangers (outsiders) as insiders and providing them with elements of life—bread and wine.
- The Trinity represents the intersection between eternity (blue) and earth (green) and the connection to the life-bringing presence of the Spirit.
- The trinity represents the establishment of home (God as tabernacle) to accommodate human beings within the hospitality of an inclusive encirclement: depicting ecclesial events as homecoming.
- There is an inter-trinitarian dynamic of encircling movement (relationality) rather than the emphasis on substantial stability (the impassible Dei)—the dazzling going around of perichoresis and divine playfulness.
- The unifying factor is not the personality and substance of the three figures but the narrative of Abraham inviting three strangers into his home: hospitality as a factor of trinitarian interconnectedness.[10]

What if this is also the framework for the gathering of the faithful? What if Christian relating was also centralized in reconciliation and forgiveness? You will note that Abraham not only fed his visitors but washed their feet (see Gen 18:4). Could this be a prefiguring of the

9. Louw, "Infiniscience of the Hospitable God," 5.
10. Louw, "Infiniscience of the Hospitable God," 6.

communion table of Christ and the washing of his disciples' feet as a form of radical hospitality and sacramental sign of mutual reconciliation and forgiveness?

What if the Haustafel was an invitation of strangers to dine within a new humanity characterized by the Paschal Lamb as king? What if the Haustafel was a people, all of whom are filled with the Holy Spirit, and who learn to breathe, move, and exist in the Spirit manifested in how we relate to one another? If indeed the Spirit is the giver of life, then each ecclesial gathering would be an issuing of this life in community. What if the Haustafel felt like coming home? What if we ached, sought after, and longed for a home to call our own, and found this in the God who tabernacles with us, mysteriously expressed in our community? What if our communities included dance, play, celebration, festivity, harvest, and cheer? Is coming home such a dreadful encounter that we avoid the very thought of it?

Therefore, if the Haustafel is meant to be table duties, manners of relating, behaviors becoming of a Christian, it should also be understood that these behaviors, if to be characterized by volitional submission, must first be understood within a Trinitarian framework of radical hospitality. If we choose to be like God, then we choose to subordinate ourselves to one another, which celebrates rather than loathes the notion of submission. The task of honor and obedience is therefore not drudgery but festive, not obligation but anticipation, not coercive but enthusiastically sought after, not interpreted through the lens of oppression but formulated through the lens of liberation. In short, the Haustafel, or perhaps the church that comes around the table, is a homecoming where laughter is heard, submission is sought, harvest is won, outsiders become insiders, dance is appreciated, love is felt, the Spirit is at work, gratitude is our language, and God is with us!

Louw ends his reflective article on Rublev's icon with a phrase that the church is emulating the Trinitarian nature of God when it acts to home in on the homeless. The duties of human relating cannot be ascertained without the motive of compassion and a prospectus that one is for another. The acts of worship, invitation, foot washing, a cup of cold water, sacrificing the calf, providing a meal, and being with God characterizes the encounter of God with Abraham in Gen 18. These acts teach us also about the Haustafel in that there are a priori virtues and dispositions that motivate ways of relating and ways of messaging. That is, the proclamation of the promise was around the table of presence. The miracle of a birth was in the context of hospitable *presencing*, God tabernacled with Abraham, and this was central to the *passio Dei*.[11]

Louw summarizes as follows:

> The formula (God of Abraham, Isaac and Jacob as an indication of ongoing, steadfast, sustainable faithfulness) challenges the church to become an inclusive caring community within the public space of life: Homing in on the homeless. Trinity is actually about establishing human dignity (*humanitas*) by means of a triadic promissiology of hospitable, divine caring: the God of Abraham, Isaac and Jacob who promised to be always the God of the estranged and the displaced other (Levinas: the perspective of the one-for-the-other—l'un pour l'autre).[12]

In summary, I would recommend a modification of Luther's Table of Duties with a preface that exposits the passions that motivate and perpetuate the duties, codes, or behaviors that dictate relating in the community of faith. That is, the Haustafel is contingent upon a people committed to emulating the perichoresis of God vis-à-vis recapitulation of the *passio Dei* in the manner of love, gratitude, compassion, mutual subordination, and being filled with the Spirit. The table duties are expressed through the means of foot washing, Eucharist, and agape feasts. Thus, the Haustafel becomes a covenant verbally esteemed amid an agape feast and one that is reiterated in the context of hospitality at the table. I would encourage pastors to restore the agape feast in their churches and call the people to covenantal relationships as iterated in the Haustafel passages of the New Testament in the context of festivity and celebration (i.e., Eucharist and Pentecost). Please see table 3 below for a summary of pathos and praxis in the Haustafel.

Haustafel Pathos	Haustafel Praxis	Scripture Citations
Parallel subordination	Foot washing	John 13, Eph 5
Filled with the Spirit	Worship/prayer	Eph 5, Col 3
Eucharist (gratitude)	Agape feast/Communion	Gen 18, Col 3
Pilgrimage	Hospitality	Gen 18, Ps 68, 1 Pet 2
New humanity	Sound doctrine	Eph 4, Col 3, Titus 2
Love	Hospitality/agape feast/foot washing	Eph 5, Col 3, 1 Pet 2

Table 3. Haustafel Pathos and Praxis

11. Louw, "Infiniscience of the Hospitable God," 8.
12. Louw, "Infiniscience of the Hospitable God," 8.

Chapter 11

Setting in Order and a New Paterfamilias

For the grace of God has appeared, bringing salvation to all, training us to renounce impiety and worldly passions and in the present age to live lives that are self-controlled, upright, and godly, while we wait for the blessed hope and the manifestation of the glory of our great God and Savior, Jesus Christ. He it is who gave himself for us that he might redeem us from all iniquity and purify for himself a people of his own who are zealous for good deeds.

Titus 2:11–14

HAUSTAFEL PATHOS

The Haustafel in Colossians is written within the backdrop that all interpersonal relatedness is to be performed as acts of worship unto the Lord (see Col 3:17). Where the Haustafel in Titus begins with pastors, both Ephesians and Colossians begin with the tasks attributed to wives. If we consider 1 Tim 2 a type of Haustafel, then we also have duties predicated upon prayer, with those prayers beginning with civil authorities. This would then also provide prayer as a primary means by which we relate to one another around the table of duties. Prayer is a way we communicate with God but also typifies Christian gatherings. The Petrine Haustafel also begins with subordination to civil authorities (see 1 Pet 2:13). The motive of the Haustafel in Peter's Epistle is one of pilgrimage, strangers, and speech (see 1 Pet 2:11–12). That is, we live as strangers here and ambassadors of another kingdom that motivates our way of honoring and submitting to one another within the rubric of the Haustafel.

Indeed, it is the disposition of alienation that compels us to welcome strangers. If we are strangers, then we become a community of strangers who welcome and invite the outcasts of society. The aliens, marginalized, and oppressed sit at the table and participate in the feast, prayer, gratitude, and mutual submission as a citizen of heaven who is sojourning. The Petrine Haustafel will utilize two essential words to communicate the premise of the subsequent ethical consideration: πάροικος (par'-oy-kos) and παρεπίδημος (par-ep-id'-ay-mos) (see 1 Pet 2:11).

This double emphasis enumerates why the praxis behaviors ought to follow. The πάροικος are aliens. They are those who live in a foreign country. Like Israel who dwelt in Egypt for so many years, we dwell upon the earth, a wholly different country than Zion. We are first and foremost citizens of heaven with a travel visa to sojourn upon the earth as ambassadors of peace and life and who proclaim and live a kingdom gospel and ethos.[13]

Israel was called to care for the stranger as a memorial that they ought never to forget that they too were strangers in a foreign land (see Lev 19:34). In like manner, the people of God sit around the table of duties and commit to such duties as a reminder that they are strangers and that these duties are countercultural to their temporary and current abode. These duties will likely be mocked by those who perceive the current civilization and its duties to be existential static categories. This manner of living characterizes πάροικος in that we are foreigners without a right to citizenship, for we belong to an other-worldly kingdom.[14]

Furthermore, παρεπίδημος intimates a type of travelling that makes a temporary residence adjacent to natives of the land. That is, we have makeshift shelters near the citizens of this earth in the hope that they, too, will become citizens of heaven through our conduct, speech, love, and compassion. Thus, we visit as a brief stay but bring with our stay a kingdom enculturation. Indeed, the Haustafel is a very concrete set of

---

13. Rogers and Rogers, *New Linguistic and Exegetical Key*, 571.
14. See Online Greek Bible, "1 Peter 2:11."

ethical behaviors that also bring a sense of kingdom inculcation in how we live and relate to one another.[15]

Moreover, the Haustafel ought to be envisaged as a concrete praxis illustrating the pathos of the new humanity. We have this allusion in both the Haustafel in Ephesians and the one in Colossians. Paul, writing to the church at Colossae, exhorts that the "new man" be put on and as such is characterized by "renewed knowledge," and a reflection of the imago Dei (see Col 3:10). In like manner, Paul, writing to the Ephesian church, will also ask the people of God to "put on the new man," which is "created in righteousness and true holiness" (Eph 4:24). These statements appear to be hinge statements to what follows, like a polemic to the household codes that follow.[16]

Finally, the Haustafel is contingent upon the Christian virtue of love. We find Paul imploring the church at Colossae that "above all these things, put on love, which is the bond of perfectness" (Col 3:14). We find that he does the same prior to expositing the Haustafel in Ephesians when he exhorts that they "walk in love, as Christ has also loved us" (Eph 5:2). Peter addressed the household of faith with an affectionate appeal to love when he stated, "Dearly beloved" (1 Pet 2:11). Indeed, parallel subordination must have as virtuous precipitants, both love and being filled with the Spirit—this kind of motive perpetuates the behaviors that follow in the Haustafel.

A NEW PATERFAMILIAS

Now where Luther begins with ecclesial authorities, I have chosen to modify his Haustafel with the ordering revealed to us through the mode of creation—that is, the marriage institution. In so doing, I would like to offer a polemic that these orders are also prioritized as such when certain commitments conflict with one another. We begin with the husband, created first and whose duty to his wife is a primary Christian duty born out of love and emulation of Christ.

---

15. See Rogers and Rogers, *New Linguistic and Exegetical Key*, 571; and Online Greek Bible, "1 Peter 2:11."

16. See Gombis, "Radically New Humanity," 319, where Gombis asserts the following: "I will argue that Paul, via the Haustafel, is laying out a manifesto for the New Humanity, painting in broad strokes a vision for how believers ought to conduct themselves in new creation communities, thus epitomizing the triumph of God in Christ."

As a husband, the following is a covenant that is verbally iterated during the agape feasts in the presence of all.

> I covenant to love my wife as Christ loves the church (Eph 5:25). I covenant to act as a conduit where she is sanctified by speaking the word of God over her (Eph 5:26). I covenant to love my wife as Christ loves the church, by sacrificially laying down selfish ambition for the sake of her welfare (Eph 5:27). I covenant to treat my wife with the same respect, love, and provision that I provide my own body (Eph 5:28). I covenant to live with my wife as one in agreement, intimacy, and unity (Eph 5:31). I covenant to refrain from bitterness toward or against my wife (Col 3:19). I covenant to honor my wife in both private and public domains while treating her as one who is an heir of grace in eternity (1 Pet 3:7).

Now, to the modern ear, this would not sound like a subversive imperative, but alas, we are not first-century Roman citizens. If we were to transport back to first-century Rome, we might find that our hearing of this would be a resounding subversion of family dynamics embedded in the antiquity of Rome and centralized in the figure known as the *paterfamilias*. The paterfamilias is a compound of cognates deciphered as *pater* (father) and *familias* (household). In short, the paterfamilias was the father of the household, which included every member in the household, family and slaves alike.

The paterfamilias was a sort of potentate whereby he was able to exercise a legal jurisdiction known as *patria potestas* or "legal authority (or power) of the head of household, and it constituted a collection of powers and responsibilities in three well-defined areas: household religious observance, rights over household property, and rights over the persons of household members."[17] The paterfamilias also held common jurisdiction to rear one's children to be "good citizens of the state or polis, as well as good stewards of the family's wealth and land."[18] The typical Graeco-Roman paterfamilias had an obligation to instruct his sons "through elementary instruction in reading and writing, as well as instruction in the social graces of table manners and etiquette."[19] This comports well with Paul's instruction, which appears to relegate instruction, discipline, and enculturation to fathers (see Eph 6:4).

17. Thompson, "Was Ancient Rome," 3.
18. Miller, "Chrysostom's Pedagogy," 161.
19. Bradley, "Roman Family at Dinner," 41.

Setting in Order

John Chrysostom emphasizes this brief but potent instruction from Paul when homiletically speaking to this congregation. He underscores that fathers are to be a pedagogue, not only in their homes but in their communities. Indeed, while not condemning relegating a child to an alternative pedagogue, he is clear that this responsibility ought not to be abrogated by the father in that the father must continually monitor the child's formation and maturation in faith and in society.[20] Good fathers will beget good fathers. Fathers are teachers by nature of being a father. Fathers cannot escape this role, neither should they, as sons and daughters cry out for mentors, teachers, models, and instructors. Too many fathers have given their children over to others, enculturated to believe that their only role is to labor and remunerate financial obligations. This has become the modern man who falsely believes that his children will get the proper formation within their schools and/or churches. We fathers forget that these institutions are meant to support the paterfamilias, not become the paterfamilias.

Chrysostom's lament is as relevant now as it was then: "Vice is hard to drive away for this reason, that no one takes thought for his children, no one discourses to them about virginity and sobriety or about contempt for wealth and fame, or of the precepts laid down in the Scriptures."[21] This kind of moral formation, Chrysostom contends, occurs within the home with the father/paterfamilias directing such formation. This is my responsibility, it doesn't belong to the teacher, coach, children's pastor, or any other pedagogue.

Chrysostom continues, introducing the topic of the child's soul with a metaphor of a city, the gates of the city being the senses—namely, the tongue, touch, sight, and hearing. The paterfamilias is responsible for directing children in terms of the most fiery and unruly member of the body: "Words that are insolent and slanderous, foolish, shameful, common, and worldly, all these we must expel."[22] Chrysostom is keen to underscore this later in his work with the following: "Stop his mouth from speaking evil. If you see him traducing another, curb him and direct his tongue toward his own faults."[23]

---

20. Miller, "Chrysostom's Pedagogy," 163–64.
21. Chrysostom, "Address On Vainglory," 94.
22. Chrysostom, "Address On Vainglory," 99.
23. Chrysostom, "Address On Vainglory," 100.

PATERFAMILIAS AS STORYTELLER

The paterfamilias (head of the household), in Chrysostom's view, is to become a compelling storyteller, and doing so in the context of the family meal.[24] In Roman antiquity, the pedagogue, or hireling instructor, would teach children the social graces of table etiquette so that they would soon graduate to eating with their parents at the table, which was typically a public affair. The meal was an apt opportunity to host guests, and it was altogether typical to have regular guests entreated for a feast. Chrysostom, however, translates this ostentatious Roman habit to a more personal family habit, exhorting fathers to share the Biblical metanarrative at the table on a regular basis to internalize the gospel in the souls of the children. Fathers, in this manner, become vivid storytellers. They share the story of the fall in a way that parallels our own fallenness. They tell and retell the stories of the patriarchs, Abraham's faith in the context of barrenness, Jacob's wrestling for a blessing, Joseph's endurance in Egypt and forgiveness for his brothers, and so on. This storytelling enables the child to see their own story in the tapestry of all the stories that have come before. The story is the template for moral formation.

In many ways, we have lost the art of telling stories. In antiquity, not only was storytelling a regular form of conversation, but it was also a form of entertainment and family synergy. The one listening becomes bonded to the one telling. It was the primary means by which Christ communicated his message of the gospel, through the medium of the parable.

Now, and lamentably so, our society has become merely the passive recipient of a few creative artists who indeed convey great storytelling, but through the means of video, capturing our attention through scintillating graphics, leaving little to the imagination, wherein we have become a consumer rather than a creator.

In essence, we are handicapped, we are passive, we let others tell the story, we no longer pass the stories on to our sons and daughters so that they in turn will do the same. Every child loves a story, they would cherish the stories told by their father. Thus, fathers must reclaim the dinner table and therein tell stories, rehearsing the ancient stories along with the modern. Become a parable-ist.

---

24. Miller, "Chrysostom's Pedagogy," 170–71.

Setting in Order

PATERFAMILIAS AS LOVE OF NEIGHBOR

The closest neighbors are those of one's own household. In this regard, the father and husband must love his wife and children in obedience to the Great Commission. We frequently look to others to serve, often at great expense to those in our own home. Our church culture has conditioned us to consider the harvest as outside the home, and as such we neglect our own family. We fail to disciple our children, and they lay strewn across the altar of building an ever-increasing following outside the home. Such is the travesty of a celebrity church culture wherein we no longer value ministry in the home as the prima facie call of any father or mother, husband or wife. Rather, we convince ourselves that our children will get what they need at school or church, and so our primary labors are misdirected. A paterfamilias's primary labor is to his wife and children; thus fulfilled, he can then pursue secondary labor in the church and/or the world.

A. B. Miller emphasizes this notion with the following sentiment: "Theologically, the rearing of children is the greatest example of love of one's neighbor; it is a fulfillment of the natural concern of a parent for a child implanted by God; and it reveals the image of God within the child."[25]

To love one's *oikos*, or household, one must model Christlike character. This seems intuitive to state but needs retelling again and again. The fires of righteous living must be stoked daily for this to become a practice or daily habit. For one method of instructing your home, and one that is likely most persuasive, is the method of emulation. Chrysostom has framed it in the following manner: "Nothing, yeah nothing, is so effective as emulation." It is a "more potent instrument than fear or promises or anything else."[26]

We say it often but hardly practice it, "Actions are stronger than words." We must consider that our patterns of behavior are a more powerful pedagogical technique than what we say in instruction. The child will see a consistent life and will eventually internalize this as his or her own in emulation of the mother and father. The child will emulate or mirror all forms of their parents, to their shame or joy. "Do what I say, not what I do" is failed rhetoric in the home and impossible to expect. The child will follow courses of action even if there is vocal prohibition. They

---

25. Miller, "Chrysostom's Pedagogy," 174.
26 Chrysostom, "Address On Vainglory," 117.

follow the father and mother, patterns of behavior become hardwired in this regard with a kind of pervasive penetration that poses a challenge to rewire later in life. So, be careful little hands what you do, for the Father up above is looking down in love, so be careful little hands what you do.

I have attempted to construct with Paul a new paterfamilias or head of the household—namely, men who are husbands and fathers. These men love their wives sacrificially, in contrast to the men of antiquity envisioning their wives as little more than slaves. These men are intentional to form their children, not only with instruction vis-à-vis parables and stories, but as a model, a pattern of living for children to follow. These men are pedagogues, not merely relegating education to others, but integrating other sources into the whole paideia or formation of the children. These men envision churches and schools as coming alongside their primary thrust in educating their children. These men cherish their wives, love their wives, serve their wives just as Christ serves his church. These men take up the cross, lay down their lives, crucify their carnality, and lead society through condescension, humility, temperance, meekness, and conviction. Thus, this call is to all men who live in a home with wife and children. Your home is your castle, it is the most powerful place and role you will ever have in promulgating holy people for the next generation. Your closest neighbor is your wife and children, so go forth and do the work of an evangelist and start in your home!

Chapter 12

Setting in Order: The Wife and the Haustafel

So that they may encourage the young women to love their husbands, to love their children, to be self-controlled, chaste, good managers of the household, kind, submissive to their husbands, so that the word of God may not be discredited.

Titus 2:4–5

We then consider the wife's covenant in the order of creation to and for her husband. Now, the marriage is the first institution God created in terms of human relations. Thus, it is to this institution that we encourage the church to return in nourishing, edifying, and discipling for certain behaviors as this is also one of the fundamental units of society. One will also notice that although much controversy has been stirred up in terms of societal implications with the wife's covenant to submit, the husband's obligations to his wife certainly abound and require a type of cruciform living. Thus, a perichoretic dance emerges where the husband loves sacrificially, creating a context whereby the wife's love in return is submission to lavish love.

However, with this being said, how can pastors help a wife navigate the response to domestic violence? If a wife is to submit to her husband and win the unbelieving husband to the Lord by her conduct, does this necessarily entail a submission to domestic violence as well (see 2 Pet

3:1)? Is this the suffering a wife must endure as underscored in Peter's Haustafel (see 1 Pet 1:3–12)?

THE SUFFERING WIFE

Betsy Bauman-Martin has written about the unique features of the Petrine Haustafel to address this very issue for the modern pastor and parish. She cites J. H. Elliot to underscore that the Petrine Haustafel is unique in that it addresses the potential conflicts between "sect and society" in Christian households. The other New Testament Haustafels address dyads that are implied to be faithful believers.[1] However, the Petrine Haustafel seems to intentionally address relationships that believers have with the society of unbelievers while omitting or modifying other dyadic relationships addressed to the believing community by the other epistolary Haustafels.[2] Bauman-Martin summarizes her polemic that the Petrine Haustafel is unique with an intended audience of believers living in unbelieving homes in the following manner:

> The omission of an address to masters, the shortening of the address to Christian husbands, and the lengthening of the addresses to slaves and women were changes that the author of 1 Peter made to the Haustafel to fit his specific purpose of writing to Christians suffering in non-Christian homes and living in what were really situations of persecution.[3]

Thus, if suffering is indeed the polemical argument of Peter's first Epistle, then Bauman-Martin has offered a hermeneutic of the Haustafel in 1 Peter that fundamentally changes the nature of how submission is viewed in the Christian community at the intersection of the unbelieving community. That is, submitting to authority would then take up the connotation that one submits to suffering that is the result of righteous living, so that dissent when competing authorities are in view is right and acceptable for the Haustafel and the duty of the subordinate in the Christian community is to suffer as Christ suffered when resisting wicked instructions or demands. Bauman-Martin's polemic is largely drawn from the paraenetic material to slaves, which she seeks to extrapolate to

---

1. Bauman-Martin, "Women on the Edge," 264.
2. Bauman-Martin, "Women on the Edge," 264.
3. Bauman-Martin, "Women on the Edge," 267.

wives who may face sinful and unethical circumstances of physical or sexual abuse.[4]

However, we must ask whether this kind of extrapolation is exegetically appropriate? That is, can we take the paraenesis to slaves as the same to other classes or cohorts of people? Does Peter intend that his exhortations cross social classes or does he, and God for that matter, have different instructions for differing cohorts of people as a means of promoting kingdom ethos and interpersonal dynamics? This kind of exegetical leap creates some confusion as there are certainly distinct paraenetic material to husbands and wives which would create ambiguity if both set of instructions were meant to be extended wholesale to both roles. I am just not sure the extrapolation of slaves to that of wives in the Petrine Haustafel is a justifiable hermeneutic within the Epistle of 1 Peter.

Nonetheless, the Petrine Haustafel contributes a unique perspective to the Haustafel literature, including the Haustafel of Titus, in that suffering becomes a pathos of Christian community as one submits to the wounds of ridicule, reviling, and rejection. For in suffering, one emulates the wounds and nonretaliation of Christ. In this regard, vulnerability, marginalization, oppression, and rejoicing in suffering become the ironic glory of a Christian. This glory is in the view of a Christian subordinate or slave within the intersection of an unbelieving society. This is also Glancy's assertion with the following remarks:

> 1 Peter does not identify servile subordination with the will of God nor of Christ. Rather, 1 Peter links the bodily violations to which the slaves were subject with the bodily violations of Jesus in his passion and death. The author of 1 Peter invites slaves to contemplate the wounds of Jesus in order to give them strength to endure their own wounds.[5]

Thus, holy dissent that leads to a *passio* of wounds is a subordination to such wounds to emulate the nature and character of Christ. In this polemic disobedience in the right context leads to obedience as one fully accepts the consequences of resistance.

---

4. Bauman-Martin, "Women on the Edge," 271, where she asserts the following: "'Accepting authority' here would then mean the slaves will not retaliate when punished for their Christian actions. The author does not ask them to end the conflict-causing activities, but only to behave submissively when confronted and punished for their nonconformity."

5. Glancy, *Slavery in Early Christianity*, 149. Cited also in Betsy Bauman-Martin, "Women on the Edge," 272.

SETTING IN ORDER: THE WIFE AND THE HAUSTAFEL

For Bauman-Martin, the notion of the "what is good" that the daughters of Sarah act upon in 1 Pet 3:6 is the good of suffering from dissenting from a non-Christian husband's requirement that she violate her conscience by engaging in the cultic activity of the household. I am not so convinced that it is the ἀγαθοποιέω (ag-ath-op-oy-eh'-o), or the doing well, as it is the resistance of φοβούμεναι, or terror that relates to holy dissent. It appears that the daughters are not to become a "prey to terror."[6]

And if this is not enough, the word πτόησις (pto'-ay-sis) is used for double emphasis in that one is not to be carried away with fear. The word conveys a sense of fluttering or perturbation incited by immense fear. And Rogers and Rogers would go on to cite Balch with the following: "Wives must fear God and not be terrified of those in house or city who oppose their faith."[7]

This would then imply that it is the polemic of resisting the fear that can come if one is to suffer for Christ whether in house or city. If indeed paraenetic exhortation is to confront the fear of consequences in a domestic sense, then the submission is to the judgment the unbelieving husband may impart rather than obedience to the sin the unbelieving husband asks of the believing wife. The "lord" may be an unjust one, but he is still lord. And yet, the "lord" is not the Lord. One's allegiance to the Lord prevails over one's allegiance to a "lord."

But would this also imply that one submits to domestic violence in the form of physical or sexual abuse? There is nothing in the Petrine Haustafel that addresses this, nor does the narrative in Gen 18 offer a judgment on this inquiry. However, although not a Haustafel, Paul does provide paraenetic material on marriage in 1 Cor 7. It is through his hermeneutical lens that I would like to offer a polemic of shalom to inform the victims and also the pastors of victims of domestic violence.

THE WIFE AND SHALOM

Paul explicates the release of obligation in the event of a departing unbelieving husband when he asserts,

---

6. See Rogers and Rogers, *New Linguistic and Exegetical Key*, 574, where this definition is used for φοβούμεναι.

7. See Rogers and Rogers, *New Linguistic and Exegetical Key*, 574.

> But if the unbeliever departs, let him depart; a brother or a sister is not under bondage in such *cases*. But God has called us to peace. (1 Cor 7:15)

Now we should note that Paul has already exhorted that believing wives ought to remain with unbelieving husbands and vice versa. He cites the soteriological potential in this housing arrangement (see 1 Cor 7:12–13). However, we should also note the caveat, "If he be pleased to dwell with her," which is a potent informant to the victim of domestic violence.

Indeed, the abusing spouse may, by verbal threat, be pleased to dwell with his victim, but displays by vehement wrath that he is indeed displeased with his spouse. This is certainly manifest in the form of physical and sexual abuse. In this case, the unbelieving spouse has already departed the relationship by removing any element of peace that otherwise may have been conferred on the household. Peace, or shalom, is the guiding principle here. The obligation to remain under the yoke of violence is broken as peace is the stalwart ethical principle that guides a believing spouse to remain or depart.

Paul utilizes δουλεύω (dool-yoo'-o) to confer a type of obligation that could be best connoted as a legal enslavement that is no longer binding if a spouse departs the codified marriage.[8] The perfect indicative passive sense also conveys that the continuing legal apparatus that binds one indefinitely is no longer a condition for the object of the law.[9]

In the event of the dissolution of this bond through a departing spouse, and I include a departing spouse vis-à-vis domestic violence, then one needs to seek shelter where there is peace. Peace becomes the ethical principle guiding the decision for a victim of domestic violence.

Paul utilizes εἰρήνη (i-ray'-nay) to iterate a concept regarding a dyadic dynamic of omission when used to mean exemption from the rage and havoc of war. Moreover, it conveys a positive sense when creating peace between individuals such as harmony or concord. And finally, it can also connote security, safety, prosperity, and felicity.[10]

In being people of εἰρήνη, we are essentially people without strife who work to bring an end to discord. It is an inner state of tranquility, and a soul motivated for righteousness through the art of peace making

---

8. Zodhiates and Baker, *Hebrew-Greek Key Word*, 1709.
9. Rogers and Rogers, *New Linguistic and Exegetical Key*, 362.
10. Online Greek Bible, "1 Corinthians 7:15."

(see Jas 3:18). It can come to mean a great deliverance from God to those faced with distress because of sin.[11] It is the very message of gospel preaching (see Rom 5:1 and Eph 2:16–17). The prepositional phrase ἐν (en) just before εἰρήνη can sometimes take on a double emphasis as in "God has called you *into* a peace *in* which He wishes you to live."[12]

Thus, the polemic I would assert is that the wife in the Haustafel operates from an ethical virtue of peace in a double sense. That is, she is both the object of peace in Christ and the peacemaker in the home. The unbelieving husband who either departs or imparts violence has, in essence, created a conundrum in terms of his wife's Christian duty to subordinate herself to her husband. In this context, the abused wife's commitment to Christ as preeminent and her call to be both an object and maker of peace stand in juxtaposition to any subordination to violence either to herself or to her children. She is released from bodily commitment to violence and from any witness to the bodily harm of her children. She creates an environment of peace to which God has called her by departing such hostilities and creating a safe harbor for her and for her children.

In this light, she has correctly subordinated herself to the chain of command, Christ before husband. She cannot submit herself to the beating hand when the peaceful hand remains outstretched. May every pastor console a victimized wife with counsel that encourages that she be an agent of peace. And if God has called her to peace, God is delivering her into peace. The theology of her marriage can be subsequently explored once she is safe and can contemplate future decisions from this place of shalom. As Paul, I do not say this as a command but as permission; it is time, pastors, that we cease from encouraging the victimization of battered spouses and rather advocate for their peace (1 Cor 7:6)!

It is in this reflection that we might add the following to the Haustafel covenants of the wife:

> I covenant to submit to my husband as unto the Lord (Eph 5:22). I covenant to engage in purity and reverence with my speech (1 Pet 3:2). I covenant to adorn my heart and spirit with meekness and a quiet spirit more than external luxuries (1 Pet 3:3–4). I covenant to love my husband and children (Titus 2:4). I covenant to be self-controlled, pure, a steward of my home, and obedient to my husband that the word of God would not

---

11. Zodhiates and Baker, *Hebrew-Greek Key Word*, 1711.
12. Rogers and Rogers, *New Linguistic and Exegetical Key*, 362.

be blasphemed (Titus 2:5). I covenant to feed my family, invest wisely, help the poor, and practice radical hospitality (Prov 31:15, 20–21). If married to an unbelieving husband, I covenant to be in subjection to him that he may be won to Christ according to my conduct (1 Pet 3:1). This covenant, however, is subordinate to my covenant to Christ, so that, if my unbelieving husband requires that I engage in sin, I must graciously dissent (1 Pet 2:1–12, 19–20). Moreover, as an agent and recipient of peace, I covenant to submit myself to Christ and depart from a physically or sexually abusive husband for the sake of my and my children's welfare, being released from bondage and being called to freedom (1 Cor 7:15).

Chapter 13

Setting in Order: The Father and the Haustafel

So that they may encourage the young women to love their husbands, to love their children.

TITUS 2:4

THE HAUSTAFEL IN TITUS does not specifically address fathers. For these covenants, we must draw conclusions from other Haustafel codes in the epistles to the Ephesians and Colossians. In keeping with the order of creation, children and parental relations would be prioritized after the marriage relationship.

Fathers are given a negative command, that they are to refrain from provocation (see Eph 6:4). The provocation is one to wrath or παροργίζω (par-org-id'-zo), which is to enrage.[1] Rogers and Rogers have provided us a comprehensive definition when they state that the word entails a strong prohibition to "attitudes, words, and actions which would drive a child to angry exasperation or resentment and thus rules out excessively severe discipline, unreasonable harsh demands, abuse of authority, arbitrariness, unfairness, constant nagging and condemnation, subjecting a child to humiliation, and all forms of gross insensitivity to a child's needs and sensibilities."[2]

---

1. Zodhiates and Baker, *Hebrew-Greek Key Word*, 56.
2. Rogers and Rogers, *New Linguistic and Exegetical Key*, 446.

This is quite a definition, and if fathers of all ages are honest with themselves, there is a sense where we could all say that we have performed such a hurtful act of provocation at some time or another with our children. And one could ask a follow up inquiry, Why is this specifically addressed to fathers? Is it possible that fathers are more likely to succumb to the temptation to provoke their children than mothers? Is it possible that fathers are filled with wrath so that they project this on to their children, forming them to be images of wrath as well? Perhaps, this is also why Paul specifically addresses men in the First Epistle to Timothy to pray without wrath (see 1 Tim 2:8). Wrath, vengeance, provocation, and aggression appear to be on the horizon of a man's soul, which requires constant crucifixion so as not to pass on a tainted legacy of an acrimonious animosity.

The Haustafel in Colossians warns fathers that the outcome of harsh provocation can discourage a child (see Col 3:21). One study has asserted this principle of gender difference in parenting as well. Shortt et al., in citing other studies and observations, note that "though overall it has been shown that unsupportive parent responses to emotion are associated with more adolescent depressive symptoms during early adolescence, the nature of the effect differed as a function of parent gender." And they go on to state that "observations of father (but not mother) emotion dismissing were linked to higher internalizing behavior problems for early adolescents."[3]

When fathers dismiss the emotions of their children, this appears to lead to greater internalization of emotions, which can be a harbinger for adolescent onset depression. Fathers who do not support children or, worse, provoke them to discouragement, shame, and exasperation are setting the stage for emotional dysregulation and isolation in their children. And, has this type of behavior not been handed down as an unwilling legacy from one father to the next? It is as if fathers know no different and simply operate as they have seen with a miserable helplessness to change. The powers of society to keep fathers away from the home, the financial bills surging, the cost of living escalating, the demands of work, societal expectations, home, and internal failures become a pressure cooker that portends trouble for their children to fathers who retreat to a tower of emotional silence or who erupt in a volcano of emotional wrath.

---

3. Shortt et al., "Emotion Socialization," 3.

SETTING IN ORDER: THE FATHER AND THE HAUSTAFEL

Shortt et al., utilizing a cohort of depressive adolescents in comparison to a nondepressive control, also found a gender distinction in terms of physiological response to anger. That is, "adolescents with depressive disorder exhibited an increase in heart rate in response to fathers' angry behavior and a decrease in heart rate in response to fathers' dysphoric behavior but no changes in heart rate in response to mothers' angry or dysphoric behavior."[4]

Fathers must take a long, hard look at themselves in the mirror and ask the difficult questions. Do you dismiss your child's negative and positive emotions? Do you respond with anger more than you respond with support? Do you stoke the flames of conflict? Do you enjoy seeing a painful response on your child's face after you have disciplined them? Do you define disrespect as a lack of sorrowful expression when correcting a child? The more anger displayed, the greater the potential for your child to suffer from depression. Fathers, this gender distinction is tangible!

Indeed, after analyzing a cohort of 107 adolescents and their parents, Shortt et al. found "that fathers of adolescents with depressive disorder were more punitive in response to adolescent sadness than were fathers of nondepressed adolescents, $F(1, 105) = 6.36, p < .05, n2 = 0.06$, but this difference was not observed in mothers' behavior."[5] The greater the wrath, the greater the child's temperament is prone to a depressive pathology. Thus, one possible conclusion and theoretical framework proposed by Shortt et al. is as follows: "That unsupportive responses, such as punitive or minimizing reactions, heighten children's emotional arousal and impair emotion regulation abilities by teaching children to avoid or suppress rather than understand and adaptively cope with negative emotions."[6] Suppression compromises adaptive coping. Suppression is learned in a child who is punished for any expression of negative emotions. You learn that silence becomes your ally, which dampens healthy expression of lamentation, and you learn greater internalization of negative affect; both lessons increase the potential for depression, despair, and self-loathing.

Perhaps the greatest temptation for a father is the display of wrath either through discipline or vis-à-vis dismissal of emotional displays from a child. The response of a father is therefore critical to child development. Moreover, the challenge of setting the church in order becomes a colossal

4. Shortt et al., "Emotion Socialization," 3.
5. Shortt et al., "Emotion Socialization," 8.
6. Shortt et al., "Emotion Socialization," 11.

mountain if families within the church are unable to set their households in order. I would hypothesize that those who undermine pastoral authority or contribute to church chaos and confusion do so in the context of a household that is also chaotic and confused. A house with unspecified gender and parental roles, one with dismissive or hostile responses, will also carry this into the *oikos*, or household, of God.

Indeed, the New Testament often will use the Greek term *oikos*, or household, of God to delineate a certain definition for the church. This seems to be the Christian effort, according to MacDonald, to offer a "community stabilizing institutionalization of early Christianity."[7]

Moreover, it appears that the function of the Haustafel was to ensure that Christianity would be passed from one generation to the next. It was the home that was necessary for the successful transmission of the gospel. Not that the church was to be minimized in this process, but that the church was to function as a household itself—nurturing and equipping individual households for the formation of disciples who would not only follow Christ in loving adherence but also transmit the faith and sound doctrine to another generation.

The locus of faithful expression, therefore, is centered in the home, operationalized by the Christian Haustafels, and more widely generalized to the church, which is a macrocosm of the home, the very household or *oikos* of God (see 1 Tim 3:15)! I believe the church has drifted from its conception as a family partly by the institutionalization of a corporation or business paradigm. Early Christians met in homes, which fostered a household environment with family dynamics that naturally penetrated the community. However, and unfortunately, the church of today focuses more on leadership development borrowed from corporate models than on development of fathers, mothers, brothers, and sisters in the household of God.

In our day, the church must concern itself with how to develop and run a human resource department, execute programs for growth of attendance and revenue, and market itself as a brand to be known in the community so that more eyes will watch the live stream. Pastors must know how to hire, fire, pander to audiences with sleek communication catch phrases, and be the CEO who orchestrates a "successful" report to church board members who often have a mentality that they hold shares in a business rather than relationships in a family. In short, we lost the

---

7. Barclay, "Family as Bearer," 76, where he cites Macdonald.

family in the church. The sooner we confess this, the sooner we can come out of our denial, repent, and ask God to help us return to the household of God.

The Christian household paradigm is further accentuated as the apostle Paul comments that it is God who is father of the entire divine and human family (*patria*) in heaven and earth (see Eph 3:14–15)! Thus, we look to our Father continually for paraenetic material, love, comfort, discipline, and direction. Fathers are to raise their children in the "discipline and instruction of the Lord (ἀλλὰ ἐκτρέφετε αὐτὰ ἐν παιδείᾳ καὶ νουθεσίᾳ κυρίου)." You will notice the emphasis on παιδεία (pahee-di'-ah) and νουθεσία (noo-thes-ee'-ah) in Paul's exhortation. I have noted elsewhere the notion of παιδεία as a comprehensive moral, emotional, and physical formation of a child. The double emphasis in Eph 6:4 is a rubric for fathers that inherent in their fatherhood is a need to transmit comprehensive moral formation and correction to their children. Specifically, this becomes a father's Christian duty in the Haustafel. This is not to exclude mothers from educating their children, but it does call upon the father to be involved in this process.

Thus, fathers, this is a call and charge to commit yourself to helping with homework, assist in physical training and exercise, correct your child by telling the truth in love, and, for the sake of the gospel, get involved in your child's life! Talk to your child about his or her dreams, aspirations, goals, struggles, and affections. Correct where necessary, train your child for spiritual warfare, pour wisdom into their hearts and souls, and invest in their moral formation. Indeed, the charge from Paul to Timothy is strong enough to illustrate a close alignment between the Christian faith and the Christian home when he states that "whoever does not provide for relatives, and especially for family members, has denied the faith and is worse than an unbeliever" (1 Tim 5:8).

My fatherly confession may be like so many others. I can recall sitting at the dinner table; there was the typical joking banter back and forth between my children. They seemed to be enjoying themselves and not taking offense at any of the comments being made. My daughter was attempting to explain to her siblings what she meant by the term *pessimism*. After defining the term as "letting people down," one of my sons jokingly remarked, "you mean like you?" There were some brief smiles until I abruptly interjected and with a harsh and punitive tone rebuked my son. Honestly, I was too strong in my condemnation. I barked and

Setting in Order

overreacted at the dinner table. My daughter attempted to intervene stating, "Dad, I knew he was joking, and we are fine."

But I persisted despite her reassurance. I severely admonished him about criticizing others and thus hurting their feelings even as I was now doing to him. His head fell and tears began to form. He was feeling the full punitive weight of my rebuke. Moreover, as the rebuke was done before the entire family, the shame or discouragement was likely amplified. He was quiet the remainder of dinner and answered in tone of sorrow or discouragement.

Noticing this posture, I apologized for my overreaction, of course at the nonverbal prompting of my wife. She could see that my remarks had rendered a crushing blow to his spirit. The next day I apologized once more, embracing him and confessing that I did not always understand his humor, but that I need not overrespond when his sibling may understand a dynamic that I do not. Our relationship can be tense at times, but I can do much more to embrace him, invest in his emotional reservoir, and provide words of affirmation.

In this instance, I had exasperated and discouraged him by invoking a kind of sadness that could be commingled with anger. I was provoking a negative affective state, likely more on the spectrum of shame than conviction. Fathers, do not take pleasure in the tears you produce by your unrighteous anger, nor justify those tears as something produced by appropriate discipline. Rather, rejoice in the tears produced by the power of the Holy Spirit convicting wrongdoing as you are used as a vessel to communicate with patience the specified wrongdoing. Clearly, I have much to learn in this area. So, Lord, please help all of us fathers to refrain from the wrath that we are tempted to produce and lay upon our children. Let us not interpret simple play for disrespect, or temperament for disobedience, or joy for reckless behavior. Rather, let us participate in the joyful development of our children. Let us refrain from the hot temper and anger that was imparted to us. Let us offer the same patience we have been given by our heavenly Father. Let us not be tempted to provoke, but to invoke the name of the Lord when we discipline.

It is in this light that I offer the following covenant for fathers:

> I covenant to refrain from attitudes, words, and actions which would drive my child to angry exasperation or resentment via excessively severe discipline, unreasonable harsh demands, abuse of authority, arbitrariness, unfairness, constant nagging, and condemnation. I covenant to refrain from subjecting a

child to humiliation, and all forms of gross insensitivity to a child's needs and sensibilities (Eph 6:4). I covenant to bring up my child in the nurture and admonition of the Lord by means of moral, cognitive, physical, and spiritual training (Eph 6:4).

Chapter 14

Setting in Order: The Mother and the Haustafel

So that they may encourage the young women to love their husbands, to love their children, to be self-controlled, chaste, good managers of the household, kind, submissive to their husbands, so that the word of God may not be discredited.

Titus 2:4–5

The Epistle to Titus does address mothers with paraenetic material, but only briefly. We find they are to love their children and keep their homes (see Titus 2:4–5). I would like to argue that the mother's role of keeping the home includes the loving of her children by fostering a home that is conducive to the work of grace. It is the mother who tends to have a nurturing role that is nuanced and necessary to the child's development. The home can become a habitation for God as the mother works and worships within its halls.

Paul has likewise written to Timothy that younger women ought to marry, bear children, and guide the house (see 1 Tim 5:14). He writes this in the broader context of addressing widows and appears to be addressing younger widows here. He notes the great temptation for women to become "idle, gadding about from house to house, and they are not merely idle but also gossips and busybodies, saying what they should not say" (1 Tim 5:13).

Thus we find a holy vocation of keeping the house along with the loving and raising of children that acts as a restraining force against the vice of slander and gossip. O how the church needs to hear this message once more as a war of words lights up the social media posts and the prayer requests behind closed doors. Where the men's temptation is anger and wrath, it appears that the female's temptation is gossip and slander. Both can dishearten, both can discourage, both can lay indelible wounds upon the hearts of a burgeoning Christian soul.

Therefore, Paul does etymologically link the bearing of children and the guiding of the house together as the table duties of the mother. Moreover, I do not believe it to be a theological leap to consider the sanctifying component of such a sacred vocation. For with such noble tasks as keeping the house and raising the children, mothers have the potential to be kept occupied so that the alternative of gossip and slander are rooted out.

My wife and I often joke that marriage and parenting are two of the most intensive acts of sanctification we have ever experienced. It is the holy fires of these relationships that burn the dross of pretense from our hearts. We keep the gold of our authentic self under duress, fatigue, and conflict. We find that we simply do not merely struggle with a certain anger here or a certain sadness there but are in need of a Savior daily. We find that we are more selfish than we ever have imagined, and that God is still working in us a cruciform and kenotic way of living. The home becomes the training ground of God. The home becomes the fiery ground where sin can be confessed and rooted out. Home becomes the place of joy, confrontation, exuberance, and godly sorrow. The home, for all its imperfections, becomes a sacred arena for God's grace to be fully formed in a soul.

And yet the home is given little attention when juxtaposed with the excitement of other works that garner peer reviews, status elevation, societal recognition, and financial remuneration. One is not paid for keeping the home. Society does not glorify domestic duties, and in some cases denigrates them as something scornful. Gone are the days when the gender roles were clearly delineated for society and the church. The mother who solely invests in her home is seen as lacking. The mother who derives great joy in the guiding of her house in grace is caricatured as lacking insight, awareness, and an intellectual drive for excellence. What happened to society? What happened to the church? It would be easy to find a scapegoat and to examine historical precedents, such as the feminist movement, that may have contributed to a changing landscape of motherly roles in the Haustafel. However, that is not the scope of this treatise and would take volumes to explicate.

Rather, I would like to explore what is meant by guiding or keeping the home as a covenantal role of mothers. Furthermore, I would like to suggest that this act alone has sanctifying potential.

When writing to Timothy, Paul uses the expression οἰκοδεσποτέω (oy-kod-es-pot-eh'-o), which has a stronger emphasis than most translations have expressed (see 1 Tim 5:14). The term has the strong connotation of one who is a master of a home, ruling a household, and managing family affairs.[1] Likewise, Paul emphasizes domestic duties again as the rule and reign of the wife and mother when writing to Titus (see Titus 2:5). This time, Paul uses a less governing word, but one nonetheless that has a sense of preservation. He asks that they be οἰκουργούς—that is, that they "keep the home." In this sense, the mother and wife look after the domestic affairs of the home with prudence and care.[2]

It is as if the Haustafels extrapolate from the wisdom literature of Proverbs in describing the glory of the domestic sphere for mothers. There is likely no more illustrious description of the wife and mother's role in the Haustafel than Prov 31. It describes the tangible manifestations of inner virtue. She is one who works with her hands. She fills her pantry with food. She cooks for her household even under restraining circumstances. She makes wise purchases for the household, indicating that she has, to some degree, power of the purse. She invests in what she buys, engendering fruit with her labor. She labors into the night for the nurture and health of her family. She blesses the poor and needy.

She clothes her family with warmth even in the deepest and most formidable snow. She fills her home with tapestry, and it becomes a lodging for those she holds dear to her. Her home is fit for kings, queens, princes, and princesses. For her home is to her as a palace of disciples. She enhances the value of her home in the marketplace. She is not clothed with the empty platitudes of the most recent trends, but rather with the enduring glory of strength and honor. This kind of raiment does not fade with the fickleness of hearts and passing human interest but remains as a cornerstone of her character. It is out of this virtue of strength and honor that she speaks the words of wisdom, and this wisdom informs a law. This law is one of kindness, mercy, lovingkindness, and nurturing encouragement.

1. Online Greek Bible, "1 Timothy 5:14."
2. See Zodhiates and Baker, *Hebrew-Greek Key Word*, 1742.

She is not idle, but works incessantly for the good of her home. Her children provide tribute after tribute concerning her goodness, character, love, and wisdom. Her husband is forever praising her in public, so that all know that there resides in this home a virtuous woman worth emulating. Above all, she fears the Lord which is the a priori and necessary bedrock from which all other virtues spring forth.

We have concrete examples of these women in Dorcus and Lydia. Dorcus is described as one "full of good works and charitable deeds" (Acts 9:36). This charity is described later in the chapter when widows presented the coats and garments that she had made while still living (see Acts 9:39). This would also imply that women can and have worked outside the home as well, which is sanctioned in the text here as "good works and charitable deeds." Thus, wives and mothers, if called to outside work, ought to move in obedience while at the same time envisioning their domestic duties also as a form of worship and obedience.

The weeping for Dorcas was profuse and the appeal was such that Peter was moved to pray for her resurrection. Indeed, this prayer was answered and Dorcas was restored to her community to continue her labor in the kingdom among the community at Joppa.

We find yet another example in Lydia, who had become quite an entrepreneur in Philippi (see Acts 16:12–14). Lydia was likely a Jewish proselyte who had come to the river to pray with other women. There was no Jewish synagogue at the time, implying there was not the minimum of ten Jewish men in the city to start one. Thus, the women of the city who sought to worship God went out of the city to the countryside to hold their Sabbath prayers. The Lord opened Lydia's heart under the preaching of Paul and she came to follow Christ (see Acts 16:14). Her entire household was baptized, implying her children and servants, and she extended an invitation of hospitality to Paul and Timothy. She longed for them to abide in her home, a gracious gift to reciprocate the immeasurable gift of having received the gospel message.

Her extension of hospitality, although not solely relegated to the role of mothers in the Haustafel, does appear to have a special role in her ministry that perhaps provides further commentary on the pathos of the home. Lydia was persistent—that is, she constrained Paul and Timothy to abide within her home. This is not altogether dissimilar to Lot's pressing request that the two angelic visitors remain in his home, have their feet washed, and feast on the meal his family prepared (see Gen 19:2–3). Just a chapter earlier, Abraham had also pleaded for the divine visitors to remain so that he could wash their feet and feed them (see Gen 18:4–5).

Moreover, we have both a potent illustration of hospitality and a horrific abuse of hospitality within the more obscure story of the Levite at Gibeah in Judges. The Levite was invited into a home as he sojourned through the city. The hospitable Benjamite washed the feet of his guests and did feed his family, servants, and livestock (see Judg 19:20–21). However, much like Sodom, the men of the city sought to sexually abuse this guest and were successful in abusing his concubine. This was followed by the tragic death of the Levite's concubine and the division of her body into twelve parts to be sent to all the tribes of Israel as a rather gruesome grievance. This abuse of hospitality sparked a civil war, the death of over sixty thousand men, and the burning of the cities of Benjamin (see Judg 19–20). This is a remarkable and often-overlooked anecdote concerning the grief, sorrow, and civil strife that can erupt when hospitality is trampled. We also have the disciples on the road to Emmaus who constrained the Lord Jesus to abide with them. It was in pressing for the Lord to remain that led to the opening of their eyes to the resurrected Lord (see Luke 24:29–31)! What a polemic for the awakening hospitality can invoke. Finally, we have the succinct exhortation from the author of Hebrews to host strangers, for who knows if you could be entertaining angels with such hospitality (see Heb 13:2).

But if we return to Lydia, we find that as a mother and Christian, she opened her home to the missionary. This is akin to the barren Shunammite who opened her home to the prophet. It appears that her hospitality was also correlated to the miracle of conception and the subsequent resurrection of her son (see 2 Kgs 4:10, 16, 35–37). Lydia's conversion and hospitality appears to have been the catalyst for the formation of a home church. This is implicit in the encounter that Paul and Silas had when comforting the Christians who had gathered at Lydia's home after his release from prison (see Acts 16:40).

Thus, hospitality can be a powerful catalyst for missionary activity, miraculous conceptions, awakenings of the soul, and illustrious of authentic community where the alien finds a home. Indeed, Jody Fleming, in citing Brandner, notes that when missionaries become the stranger and guest in the city where they have been sent, they

> voluntarily [expose] themselves to an alien environment, dependent on the benign hospitality of the host country/church, and accepting the vulnerability that comes with existence as

a stranger, they touch all those who themselves experience alienation.[3]

And so we imagine that the power of hospitality is to convey a sense of belonging to the outcast, a sense of community to the estranged, a sense of family to the alien, a sense of home to the homeless, and a sense of love to the lonely. Hospitality is a vital filial component of the church that has been lost in the modern church culture of events that encourage attendance but no relationship. The bonds of belonging are sacrificed in a society that burns to work, keep status quo, objectify gatherings, and idolize autonomy and isolationism. This lamentably has been exacerbated by social media and technological platforms that create silos of loneliness as online relationships become a pressure cooker of status checks rather than heart conversations.

Frederick Faber identified a certain kind of hospitality bathed in kindness that has a missiological component for the church: "Kindness has converted more sinners than zeal, eloquence, or learning."[4] Hospitality is the conspicuous expression of kindness in a radical fashion where the home is open, becoming a spiritual metaphor for open hearts.

Rosaria Butterfield, a wife and mother, has written an entire monograph on hospitality, having come to know Christ through such ministry. She begins her work by asserting the following: "Radically ordinary hospitality is accompanied suffering."[5] I am fond of the paradox inherent in her description of hospitality as both radical and ordinary. It is radical as it upends a typical culture of individualism, and it is ordinary as it can become a daily phenomenon. That is, when eyes are open to the manifold opportunities, radical hospitality can become a regular rhythm to one's life (i.e., liturgical). However, if indeed suffering is a primary component, why would we pursue what is certainly noble, but also at the expense of our lives or livelihood? I suppose the answer is in the life that springs forth from this kind of compassionate display. Suffering with someone, *co-passio*, is the seedbed for an abundant life.

After sharing a couple of personal anecdotes illustrating radical ordinary hospitality, Butterfield comes to a definition: "Radically ordinary hospitality is this: using your Christian home in a daily way that seeks to

---

3. Fleming, "Spiritual Generosity," 57.

4. Gress and Mering, *Theology of the Home*, 145, where they cite Frederick Faber in a chapter dealing with hospitality.

5. Butterfield, *Gospel Comes with a House Key*, 13.

make strangers neighbors, and neighbors family of God."[6] Of course, this requires a kind of courageous vulnerability to open the garage door, to sit on the front porch, to take walks and engage in neighborly discourse, to open the doors wide to our clutter-filled homes. It is to let our guard down and risk the rejection we all fear. Our minds are often filled with "what if" questions that prohibit our open hearts and open doors. We also, and let me personalize this, I also justify my insulation as being protective of my family—as if I am protecting my children from an outside evil influence. However, perhaps this justification actually paralyzes our families from experiencing the depths of grace extended to us all—the fact that we are all sinners in need of rescuing.

Butterfield utilizes a lexical aid to describe her concept of radical ordinary hospitality when she appeals to the Greek word *philoxenia*, "which means 'love of the stranger.'"[7] And it is this love of strangers that becomes the ethos and cornerstone of radical hospitality. But love of strangers can bring so many fears of hurt, rejection, abandonment, and reinforcement of a false emotional claim that I am somehow fundamentally flawed and misunderstood. Butterfield exhorts that universal adulation and acceptance is a kind of "sentimentality that makes us stupid." Therefore, we must "snap ourselves out of this self-pitying reverie," for "the best days are ahead." "Jesus advances from the front of the line."[8]

I must admit that I was arrested by Butterfield's citation of Ps 68:6.[9] As a Pentecostal, I can recall the recitation of Ps 68:1 in several prayer meetings as we would prepare our hearts for spiritual warfare in prayer. However, what if the first verse is correlated with the fifth and sixth verses (which I include here for your reflection)?

> Father of orphans and protector of widows
>   is God in his holy habitation.
> God gives the desolate a home to live in;
>   he leads out the prisoners to prosperity,
>   but the rebellious live in a parched land.
> (Ps 68:5–6)

What if when God arises to the scattering of his enemies, it is within the context of upending the sinful structures and oppressive embattlements

---

6. Butterfield, *Gospel Comes with a House Key*, 31.
7. Butterfield, *Gospel Comes with a House Key*, 35.
8. Butterfield, *Gospel Comes with a House Key*, 35.
9. Butterfield, *Gospel Comes with a House Key*, 37.

of our society? What if it is by fathering that he prevails? What if it is by creating belonging that the enemies flee? What if it is justice for the marginalized widow that creates victory? What if it is the quintessential defeat of loneliness that marks the shout of heaven? God creates community as a stamp of sovereign community that we are often so quick to reject as fear becomes a stalwart in our hearts. Let me confess, I am afraid. Pure and simple. I am afraid of God's victory as it may be this victory that fundamentally changes my social structure and carnal comfort.

This kind of victory, the victory of belonging, is not altogether foreign to Scripture. It was the exuberant prayer of Hannah, upon learning she was with child, who boldly declared the following hymn:

> Hannah prayed and said,
> "My heart exults in the Lord;
> my strength is exalted in my God.
> My mouth derides my enemies
> because I rejoice in your victory.
> There is no Holy One like the Lord,
> no one besides you;
> there is no Rock like our God.
> Talk no more so very proudly;
> let not arrogance come from your mouth,
> for the Lord is a God of knowledge,
> and by him actions are weighed.
> The bows of the mighty are broken,
> but the feeble gird on strength."
> (1 Sam 2:1–4)

What an example of prevailing victory, all due to a pregnancy. Do we speak like this when a child comes into our home? Do we speak like this when we host a stranger around a dinner table? Do we speak like this when someone becomes vulnerable enough to open up about their heart's dilemmas and questions? Do we talk like this when the barren is given new life, when an orphan is adopted, when a widow finds a family, or when a single mother is invited to a play date? I dare say, if we did conceptualize these seemingly mundane encounters as spiritual victories, we might recite Ps 68:1 within a different context and the landscapes of our prayers might change. Our prayer might exchange the eloquence and obtuse language of esoteric and cosmic victory for the victory of a newly formed relationship.

Setting in Order

Indeed, as our study is on the household and, by extension, God's household, we find a term in the Hebrew text of the Psalm that encapsulates this human phenomenon. It is the word *bayith*, which for the psalmist refers to the placement of the lonely in families (see Ps 68:6). *Bayith* is a noun that originates from the verb *banah*, which conveys the practice of building. The building can be a tent, house, palace, or temple. The word also conveys the building of a family, race, descendants, or household. Essentially, a *bayith* is anywhere someone might live. Where there is a lodging of image bearers, there constitutes a *bayith*.[10] Therefore, God seeks out these families for the lonely to lodge in so that transformation from unbelonging to belonging can occur. This transformation is also the power of the gospel to save and deliver from the enemy that promulgates loneliness to the victory of community.

I remember the first time Aubrey sat me down and began to unfold a burden of her heart to adopt an international child. This burden began with a dream that entailed her picking up a small Asian child from a watery trap and embracing her as if she were her own. This dream birthed many prayers and these prayers birthed expressing this desire to me that I also would join her in praying about whether God was leading us to adopt. I was initially reluctant, thinking of the enormous financial investment and wondering how such a move would be financed. We had already given birth to four dear children, and in my mind at the time, this was the number we had always discussed when planning out our family. However, God was performing a work in my wife's heart and little did I know that this work would also consume and change my heart as well. The work of God would serve to revolutionize the way I came to view children.

As we were praying about adoption, I was alone specifically seeking the Lord on how to invest our tax return that was coming. God, rather bluntly, posed a question to my soul: "Do you recall the rich young ruler?" This question came quite unexpectedly, and my answer was, "Why, yes Lord." God's reply was along the following line of thought: "I would like that you do not respond as he did when I ask that you invest in the soul of an orphan." He followed by stating that the work in my wife's heart was from him, and not simply a mere desire, fancy, or sentimental imagination.

Therefore, I relinquished my thinking of investing in my retirement or paying down debts, I gave the tax return to the cause of adoption as a deposit that we were committed to raising the funds and investing in this

---

10. Zodhiates and Baker, *Hebrew-Greek Key Word*, 1602.

soul who would become a Jensen. To say that the adoption process was a utopian journey filled with only ecstatic moments would be disingenuous. Certainly there were and are challenges that we must navigate, but the challenges have served for our sanctification. We opened our home to Naomi Jensen, and our view of children changed that day as we added two more children after her to our family. I remember the day we finally met Naomi and she looked quite suspiciously at us, as we were strangers. We looked entirely different than what she had ever known. We spoke a foreign tongue and she understood nothing but perhaps the tone of our voices. I remember the fighting as we held her and prepared to drive to our hotel. She kicked and screamed, perhaps in a panic that her entire world was changing and that she was in the arms of a man who was strange and foreign. She kicked and screamed until, exhausted from her efforts, she collapsed into a deep sleep holding to my finger.

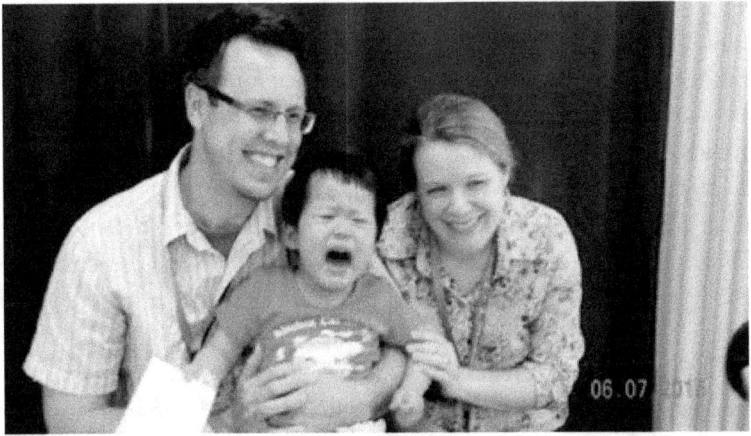

Figure 6. Gotcha Day

Perhaps her hold on my finger was unintentional. Perhaps it was a reflexive action amid her internal chaos and the upheaval of assorted emotions. Nonetheless, this small action had colossal implications for my soul. It opened in me a floodgate of love that had only been imagined up to this point. But now I was experiencing this love and it was changing me. I began to look at family in a whole new way, a family that can become a habitation of God's invitation to the lonely. Perhaps, the spiritual victory of Ps 68:6 was taking hold in my heart. Perhaps, my definition of family was broadening. Perhaps, spiritual warfare was taking on a greater nuance in my soul.

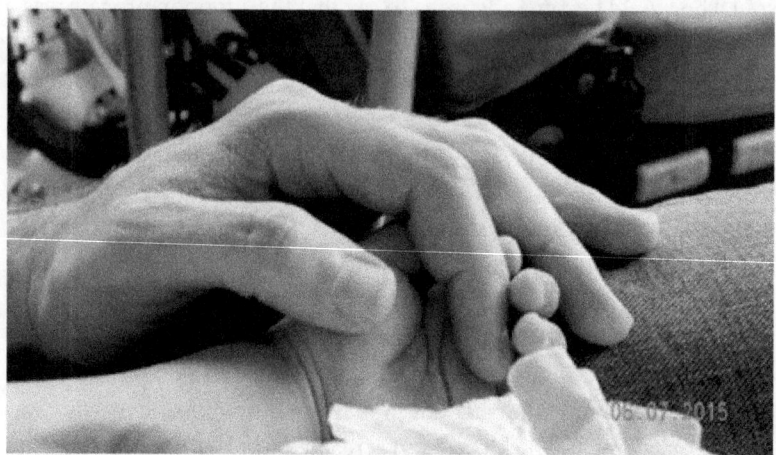

Figure 7. The Grasp

I am not quite sure what happened, but it had an aroma of grace about it. And to be honest, I have not lived out the charge that Butterfield commends to us. I find that there is a longing for radical hospitality, but also a great fear. This fear is fear of rejection, discomfort, burnout, stress, and loss of self-care. The fear of rejection looms large in my heart for I have been rejected by my very own in the body of Christ. I fear a reoccurrence if I am to open my heart once again. And so, I find myself at times repenting over these fears and by no means wanting to criticize those who have set up healthy boundaries of self-care. If I am honest, I read Butterfield's expressions of daily life and feel overwhelmed at the prospect of it all. But wasn't this my initial feeling about the adoption process? Sure, it was a two-year journey with formidable labor, paperwork, travel, and sacrifices. The sacrifices were not just with time or money, but also emotional sacrifices. There is the notion that one takes up the cross whenever embarking on a call from the Lord. So here I find myself again, standing at a crossroad of radical hospitality and how or when or if to express such hospitality. Will I take the first step? And if I do, to what or to whom do I take this next step? If the Haustafel is characterized by radical hospitality, then I must confess that this must become a regular spiritual ethos and praxis of our home. The expression of this may be different for our homes, which is why being filled with the Spirit is so necessary. It is the Spirit of the Lord who will reveal the expression of radical hospitality.

O Beloved, immerse yourself in prayer, seek his face in the prayer closet, and find that the charge of hospitality may come. But it will come

SETTING IN ORDER: THE MOTHER AND THE HAUSTAFEL

in the way the Lord has chosen for you. It will come to form you in his image with specific actions and pathos to make you more like the Son.

Butterfield ends her chapter on "The Jesus Paradox" by expositing the outcome of Christian hospitality, which is a fitting way to summarize hospitality in the Haustafel. She asserts that Christian hospitality

> beckons mystery, births community, and bequeaths truth telling. Hospitality commands the kind of truth telling that makes your teeth stand on edge. It sounds domestic, but it really shakes the gates of heaven for the souls of the people you feed, hold, and love.... Jesus foregrounds the trust that says, "I love my neighbor because she is mine, and not because she loves me back."[11]

Therefore, though not exclusive to the female gender, the role of hospitality is implicitly noted in the covenants involving the wife and mother in the epistolary texts. Thus, they are included as a primary task of both wife and mother in the covenants. However, we should note that it was the radical hospitality of Abraham in Gen 18 toward God that resulted in the blessing of pronouncement and the miracle of a child. It is in this way—the way of the entire family—that radical hospitality can be expressed.

And so, mothers covenant in the following manner within the Haustafel:

> I covenant to love my children, to be discreet, chaste, keepers of the home, good, and obedient to my husband so that the word of God will not be blasphemed (Titus 2:5). I covenant to guide the house by managing my home affairs in wisdom so that I give no occasion for the adversary to speak reproachfully (1 Tim 5:14). I covenant to work willingly with my hands for the nurturance of my family (Prov 31:13). I covenant to feed my family, invest wisely, help the poor, clothe my children, and practice radical hospitality (Prov 31:15, 20–21). I covenant to clothe myself with strength and honor so that I may speak wisdom with the law of kindness (Prov 31:25–26). If working outside the home, I covenant to implement healthy boundaries so that I do not neglect my domestic duties of the home (Prov 31:24, Acts 16:14).

---

11. Butterfield, *Gospel Comes with a House Key*, 45–46.

Chapter 15

Setting in Order: The Child and the Haustafel

Likewise, urge the younger men to be self-controlled.
TITUS 2:6

AS WE CONTINUE TO move in the order of creation, we come to sons and daughters. We have already identified the immeasurably important roles of husband and wife, father and mother, and the order of prioritization. The children now commit to a covenant in their operational behavior with their parents. We begin with the Haustafel in Ephesians where the charge is as follows:

> Children, obey your parents in the Lord, for this is right.
> "Honor your father and mother"—this is the first commandment with a promise—"so that it may be well with you and you may live long on the earth." (Eph 6:1–3)

The charge is one of obedience, or ὑπακούω (hoop-ak-oo'-), which is to "hear under." Other connotations include giving heed and yielding and are typically contextualized to servants, soldiers, or pupils. The word has also been used to those who receive and believe the gospel message (see Acts 6:7; Rom 6:17; 10:16; 2 Thess 1:8; 3:14; Heb 5:9; 11:8). ὑπακούω is exercised when one submits to the preached word or keeps the word in daily practice of faithful obedience.[1]

---

1. Zodhiates and Baker, *Hebrew-Greek Key Word*, 1764.

Indeed, it appears Paul is borrowing from the wisdom literature in his exhortation and extrapolating on the fruit of such obedience. There is a similar charge in the book of Proverbs:

> Listen to your father who begot you,
> and do not despise your mother when she is old. (Prov 23:22)

The ancillary explanation for the charge to obey is an appeal to righteousness. A child's obedience is the right course of action resulting in divine blessing. It does appear that a heavenly order is being prescribed for earthly relational dynamics. Indeed, God focuses on this kind of "right ordering" relationships in the family as this acts as a microcosm in rightly ordering the church. Paul repeats this appeal to righteousness in the Colossian Haustafel when he says the following: "Children, obey your parents in everything, for this is your acceptable duty in the Lord" (Col 3:20).

DIAKOSUNE AND RIGHTS

The righteousness or δίκαιος (dik'-ah-yos) of obedience is an appeal to justice and expectation. Indeed, the entirety of the Haustafel implies this very concept. The table of duties is a kind of expectation or obligation that is exercised by faith in desire for righteous living. But this ethos is not merely an obligation. It is a volitional duty accepted in a missional way by those who long to adopt a kingdom ethos and praxis in how they relate to others. Thus, painted in a more freeing sense, we might coin the term *right* or *table of rights*. The right is an opportunity or privilege to exercise one's faith in the not so ordinary day-to-day interactions with others. Every day is chock-full of opportunities to submit to authority, serve the marginalized, feed your children, love your wife, and respect your husband. These day-to-day interactions become a laboratory of human relatedness where one can grow more and more into the divine order of relating so that by the time one enters the church, these practices are innate, having become intuitive.[2]

The Haustafel then becomes something much more than interpersonal covenants, although this is included. It becomes an exercise in being conformed to the just character of God. The tables duties are not

---

2. See Zodhiates and Baker, *Hebrew-Greek Key Word*, 1705–06, for a more nuanced definition of δίκαιος.

coerced or unwilfully imposed. Rather, the table of duties are self-imposed, a volitional acceptance and practice of restraint in how we interact with others based on our role in that family or community.

Certainly, we can say with Paul that there is none righteous in the most culminating of ways (see Rom 3:10). That is, complete righteousness is inherited as a deposit upon salvation but is fully realized in the eschaton. Moreover, we must also commit to the understanding that the Haustafel is not only a behavioral paradigm of rules and regulations governing communities. To do this would be to live in the error of the Pharisees, who contrived several regulations for behavioral codification that created a system of self-righteousness without the internal milieu of God's mercy and justice. Let it not be said of us who are likely tempted to codify the covenants without a soul transformed and a heart circumcised. Here is the warning from Paul: "Not knowing the righteousness of God and seeking to establish their own, they have not submitted to God's righteousness" (Rom 10:3).

Let us also be careful in all covenants that the focus is not merely on behavior but rather the focus is on relationships that attune to behaviors. The δίκαιος exhibit righteous behavior because they are walking with God. The dos and don'ts in interpersonal relation can become cold and austere and, at worst, oppressive if there is no relationship to fuel the covenants with a burning love and expressed mutual subordination. This is why the Haustafel begins with pathos and virtues before addressing behaviors and covenants. In walking with God, we find that the cultural euphemism of one's duty being one's right is juxtaposed with a Christian community whose right is one's duty—or, said in other terms, one's right is one's covenantal relating.[3]

There is a profound difference here. The Christian views the pathos and praxis of the Haustafel as Christian witness and mission. It is his or her duty to commit to such dispositional virtues and interpersonal covenants. This is juxtaposed by a society that is increasingly autonomous and individualistic, desperately clinging to an existential privacy rather than covenanting to commit and submit to δίκαιος relationships.

E. A. Havelock has written a dated but insightful article on the development of δίκαιος in Greek and later in Western civilizations. He provides a nuanced distinction between δίκαιος and δικαιοσυνε: "δίκαιος refers to the maintenance of reciprocal relationships of right: they connote 'rights'

---

3. See Zodhiates and Baker, *Hebrew-Greek Key Word*, 1706, for a comparison of Western relating derived from autonomy and Christian relating derived from δίκαιος.

rather than 'righteousness'; they were indexes of purely external behaviors." He goes on to delineate this distinction further when he asserts that "with the appearance of δικαιοσυνε it had occurred to some that this kind of reciprocal propriety corresponded to a personal virtue, the property of an individual."[4]

So, the question that then follows is did the apostle Paul intend to refer to mere external behaviors with δίκαιος when exhorting children to obedience? Or did Paul also intend to appeal to a moral virtue of righteousness that was intended to communicate the relational preservation between child and parent based on the child's sincere desire for righteousness? By seeking relational posterity with God, the child then desires relational posterity with his or her parents, all of which is part and parcel to living out what is right.

My polemic is that Paul is not appealing to mere external behaviors, although that is included. I believe he argues for obedience from the premise of promise. That is, although one assertion is that obedience is given to parents as it is the right thing to do before God and before humanity, a corollary to this is the child not only obeys but also honors his or her parents as it is accompanied by promise. God's promise motivates the honor. God's promise appeals to the inner virtue forming within the child's soul, which is behaviorally operationalized with obedience and honor. The promise of God motivates, enthuses, inspires, and fills the child's heart with a certain purpose.

The promise is explicated in Exodus in the following manner: "Honor your father and your mother, so that your days may be long in the land that the Lord your God is giving you" (Exod 20:12).

What we find is a dual promise of longevity and land. A full and long life along with an inheritance of land from the Lord himself is the promise associated with the honor given to parents. What comes before this command in the Decalogue are rationales for obedience and consequences for disobedience, but Paul is keen to identify the first command with a promise. It is the promises of God that can be cultivated in the heart of a child that may act as a relational catalyst that draws her near to God's heart. This drawing near to God is the seed for honor and obedience that results in longevity and land.

Perhaps Paul's use of δίκαιος indicates the external behaviors of obedience whereas his call to honor is a cry to the soul, a virtuous kerygmatic

---

4. Havelock, "Dikaiosune," 51.

Setting in Order

appeal built on relational and reciprocal propriety that the child is catching one precept at a time.

Furthermore, in attempting to define δικαιοσυνε, Havelock brings to us a story of Greek antiquity where the word was used to describe a Spartan of great notoriety, Glaucus. Leotychides is the narrator, rehearsing the narrative as a rhetorical polemic that he and Athens have been wronged and deserve a tangible remedy for their grievance. He tells of Glaucus, a Spartan of import known for his δικαιοσυνε. The tradition ensues that a Milesian arrived to make a deposit with Glaucus given his stature of δικαιοσυνε. The Milesian believes that his deposit will be quite secure with Glaucus contingent upon the attribute of δικαιοσυνε.

Much time passes and the children of the Milesian who made the deposit produce the tokens of this deposit asking for the inheritance that was secure with Glaucus. Glaucus replies with a forgetful reply that he cannot recall such a deposit being made. He is explicit in that he informs the inquirers that he would like to do the "right" (δίκαιος) thing in this exchange between them but requests more time to investigate the veracity of their claim. The Milesians depart, denouncing Glaucus's hesitation and delay, claiming to have been robbed.

Glaucus presents himself to the oracle at Delphi to assist him in finding a solution to his inner conflict. He asks whether he should take an oath to plunder the money. The oracle provides an answer in seven hexameter verses. First, the obvious is stated in that Glaucus would surely profit if he took an oath to plunder the money. In this regard, he would prevail and profit. However, what is ominous in the oracle's prediction is that this oath would spawn a demonic offspring. This demonic oath reserves the potential to exterminate a man's lineage and posterity. In contrast, the man who is faithful in his pledges would enjoy a prevailing lineage.

Glaucus seeks repentance after the oracle is provided and longs for pardon from the oracle of Delphi. He seeks to evade such an ominous prediction. The oracle refuses Glaucus's request with the rationale that to tempt the violation of a pledge is the same as performing the deed. That is, intention appears to be attached to the meaning of δικαιοσυνε in Greek antiquity. Glaucus does repay the money, but it is too late for him. Leotychides provides for his audience the moral of the story. Why does he tell the story? He claims that the oracle of Delphi was vindicated; by his time, there was no root or mention of the line of Glaucus in Sparta.

SETTING IN ORDER: THE CHILD AND THE HAUSTAFEL

"In the case of a deposit, do not even harbor intention of refusing payment to a claimant."[5]

Now, it is impossible to know if Paul's use of δίκαιος has in mind the history of the word's use in Greek history, or even Herodotus's history. However, he is using the Greek language that has a history of nuance. Therefore, I do wonder if the nuance of intention is communicated through his appeal to honor and obey. If this is the case, then the children's Haustafel role in the covenant community is more than external conformity to the instruction of a parent, but an inner intention and, I might say, affection for obedience.

LOGOS VS. LALIA

If we look at the construct of "obey," there is an undertone of the Shema which may be alluded to. The word ὑπακούω (oop-ak-oo'-o) is derived from an act of listening.[6] That is, one cannot obey without first fully listening to the one speaking, issuing commands, or giving instruction. Even Jesus points out the great contrast between hearing and listening when he provides us with a word play when admonishing the religious leaders of his time.

Jesus provides for us this listening conundrum in John 8:43 when he states the following: "Why do ye not understand my speech? Even because ye cannot hear my word" (John 8:43). Here, Jesus weaves two Greek constructs together to emphasize his point. He begins with λαλιά, (lal-ee-ah') to illustrate the misunderstanding the Pharisees conveyed in regard to the words of Jesus. In this sense, λαλιά conveys a kind of incapacity to understand, as if Jesus's speech is received as unintelligible sounds. The deeper admonishment could be reiterated in the following manner: "What I am saying to you is as if it had no meaning whatsoever."[7] That is, a heart that is cold or hardened against the λόγος (log'-os) of Christ will only hear what it would like to hear. The words of Christ then become fodder to the incensed for the sound is only perceived as a threat to the power the Pharisees currently maintain.

---

5. Havelock, "Dikaiosune," 56.

6. See Online Greek Bible, "Ephesians 6:1," where the following definition is provided: "To listen, to harken; 1a) of one who on the knock at the door comes to listen who it is, (the duty of a porter); 2) to harken to a command; 2a) to obey, be obedient to, submit to."

7. Zodhiates and Baker, *Hebrew-Greek Key Word*, 1734.

Christ will appeal to λόγος (log'-os) in the second half of John 8:43 to again illustrate the reality that to hear Christ's λόγος has a precondition of a heart that is open to attend to obedience. The heart malleable to obedience has greater capacity to understand the λόγος conveyed by the speech of Christ. The intended meaning of Christ's λόγος is understood upon the bedrock of a heart whose doors are open to surrender. The heart that is embedded with stone hears the speech of Christ as incendiary and thus hears the λαλιά of Christ with no meaning rather than the λόγος of Christ with a targeted meaning of reform, renewal, and salvation.[8]

The content of Christ's speech does not change, but the context of the heart alters the meaning that is received. We might refer to this phenomenon with other words that are reflective to cognitive neuroscience. That is, semantic conclusions activate a specific neural network that takes into consideration not only the content of speech but the visual analogues of the speaker along with the a priori information concerning the speaker's identity.

Roel Willems et al. sought to better understand this assimilation of hearing and meaning when experimenting with speech and visual constructs and how these phenomena interact with neural networks. They cite earlier studies that have established the use of ERPs (event-related potentials vis-à-vis EEG recordings) to identify when there is either an incongruent semantic sentence structure or an unexpected word placement within a sentence. The ERP consistency displays what has become known as an N400 effect whenever a person is confronted with incongruence or unexpected word placement. They further found that the N400 effect occurs between 250 and 500 msec. after the incongruent word and is typically potentiated at central and posterior electrodes.[9]

Moreover, functional MRI studies have provided us with a locus for semantic integration. Several studies have identified increased activation or metabolism in the left inferior frontal and/or temporal areas of the brain when posed with semantic ambiguity.[10] These studies confirm that the brain has learned semantic rules when deciphering speech and,

---

8. Zodhiates and Baker, *Hebrew-Greek Key Word*, 1734.

9. Willems et al., "Seeing and Hearing Meaning," 1235, where they provide an example of an N400 ERP. They give the following example: "For example, the sentence-final word of the sentence, 'She spread her bread with socks,' leads to a negative deflection in the ERP waveform in comparison to the ERP for a congruous ending as in 'She spread her bread with butter.'"

10. Willems et al., "Seeing and Hearing Meaning," 1236.

when these rules are violated, there is an activation of understanding centers with remarkable ERPs and increased metabolism of certain neural networks utilized in making meaning of unexpected speech and visual anomalies. Willems et al. sought to better understand visual cues when making meaning. They cite several other studies that have found semantic processing leads to selective cortical activation. For example, ventral temporal activation occurs when there is "semantic knowledge of an object," whereas inferior frontal activation occurs during the action of "semantic selection or retrieval."[11]

They go on to assert a theoretical paradigm in the processing of language that is important to our current discussion on hearing, words, honor, and obedience. They sought to understand whether the brain preforms a one-step immediate integration of speech and visual analogs versus a two-step process. Ultimately, their study affirmed an "'immediacy assumption,' that is, the idea that every source of information that constrains the interpretation of an utterance (syntax, prosody, word-level semantics, prior discourse, world knowledge, knowledge about the speaker, gestures, etc.) can, in principle, operate immediately."[12] This is important as the identity of the speaker is just as important as the content of the speech in the phenomenology of making semantic meaning. Willem appeals to a prior meaning-making model known as Fregean compositionality, which "states that the meaning of an utterance is a function of the meaning of its parts and of the syntactic rules by which these parts are combined."[13] To integrate this finding into the word play of Jesus, we find that the Pharisees were unable to understand his speech because of preconceived notions about his identity that formed a conclusion regardless of his words so that whatever he said was mere sound (λαλιά) rather than intelligible speech (λόγος).

CONTEMPORARY APPLICATION

Does this kind of misunderstanding, preconceived construction, and hindrance to meaning making occur in contemporary pastoral contexts? Certainly; for example, we find that Pastor Pascal was invited to a meeting by one of his church board members to "clear the air" after several

---

11. Willems et al., "Seeing and Hearing Meaning," 1236.
12. Willems et al., "Seeing and Hearing Meaning," 1237.
13. Willems et al., "Seeing and Hearing Meaning," 1237.

months of difficult budget conversations within the board. This church board member accused Pastor Pascal of attempting to destroy the church by putting forth a budget plan that she initially agreed with then later sought to reverse after conversations with disgruntled staff members.

Pastor Pascal conceived that her desire to meet was for reconciliatory reasons. However, he was sadly mistaken when this board member fired off various accusations over grievances that the board member never experienced and was not a direct witness to. Rather, it is likely that she took hearsay conversations from disgruntled staff members to create a rubric of accusation. And thus, for an hour she accused Pastor Pascal of corruption, manipulation, and of being at risk of being sued. Each and every time Pastor Pascal attempted to bring nuance to the history she had formulated in her mind, he would be interrupted with yet another accusation. That is, she never sought to understand the words of Pastor Pascal, likely because she did not want the preformed archetype of a corrupt leader to be disrupted. Anything contrary to this image she had concocted could not be entertained. It is likely that Pastor Pascal's words were mere sounds (λαλιά) rather than intelligible speech (λόγος).

Pastors, be quite cautious when you get an invitation to "clear the air." It is quite possible that this is a code to air grievances so that you will be demoralized, marginalized, or so that you will resign. If one already has a preconceived construction concerning your identity, these concepts may have already been etched as a firm caricature of your identity and may do more harm than good. If you perceive that this is happening in any meeting, it is appropriate to end the meeting rather than being abused with a kind of emotional violence that seeks to unravel your call.

Now, why is this important? It is that we learn to formulate identities of others quite early on in childhood. We learn meaning making and interactions with authority figures as a child. Children learn to listen, attend, obey, and attune themselves to their parents. If this is not occurring in the home, then of course unhealthy dynamics will also enter the church for the pastor to contend with. Indeed, I have once asserted that rather than an obsession with learning leadership within a paradigmatic rubric of corporate leadership principles, pastors might do well to study family dynamics as the church functions more like a family than a corporation.

THE FAMILY AND THE CHURCH
AS BOWEN FAMILY SYSTEM

This is where Murray Bowen becomes relevant. He was a psychiatrist at the Menninger Clinic who studied mental illness and its relation within the family system. His observations led him to develop what is now known as the Bowen family systems theory to describe components of mental illness within families. Bowen asserts that an individual in a family acts in an integral role in the one emotional system that represents the family, so that the mental illness or the severity of the mental illness is influenced by, or in some cases caused by, certain dysfunction in the emotional system of the family. Bowen and his colleagues describe the family system as an "automatic functioning and reactivity expressed in habitual processes that are expressed beyond conscious choice or control."[14] And to add greater clarity, the family system is "the existence of a naturally occurring system in all forms of life that enables an organism to receive information (from within itself and from the environment), to integrate that information, and to respond on the basis of it."[15]

As we have noted, it is important for children to not only obey, but to honor their parents as an expression of the Haustafel. And, as we have looked at obedience as a secondary step to first correctly attuning to and hearing the speech of the parents, and as we have seen that the listening is often preconditioned upon the identity of the speaker, we now consider that automatic responses of individuals in family is sometimes habitual and performed without thought, but rather a process that can sometimes be performed outside of one's awareness. For example, family dynamics can be likened to one following a script in a narrative or an elaborate play. And yet the one playing the role does not know that lines of that script are embedded in his or her mind. The compulsion is to simply rehearse the script, for he or she has often been pigeonholed into this role by the pressures of the family dynamic. The script becomes inherent and automated. It becomes integrated into behaviors and often you may hear lamentations from these same individuals, "I don't know why I keep doing this, I just can't help myself."

Bowen asserts that these behaviors are not an individual in isolation, but rather emblematic of a system at work. For the system to function,

---

14. See Son, "Anxiety as a Main Cause," 11, who references definitions of the Bowen Family Systems theory.
15. Son, "Anxiety as a Main Cause," 11.

or in many cases to dysfunction, the individual has a role or script to preserve in the system maintaining a sense of status quo. When the status quo becomes upended through crisis, loss, grief, additions, or immense change, the patterns of behavior escalate to return to the previous system dynamics. Acting out can sometimes be perceived thus as a cry to return to a system that provided some semblance of stability or comfort. Or, acting out is just what some do because it provides a redirection of focus back on the individual who is wounded, alone, and in need of consolation. As pastors, we would do well to study the family dynamics within the parish. Chances are that the same dynamics are at work in the church, which is also an emotional system.

Let us consider Pastor Connie. She began hearing complaints from a church member. This member had lodged several complaints against the children's pastor. The church member did not isolate her complaints but began expressing such grievances to other staff members who promoted these complaints to Pastor Connie asking for action. Pastor Connie placates the church member and anxious staff members by mentoring the children's pastor. This action, although an attempt to help the church and assuage the church member, emboldened the church member to not only continue to air grievances but to broaden the grievances to now include Pastor Connie. Now Pastor Connie was emotionally unhealthy, too busy, or anything else that would suffice to fit into the script the church member was carrying out. The church member began including the entire staff and state leadership in expressing her grievances. There was no boundary or barrier that she would not traverse.

This example illustrates a family system at work in a dysfunctional manner. The church member was emboldened as the "savior" of the church since her grievances acted upon the anxiety within the staff leadership concerning the publicity of this church member's grievances. Pastor Connie sought to confront these grievances but then became the object of such grievances.

The church member had, in many ways, also become enmeshed with other staff members so that she was able to wield her influence of grievance, which persuaded others as well serving to accuse Pastor Connie as inadequate or unable to lead. Other staff members then persuaded Pastor Connie to placate rather than confront. And when Pastor Connie attempted to confront, this was evaded with more grievances being expressed at the notion of being confronted. The grievances expanded to include the church board, all staff, state, and even international leadership.

SETTING IN ORDER: THE CHILD AND THE HAUSTAFEL

Two processes may have contributed to the dysfunction in this system. One is enmeshment, which is a lack of differentiation, and the other is triangulation. The church member had become enmeshed with certain leadership so that there was a lack of differentiation between the staff and the church member. This perpetuated a grievance culture by placating and emboldening the church member. Furthermore, the church member appeared to voice a strong concern for the church health, perhaps seeing herself in a savior role and the church staff in the saved role. She triangulated certain staff members to rally to her cause. This role led to further entrenched and dysfunctional dynamics that eventually resulted in the church member's disfellowship by state leadership. Families and churches experience both fusion and emotional cut off. The pattern that families and churches often experience is the following progression: fusion or enmeshment that then leads to emotional cut off or exile.

Bowen calls for a healthy differentiation within family systems that has the potential for one to better objectify the conflict and observe the scripts at play within congregational life. However, the pastor, like a father or child within a family system, must also have a healthy sense of differentiation apart from the family system to make such observations. Therefore, church conflict often requires neutral third-party arbiters to bring awareness to the sick family system and provide recommendations for healthy structures and healthy relationships. For example, church families are often connected by marriage and business relationships or splintered by divorce and death. These dynamics can complicate the one emotional system of the church.

Bowen observes a kind of dialectic between individuality and togetherness. He defines individuality as "the capacity to be an individual while part of a group."[16] One should not consider individuality in Bowen family systems as autonomy; rather, one is able to preserve individual identity while at the same time belonging to a community. The identity does not become the community. Bowen uses yet another term to describe this phenomenon, *fusion*. This is when one is unable to construct any meaningful identity outside the community to which she or he belongs. Now, we should be clear that Bowen is writing about families when using such terms, but many have extrapolated his theories to include larger communities with similar dynamics.

---

16. Son, "Anxiety as a Main Cause," 12.

Setting in Order

Bowen calls for a kind of emotional autonomy within the context of interpersonal relatedness. That is, one is together with a family or community in relationships, but not dependent on said family or community for emotional meaning making or function. This is the complicated dance of the dialectic, like the eschatological construct we often quote, "already and not yet." Healthy family systems function within a dialectic of an emotional distinction and differentiation known as an interpersonal togetherness paradigm. One could imagine that this could become complicated quite quickly, for it is not always intuitive to function in such a manner. People in family systems will often default to an emotional template constructed early on in life. This could be an emotional template of estrangement or enmeshment, which is the boundary of differentiation taken to its uppermost limit on one hand, contrasted with no differentiation at all on the other. The other tragic possibility here is that enmeshment can often be a harbinger of future estrangement. For when an identity of togetherness is threatened in any way, one can sometimes envision preservation by any means necessary by annihilating the threat. The annihilation, unfortunately, is usually the destruction of someone else in the community to preserve the self in an enmeshed family.[17]

Friedman, in consulting the Bowen family systems theory, provides for us five ways in which a church may be able to identify minister burnout and church factions with the following:

1. Degree of isolation between the congregation and other congregations in its own faith community or in its local community.

2. Degree of distance between the lay leadership and the general membership.

3. Extent to which the lay leadership allows the congregation to preempt its entire emotional life (no other friends or social networks).

4. Degree to which the lay leadership has intense interdependent relationships with one another beyond their congregational functioning, such as being related through blood, marriage, or business.

5. Inability of the lay leadership, particularly the "president" or the senior warden, to take well-defined positions, independent of the complainers.[18]

---

17. Son, "Anxiety as a Main Cause," 12.

18. Friedman, *Generation to Generation*, 217. Also cited in Son, "Anxiety as a Main Cause," 17.

Though not a comprehensive list by any means, Friedman starts the church on a journey of family considerations. For example, the first recommendation is a principle around estrangement or emotional cut off. If one local church distances itself from other community churches within the same tradition, movement, denomination, or mission, this isolationism will soon begin to operate within the church itself. For example, the congregants will also emotionally distance themselves from each other. There can be all kinds of implicit etiologies to the emotional distance of one congregation from another. Perhaps there is a high sense of autonomy. Or perhaps there is a self-righteous disposition of spiritual elitism. Or perhaps it is grief or wounds that lead one to isolation to cover the shame. Whatever the source, the dynamic of separation needs to be recognized and acknowledged and prayerful guidance given on how to reintegrate with the community at large. The second recommendation is, like the first, around a level of estrangement on a microcosmic level within the congregation itself. If the entire church is distant from other churches, this can spill over into the distance between the leadership and members.

The third recommendation is one birthed from the opposite principle around estrangement, that of enmeshment. Estrangement and enmeshment can be equally dangerous to a family system. For example, the wife feels emotionally distanced from her husband and so redirects her emotional investment to the children, only to find that there is no relationship remaining with her husband when they become empty nesters. Or the husband feels emotionally cut off from his wife and so invests his emotional energy into his work, again only to find that when he retires, he is restless and depressed, having no relational investment with his wife. Unfortunately, this can have multigenerational effects where children isolate from one another, rehearsing a narrative that "I am different from my brother or sister," leading to an emotional estrangement within the family system. Or, in contrast as noted above, the child who is enmeshed with his or her mother has difficulty leaving the family of origin and uniting with the spouse, seeking decision-making approval from the mother rather than a cooperative decision-making paradigm with the spouse.

Enmeshment resembles a fusion of two identities. The greater the level of enmeshment, the greater the rigidity during decision-making processes. The greater the level of differentiation, the more one can objectify the conflict and emotionally disentangle oneself. This kind of enmeshment can invade the church family as well. If the only relationships in one's sphere are church members, then one can hardly be objective or rational. If there is the least threat to the relationship, extreme measures must be taken to preserve the relationships, which can sometimes lead to sinful behaviors in how one preserves the enmeshed relationship.

That is, if one's entire identity is defined by the role within the church body, then one will fight tooth and nail to preserve this identity, sometimes not quite aware of why one is fighting so intensely. Sinful undermining of leadership and the leveraging of influence or the spreading of slander can sometimes be justified in the name of Jesus. For it is the perception that one's identity as perceived by one's role in the church surely must be from a divine origin. This is to not make light of the call of God. For it is a sober and holy calling indeed. I am merely attempting to bring awareness of how enmeshment, first learned in the family, can find its way into the church in unhealthy relational dynamics.

For example, Rose, a staff member who operated in her home as mother, grandmother, priest, and leader of the family, brought this same kind of operation to her role in the church. She was the primary provider of her household and was still living with her adult children, who may have had a difficult time differentiating. She had separated from her husband before he died and may have assumed many leadership roles within the family system as a result.

Perhaps, unaware she was doing so, Rose was also becoming enmeshed with other staff members and dynamically relating to individuals, including the lead pastor, as their mother. When budget cuts came to this church with chronic anxiety and her position was being discussed as for elimination, this was a threat to her identity, which may have been consumed by her perceived role within the church itself. Rose retaliated by leveraging her influence with other staff members and church board members in secret. She decided to cut herself off from the pastor who was negotiating the budget with the church board. If the pastor was the threat, he then needed to be eliminated. If the pastor was not following Rose's vision for the church staff structure or direction of the church, then surely he had missed God's revelation for the church. By leveraging her maternal influence, she was successful in convincing a few church board members to call for a reversal of the church budget and even the pastor's resignation if he did not acquiesce to the request.

Sadly, this kind of enmeshment dynamic plays out time and time again in the church. The enmeshment begins in the home and is extrapolated to the church. Rose's story is not unique. Rose sought to preserve her role in the church family as maternal leader and entrench that role by creating an influence that was unfortunately substantiated by church leadership. This leads to an empowerment of enmeshment because it was reinforced. If Rose can experience a kind of prevailing victory utilizing the principles of enmeshment, it is likely that this behavior will be repeated. This is where the rub can become so very painful for pastors. For they will likely inherit a church infrastructure that is united by marriage and business relationships. Teasing out these conflicts of interest is emotionally painful.

For example, I was talking with a pastor not too long ago who was describing his elder board. He cited more than one board member who had family members or even a spouse who were also staff members of the church. Thus, there is likely to be great inherent conflict if budget discussions inch anywhere near cutting those positions. Another pastor was attempting to hire a new staff member and interviewed a candidate whose son was engaged to a current staff member's daughter. If this potential candidate is not hired, the lead pastor will likely face not only the ire of the candidate's scorn for being looked over but the ire of the staff member who advocated for this candidate with some level of motivation from the in-law dynamic. Can you see how messy these relationships can become? A pastor walks into a world of intertwined, enmeshed relationships, ones that are also estranged because of wounds over the history of the church.

Remember, the pastor inherits the history of relationships. You are not only inheriting the here and now, but a history of conflict, fractures, fusion, and cut offs. To say this is a daunting task for pastors is an understatement. Pastors must work to minimize or eliminate these conflicts of interest by defining roles precisely. Elders should not be related to staff members either by business or marriage. Staff members should not privately influence elders but ought to make whatever remarks necessary in the public forum of a joint meeting. A church who differentiates in this manner will create healthy boundaries to objectify and negotiate conflict in a constructive manner.

And this is the exhortation of the fourth principle noted above. A pastor would do well to make attempts to ensure that there are little to no conflicts of interest concerning leadership with both familial and business relationships. This can lead to enmeshed alliances and possible persecution of others who may disagree with the alliance. The final and fifth recommendation is one of precision. Friedman contends that the more precise and defined the pastor's position and role, the more objective he or she can be in conflict. The pastor must explain his or her position in redundant and consistent manners to dispel myths or misunderstandings that may arise from projection or persecution of those who oppose the pastor.

We were all once children and in many ways the dynamics of relating were forged during these years. Perhaps a foray into a genogram would be helpful in elucidating one's pattern that persists in communities or church families.

Bowen asserts that an individual can retain an aspect of autonomy but also live by a kind of family system that governs his or her actions. In this respect, when illness become obvious, "it is the product of a total family problem," and "when this simple concept is extended to its ultimate, then all mankind becomes responsible for the ills of all mankind."[19]

This then creates an inquiry for all to consider. What parts of myself—thoughts, decisions, and actions—are derived from the family system from which I came? Have I inherited restlessness from my family system? Did I cope through estrangement as my mother had done before me? Have I inherited an addiction from my father that manifests itself in the form of relentless work? Do I push my children away from me with the same expression of rigidity that I experienced as a child? Have you asked these questions? Do pastors look at their families to see what they may bring into a church family?

Did the bankruptcy my family experienced influence me to the degree that in anxiety I proposed radical financial ideas to save money in our church family? Did I leave a church system when I could not absorb the anxiety any longer only to find that my community was not deep or profound enough to endure it? Pastors, we can push differentiation to the extreme and find that it is a lonely island. In contrast, we can fuse with members within a congregation and find that we have lost our identity. Both dynamics are dangerous, and both create dysfunction and individual illness. The fusion of one with another can lead to an overemphasis on accommodation and the one who accommodates excessively eventually becomes the one who absorbs the communal anxiety of the

---

19. Bowen, *Family Therapy in Clinical Practice*, 289.

SETTING IN ORDER: THE CHILD AND THE HAUSTAFEL

congregation, leading to anxiety disorders, panic attacks, and emotional paralysis. We might call this burnout today!

Bowen is keen to assert that "far more human activity is governed by man's emotional system than he has been willing to admit."[20] We make good-intentioned efforts to intellectualize and objectify a conflict, perhaps even boasting of our own rational approach, but are seemingly blinded to our own emotional solution to the conflict. I think if we become honest with ourselves, we would confess that seminal decisions have been crafted in part by emotional reasoning. We are not the pure rational and objective creatures that we tend to boast of. Joy, excitement, pride, shame, sorrow, and condemnation have all played a role in our decisions. The brokenness of the fall has created a context for us all to entertain erroneous imaginations that have influenced our affairs of human relations. In many cases, we are simply operating in the same way that we did in the family system we grew up in.

For example, I defaulted to being silent amid false accusations and slander. I returned to being the child that was silent in the face of my father's anger. I assumed the role of a child who said nothing, hoping and praying the moment would pass and the family system would reset. Or I was the child who hoped my mother would come to rescue me from the anger of my father and take me away to the hotel for a time of peace and rest. Perhaps this is why I imagined fantasies where someone, anyone, would come to my defense as a pastor. Perhaps God was nudging me to be somewhat more assertive in the conflict, to defend the call much like Paul did when his call to apostleship came under assault.

It is so very easy to fall back into family default roles or temperaments without being aware of it. Perhaps you were the hero child destined to save the entire family system, so you enter the pastorate as a messiah figure only to burn out when nothing you plan is executed and you finally realize your weakness and limitations. Boundaries become blurred and there is no margin for your family because you continue your relentless efforts to resurrect the church. Or perhaps you were the scapegoat in your family and enter the congregation absorbing the blame for all that goes wrong. This dynamic can quickly lead to sorrow, despair, depression, and escalating self-loathing. Or perhaps you were the middle child, often overlooked with attention being directed to the oldest or youngest. In this context, one defaults to a kind of feigned contentment

---

20. Bowen, *Family Therapy in Clinical Practice*, 305.

of remaining in the shadows and perhaps delegating leadership decisions to others who can potentially use their influence to denigrate or undermine your authority. Pastors, you are children as well. What did you learn as a child? How is it playing out right now in your parish? Who is taking advantage of your interpersonal dynamics? How can you become aware of your blind spots? I would contend that looking earnestly into your own family system is a place to start.

AMBIGUITY AND THREAT INTERPRETATION BIAS

Muris et al. have identified a possible heuristic explanation to the burgeoning emotional reasoning templates that can occur in children. In citing other studies, they assert that "there is evidence for at least two distinct types of cognitive biases in anxious children: attentional bias which refers to hyperattention toward irrelevant, but threat-related stimuli, and interpretational bias which pertains to the tendency to interpret ambiguous situations as threatening."[21]

Therefore, is it possible that as we navigate anxiety, panic, worry, and somatic tension that there is a hyperattention on the irrelevant or alternative models of "threat" stimuli? And of course, when we speak of threat in pastoral family models, we tend to refer to church conflicts of any kind. That is, a pastor may vigilantly attune to conflict within his or her staff, church board, or influential members, paying little to no attention to most of the congregation who supports, prays for, and loves the pastor. This is an attentional bias that is the a priori source of emotional reasoning. Moreover, interpretational bias can also be a dynamic looming large in the mind of a pastor, originating in the anxious child who misinterprets ambiguity as a threat. Ambiguity is often neutral and calls for clarity. However, in an anxious child and, I dare assert, an anxious pastor, the tempting interpretation is one driven by the emotions of fear, apprehension, or anxiety that one's very existence and identity are under assault.

In many ways, I am more anxious than I would like to admit. I secretly tremble when on zoom calls, I internally denigrate my education, calling, and credentials to be speaking. I gave so much attention to smaller conflicts and could not see the broader landscape. I envisaged ambiguity as a threat to my call as pastor. And perhaps some of the conversations were indeed a threat, a slander, and a serious questioning

---

21. Muris et al., "Emotional Reasoning Heuristic in Children," 262.

of my pastoral role. But perhaps some of the ambiguity concerning direction, budgets, and personnel was given an automatic heuristic of threat. Why do I tremble when among leaders? Why do I feel a sense of anxiety since the emotional trauma of transition? Could it be that what happened is a reminder of prior emotional trauma and a reinforcement of internal ambiguity? To be accepted can be a strong human inclination. To be rejected can reinforce emotional reasoning to the extent that one implodes under the pressure of an anxious hermeneutic.

Therefore, this phenomenon of attentional or interpretation bias can persist so that the feelings become the rod of discernment. That is, the pastor can be tempted to believe that "if I am anxious, then there must be danger." This can perpetuate persistent anxiety and depression. The proposed intervention here is to disentangle emotional responses from perception and belief. Emotions do not always evaluate experience with an objective lens. Reorientation to objectivity can assist in erroneous threat perception. And yet, there is a history of threat that becomes the hermeneutic of the pastor. The threat began long ago in a family where subjective and objective threat was blurred so that ambiguity cannot be tolerated in one's internal milieu. Ambiguity itself is a threat.

Then, there is the multigenerational inheritance model of family systems that a pastor may default to if not aware of his or her own family of origin. P. Klever sought to study such transmission when working with several multigenerational families. He notes that the literature is itself somewhat ambiguous but appears to affirm multigenerational transmission with a differentiation of manifestations. That is, a nuclear family may have undergone the turmoil of multiple divorces, which is manifest in marital strife or parent-child conflict in the next generation. The dynamic remains, but the manifestation varies. Divorce does not necessitate a future divorce in the next generation—and thank God for his grace! However, a divorce may be replicated in an altogether different manifestation such as dyadic ambiguity, distance, estrangement, or parent-child fusion.[22]

For example, every pastor should undertake the task of writing his or her own genogram. Please see appendix G for my own. My father's mother divorced and remarried. My paternal grandfather likely suffered from PTSD after World War II and turned to alcoholism to cope. This led to the family splintering only for my paternal grandmother to marry yet

---

22. Klever, "Multigenerational Transmission," 255–56.

another alcoholic. My father's stepfather modeled a home environment of rage, which set up a replicating cycle of anger outbursts that laid an emotional framework for the nuclear family that was passed on as well. My father inherited the same coping mechanism and turned to alcohol to cope with the anxieties of life. The same anger displayed in my father's stepfather had taken hold of him and he walked the same path of anger outbursts and a drunken escapist paradigm.

My mother was initially raised by her maternal grandparents as her paternal grandparents disapproved of the marriage between her father and mother. For some mysterious reason she was abruptly taken from her grandparents' home and began living with her mother and father. Though not altogether confirmed, it may have been abuse that led to the abrupt transition for my mother. Thus, my mother's developmental years were spent in sudden transition and possible trauma. She married an abusive man from whom she was divorced not long after. This was a family secret until she disclosed this information to me when in my twenties. She moved from her family of origin across the country to escape the toxic family dynamics that she found contributed to her own fears for her children. I grew up with very little contact with my extended family, some of whom I have never met. My mother was estranged from her parents, likely starting early on when being raised by her grandparents.

She fled from her family, but the dynamics followed her. Both my father's and my mother's family histories are riddled with substance use and divorce. This would then translate to a feverish attempt to flee these dynamics, which appeared to be manifested in a kind of restlessness that translated to moving nearly every four years. My childhood was one move after the next. Sometimes these moves were because of financial necessity, at other times it was because of a financial venture as my parents sought to make money by flipping houses.

As the first born, I grew up with enormous expectations that I would redeem the family system by going to college and advancing in some career in medicine. My mother continuously groomed me for such a career. The moment I entered college, my level of differentiation escalated, and I began to repeat the same pattern of estrangement that was in the generation before me. I contacted my parents and siblings less and less as I lost myself in my studies. I became enamored with academia, and this appeared to be my alcoholism. The seeds of study and work began to blossom, which could become a strong temptation as an addiction. I married, began my own family, which led to further estrangement with my nuclear family. I also moved away from my family as I continued the pursuit of one degree after the next. I became acutely aware of my preponderance to work to the detriment of relationships when my fiancé and now wife began to lament how little time we spent together.

My sister married an abusive husband from whom she was divorced not too long after, remarried only a few short months later, had two children, and then divorced her second husband. She lived with our parents even during her second marriage where a kind of fusion took place between her and our mother. That is, it appeared that her decisions were made collaboratively more with our mother than with her spouse. She moved across the country like our parents did a generation earlier. There, she divorced her second husband, married a third time. My parents followed my sister to live with her on the west coast. My father has become a sort of de facto father figure for my nephews.

My brothers, the youngest of the family, have suffered from anxiety and substance use disorders intermittently throughout their adolescence and adulthood. They are emotionally fused together, being twins, and are quite estranged from the family as well. One of my brothers did successfully complete a Teen Challenge program, but their status and spiritual state remain a mystery as they choose not to communicate with the family. My contact with my brothers consists of me initiating a phone call on major holidays only to get their voicemail and me leaving a generic voicemail desiring to catch up and praying for a blessing during whatever holiday season I am calling.

Therefore, if one were to summarize nuclear family dynamics, one would discover estrangement, fusion, divorce, secrets, denial, substance use, and restlessness as major themes. Now, one must face the difficult reality of investigating how these dynamics manifest in one's decisions and life trajectory. For example, restlessness has manifested in my decisions to pursue several degrees as I have recapitulated my family dynamic of moving approximately every four years. I have also moved away from my family of origin, not aware that I was becoming more and more estranged from them, fulfilling the same dynamic that occurred when my father and mother moved away from their respective families. My children have had little contact with their aunt and uncles with some level of greater contact with my parents, perhaps a lining of grace but with the same dynamic principle of estrangement.

My substance use disorder became my work, a way of escaping dyadic dysfunction as I need not understand or face it if I was solitary among my books. And what has become a painful awareness for me is that divorce also manifested when I was asked to resign from my former pastorate by the church board. I still remember a couple of the staff members defining this moment as a "divorce." That is, I was moving out of state to become later estranged from this congregation. It was yet another manifestation of estrangement that had always been there, but one I thought would not affect me within my church family. But it indeed followed me; the principle remained even if the manifestation was different. I have very little contact with the very church members I have poured into for several years. They have moved on and yet I have not. There is something that persistently draws me back to the disruptive split. My conversations seem to pull me back to this prior congregation. Even though I have made several attempts to find a place within a new church, my thoughts and reflections pull me back.

I was not supposed to become a statistic. I always thought that, with God's help, I would rise above the disappointing statistic that most pastors will leave their first pastorate after five years of serving. I thought my training in mental health would assist me in navigating even the most tumultuous conflicts. But alas, those tools failed me. I must accept that I did become a statistic and that this is a part of my story. I must go on sharing my story with others, finding a listening ear that may be the source of my healing and perhaps form a template for healing others. I longed to overcome the divorce principle so ingrained in my family by being a committed husband and, in many ways, this continues as I seek to love and serve my wife and seek her counsel when making family decisions. Indeed, our decision to resign from the church was one sought after by much prayer, counsel, fasting, and discussion. We made it together and for the good of our family.

I also feel the pain of divorce here. The staff member who described it as a divorce was more accurate than I was prepared to believe at the time. Even now, years later, I feel the pain of divorce and estrangement. My wife always said, "We went to be married to the land." This metaphor is an apt one and is now even more emotionally relevant. It was a wedding, and we left as Abraham from Ur, we gave up what we had with great joy to enter a marriage that resulted in dissolution and divorce.

It is the genogram that enables a pastor to discover implicit dynamics that may follow him or her into the congregation. It creates awareness so that one is not altogether blindsided by certain interrelational patterns that may seem to emerge in the congregation. You were once a child and

SETTING IN ORDER: THE CHILD AND THE HAUSTAFEL

to some extent you became a parent when pastoring a congregation. So, it is to the covenant children make to their parents that we now delineate below, and if children are reminded of this covenant and practice this covenant, perhaps they will likewise do so in a church family.

> I covenant to obey my parents in the Lord, as this is right (Eph 6:1). That is, it is my right to preserve my relationship with God and my parents, and obedience mediates the formation of this righteousness as an internal virtue. I covenant to honor my father and mother, which is the first command, and one with an associated promise (Eph 6:2). I am grateful that the fruit of honor is well-being and long life (Eph 6:2). I covenant to not only hear the encouragement and admonition of my parents but will attune my soul to listen to their instruction (John 8:43). I covenant to not only obey in practice, but also with a pure intent.

Chapter 16

Setting in Order: The Servant and the Haustafel

> Urge slaves to be submissive to their masters in everything, to be pleasing, not talking back, not stealing, but showing complete and perfect fidelity, so that in everything they may be an ornament to the teaching of God our Savior.
>
> TITUS 2:9–10

DEFINITIONS

IF WE CONTINUE TO peer into the order of creation as a template to order the prioritization of the Haustafel duties, we will find the book of Genesis to be a litany of family interactions until we come to God's intent to create a nation from the seed of Abraham (see Gen 17:4). That is, God promises that Abraham would be a father of many nations! Moreover, he states that kings would also come from Abraham's lineage (see Gen 17:6). What comes next is remarkable. God expands his covenant with Abraham's family to the nation that would eventually form from Abraham's family (see Gen 17:7). The tangible expression of this covenant would become circumcision, setting apart a nation as a peculiar people belonging to God (see Gen 17:11).

SETTING IN ORDER: THE SERVANT AND THE HAUSTAFEL

We find an extrafilial interaction in the story of Joseph and Egypt (see Gen 39). Interestingly, the relationship is one of servitude. Joseph was a slave to Potiphar, having been sold into slavery by his brothers. It is to this interaction in the Haustafel that we now turn. Joseph's praxis as a slave is given apt description beginning with the presence of God (see Gen 39:2). Moreover, Joseph became prosperous even as a slave (see Gen 39:2). The presence of the Lord with and upon Joseph was quite conspicuous, even to Potiphar, an unbelieving Egyptian (see Gen 39:3). This then provides a polemic that servants display an obvious fidelity to the Lord and that this expresses itself in integrity with leaders so that our conduct and behavior is above reproach and unbelievers can remark, "God is with him/her."

The Lord made Joseph prosper, even as a slave (see Gen 39:3)! What we are exploring here, then, is Joseph as the servant exemplar. He models servitude in the Haustafel and is the prototype for the conduct of servants that follow. God graced Joseph, and his master Potiphar also provided grace in response to Joseph's excellent character and contribution to his home (see Gen 39:4).

In the Hebrew, the word *sharath* is used to convey Joseph's servitude to Potiphar. The word encapsulates service, but can also mean to minister to, attend, wait on, or to act as a priest, and has been used to illustrate the worship of Jehovah. Elisha ministered (*sharath*) to Elijah (see 1 Kgs 19:21). Abishag waited (*sharath*) upon David (see 1 Kgs 1:15). Amnon had a valet who served (*sharath*) him (see 2 Sam 13:17). King Ahazuerus had personal servants who attended (*sharath*) to his needs (see Esth 2:2).[1]

The word is used in the Old Testament to convey a servant of high rank or status as in our anecdote with Joseph in Potiphar's house above. Interestingly, the word *sharath* is used sixty times to convey a ministry of worship (see Exod 29:30, 1 Sam 2:11, and 3:1). The Levitical priests would conduct special services of worship within their specified duties and indeed the word *sharath* is used to describe these acts of worship. More specifically, the word *sharath* was used to describe the priestly role of the Levites altogether. This could then lead to the inquiry into whether God designed this role in nations as an expression of worship. That is, servants worship the Lord in providing their service to God by attending to others.[2]

---

1. Zodhiates and Baker, *Hebrew-Greek Key Word*, 1673.
2. Zodhiates and Baker, *Hebrew-Greek Key Word*, 1673.

Setting in Order

We are now moving into territory outside of the nuclear family and exploring the Haustafel relationships within greater networks of people, such as nations. Joseph is one of the first examples we have of how one can interact in a covenantal way within a national system and gives us an illustration of a faithful servant and an excellent leader. His display of both roles over his lifetime is a model for relationships in the Haustafel outside of the nuclear family and in the nation, which can likewise be extrapolated to the church as well. Joseph's act of worship moved the heart of God to bless him, and Potiphar's house for Joseph's sake (see Gen 39:5).

Now, we cannot ignore the fact that Joseph's servitude was compulsory and yet he served with great fidelity and enthusiasm. This is an immense challenge beyond the scope of this monograph. That is, I do not intend on commenting on the ethical challenge of slavery as this would need an entire work dedicated to exploring its ethos, justice, and injustice. However, what I would like to underscore is that all societies have institutions or structures in place where the roles of being a servant in one form or another are obvious. God has spoken into these structures and has a word for those who serve in these structures in roles as subordinates.

The Haustafel in Ephesians, in similar fashion to the paraenetic material to children, exhorts servants to obedience (see Eph 6:5). One will also notice that servants are the next people group addressed in order after the address to the nuclear family. The implicit context is the church, but one could also imagine society as well. We have already explored the concept of ὑπακούω (hoop-ak-oo'-o) in the paraenetic material on children in terms of obedience, attuning to, and hearkening to the commands of others. However, I would like to draw attention to how obedience is rendered. The emphasis for the servant is obedience out of "fear and trembling," or φόβος (fob'-os), which has caused some to assert that the words "express anxious solicitude about the performance of duty."[3]

That is, one is to be *anxious*, or perhaps a clearer rendering would be *enthusiastic*, about serving one's "master" or, in our colloquial sense, leader, head, boss, etc. When one is serving with fear and trembling, one seeks the content of the duty with an eagerness to perform and complete the task designated. But we cannot ignore the denotation of φόβος, which is where we derive the English "phobia." Therefore, there is also a sense of dread, terror, or fear in the service rendered, which to our modern mind

---

3. Rogers and Rogers, *New Linguistic and Exegetical Key*, 446.

can be quite impugning. One would think that we ought to serve with a motivation of immense joy, not out of a disposition of fear, dread, or anxiety about judgment.

And yet we have the word to contend with. It is the same word Paul employs when he asks the Philippian church to work out their salvation with "fear and trembling" (Phil 2:12).

SERVITUDE AND THE HEART

Joseph Parker notes that the relations between master and servant are always a definitive fixture in all societies in human history. It is a static category though the terms may change.

> There will always be masters, and there will always be servants. It is none of our doing—it is a law from the beginning; and if it be properly accepted and properly worked out, it is a beneficent law.[4]

Thus, it is a human category likely inherent in the design of nations, and thus relates to the next created order, that of the nation first prophesied to Abraham and finding fulfillment in Israel as a nation and Moses as its leader. The first systematic and codified law was given to Moses for a nation. The last of these commands address the implicit notion that there will be servants in the nation, and those servants are not to be coveted (see Exod 20:17).

Parker goes on to assert that it is contentment in Christ, that when one serves one does so with the gestalt that one is serving Christ. In such an inner state, one may find joy even in the menial tasks of one's duties.

> Meanness of heart, discontentment of spirit, peevishness of soul, cannot find sunshine in midsummer's longest day; but sweetness of soul and true obedience and right-minded manhood can find sunshine amid the snows of winter, amid the gloom of December . . . in the Lord. That is the centre, and that is the explanation, and that is the music of it all.[5]

There is a singleness of heart that Paul espouses as the catalyst by which a servant finds his or her joy in the Lord. This singleness or

---

4. Parker, *Epistle to the Ephesians*, 226–27.
5. Parker, *Epistle to the Ephesians*, 228–29.

ἁπλότητι is pure intention and wholehearted devotion to service.[6] As noted above, we come again to the import of intention in the expression of obedience. The heart is as much if not more important than the tangible behavior observed. The heart must first find the music of the Lord in the acts of service before the acts genuinely become the expression of sincere worship and the offering of incense before the Lord. What does the heart of the servant sing? What is her melody as she goes about her duties? Can you sing in worship as you work? Does your soul cry out to the Lord the song of eternity, "What I do I do for the Lord?"

This notion cannot be overemphasized, because Paul would go on to offer greater clarity. It is not enough to be seen in obedience. Indeed, the Christian servant seeks no certain recognition. Rather, the Christian servant does his duties whether seen or not. For he knows that his service is to the One who sees all! And the service is not simply for remuneration or obligation with a gritting of the teeth. It is not merely a submission to the curse and fall of the first Adam. Rather, Paul will again cut right to the heart of the matter. Servants work from their hearts in worship unto Christ.

The servant who works diligently when observed but takes his leisure in sundry lazy ways does not perform the will of God from the heart. This servant remains ignorant of the omniscient One, the Master from heaven who sees the true intent of the heart of the servant whose slothfulness cannot altogether be hidden in the secret places of his duties.[7]

Paul's admonition continues in that the servant who seeks to please simply the corporeal sense of his earthly transactions is at risk of sacrificing his principles. The men pleaser or ἀνθρωπάρεσκος (anth-ro-par'-es-kos), seeks merely the adulation of men, satisfied that this praise is sufficient for the soul. This then can become an idol whereby men and women substitute their worship of God in service to others for worship of men in desperate need for affirmation. Servants in all professions and walks of life ought to ask the question, Who does my soul long to please? If it is the Lord, you will always work diligently and in excellence as one who worships the living God. If it is men, then one might either work feverishly for praise and promotion leaning into a proverbial idolatry. In

---

6. See Rogers and Rogers, *New Linguistic and Exegetical Key*, 446, for the definition of ἁπλότης.

7. See Rogers and Rogers, *New Linguistic and Exegetical Key*, 446, for the definition of ὀφθαλμοδουλίαν.

SETTING IN ORDER: THE SERVANT AND THE HAUSTAFEL

contrast, one may resent the task and find a kind of cynicism that works only when seen, thus begetting a slothful disposition.

Zodhiates provides nuance to God's will, or θέλημα (thel'-ay-mah), in Eph 6:6 when he states the following:

> It [θέλημα] does designate what occurs or what should be done by others as the object of God's good pleasure in the carrying out of the divine purpose or the accomplishment of what He would have.[8]

In other words, the servant is the object of God's pleasure, and this pleasure is experienced or manifest in a culminating sense when the servant carries out the divine purposes of the Master. The servant finds pleasure in the menial tasks of her job or duties. The servant sees the divine in everything he does. The servant folds laundry, makes meals, cleans the kitchen, works in the office, or scrubs toilets as if this act is just as filled with the pleasure of God as if we were singing glorious songs in the gathering of the saints to worship the living God. The servant in the Haustafel is challenged to find glory in the everyday, not-so-ordinary tasks of her duties.

WORK AND WORSHIP

Rod Dreher, in his book *The Benedict Option*, undertakes a chapter on labor underscoring the Benedictine way and polemic in how one understands work. He asserts the following:

> In the Benedictine tradition, our labor is one way we participate in God's creative work of ordering Creation and bringing forth good fruit from it. When undertaken in the right spirit, our labor is also a means God uses to order us inwardly.[9]

In other words, part of ordering creation and within the context of Titus, the church is for the servant-master relationship to work in harmony. That is, the soul must first be ordered before the church can be ordered. The exhortation of Paul to servants is for one to see worship in duties of work. One can conceive that there is a sanctifying component to one's work. Indeed, the Haustafel material throughout the Epistles (orthodoxy) drills down to an ordered soul that expresses itself in ordered

8. Zodhiates and Baker, *Hebrew-Greek Key Word*, 1721.
9. Dreher, *Benedict Option*, 178.

(orthopraxy) relationships or, put in another way, right affections (orthopathy) in relationship.

So, what must the servant in the Haustafel conceive when she works? None other than to consider her work as a "gift to God—as participation in His ordering of Creation."[10] In this light, one can begin to utter expressions of praise when fixing the toilet or reverberate sounds of worship when teaching a child math or glorify our Maker when prescribing a remedy for illness or resound with joy when completing the accounting for a fiscal year.

The Benedictine order lives by a mantra that encapsulates their day-to-day existence, *Ora et labora*, Latin for "prayer and work." This rule, if you will, on one hand relieves one of idleness that can be an "open door to slothfulness." And on the other hand, more than resisting a sinful posture, the servant who works well participates in his sanctification so that every Benedictine monk's daily labors are "opportunities to glorify God."[11]

The servant, laborer, or subordinate who is a Christian must move away from a paradigm that views work as merely a means to an end with that end being advancement of a career, paying the bills, living in a comfortable home, or paying for a child's sporting events and music lessons. Although this litany is not necessarily averse to the Christian servant, the perspective omits the primary impetus derived from labor and service to one's master—that is, seeing it as service and worship to the One Master. Work can be viewed as a gift from God and thus with sacred underpinnings. We might go further and create a polemic that work can be sacramental—a very ordinance from the Lord.[12] This hearkens to creation and a pre-fall epistemology where God put Adam in the garden to "dress it and keep it" (Gen 2:15). In this way, one could assert that God always intended humanity to labor, but not with drudgery as it has become after the fall, but with great joy—participating with God in the very ordering of creation. Work can take us back to the garden, if we are willing to let our mind attune to the Spirit of God in this way. As Father Martin Bernhard asserts, "Any time we take something neutral, something material, and we make something out of it for the sake of giving glory to God, it becomes sacramental, it becomes a channel of grace."[13]

10. Dreher, *Benedict Option*, 179.
11. Dreher, *Benedict Option*, 60, 61.
12. See Dreher, *Benedict Option*, 61, for his thoughts on work as sacrament.
13. Quoted in Dreher, *Benedict Option*, 61.

SETTING IN ORDER: THE SERVANT AND THE HAUSTAFEL

WORK AND INHERITANCE

The servants are likewise given a promise like that of the children. The promise is that the good done in service unto another will be likewise received by the servant from the Lord (see Eph 6:8). The Haustafel in Colossians adds clarity to this promise when it describes the *good* as *inheritance* (see Col 3:24). There are terms utilized by Paul for emphasis as he extrapolates the servant's reward here. The first is the notion that one receives or ἀπολαμβάνω (ap-ol-am-ban'-o). The prepositional arrangement of the word underscores an immediate reception, and that this is from Christ who is the immediate possessor of the reward. Second, the word ἀνταπόδοσις (an-tap-od'-os-is), which expresses the idea of a full or complete return. And finally, the term κληρονομία (klay-ron-om-ee'-ah), which is the inheritance itself. The genitive apposition is used to provide special emphasis that the kingdom is other-worldly in that slaves become benefactors of an inheritance.

There does not exist within the confines of our earthly system a model by which slaves receive an inheritance, as this was solely delegated to family members. Slaves possessed no property they could pass on to their children. The kingdom upends this notion and attaches this specific promise, which was null and void in our fallen system, and provides promise with gravitas, a weightier inheritance, implying eternal salvation and a home that can never be disinherited.[14]

HONORING AUTHORITY

Now, we also come to the Haustafel in Titus with paraenetic material urging obedience and a disposition that longs to please one's master (see Titus 2:9). Paul again underscores a reference to sound doctrine, a main theme of the Pastoral Epistles when writing to Timothy: "Let all who are under the yoke of slavery regard their masters as worthy of all honor, so that the name of God and the teaching may not be blasphemed" (1 Tim 6:1).

That is, obedience is a means of adorning sound doctrine. Honoring those in authority is the catalyst by which sound doctrine is expressed. I have written elsewhere asserting that we have lost a culture of honor, mistaking it for somehow propping up an oppressive regime and undermining the priesthood of all believers. That is, the individual

---

14. Rogers and Rogers, *New Linguistic and Exegetical Key*, 469.

is king in our new culture, and to honor one as being in authority over the individual is repugnant as our culture attempts to dismantle forms of authority. And God forbid that those in leadership in the church would disagree with a particular vision of a member with influence. What we find in too many instances is an attempt to slander a pastor in the name of Christ because he or she is not aligning with the vision or direction of the slanderer.

Paul, however, gives us a kingdom lens of honor and obedience in the Haustafel. This is first practiced in the home and then becomes an ethos in the nation and can also be expressed within the church.

Paul also broaches the topic of blasphemy, which has been addressed before. When servants obey and honor their leaders, they have potential to also obey and honor God. When servants undermine, slander, dishonor, and spread sinister influence in the home, church, or any other community, then this creates the context for blasphemy, which is to repudiate one's character, calling, and existence.

Paul perhaps has insight into human character and temptation as he illustrates the temptation of the servant to despise her master. Perhaps this despising is because the master is a believer and should not be a master at all in the Christian community. Indeed, we are all equal at the cross. And this is true in terms of soteriological inheritance. But this does not imply that God no longer cares about authority or that there is now therefore no dynamic of master-servant relationships. Quite the contrary; Paul urges the servant to envision his master as a recipient of grace and that this conceptualization breeds honor.

The one who despises has not fully considered the state of the other man's soul and station in life. The present imperfect sense of the term *to despise*, καταφρονέω (kat-af-ron-eh'-o), indicates that one must continually resist what seems to be always knocking at the door of the human heart.[15] Despising is a matter of habit. It comes gaining access to the regular rhythm of human interaction and is a scheme of the enemy to destroy dyadic relationships. It is easy to despise what we do not know or what we have not experienced. The master has a burden to carry just as the slave. The burden may be different in scope, practice, and weight—but a burden, nonetheless. Seeing the burden that all of us carry will guard against the disposition to despise and perhaps compel us to the antithesis—service and honor.

15. See Rogers and Rogers, *New Linguistic and Exegetical Key*, 497, for more on the meaning of καταφρονέω.

SETTING IN ORDER: THE SERVANT AND THE HAUSTAFEL

The slave serves the master who has received the same benefit of salvation, the same riches of glory, the same inheritance of eternity, and the same grace from God. Servants, honor your masters, serve them with great diligence and excellence. Perhaps you will find great joy in the Holy Spirit as you begin to sense your service transform to service unto the Lord.

The servants, in Paul's view, have come under the yoke or ζυγός (dzoo-gos), which often indicated slavery by captivity. The slaves in this manner were made to "pass underneath three spears lashed together to form a doorway outline, thus requiring them to bow their heads and 'pass under the yoke.'"[16]

The yoke is a means to give honor. The yoke of captivity can be grievous but also creates an opportunity for a display of ironic grace in the life of the servant who honors his master, and by doing so honors the living God. The yoke is lighter with the gift of service. Indeed, this is love expressed when a master is honored, when a master's feet are washed, when a master need not concern him- or herself with the nature of the task, but with great confidence believes the performance will indeed be completed with meticulous care and attention. As a servant, we grant a gift to masters when the creativity of our soul is channeled into the completion of the master's request. Therefore, to the subordinates in any family, community, organization, or church—serve with excellence, take upon yourself the mantle of Joseph and find that you are giving a gift to your superior who may indeed glorify the God you serve because of your diligent, compassionate, and excellent disposition.

The Haustafel in Titus likewise addresses servants in the home and by extrapolation, the church. One nuance in the Titus Haustafel is for the servants to desire to please their masters well (see Titus 2:9). And Paul adds that servants are not to talk back to their masters (see Titus 2:9). He uses the word ἀντιλέγω (an-til'-eg-o), which has come to have a rather strong meaning in Greek. That is, if one were to envision the behavior associated with ἀντιλέγω, one would see a servant who speaks against her master. The word also carries the connotation of contradiction, so that a servant not only undermines but says and does the opposite of the master's injunction. The servant who ἀντιλέγω also may engage in the audacious action of opposing her master openly, making a public testimony of setting herself against her master. And finally, the servant who

---

16. Rogers and Rogers, *New Linguistic and Exegetical Key*, 497.

ἀντιλέγω can in time refuse to even associate with his master, decrying his station and post.[17]

Now time does not permit a deep foray into the ethos of slavery and the years of advocacy that have come, rightly so, for the freedom of slaves in many countries throughout the epochs of humanity. I am not asserting a polemic that slaves ought not resist tyranny, oppression, and brutality by means of advocating for freedom and speaking out against injustice. Rather, I am asserting that within the framework of an ethical dyadic relationship of superior-subordinate relationship, servants have a spiritual duty to serve, honor, obey, and please their superiors as an expression of worship unto the Lord.

SERVICE AND STEWARDSHIP

Paul's counsel to Titus brings up yet another notion and temptation for servants—the notion of embezzlement (see Titus 2:10). Paul admonishes servants to refrain from νοσφίζομαι (nos-fid'-zom-ahee), which is to secretly stash away the master's belongings, profits, or possessions for the servant's personal use without the permissive directive of the master. In other words, it is the illegal activity of embezzling the master's possessions.[18] The temptation looms large that the master would not notice if a portion of his account were to be redirected into another account that may personally benefit the servant. This misappropriation of funds has an illegal ethos which has landed many servants in jail. The recent scandal of Bernie Madoff is a lesson to all who serve others, that there are dire consequences for those who embezzle money from those they should be serving with utmost fidelity.[19]

When servants are faithful in stewarding the master's accounts, it is an act that adorns the doctrine of God, for it is a microcosm of what God has entrusted to us—the stewardship of the earth! Paul uses the word κοσμέω (kos-meh'-o) to illustrate the dynamic of beautifying God's

---

17. See Online Greek Bible, "Titus 2:9."
18. Zodhiates and Baker, *Hebrew-Greek Key Word*, 1741.
19. See Campbell, *Madoff Talks*, xvii–xviii, where he reminds the reader that Madoff was able to "rack up an incredible $65 billion of cumulative gains from unsuspecting and often unsophisticated investors, many of whom were friends and family." And see also where he illustrates that Madoff "had done in some 16,000 investors domestically and as many as 720,000 internationally," in what was likely the largest Ponzi embezzlement scheme in US history.

doctrine with economic fidelity. Ironically, this word also provides a connotation of ordering which we have taken as a theme for the book of Titus. Thus, why would we not also find this concept in the Haustafel as Paul provides a sense of kingdom ordering to dyadic relationships? κοσμέω is often used for the arrangement or encasement of jewels in a way that encapsulates their full beauty.[20]

What a beautiful metaphor for all servants to embrace. When they honor their masters, steward his or her possessions well, refrain from a sinister or public resistance to authority, they set themselves as a jewel to reflect the light of God's kingdom. God has ordered creation in a way that may fly in the face of modernity. His ways are beyond our ways. Indeed, many may bristle at his ordering, thinking it to be archaic and antiquated. They further conceive, to their own deception, that there is a better way to live and exist. They strive to create a society free from the domestic and national codes God has provided to us in the Scriptures. I think what we have created in our pursuit of ultimate autonomy has left us disoriented, lonely, and bitter. When "I" is the cause for existence, then walls tend to rise around the individual with no room for community to operate in the overrealized autonomous individual. God has set forth a pattern of ordering relationships; the Haustafel focuses on these dyads for the benefit of all and the doctrine of God to be fleshed out in how we relate to one another.

SERVICE AND GRACE

Paul will next introduce us to the polemic for the master-servant dynamic, the great leveler of humankind—the grace of God (see Titus 2:11). Paul uses the grace of God for all as a motivating ethos for servants to honor their masters. Grace is available to all! Whether slave or free, Jew or gentile, wealthy or poor, male or female—grace has appeared to all regardless of socioeconomic status.

And it is this grace that compels us to deny ungodliness and worldly lust. It is grace that compels us to be sober, righteous, and godly in a world that moves increasingly away from such virtues (see Titus 2:12). The servant, or rather all of us, must look for the blessed hope, the parousia of Christ, the glorious return of our Savior, which in a sense stirs us to live amicably in the station God has placed us in (see Titus 2:13). Indeed,

---

20. Rogers and Rogers, *New Linguistic and Exegetical Key*, 510.

the Haustafel is the operationalization of being a peculiar people. The world should really scratch their head in wonder and confusion when they see the community of God in action. It should be like nothing they have experienced before in contrast with the pattern of this world's dynamic of interrelatedness.

PETER AND SERVANTS

I do think it would be helpful to include Peter's paraenetic material on servants as a dialogical partner with Paul in Titus. His exhortations can be a difficult directive for all of those who have felt the sting of an austere master. Peter anticipates that there will be both gentle and severe masters but exhorts that the servant's reply in both situations ought to be the same. They are to be subject, with the fear of the Lord as their motive (see 1 Pet 2:18).

Peter uses the adjective σκολιός (skol-ee-os'), which indicates a master who is crooked, austere, hard to deal with, and harsh.[21] This surly presentation creates a kind of initial response of antagonism. That is, why would anyone submit to what appears to be an oppressive dynamic like the one the apostle Peter describes?

Perhaps it is because suffering, and, more precisely, suffering wrongfully, holds a mysterious key to the formation of character. In the Christian paideia, suffering is a teacher. Peter broadens his appeal using the master-servant dyad as an illustration (see 1 Pet 2:19). He describes one who endures suffering due to his or her belonging to God or his or her conscience to adhere to God's ways. From the Greek συνείδησις (soon-i'-day-sis), "conscience" implies a moral right from wrong. It is a seed born in the soul of humanity that compels one to a certain ethical duty.[22] συνείδησις precedes action and is a manifestation of conduct with oral confirmation vis-à-vis testimony.

Indeed, one can endure unjust suffering as one surrenders to the ironic virtue of gratitude. This is the nuanced sense of χάρις (khar'-ece), where Peter employs the word *grace* as a specific means of implying a sense of gratitude for the goodness of God toward us even in the face of suffering.

---

21. Rogers and Rogers, *New Linguistic and Exegetical Key*, 572.
22. See Zodhiates and Baker, *Hebrew-Greek Key Word*, 1759.

SETTING IN ORDER: THE SERVANT AND THE HAUSTAFEL

It is the blessed state communicated by our Lord when he asserts, "Blessed are you when people revile you and persecute you and utter all kinds of evil against you falsely on my account" (Matt 5:11).

It is the higher-order love described by our Lord in the following manner: "Instead, love your enemies, do good, and lend, expecting nothing in return. Your reward will be great, and you will be children of the Most High, for he himself is kind to the ungrateful and the wicked" (Luke 6:35).

Paul will elsewhere appeal to conscience again as a mediation to obedience. He appeals to conscience as a catalyst to awaken our souls to obey authority. Listen again to his exhortation: "Therefore one must be subject, not only because of wrath but also because of conscience" (Rom 13:5).

And we should note that the glory of suffering is in the context of unjust suffering. There is no glory in suffering for wrongdoing, sin, slander, or wickedness, so that a servant does not boast of suffering from having stolen, disobeyed, or maligned her master. The boasting of suffering is when a servant, within his conscience, testifies to the ways of God, and then suffers harm unjustly for preserving such a conscience or συνείδησις.

Peter is clear about this when likewise, he asserts the following: "If you endure when you are beaten for doing wrong, what credit is that? But if you endure when you do good and suffer for it, this is a commendable thing before God" (1 Pet 2:20).

Peter clearly delineates the glory of suffering for doing well from the shame of suffering for doing wrong. The servant who suffers injustice is commended by God. The servant who is buffeted for having served the Lord is honored of the Lord. The servant who adheres to God while still loving her enemies finds enjoyment in God's presence and is given a kingdom joy that persists amid the beatings, imprisonments, confinements, and unjust wrath of her master. This is not the masochistic display of a nonflinching face amid being punished for wrongdoing. This is not the comparison of those who suffered the greatest without an affective display during the lashes. Indeed, Rogers and Rogers assert the following:

> Mere endurance is no cause for pride. Slaves, like schoolboys, sometimes vied with one another in the ability to endure corporal punishment without flinching. If the beating is deserved,

there is no glory in bearing it; but to show patience in the face of injustice is true evidence of Christian character.²³

The Haustafel is thus a code of Christian duty, addressing those in various roles of family and society. It is difficult to our modern ear, but those in subordinate roles can resist authority in an honoring way if the task being asked violates one's conscience toward God. However, in the resistance, one accepts the unjust punishment and indeed rejoices in it. However, when a servant does wrong, repentance is the Christian response. The servant honors and obeys the master in the Haustafel. In a mysterious way, this glorifies God and is an illustration of the servant's obedience to the Lord as well.

Peter will reiterate this concept of acceptable and unacceptable suffering throughout the epistle. We find that the one who suffers for the sake of righteousness is μακάριος (mak-ar'-ee-os), or blessed and fully satisfied (see Pet 3:14).²⁴ He goes on to assert the distinction when he says, "For it is better to suffer for doing good, if suffering should be God's will, than to suffer for doing evil" (1 Pet 3:17).

Finally, we have Peter aligning the spirit of the Lord resting upon the sufferer who endures for Christ's sake. And again, as he's done before, Peter is quick to note the contrast of those who suffer for the sake of sin. Note the contrast once more:

> If you are reviled for the name of Christ, you are blessed, because the spirit of glory, which is the Spirit of God, is resting on you. But let none of you suffer as a murderer, a thief, a criminal, or even as a mischief maker. (1 Pet 4:14–15)

We should note the final admonition. Peter advises that we refrain from being the busybody, or ἀλλοτριεπίσκοπος (al-lot-ree-ep-is'-kop-os), which is rendered as "one who looks after the affairs of another, agitator, mischief maker, [and one who] meddl[es] in domestic affairs."²⁵

CONTEMPORARY APPLICATION

Pastor Gloria had taken a trip to Israel. She was invited by a friend to visit the Holy Land and tour the seminal sites where the stories of the Bible

---

23. See Rogers and Rogers, *New Linguistic and Exegetical Key*, 572.
24. Rogers and Rogers, *New Linguistic and Exegetical Key*, 575.
25. Rogers and Rogers, *New Linguistic and Exegetical Key*, 578.

come alive in the landscapes of history. She was surprised when a church member rebuked her on her return that she had not been informed of the trip. She supposed that the friendship between Pastor Gloria and herself would have necessitated she know about the trip and be first informed when she returned. Pastor Gloria had mentioned the trip in a sermon as an illustration, which prompted the church member's grievance.

Afterward, the church member retaliated, attempting to investigate the personal state of Pastor Gloria. She sought information that she later attempted to use to argue that Pastor Gloria was seemingly unfit for ministry because of postpartum depression. This content was included in a letter written to Pastor Gloria's supervising pastor.

The church member as an subordinate to Pastor Gloria who was the appointed authority is an illustration to not only servants but to all. The ἀλλοτριεπίσκοπος seeks to meddle in the affairs of others for the direct purpose of stirring agitation. Pastors must beware of the church member who perseveres to know his or her personal affairs. It is possible that a litany of grievances is being compiled for future use of slandering the pastor if the church member is crossed in any form or fashion.

The message is clear, respect and honor a person's private affairs, do not seek to know or unveil such matters, but commit all things to the Lord who will unveil such matters in his own providence. The servant does not meddle, but meticulously serves. The servant does not agitate, but assimilates the instructions given to her. The servant does not seek to cause mischief but is magnanimous in his work ethic and gratitude, even if he is to suffer for Christ's sake.

Peter will point to the exemplar for the servant who suffers for righteousness—Jesus Christ. The servant follows the Suffering Servant—step by step, lash by lash, stripe by stripe (see 1 Pet 2:21). The servant does not return reviling for having been reviled. The servant does not issue threats. Rather, the servant commits herself to God, who will judge righteously on all occasions (see 1 Pet 2:23). The stripes of Christ do heal our souls but also heal injustice. The healing may not always be in the already but certainly is in the not yet. For the servant who suffers injustice, for the pastor who was unjustly maligned, for the prophet who was stoned, for the missionary who was rejected, for the ambassador who was rejected by the religious, and for the innocent who had to make difficult decisions—receive the healing of Christ's stripes as in the end all will be made right. Looking for his coming is the source of consolation for the one who suffers!

It is in this light that we must again remember that the Haustafel is rooted in creation and is a semblance of new creation order. The emphasis is not necessarily on upending contemporary social hierarchy but inserting new creation dynamics into these settings as a kingdom paradigm of interpersonal relating. As Parsons has noted, "Equality is not dependent upon social status, but upon creation reasserted in re-creation."[26]

CHRYSOSTOM AND THE SERVANT

John Chrysostom, in his homily on Philemon, addresses the role of a servant in the Haustafel. He utilizes Philemon as an occasion to extrapolate the Christian's disposition as a servant. After a litany of Biblical figures who stand as pictures of humility, he asserts the following: "This is the part of well-disposed servants, not only in His mercies, but in His corrections, and in punishments wholly to submit to Him."[27]

Providence is the key to the freedom that accompanies submission. We trust in God's sovereignty, goodness, and providence that mercy, correction, and punishment are for the advancement of our character and conformation to the image of the Son. For Chrysostom, humility is the virtue of submission. We can either willingly humble ourselves or be humbled. The former is a reward in this life, the latter a judgment in the next. Or consider, that if "we are not humble for His sake, we shall be made humble by tribulations, by calamities, by overruling powers. Seest thou therefore how great is the grace!"[28]

The calamity itself can be an observance of grace! But one will bristle at the thought that correction can be favor, punishment can be merciful, and tribulation can enact forgiveness. This is a paradox indeed and serves as a dialectic in tension. Christ learns obedience in suffering (see Heb 5:8). Suffering or tribulation, therefore, is the master who instructs the Christian in humility, which equips the servant for entire surrender. Entire surrender is freedom that accompanies a servant's service. The servant trusts God's decision for her post and works diligently as unto the Lord. The servant submits to admonition as a form of grace! Love is not love unless it is love not only merited as mercy but also as correction.

---

26. Parsons, "Slavery and the New Testament," 92.
27. Chrysostom, "Homily on Philemon," 106.
28. Chrysostom, "Homily on Philemon," 107.

SETTING IN ORDER: THE SERVANT AND THE HAUSTAFEL

Correction mediates humility and humility is a necessary attribute for the Christian servant.

Chrysostom is so moved as to exclaim the paradox of joy in suffering as the good teacher of humility and as the suffering servant who does so with increasing delight. Not as a masochist, but as one who trusts in God's sovereignty over all things, whether easy or hard. He sums up his homily with the following: "They think that they are receiving favours, when they are suffering wrong for the sake of their beloved."[29] This appears to be a direct allusion to the Epistle of Peter (1 Pet 4:12–14), who does well to compare wrongful suffering to the very same suffering of our Lord as a form of consolation and even joy for the servant who likewise suffers. The servant who suffers wrongfully can perceive that he suffers rightfully if able to conceive that the work of suffering serves a teleological end.

Martin Luther King Jr., writing on shattered dreams, warns against the resignation of segregation to the embitterment of the soul, admonishes against fatalism to the bondage of the will. He goes on to assert a posture for the servant:

> Some of us, of course, will die without having received the realization of freedom, but we must continue to sail on our charted course. We must accept finite disappointment, but we must never lose infinite hope. Only in this way shall we live without the fatigue of bitterness and the drain of resentment.[30]

Hope, then, also becomes the existential polemic of the servants, being willing to accept disappointment, shattered dreams, unrealized expectations, and to continue pursuing the high mark of one's calling. One's situation need not determine one's future dream. The servant is content, but this contentment does not thwart the persistent and unrelenting dream that can be a "bottomless vitality" transforming the "darkness of frustration into the light of hope."[31]

Therefore, we come to the covenant of the servant in the Haustafel. This is summarized below and can be reiterated during the agape feasts around the table fellowship.

> I covenant to be faithful to the Lord so that my superior and all with whom I work may know that God is with me (Gen 39:2–3).
> I covenant to diligently work to advance a conduct of pure

---

29. Chrysostom, "Homily on Philemon," 108.
30. King, "Shattered Dreams," 389.
31. King, "Shattered Dreams," 389.

character and integrity (Gen 39:4). I covenant to serve others as if I am serving the Lord, worshipping Christ through my service (Gen 39:5). I covenant to obey those in both ecclesial and secular leadership with sincere solicitude concerning my performance of duties (Eph 6:5). I covenant to serve with immense devotion and singleness of heart (Eph 6:5). I covenant to serve with excellence, not to be seen by others, but in knowledge that God sees all (Eph 6:6). I covenant to order my soul unto service as I realize that God is ordering my role in creation—*ora et labora*, "for prayer and work" (Gen 2:15). I covenant to submit to the sanctification that service can create in my discipleship and walk with the Lord. I covenant to obey those in leadership over me, knowing that a promise of inheritance awaits me and that by doing so, I adorn the doctrine of God (Col 3:24 and 1 Tim 6:1). I covenant to refrain from despising those in leadership (Titus 2:9). I covenant to steward the tasks and money of those in leadership over me, refraining from all forms of embezzlement (Titus 2:10). I covenant to obey leaders who may have an austere nature and prepare for suffering injustice for the glory of God (1 Pet 2:19–20).

Chapter 17

Setting in Order: The Master and the Haustafel

Tell the older men to be temperate, serious, self-controlled, and sound in faith, in love, and in endurance.

TITUS 2:2

MASTERS ARE NOT SPECIFICALLY addressed in the paraenetic material in Titus. However, Paul implies an address to masters when qualifying the elderly for Titus at Crete. In that regard, leaders are given attributes which ought to inform their relationships. That is, leaders remain sober, reverent, temperate, sound in the faith, permeated with love, and patient in trial. Temperance and patience are mentioned in one breath to provide a double emphasis on the need for endurance for anyone who would carry the burden of leadership. Patient with people is a hallmark trait of any aspiring leader and is often born through experience in leadership. One failure ought not to capitulate surrender. Rather, pick up the baton once more and learn the lesson of temperance as you once again lead the people to Zion. The more failure, the greater temperance. Difficulty is the oven that forges a masterful weapon for use in the kingdom.

Paul does address masters in the Ephesian Haustafel and will become our beginning in addressing the role of masters in the covenantal relationships within the Haustafel. Paul anticipates that masters will be tempted to intimidate their servants (see Eph 6:9). This is a key insight and one all leaders should take seriously. Perhaps Paul is keenly aware of human nature.

Paul underscores the true Master of heaven as the central polemic for enduring threats. He states that the Master in heaven is no respecter of persons. That is, the same judgment that comes upon a leader will also be rendered to a servant. Sin is sin, no matter the socioeconomic status of the sinner. Love rather than intimidation and mercy rather than threats are the behaviors for the master within the Haustafel.

The Colossians Haustafel will convey just and equal treatment of the slave with the same appeal given to our Master in heaven (see Col 4:1). Masters upon the earth are to operationalize their relatedness to subordinates in the same manner our Master in heaven relates to us.

We also have a type of Haustafel in Rom 13:1 that is extrapolated to a national meaning. That is, Paul aptly describes powers (ἐξουσία, ex-oo-see'-ah) as being ordained (τάσσω, tas'-so). So, masters or those in authority are, in a sense, ordered and appointed by God. The perfect tense of τάσσω would indicate the state or condition of the magistrate, so that one could translate Paul as stating that the ἐξουσία stands ordained (τάσσω) by God.[1] This is difficult to comprehend when you have those in authority such as Nero, Caligula, or Hitler.

Paul continues to assert that to resist the powers in place is to resist the ordinance of God (Rom 13:2). There is a punitive judgment (κρίμα, kree'-mah) for those who resist such ordained authority. Rogers and Rogers argue that the "sword is the symbol of the executive and criminal jurisdiction of a magistrate and is therefore used of the power of punishing inherent in the government."[2] Paul further explains that those in power are ministers (διάκονος, dee-ak'-on-os) of God (Rom 13:4). This seems impossible in our current political climate where the suspicion of corruption lurks behind many authority figures. Those in authority are deacons of God in that they are wittingly or unwittingly executing his will. The magistrate is under the employment of the Lord.[3]

---

1. See Rogers and Rogers, *New Linguistic and Exegetical Key*, 340, for a more nuanced reflection on τάσσω.

2. Rogers and Rogers, *New Linguistic and Exegetical Key*, 340.

3. See Zodhiates and Baker, *Hebrew-Greek Key Word*, 1704, for a definition of διάκονος.

MASTERS AND ROMANS 13

Robert Stein has set forth a paper as an attempt to understand the argument of Paul in Rom 13. While pointing out the logical connections with the passage that comes before Rom 13, Stein concludes that Rom 13:1–7 is an *eine selbstandige Einlage* (an independent deposit), an autonomous thought in Paul's writing. However, I would like to underscore Stein's own insightful parallels to argue the opposite.[4]

Stein notes that Rom 12:18, "Live peaceably among all men," is a thesis that logically flows to addressing the Christian's response to the governing powers of the day. He likewise notes that parallel of vengeance that Paul is explicating. In Rom 12:19, Paul is clear that Christians do not respond to evil with vengeance, as vengeance is the Lord's. Moreover, he, or rather God places the sword of vengeance in the hands of governing authorities to mete out punitive consequences for evil in Rom 13:4. Finally, Stein notes the parallel use of the word (ἀποδίδωμι, ap-od-eed'-o-mee), which is often rendered "pay" in Rom 13:7. This same word is used in 12:17 to caution Christians against "paying" one's evil deeds with retaliatory evil. The word is utilized again in Rom 13:8 to emphasize the only debt any Christian should owe and continue to pay, that of the love debt. Love is owed to all and is a continuum that every Christian should pay bountifully.[5]

Therefore, noting Stein's observations, I would like to assert that Paul is developing an argument for obedience while describing the ordained role of governing authorities or, in our case, the role of the master in a larger Haustafel. He begins with Rom 12:17 and ends in 13:10. Utilizing the ἀποδίδωμι notion "to render or pay back," the pericope is neatly divided into economic categories defining what kinds of existential and material aspects of human living we render to others. Note the following structure:

A. Rendering good to evil (12:17–21)

B. Rendering obedience to authorities (13:1–6)

C. Rendering taxes to civil government (13:7–8)

D. Rendering love to all (13:9–10)

---

4. Stein, "Argument of Romans 13:1–7," 326.
5. Stein, "Argument of Romans 13:1–7," 326.

Setting in Order

In this regard, there should be no Christian debt with exception of the love that we constantly render to all. Christians are called to render goodness, generosity, and prayers even when under the most reviling of circumstances. Christians are to obey authorities, be ambassadors of peace, and submit to penalties if the secular government attempts to violate one's conscience before God. The Christian is to render all taxes, fear, and honor to those in authority, regardless of the system of government. The Christian is, above all, to love unrelentingly. To return to Titus, this will be further explored in the next chapter when Paul instructs Titus to exhort the church at Crete with the following:

> Remind them to be subject to rulers and authorities, to be obedient, to be ready for every good work, to speak evil of no one, to avoid quarreling, to be gentle, and to show every courtesy to everyone. (Titus 3:1–2)

Now, embedded in Paul's instructions on authority are extrapolated roles of masters or authority figures in the macro-Haustafel that we can reasonably extract. For example, masters or authority figures will and must render judgment or discipline. Paul uses the Greek κρίμα (kree'-mah), which can be rendered "a solemn judgment, judicial trial, or judicial sentence."[6] The word also takes on connotations such as a sentence, condemnation, lawsuit, or legal sentence. It certainly invokes a forensic sense and indicates those who arbitrate conflict and execute judgment, including punishment to those who commit wrongdoing.

In this regard, a master, leader, magistrate, or ruler must learn and become accustomed to rendering discipline. This is a necessary component of the appointment. But as Jesus has challenged all who operate in this forensic role, take heed:

> Do not judge, so that you may not be judged. For the judgment you give will be the judgment you get, and the measure you give will be the measure you get. Why do you see the speck in your neighbor's eye but do not notice the log in your own eye? Or how can you say to your neighbor, "Let me take the speck out of your eye," while the log is in your own eye? You hypocrite, first take the log out of your own eye, and then you will see clearly to take the speck out of your neighbor's eye. (Matt 7:1–5)

Therefore, we have been warned and admonished. Certainly, Jesus's words apply to all, but quite acutely to those in leadership as this

---

6. Zodhiates and Baker, *Hebrew-Greek Key Word*, 1731.

is a routine component of their assignment. He or she who leads must always constantly engage in self-reflection before rendering judgment. The beam so easily besets the best of humanity. We must be careful to remove this beam through daily reflection, continuous and quick repentance when a slight is discovered, and thorough penitence. The leader who judges his or her own heart will lean into more precise judgment of others when the time comes. We must all consider that we will be judged by the same rubric of judgment we have given to others. Let this be a constant reminder, a resounding principle for all in leadership. Do not be quick to render a verdict, but allow space for counsel, time, testimony, Scripture, and prayer to integrate into any discipline that is forthcoming.

Furthermore, although Paul is addressing state leaders specifically, the notion that authority is God's business can be extrapolated to leadership in general. That is, a leader or master ought to consider that he or she is God's minister (διάκονος, dee-ak'-on-os) or deacon (see Rom 13:4). In this regard, one in authority would ideally seek to execute God's will in a judicial manner, perceiving that his or her very office has a divine origin.[7] In this regard, the state authorities "have a part to play, alongside that of the apostles and their helpers," in furthering "God's eschatological purposes."[8]

Furthermore, the ministry or service that the authorities of the state perform in service of God is as a body who executes his wrath upon evil or evildoers. "It is thus, paradoxically, an instrument of God's long-suffering [Rom 2:4], for through this partial manifestation of his wrath the power of evil is restrained, and its final judgment and defeat deferred [2 Thess 2:6]."[9]

Masters in the Haustafel therefore are appointed as those who restrain evil by executing the wrath of God in the microcosm and as a proleptic reminder of the wrath of God to come. Those in authority have the rite of *ius gladii* (the rite of the sword) but must be aware that the One with the double-edged sword will execute judgment in the eschaton (Rev 3:12, 16). Therefore, those in authority must wield the sword or

---

7. See Stein, "Argument of Romans 13:1–7," 334, where he asserts the following: "Paul speaks of the state possessing divine authority, here he develops this thought further by asserting that the state functions as God's διάκονος ('servant') for the advantage of the believer."

8. See Barrett, *Epistle to the Romans*, 246, for Barrett's inference on the state being ordained by God's providence.

9. Barrett, *Epistle to the Romans*, 247.

discipline with immense discernment, knowing that a posture quick to wrath may result in a measured judgment upon the self.

PHILEMON AND THE MASTER-SLAVE DYAD

Now I would like to explore what is likely the most intentional address to the master-slave relationship in the New Testament, the Letter to Philemon. In doing so, perhaps we can obtain greater clarity on how those in authority relate toward subordinates.

I would like to explore the following chiastic structure for Phlm 1:8–19:

> A. New profitability (Phlm 1:8–11)
>   B. A new reception (Phlm 1:12–14)
>   B'. An eternal reception (1:15–17)
> A'. Profitable restitution (1:18–19)

After initial greetings and thanksgiving, typical of Pauline introductions, Paul appeals to Philemon on behalf of Onesimus. It is conjectured here that Onesimus is a runaway slave who has served Paul in "my bonds" (Phlm 1:10). And it is during this time that Onesimus has endeared himself to Paul, who designates Onesimus with a title similar to that given to Timothy and Titus. That is, he refers to Onesimus with the beloved τέκνον (tek'-non), which is to say, "my son" (Phlm 1:10). The birthing of this son appears to have occurred in Paul's imprisonment as Onesimus ministered, or διακονέω (dee-ak-on-eh'-o), to Paul in the persecution that accompanied the preaching of the gospel (Phlm 1:13). Paul again implements deacon language here to esteem Onesimus as a fellow worker in God's kingdom and perhaps as a polemic for Onesimus's newfound profitability (Phlm 1:11). Indeed, this kind of profitability is invaluable. It appears that Onesimus served Paul's personal needs. The term διακονέω is combined with δεσμοῖς, perhaps to etymologically associate service with chains, and thus implies comfort, companionship, and material service in the context of the suffering that Paul is enduring.

Let us begin with the notion of a new profitability regarding Onesimus. Paul may have been adhering to the fugitive law of Deuteronomy where the following is issued to the Israelite community:

> You shall not return to their owners slaves who have escaped to you from their owners. They shall reside with you, in your

midst, in any place they choose in any one of your towns, wherever they please; you shall not oppress them. (Deut 23:15–16)

Thus Paul had provided safe harbor for Onesimus where it is implied that Onesimus received the gospel and began serving Paul in his chains. The use of τέκνον (son) and γεννάω (begotten) both provide implicit evidence of Onesimus's conversion (Phlm 1:10). Moreover, Paul's appeal that Philemon receive Onesimus now as an ἀδελφός (brother) also gives credence to Onesimus's reception of the gospel (Phlm 1:16). It is also conjectured that Onesimus may have stolen from Philemon and fled the anticipated punitive action, for Paul offers to repay any debts owed by Onesimus (Phlm 1:18).

It appears that the birth of the τέκνον preceded the ministry as a διακονέω. And as Frilingos provocatively asserts, "In this new setting Onesimus becomes the apostle's mechanism, technology, or what I term Paul's τέκνο-ology of power."[10] That is, the filial metaphor is not simply a rhetorical device to appeal to Philemon's emotions. Rather, it is a new concept from spirit-infused relationships that defines a new community/humanity radically altered by soteriology. It is the power of God that produces the τέκνον (son) of God, which subsequently equips the διακονέω (deacon/minister) of God, and which breaks the fetters of relational wounds to create the ἀδελφός ἀγαπητός (beloved brother).

What profundity of power wherein God confounds the social structures of our day! Paul is writing to the traditional paterfamilias, Philemon, and includes the *domus* or household that is also the church or *ecclesia*. One can take note of that by acknowledging the multiple recipients of the letter (see Phlm 1:2). The leader, Philemon, is being led by Paul. And, as we will see later, the mystery of Christian leadership and authority can be summed up in such a notion and begs the question, Are you leading by being led?

Paul begins his polemic with a new sense of profitability, which is a principle for all masters in the Haustafel. Where Onesimus was once unprofitable and perhaps even diminished Philemon's profits by not only fleeing from the works and tasks on the estate but by possible thievery as well, he is now profitable. But what sense does Paul convey? Paul uses the Greek εὔχρηστος (yoo'-khrays-tos) to exposit his profitability argument to Philemon. Paul has used εὔχρηστος elsewhere in the Pastoral Epistles to provide clarity on his intended meaning. For example, when writing

---

10. Frilingos, "For My Child, Onesimus," 93.

to Timothy he asserts the following: "All who cleanse themselves of the things I have mentioned will become special utensils, dedicated and useful to the owner of the house, ready for every good work" (2 Tim 2:21).

The usefulness or εὔχρηστος is couched in the language of sanctification and cleansing, so that the useful servant is one who is cleansed from the works of the flesh. Paul describes this as cleansing from youthful lusts, foolish arguments, unlearned questions, and engendering strife (see 2 Tim 2:22–23). The good work of the εὔχρηστος servant is also described further as one who has righteous faith, is gentle with interpersonal relations, apt to teach, patient, and meek. Therefore, the εὔχρηστος of Onesimus has as much to do, if not more, with his newfound character than any tangible skill that he has ascertained.

The new profitability for Philemon is a qualitatively new person with a new soul, new perspective, and new character, which translates into a heart that is obedient to the Master by way of serving his earthly master. And, as we will see, Paul is appealing for a new interpersonal relation between Onesimus and Philemon vis-à-vis Onesimus's transformation.

Paul uses εὔχρηστο once again when he requests something of Timothy: "Only Luke is with me. Get Mark and bring him with you, for he is useful to me in ministry" (2 Tim 4:11). We find here again that Paul's use of εὔχρηστο is one that implies usefulness or profitability in ministry or service either to Paul's personal needs or in a broader sense, in propagating the gospel.

Second, Paul implores that Philemon receive, or ἀπέχω (ap-ekh'-o), Onesimus, which brings us to the second operational principle for masters or leaders. Where the first polemic is for masters to view subordinates with a different kind or profitability that circumscribes values as relationships, the second principle appeals to the master that he would receive again the subordinates who have drifted away.

This appeal integrates many Christian virtues such as forgiveness, mercy, and hospitality. Paul may be employing a play on words as he "sends" Onesimus, utilizing ἀναπέμπω (an-ap-em'-po), so that Philemon would "receive" Onesimus, or ἀπέχω (ap-ekh'-o). One should also note that Paul connotes the authoritative station of Philemon using ἀναπέμπω, as this typically illustrates the sending of someone or something to a person of higher office, authority, or power.[11]

---

11. See Online Greek Bible, "Philemon 1:12."

SETTING IN ORDER: THE MASTER AND THE HAUSTAFEL

Moreover, some have hypothesized that the epistolary aorist use of ἀναπέμπω indicates that Onesimus himself carried Paul's letter to hand deliver it to Philemon.[12] One could imagine the mixed emotions of Philemon as he is reacquainted with Onesimus and reads Paul's letter.

For pastors, we can imagine a staff member, elder, or deacon who has drifted from faith or undermined authority within the congregation. As such a one returns, how do you receive him or her? What kind of reception is expressed? How do those in authority overcome the hurt or destruction of one who had stolen one's reputation or denigrated one's character? Or, in a more material sense, how does one receive back an employee who orchestrated the loss of profit, stake, or presence in the community? Does one take a risk in profit loss once again?

One should note that the key to Paul's appeal to Philemon to receive Onesimus is predicated upon Onesimus's conversion. That is, Onesimus is new in character, behavior, and perspective. That would then convey an altogether kingdom way of interpersonal interactions. And as we will see, Paul is getting at manumission here. He would like Philemon to receive Onesimus as a brother and not a slave. This would have been a radically alternative way of expressing hospitality to the one who diminished your bottom line. The way of the kingdom is often puzzling to our current institutions and practices.

Now Paul spares no expense in his emotional rhetoric. He asks that Philemon receive Onesimus as if Paul himself had begotten him as a child (Phlm 1:12). Paul employs several filial appeals conveying that Onesimus is Philemon's brother and Paul's son. As such, he is requesting an honorable reception with a filial embrace, feast, fellowship, and love. The words of the famed Christmas carol "O Holy Night" comes to mind:

> Truly He taught us to love one another;
> His law is love and His gospel is peace.
> Chains shall He break, for the slave is our brother,
> And in His name all oppression shall cease.[13]

Paul's view of the gospel radically changing hearts and relationships is also encapsulated by his view that Onesimus is not merely a runaway slave who is seeking refuge, but he is an ambassador from the home of Philemon divinely sent to represent Philemon as one who ministered to Paul's material and immaterial needs (Phlm 1:13).

---

12. See Rogers and Rogers, *New Linguistic and Exegetical Key*, 514.
13. Cappeau, "O Holy Night."

Paul views Onesimus as an extending gift of help from Philemon, even if it was nonvolitional. God intended for Onesimus to find Paul and subsequently serve Paul. This language of vicarious service is not foreign to Paul. He was grateful for Stephanas, Fortunatus, and Achaicus, who came to minister to him; "that which was lacking" on the part of the Corinthian church "they have supplied" (1 Cor 16:17). That is, the household of Stephanas seems to have taken upon themselves a commission of sorts; they were ordered, ordained, and driven to supply refreshment to the saints through the spiritual gift of hospitality.

Paul utilizes this vicarious language again in Philippians when describing Epaphroditus as a fellow soldier, messenger, and minister "to my need," and who "suppl[ied] what was lacking in your [the Philippian's church's] service to me" (Phil 2:25, 30). Thus, we have at least three examples of presumed or explicit ambassadors from the household of Philemon, the church at Corinth, and the church at Philippi, whose mission was to serve Paul's needs as he suffered in chains for the sake of the gospel. Onesimus, being listed as such an ambassador, provides a kingdom lens of viewing subordinates in the Haustafel. No doubt, Onesimus was a part of Philemon's household. He was his slave and subordinate. As his master, Philemon had the authority to discipline Onesimus for the injustice incurred upon him. Paul here appeals for mercy to triumph over judgment. The leader of the Haustafel thus receives subordinates with a hospitality unmatched. The master feeds, rejoices over, celebrates, and nurtures the kingdom's relationship between them. This is not to say that a leader need not ever render discipline, but that he or she expresses mercy upon the repentant subordinate and receives one as the father receives the prodigal son.

The reception Paul speaks of is then translated into eschatological terms when he appeals for an eternal reception (Phlm 1:15). This appears to be the central theme of Paul's polemic and represents the inner core of the chiastic structure within this pericope. Indeed, Paul sees the hand of God in Onesimus's departure, which strikes of irony. How does one view a runaway slave as a divine act? It would seem most natural to conceive of this as a carnal and, indeed, sinful act of defiance (Phlm 1:18). Indeed, his ill-intended absconding with material goods naturally would be met with punitive action. Or perhaps it was the withholding of profitable labor that was his crime (Phlm 1:11). In any case, one would be hard pressed to see the hand of God in the act of being a fugitive. And yet, Paul will press the difficult polemic, providing all who face such a challenging interpersonal dynamic a varied lens with which to comprehend such an affair.

Now we do not know if Paul has the example of Joseph in mind when writing to Philemon, but surely the accounts run in parallel fashion. For Joseph ascribes the hand of God to his own captivity. He asserts that it was God's hand which sent him to Egypt (Gen 45:7). Joseph emphasizes this again, perhaps in part to console his brothers who wounded him so, and perhaps also in part to note the sovereignty of God to bring about redemptive kingdom acts despite acts of wickedness. Therefore, Joseph emphasizes the point by again noting that it "was not you who sent me here; but God" (Gen 45:8). Joseph explicates the plans of God further when he states that the rationale for such a departure includes the preservation of posterity for the house of Jacob upon the earth and the saving of "your lives by a great deliverance" (Gen 45:7) Moreover, God's plan includes a reversal of roles for Joseph. He was initially a slave, but by now has become "a father to Pharaoh, lord of all his house, and a ruler throughout all the land of Egypt" (Gen 45:8).

Even if Paul does not have the patriarch's narrative in mind, he surely emphasizes a similar polemic. That is, Onesimus's departure, painful as it may have been for Philemon, is providential. As Joseph was teleologically ordained for the posterity of his family, Onesimus may also have such an appointment to bring Philemon's house to an appointed end. Indeed, Paul provides the aorist indicative passive use of "send away" with χωρίζω (kho-rid'-zo). Such an etymological construction hints that this may be the divine passive, which in the Hebrew language would indicate the secret or hidden action of God (Phlm 1:15).[14]

Furthermore, Paul desires that a kingdom inculcation occur; that is, let the kingdom's way of interacting so infuse the house of Philemon that, once received, one is always received. Onesimus is to be received with eternity in mind. Paul uses αἰώνιος (ahee-o'-nee-os) to indicate permanence, an enduring hospitality that hints at kingdom relations. There is to be no further breach, no schism or divisive barrier between the two. By receiving Onesimus, Philemon is receiving Paul's son, Paul himself, and perhaps more is implied here: Philemon is receiving God's child![15]

Paul explains further by implementing an ordinary commercial transaction, nuanced now with eschatological language. He states that

---

14. Rogers and Rogers, *New Linguistic and Exegetical Key*, 514.
15. Rogers and Rogers, *New Linguistic and Exegetical Key*, 514.

Philemon ought to receive, or ἀπέχω (ap-ekh'-o), Onesimus as one might receive a sum in full, having received a receipt for such a transaction. By inserting the commercial term ἀπέχω, Paul implies that Philemon is receiving the kind of profitability that was lost because he receives a new man, a changed heart, a new brother, and a servant of the Lord into his own home. The term also intimates that Philemon was to *keep* Onesimus for *himself*.[16]

This may be Paul's way of illustrating the relationship between Philemon and Onesimus as a proleptic arrangement that foreshadows the reception of the church by Christ. As Philemon keeps Onesimus for himself, Christ keeps the church for himself. The reception is covenantal and intimate, the reception is filial and speaks of the heavenly bond that is everlasting in substance. In such a light, a master ought to receive subordinates with such terms of endearment even amid a culture that may bemoan such an arrangement. This is a hard saying indeed! If one were to distill a principle here, I suppose a leader would ask on every occasion, Do I entreat my team, servants, employees, or subordinates as if I will spend eternity with them? Let this thought therefore be a guide to your every interpersonal interaction.

If Philemon is to receive Onesimus reflecting on eternity, then the nature of the relationship must change and take on kingdom dynamics. Paul notes this when he asks that Onesimus be received as a beloved brother. Paul's use of ἀδελφός ἀγαπητός (ad-el-fos' ag-ap-ay-tos') implies a qualitatively new relationship that has been birthed predicated on Onesimus's conversion and what appears to be a penitential return. The term ἀδελφός can be literally translated "from the womb of a sister." It has been utilized more broadly to connote a common origin (i.e., members of the same tribe or countrymen). Neighbors were also illustrated by ἀδελφός as a term of affection for those in proximity.[17]

Paul's use of ἀδελφός, however, is likely a reference to a community of love with Christ and his work as the foundation of such a community. The context of Philemon seems to fit this definition most precisely. Such is the use of ἀδελφός in passages such as Matt 12:50 where Jesus broadens the eschatological family with the following: "For whoever does the will of My Father in heaven is My brother and sister and mother." Furthermore,

---

16. Ellicott, *Ellicott's Commentaries*, 227.

17. See Zodhiates and Baker, *Hebrew-Greek Key Word*, 1682, for more on the definition of ἀδελφός.

the use of ἀδελφός is given nuance in Mark 10:29–30, where Jesus speaks of loss and gain:

> Jesus said, "Truly I tell you, there is no one who has left house or brothers or sisters or mother or father or children or fields for my sake and for the sake of the good news who will not receive a hundredfold now in this age—houses, brothers and sisters, mothers and children, and fields, with persecutions— and in the age to come eternal life.

So we find that Jesus will reorient us to a new definition of ἀδελφός as those who do his will and who receive an exponential reward of filial relations in the eschaton, so that, if the gospel does cause a loss of filial relations secondary to unbelief, the believer can be encouraged in that filial relationships are bountifully restored with immeasurable propensity.

This then leads to the inquiry as to whether Paul is arguing for manumission; that is, can Philemon continue as Onesimus's master, or is he now no longer in a leader-subordinate relationship? This is a key question for the Haustafel. Certainly, God does not do away with all roles of authority and Paul himself has argued for roles of leadership within the church and Haustafel when he writes of bishop, deacon, husband, and parental relationships. Is it still possible for those in leadership to interact with the subordinate as an ἀδελφός?

It is not my contention to assert that slavery can exist within the ethos of Christian fellowship. I would rather argue the antithesis: slavery is outside the kingdom ethic. For the kingdom is one of freedom, love, and voluntary servitude. If Onesimus is to serve Philemon once more, it is because he longs to do so out of his love for Christ and Philemon. The obligation has been terminated, but love may still compel servitude. We just do not know enough to assert how Onesimus and Philemon navigated Paul's appeals upon his return. For the Christian leader, we look to the family as a rubric that acts as a compass to navigate us through challenging decisions that certainly face all that take up the mantle of leadership.

Jesus strikes at the heart of the leader when addressing the scribes and Pharisees in Matthew's Gospel. Listen once more Beloved:

> They do all their deeds to be seen by others, for they make their phylacteries broad and their fringes long. They love to have the place of honor at banquets and the best seats in the synagogues and to be greeted with respect in the marketplaces and to have

people call them rabbi. But you are not to be called rabbi, for you have one teacher, and you are all brothers and sisters. And call no one your father on earth, for you have one Father, the one in heaven. Nor are you to be called instructors, for you have one instructor, the Messiah. The greatest among you will be your servant. All who exalt themselves will be humbled, and all who humble themselves will be exalted. (Matt 23:5–12)

The full passage is cited above so that we would all once again meditate on the words of Christ and let the convicting tone find every corner of our hearts. How many of us enjoy the title given to us by our deeds, great learning, accomplishments, and elevation? How many of us enjoy the perks of leadership? How many of us enjoy the feasts called in our honor? How many of us enjoy the conspicuous marks of leadership, authority, and superiority? How many of us is Christ even now addressing who lead homes, companies, churches, cities, states, and nations? How many of us would conceive servitude as the great station of this life and the next? How many of us would volitionally humble ourselves, prefer our fellow neighbor, brother, or sister, and condescend in this life? How many, I ask?

My confession is that I came to enjoy hearing the designation *pastor*. When I transitioned from pastoring, I grieved the loss of this apparent identity. But did I enjoy this title too much? Did I enjoy the corporeal manifestation of what this term entailed? If so, perhaps it was good to lose it for a season, so that I can take up the mantle of a servant—for this is a much greater designation. Indeed, the most glorious title one could have would be servant! O how the kingdom is so unlike our earthly patterns! We can all be tempted by leaving a mark, achieving greatness, only to be left with an empty pang of vainglory. The glory isn't real, isn't genuine, but rather vanity upon vanity.

Do we love the sound of *rabbi*? Has it become an idolatrous cacophony of noise guiding our every move and every decision? Has the sound of *master* become so entrenched in our identity that we feverishly chase every wind of opportunity to hear it again? Could it be that Paul has Christ's words in mind when he is writing to Philemon? How do Christ's words reconcile with the many Haustafel passages we have thus far been exploring? Perhaps the suggestion is as such: if one is exalted into leadership, then condescend to voluntary servitude.

Perhaps this is why the apostle James cautions ambition with the following: "Not many of you should become teachers, my brothers and sisters, for you know that we who teach will face stricter judgment" (Jas 3:1). If we knew the judgment that can come with leadership, perhaps we would not blindly accept the elevation that can come from human endeavors.

The apostle Peter also weighs in on Christian leadership with the following remarks: "Tend the flock of God that is in your charge, exercising the oversight, not under compulsion but willingly, as God would have you do it, not for sordid gain but eagerly. Do not lord it over those in your charge, but be examples to the flock" (1 Pet 5:2–3). The elder serves willingly, eagerly, and by example. The leader who does so by compulsion, lust for power, and for mere monetary gain is incompatible with Christian leadership. Lord, help us to discern this in your body!

The key is servitude—condescension, kenosis, and being lowly of mind and heart. The greatest strip themselves of designations, titles, earthly ambitions, and lead through service.

Unfortunately, the corporate ethos has infiltrated the church where the pastor is more CEO than pastoral counselor, more executive than earnest intercessor, more entertainer than purveyor of sacraments, more celebrity than servant, and more of a facility curator than a soul shepherd. As a result, the church has experienced a cultural shift. Where the pathos of prayer, words, and sacraments were the focus, the church has now embraced a celebrity, carnival, and curb-appeal ethos to its own detriment. We would rather invest thousands of dollars in sound and video systems than in marriages and families. We would rather invest thousands if not hundreds of thousands of dollars in sleek lobbies, state-of-the-art gymnasiums, Disneyesque childcare rooms, and coffee bars rather than orphans, widows, and the lost. We are sensual people, forgetting the discipline of contemplation and denying the true value of that which is unseen. And as a personal confession, I am caught in this ethos, desperately looking for a way to navigate this church culture without being overly critical, but nonetheless sounding the alarm.

Finally, we have the *inclusio* of Phlm 18, the profitable restitution. Paul agrees to whatever debt Onesimus owes Philemon. If there is a tangible deficit, Paul agrees to pay it. The principle here is forgiveness, mercy, and jubilee. Jubilee, manumission, and the sponging away of debt is noted here just as it occurred in Israel's history during the year of Jubilee. The fiftieth year of Jubilee was a radical reset of all history. Even land was given back to those who lost it due to misfortune. The seminal Jubilee year had divisions of seven called the year of release, which was a reminder of the fiftieth year to come and which included forgiveness of debts as well. The year of release, Jubilee, and here, Philemon's pardon of any debt, are both potent reminders of the soteriological mercy and pardon God has given us through the death of our Lord.

Paul uses the word ἐλλογέω (el-log-eh'-o) to confer a commercial meaning.[18] Paul uses the term again in the Epistle to the Romans to explicate the notion of a soul account to which sin is charged or imputed contingent upon the law (Rom 5:13). That is, though sin always remains, it is not charged to one's soteriological account without the law. The law becomes the mediator of imputing sin. In the same sense, Paul is voluntarily offering his commercial account to be charged for any tangible losses incurred by Philemon.

NOUWEN AND CHRISTIAN LEADERSHIP

Finally, I would like to explore Henri Nouwen's reflections on Christian leadership in his small but cogent monograph *In the Name of Jesus*. In the final section of the book, he provides a thesis for all in Christian leadership when he states, "But I am also getting in touch with the mystery that leadership, for a large part, means to be led."[19]

It is a mystery, for conventional leadership is going ahead with followers behind but Christian leadership is often being led to a place that may be undesirable. Indeed, Christian leadership will often entail an incarceration of some sort—if not tangible, then emotional. If we are indeed leading in the kingdom, then we are an irritant to the old-world order. The consequences of such leadership will typically invite persecution—and often the most painful is persecution from within.

Henri Nouwen was experiencing a new kind of leadership when he left the decadence of Harvard and made his home among the intellectually disabled who cared nothing for his achievements or education. These members of the Haustafel, would interject during mass and offer antithetical opinions even as Nouwen preached. Imagine this!

Nouwen continues to opine when he reflects on the temptation of power. He asks,

> What makes the temptation of power so seemingly irresistible? Maybe it is that power offers an easy substitute for the hard task

18. Rogers and Rogers, *New Linguistic and Exegetical Key*, 514.
19. Nouwen, *In the Name of Jesus*, 75.

of love. It seems easier to be God than to love God, easier to control people than to love people, easier to own life than to love life.[20]

And indeed, the temptation of all in leadership is to be relevant, spectacular, and powerful. Unfortunately, the church culture reinforces this in our pastors and leaders. Church culture has become an institution of event planners, feverishly analyzing each event to fine-tune its ability to draw the crowds and help us feel better about our ministry. If crowds are the primary outcome, then we have become a body in vain pursuit of growing an empire with our brand. Lord, help the church to rid itself of such idols.

Nouwen continues with an insightful assertion: "The temptation of power is greatest when intimacy is a threat. . . . Many Christian empire-builders have been people unable to give and receive love."[21] And what is it that makes intimacy such a threat? Do leaders avoid such intimacy because of the manifold wounds received in the past? To avoid intimacy is to avoid the potential hurt that comes along with it. Do leaders avoid intimacy and choose power because it is easier? Is it easier to control rather than love? Is the default character of humanity that one would rather create systems than love people, create policies rather than sit with people, talk to the sheep rather than walk with the sheep? And the tragic teleological end of one who seeks power over and against love is to awaken one day to find him- or herself devoid of loving, healthy, and intimate relationships. O what a tragic end indeed, to find at the end of a ministerial journey one is without true intimacy.

If one is to challenge the sirens of power, Nouwen asserts that one must find an "ability and willingness to be led where you would rather not go . . . the servant-leader is the leader who is being led to unknown, undesirable, and painful places."[22] Nouwen reflects on John 21:18 where Peter would go from leading to being led, even coercively to a place of persecution. The leader must sacrifice ambition, acclaim, renown, fame, and even goodly goals for the telos of God's end for him or her. The master who would interact with subordinates must first be led by sometimes inexplicable forces and there find a sense of contentment that is other-worldly.

---

20. Nouwen, *In the Name of Jesus*, 77.
21. Nouwen, *In the Name of Jesus*, 79.
22. Nouwen, *In the Name of Jesus*, 81.

Finally, Nouwen calls for a radically poor church as perhaps another remedy for the temptation of power. Invoking Mark 6:8 and 1 Tim 6:9, he asserts that "wealth and riches prevent us from truly discerning the way of Jesus. . . . If there is any hope for the church in the future, it will be hope for a poor church in which its leaders are willing to be led."[23]

What a challenge. The Christian leader pauses to reflect on what he or she should take on the journey. Perhaps it is the sole staff member that keeps them company, having forsaken the bread, haversack, money, and spare tunic (see Mark 6:8). Perhaps it is with this staff member that a great meany seas will be parted and waters spring forth from a wilderness rock. Nouwen is not naïve to realize the consequence of such an assertion when he states, "We will become dependent on the positive and negative responses of those to whom we go and thus be truly led where the Spirit of Jesus wants to lead us."[24]

Dependent on others is not the typical way of the leader. The conventional leader is quite independent, with subordinates dependent on him or her. The master or leader in the Haustafel bears the burden of responsibility to ascertain provision for the members to whom he or she is entrusted. And yet, Nouwen calls for a different kind of leader in the church. He calls for condescension, humility, powerlessness, and obedience. Wealth itself is not the snare, but for so many it is the desire for wealth that becomes the catalyst for ruin and destruction (see 1 Tim 6:10).

As I prepare to welcome my eighth child to our bustling family, I feel caught in the tension Nouwen espouses. On one hand, I feel the enormous need to provide for my family—home, shelter, education, opportunities in the arts and sports, and a refuge for them to take safe harbor in. On the other hand, I also long for them to be pupils of obedience. I understand that Nouwen was a priest with no children and so made a new way of living among the intellectually disabled whereby he found a new family to instruct him in the way of the Lord. However, would I take such a pilgrimage with a wife and eight children? Would I depend on others for meat and bread, beholden to their whims, pleasures, and displeasures? As a pastor, I brought my family to a church in sole obedience to the call. But what does a pastor do when there is a call to resign his bivocational status in the context of personal slander with little assurance

---

23. Nouwen, *In the Name of Jesus*, 84.
24. Nouwen, *In the Name of Jesus*, 84.

of compensation for his family? It is difficult to discern this call of resignation as God's call in the context of overt and slanderous behavior.

Both the call to poverty and the call to support a large family need not be mutually exclusive. Both are compatible with the kingdom. Both can serve the Lord with obedience to the station they were given. Paul himself noted his own work to alleviate the financial burden of the church (see Acts 20:34–35). And perhaps stripping the church of the professional vocation of minister may be a hidden blessing for the church. For the role of pastor has become so very corporate that it is often difficult to discern theological leadership from corporate leadership. Perhaps God would like to remove this temptation altogether by moving the church to a place of radical generosity, voluntary poverty, and bivocational ministers. In this regard, perhaps the days of Christian empires are numbered, the handwriting is on the wall, for we have been weighed in the balances and found wanting (Dan 5:27). Perhaps COVID-19 was a catalyst to dismantle the age of Christian imperialism and once and for all remove the scepter of Pharaoh from among us. And perhaps, just perhaps, in this new way of living together we just might find the kingdom way of the master or leader in the Haustafel. And now we come to an integrative covenant for leaders to be iterated at the agape feast:

> I covenant to refrain from threatening those under my leadership (Eph 6:9). I covenant to render just judgment and discipline when necessary (Rom 13:1–4). I covenant to engage in self-reflection, counsel, time, Scriptural meditation, prayer, and, if necessary, repentance prior to rendering judgment or discipline upon anyone else (Matt 7:1–7). I covenant to lead by searching the heart of God and executing his will (being a deacon of God) within my sphere of leadership (Rom 13:4). I covenant to view subordinates with a new kind of profitability that encapsulates them as servants of the Lord first and servants of the task second (Phlm 1:11). I covenant to receive those under my leadership with intentional hospitality and interact with them in a way that confers eternal relationships; that is, how we relate in heaven acts as a dictum to how we relate here upon the earth (Phlm 1:15). I covenant to care for those under my leadership as if he was my brother and she was my sister (Phlm 1:16). I covenant to condescend to voluntary servitude, ministering to those under my care (Matt 23:5–12).

Chapter 18

Setting in Order: The Elderly Men and the Haustafel

Tell the older men to be temperate, serious, self-controlled, and sound in faith, in love, and in endurance.

Titus 2:2

Paul is unique when addressing the Haustafel in Titus. That is, he addresses the elderly and the youth. This is not performed in the other Haustafel passages of the Epistles and thus provides a nuance to the paraenetic material in Titus. The church is implied in his address. Or could it also be asserted that Paul is addressing households with multiple generations? So, if grandparents were indeed living within the same home, could this be an address for them? I am going to contend that the audience here is multimodal. That is, the address is indeed to the church at Crete along with the same covenants to be displayed in the home.

And so, we have a Haustafel description of the elder men encapsulated within this one verse. They are to be νηφαλίους (sober), σεμνός (honorable or dignified), σώφρονας (temperate), ὑγιαίνοντας τῇ πίστει (sound in the faith), ἀγάπη (sound in sacrificial love), and ὑπομονή (sound in endurance).

SETTING IN ORDER: THE ELDERLY MEN AND THE HAUSTAFEL

VIRTUES FOR AGED MEN

Rogers and Rogers describe νηφαλίους as one who exercises restraint in indulging desires.[1] The antithesis of this is found in Paul's Epistle to Timothy when he describes men of all ages in the perilous times who are lovers of themselves (see 2 Tim 3:2). The elderly man in the Haustafel is a dissident of such self-indulgent luxuries, offering a tangible polemic for the younger men to pattern their lives after. Restraint is one of the greatest lessons one can teach as impulsive thoughts or actions are a constant temptation. Like the beating of a constant drum, the despotism of longing is to feed desire that can haunt the soul. Deferring satisfaction, restraint in the face of strong impulse, and the ability to say no are virtuous lessons indeed for the elderly men to model for generations following.

The elderly man conveys a sense of σεμνός (sem-nos). That is, he is dignified, honorable, and owing his modesty to a heavenly citizenship. In this way, the elderly men inspire the younger men to live lives of veneration. The kind of dignity that σεμνός conveys is not one of arrogance that pushes away, but one of virtue that attracts and invites.[2] The elderly man full of dignity then lives as one immersed in the sacred. It is sacred honor rather than earthly dignity that motivates the elderly man who is σεμνός. This sacred honor is one lived in restraint, one lived with faith, love, and endurance, as we will soon see.

Furthermore, the aged or elder men are to be temperate or σώφρονας (sophronos). The older man who is σώφρονας has sound cognitive abilities. He is discreet and will place boundaries on his own freedom and ability, conveying self-control. He volitionally inhibits passions and desires, is sober, cognitively vigilant, and prudent.[3]

One will recall that this personal trait or virtue is one of the qualifications for being a bishop or overseer as well. "Now a bishop must be above reproach, married only once, temperate, self-controlled, respectable, hospitable, an apt teacher" (1 Tim 3:2).

Paul likewise addresses the aged women with the same exhortation that they would be σώφρονας, chaste, and keepers of the home (Titus 2:5). Moreover, Paul addresses the younger men in the Haustafel with the same exhortation that they would be σώφρονας, discreet, and sober-minded (Titus 2:6). Therefore, σώφρονας appears to be a ubiquitous virtue in the

---

1. Rogers and Rogers, *New Linguistic and Exegetical Key*, 509.
2. See Zodhiates and Baker, *Hebrew-Greek Key Word*, 1756.
3. Zodhiates and Baker, *Hebrew-Greek Key Word*, 1761.

Haustafel, on display by both genders and across the generations. Perhaps, this seminal virtue of temperance is foundational to communal living. Or perhaps it is a virtue that signals a healthy body. Or perhaps it is a virtue that mitigates conflict. Perhaps all the above are facilitated by σώφρονας. And oh, how important it is today to limit our freedoms and to exercise voluntary restraint in a world that experiments with sexuality, gender, and death in the name of freedom and choice. Show me an aged man who practices restraint and there you will find wisdom.

Paul explicates further that σώφρονας can be taught as he exhorts the elderly women to "teach" the young women to be σώφρονας (Titus 2:4). I suppose we ought to ask ourselves, In what manner is σώφρονας taught or conveyed in the paideia of the Lord? Is this virtue communicated merely by example? Paul intimates this by inserting a conditional "that" between Titus 2:3 and 2:4. In this manner, holiness, refusal to falsely accuse, voluntary abstention from alcohol, and active teaching appear to be the exemplary conduits of σώφρονας (Titus 2:3).

We also derive a sense that σώφρονας is a gift from God, perhaps a virtue of grace (2 Tim 1:7). So, perhaps σώφρονας is initially gifted through the Holy Spirit and furthermore conveyed through both the fruit of the Spirit and behavioral expressions of holiness.

Moreover, we have the aged men being ὑγιαίνοντας τῇ πίστει, or sound in the faith. The tense is the present participle indicating a continuous or repeated action.[4] Therefore, the elderly men remain sound in the faith as a perpetual practice. There is a searching of the Scriptures and praxis of the great doctrines that accompanies the elderly men. They are discerning, stamping out heresy, identifying wayward trends in the church, and calling the church back to standards of God's holiness. The elderly men are not tempted by the winds of false doctrine or the trendy new methods that jettison prayer, word, and sacraments. Being sound in faith is a lifestyle.

Perhaps being ὑγιαίνοντας τῇ πίστει is a result of having received sharp rebukes or corrections over his life (see Titus 1:13). In this way, the rebuke is a loving gesture, molding the man into a true man of God over the years of having had missteps, mistakes, ambitious errors, prideful self-assertions, and temptations to be popular. Having received sharp rebukes from his elders, he now has incorporated a kind of soundness that is steady, firm, with a resolve to emulate the character of Christ and

---

4. Zodhiates and Baker, *Hebrew-Greek Key Word*, 1587.

promote his gospel without the trappings of the idols of this age. Perhaps rebuke is the laboratory that forges a man for sound faith!

Now we should note that the following virtues are listed as types or categories of the present participle ὑγιαίνοντας, which is to be sound. The elderly men are sound in faith, love, and patience. This litany implies a tripartite collection of virtues that can be corrupted. That is, faith can be corrupted by wounds that create a type of cynicism that casts a shadow of doubt on the promises of God. Idols that seem to provide all the answers leave one empty at the end. The winds of doctrine that sound exciting fizzle out when the new church trend supplants it. Love can wax cold in the context of lawlessness. Love can fade when, in isolation, one begins to perceive oneself as unwanted, unlovable, and the scapegoat of all interpersonal conflict. Patience can wane in a society that expects immediate satisfaction, immediate results, and conventional outcomes. If the measures we utilize are built upon a faulty foundation of superficial growth, then our patience may be exhausted on the altar of building sizes, crowds, and an annual budget. The elderly men live their lives resisting the temptation of these idols so that they may posit an altogether different way of living. They continue in the same faith delivered through Christ and his apostles. They practice love in the most loveless of situations. They endure with great patience in prayer, ministry of the word, and sacraments in community despite the church trends that speak otherwise.

The love herein employed is ἀγάπη (ag-ah'-pay), which indicates a kind of benevolent expression where the one loving acts in accordance with what the object of the love needs rather than desires.[5] In this way, the elderly man can say with Job, Should we not accept both good and bad from God (Job 2:10)? Even the trouble or adversity we receive from the hand of God is a result of his ἀγάπη. The elderly man discerns this and receives trouble with earnest gladness, knowing that God's love is mysteriously involved and, as such, his character is being formed in the image of the Son.

And finally, we have ὑπομονή (hoop-om-on-ay'), which is to abide under whatever circumstance you find yourself in.[6] It does not necessarily mean that you remain in the circumstance; this is an altogether different notion of discernment. Rather, the elderly man who is ὑπομονή remains in the faith despite whatever sufferings, trials, vexations, or

---

5. Zodhiates and Baker, *Hebrew-Greek Key Word*, 1680.
6. Zodhiates and Baker, *Hebrew-Greek Key Word*, 1765.

persecutions he may endure. His pursuit of the Lord is not shaken. His pure affection for the kingdom does not fade. His longing for communion with Christ remains. And perhaps what enables the elderly man to ὑπομονή is the sometimes-elusive phenomenon known as hope.

ERIKSON AND HOPE

Let us hear Paul's exhortation to the Thessalonians wherein he seems to link the two ideas:

> Remembering before our God and Father your work of faith and labor of love and steadfastness of hope in our Lord Jesus Christ. For we know, brothers and sisters beloved by God, that he has chosen you. (1 Thess 1:3–4)

Hope in Christ and a perspective that, somehow, we are ordained to navigate the messiest of circumstances adds fuel to the flame of patient endurance. We were chosen to endure the evil of men. We were chosen to endure slander and blasphemy of all sorts. We were chosen to endure the undermining of authority. We were chosen to hope in Christ even as our fellow brother and sister seeks our destruction. It is hope in the faithfulness of Christ that aids in our endurance in the infidelity of humanity. Our faith grows, and as an aged man, one can look back and thank God for holding one amid his most dire of circumstances.

Erik Erikson reflects on the stages of the life cycle and specifically addresses hope in old age with the following remarks: "And indeed, in whatever language, hope connotes the most basic quality of 'I'-ness, without which life could not begin or meaningfully end."[7]

So, hope becomes essential to ego, strengthening the self with a kind of integrity that brings meaning to the end of a chapter, or perhaps the end of a book. Life begins with hopes and dreams, filling the imagination as the child grows, matriculating through the stages of development. Hope is tested and tried through tragedy, trial, and disillusionment. Hope, according to Erikson, is matured into its final manifestation, faith. And Erikson continues to opine, with Biblical allusion, that the most mature of faiths is contingent upon returning to the beginning. That is, "unless [we] turn and become like children," we cannot enter the kingdom (Matt 18:3).[8] It is ironic that the end is a return to the beginning. And yet

---

7. Erikson, *Life Cycle Completed*, 62.
8. Erikson, *Life Cycle Completed*, 62.

it must be so, from dust we were formed and to dust we will return (Eccl 3:20). Why would this not also be the case with our psychosocial development? We are born with a kind of hope that dreams for the impossible, and if or when hope matures as an old man, we return to this kind of hope to prepare for a homecoming that is nothing short of miraculous.

In *Legacy*, I have already written concerning Erikson's concept of integrality. It bears reiterating here:

> This in its simplest meaning is, of course, a sense of coherence and wholeness that is, no doubt, at supreme risk under such terminal conditions as include a loss of linkages in all three organizing processes: in the Soma, the pervasive weakening of tonic interplay in connecting tissues, blood distributing vessels, and the muscle system; in the Psyche, the gradual loss of mnemonic coherence in experience, past and present; and in the Ethos, the threat of a sudden and nearly total loss of responsible function in generative interplay.[9]

The entire citation is reproduced to provide Erikson's comprehensive definition of integrity, which is summarized in integrality, or the ability to hold things together. Therefore, Erikson posits that the elderly, if able to live in integrity, resist the disintegration of their Soma, Psyche, and Ethos. For a more theological framework, we may suggest, Flesh, Soul, and Spirit.

Moreover, Erikson's use of wholeness suggests a work of shalom at the end of life. That is, peace, unity of self, resolve for the kingdom, and self-forgiveness for the past produces a type of integrity that instills a sense of shalom that can be further communicated to the next generation. Furthermore, it becomes the passing of a kind of generativity as well. The despair can creep into the soul whenever one envisages that one's generativity is lost. But, if one can imagine that the generativity is not loss but translated, then perhaps one can hold in dialectical fashion a new kind of generativity. For this to occur, the old archetypes that define generativity must also be redefined. The once-safe cognitive schemas that defined our identity and production must be given new terms, new definitions, a different rubric that aids in the integration of the self in old age.

Often overlooked, Erikson also posits the development of virtues that emerge from each dialectical psychosocial crisis that occurs over the life cycle. Although not limited to faith, hope and love, he does emphasize

---

9. Erikson, *Life Cycle Completed*, 65.

these virtues as a *cardinalium virtutum distincio* (the distinction of or among the cardinal virtues). That is, rather than the traditional cardinal virtues of prudence, justice, fortitude, and temperance, Erikson rightly underscores faith, hope, and love. However, he does not register these virtues as successive in development. There are other virtues that occur in between these acquired virtues as one develops. Moreover, he aspires to assert that wisdom is the virtue that accompanies the psychosocial crisis of integrity vs. despair.

I do agree with Erikson on the cardinal virtues of faith, hope, and love as Paul also posits that these virtues remain or last (see1 Cor 13:13). Moreover, as we look intently at elderly men and their place in the Haustafel, we can also see Paul working to underscore these three cardinal virtues once more in Titus. That is, elderly men are to be sound in faith, charity, and patience (Titus 2:2). And if patience is associated with hope as it is in 1 Thess 1:3, then we have the triad *virtutum distincio* (distinct virtues) once again reiterated or perhaps integrated with wisdom at the end of life for the benefit of the Haustafel.

It is interesting to note that Erikson defines hope as "expectant desire," and utilizes the following extrapolation for more of his meaning when he says that it is "a vague instinctual drivenness."[10] And of course, for Erikson to define hope in such matter fits his rubric of situating the developing hope in infancy, during the trust vs. mistrust dialectic of human development. That is, if one cannot trust his or her caregivers to meet fundamental human needs, then perhaps this insult creates a kind of overall suspicion of God and others while also predisposing one to a kind of hopelessness that is not easily overcome. And if wisdom at the end of life is predicated on virtue assimilation over the lifespan, then it is not altogether illogical to ponder that hope is required for wisdom, and that wisdom is required for integrity. The elderly are to experience and convey a kind of integration of hope with faith and love as a praxis for the Haustafel.

Erikson places the virtue of fidelity in adolescence amid the dialectic of identity vs. identity confusion. Herein, he states that fidelity is "the capacity to trust (and to trust oneself), but also the claim to be trustworthy, and to be able to commit one's loyalty to a cause of whatever ideological denomination."[11] Loyalty and commitment become the praxis of fidelity

---

10. Erikson, *Life Cycle Completed*, 59.
11. Erikson, *Life Cycle Completed*, 60.

or faith. And, according to Erikson, this springs from identity formation that typically occurs in the adolescent phase of human development.

Finally, Erikson places love logically in young adulthood where the crisis dialectic is intimacy vs. isolation. Here, one determines associations that portend to covenants of mutual living. The most obvious of these is marriage but it is certainly not the only enduring human covenant. Erikson defines the virtue of love as "that mutuality of mature devotion that promises to resolve the antagonisms inherent in divided function."[12] One learns to live with oneself when able to experience and give love to another.

Erikson notes the antipathic force of this stage, which he asserts is exclusivity related to rejection experienced in adulthood. Rejection, if painful enough, can compel one to live in a state of exclusivity, perhaps returning to the dialectical tension of intimacy vs. isolation. The one rejected becomes the one rejecting to secure, perhaps falsely, a place free of future hurt. Ironically, Erikson asserts that some form of exclusion can be dynamically healthy and will go as far to say that the one who is unable or incapable of rejecting or excluding anything at all "can only lead to (or be the result of) excessive self-rejection and, as it were, self-exclusion."[13]

As a means of confession, I do wonder if my lamentation over lacking community derives in part from my rejection of the self. If I devalue myself, then perhaps there is a certain dread when contemplating fellowship for fear that I will once again be rejected. Perhaps there was a certain birth of this during my time of pastoring. I was pastoring at the stage of development that was on the border of intimacy vs. isolation and generativity vs. stagnation. I was in my late thirties and when insulted and blamed for the church's decline, I internalized a wound that has befuddled a cure (Jer 30:12). The insult injured my trust for intimate relationships and threatened the beginning stages of generativity. The model of ministry that I had spent twelve years investing toward disintegrated before my eyes in mere months. This led to a distrust in my discernment, imagination, and creativity. I now contemplate a new imagination only to talk myself out of it, moments later. I often wonder if God can entrust me with another work—a false premise, but one that resounds like rolling thunder in my mind as I enter the stage of generativity vs. stagnation with an existential insult to my identity. During the pastorate, not

---

12. Erikson, *Life Cycle Completed*, 71.
13. Erikson, *Life Cycle Completed*, 71.

only was my call questioned, but my very salvation. It was determined that I could not integrate medicine and ministry by a board of less than twelve people who never walked the twelve-year journey of investment. However, where I thought I could simply move on, I have found a kind of stagnation that has accompanied my recovery over the past two years. I fear the new, the start-up, the church plant, the knocking on doors to pastor again. I fear damage to my family, my marriage, and my identity. Most of all, I question the accuracy of hearing from God. Excited at a certain prospect, I remain reticent to act. I both long for but find I am unable to muster the energy for an intimate and authentic community.

When attempting to find or invest in community, a counseling relationship often ensues that mitigates community as there needs to be some form of boundary to maintain a therapeutic relationship. When letting my imagination run wild with possible venues of creativity, stagnation lurks around the corner with statements such as, "It is not time, you are unable, you will be rejected, etc." I find myself wondering if the insult at the hinge point of intimacy and generativity has created an emotional barrier to resolving the dialectic developmental crisis. Do I choose intimacy or isolation? Do I choose generativity or resign myself to stagnation? Insults at certain stages of development have a way of prolonging the dialectic resolution. However, if I or anyone who has experienced an offense along the stages of development long to arrive at a place of wisdom where faith, hope, and love are integrated, a work of shalom in the soul in and through the Holy Spirit is often the catalyst that aids in compelling us toward such integration. And sometimes this requires the beautiful risk of trusting someone else with your heart once more. Will you take the risk, even if you find yourself in your latter years?

Below is the covenant that elderly men take at the gathered agape feast:

> I covenant to live a life of restraint, deferring immediate satisfaction of impulsive desires until a more prayerful consideration can be made (Titus 2:2). I covenant to live a life of dignity and honor by immersing myself in the sacred (Titus 2:2). I covenant to be temperate, voluntarily placing restriction on my freedom for the sake of the next generation (Titus 2:2). I covenant to be sound in faith by practicing sound doctrine (Titus 2:2). I covenant to integrate all the admonitions over my life as a way of passing a legacy of sound faith. I covenant to be sound in sacrificial love by living with and in sacred community (Titus 2:2). I covenant to endure in the faith by being trustworthy through manifold trials with a determined hope that Christ is all in all

(Titus 2:2). I covenant to hold to the faith as a child holds to his beloved Father (Matt 18:3). I covenant to integrate faith, hope, and love in my old age as a means of passing a sound legacy to younger men (1 Cor 13:13).

Chapter 19

Setting in Order: The Elderly Women and the Haustafel

> Likewise, tell the older women to be reverent in behavior, not to be slanderers or enslaved to much wine; they are to teach what is good.
>
> TITUS 2:3

PAUL ADDRESSES ELDERLY WOMEN in the Haustafel by first qualifying holiness. The Greek ἱεροπρεπεῖς is used only here in Titus to convey holiness. It connotes a kind of becoming, an existential quality of matriculating in the sacred. Thus, it is to live resolutely in, practice with fidelity, and become qualitatively sacred.[1] Rogers and Rogers will go so far as to connote that ἱεροπρεπεῖς is to become "temple-like" in character. This hearkens to Paul's emphasis on the human body now becoming the temple of the Holy Spirit in the new covenant ratified with Christ's blood (1 Cor 6:15–20). In this regard, the aged woman is engaged in duties of the sacred, performing services of holiness and consecration. She confounds the secular, because she acts with an other-worldly praxis. The elderly woman thus is a priestess, preparing the shewbread of her home, offering incense as worship, preparing the sacrifice of her time, washing the feet of others, and immersing herself in the sacred.[2]

Paul addresses the holy conduct of women in the Haustafel in his first Epistle to Timothy when he asserts the following:

1. Zodhiates and Baker, *Hebrew-Greek Key Word*, 1724.
2. Rogers and Rogers, *New Linguistic and Exegetical Key*, 509.

> Also that the women should dress themselves in moderate clothing with reverence and self-control, not with their hair braided or with gold, pearls, or expensive clothes, but with good works, as is proper for women who profess reverence for God. (1 Tim 2:9–10)

In this regard, holiness does have external qualities in addition to internal virtues. Modesty, which is quickly becoming a lost virtue in Christian community, is one such external attribute. The Christian community has in large part adopted the fashion of our age, which is a fashion that prides itself on the revealing nature of its clothes. In contrast, the elderly woman does not succumb to such fads but remains modest in her appearance as a model for the younger women. This modesty is a simple but powerful expression of her holiness.

Holiness also includes a sense of propriety. The Greek αἰδώς (ahee-doce') connotes an "innate repugnance to a dishonorable act."[3] Propriety in this regard may invoke a kind of inner distaste for the irreverent, a bad taste for the dishonorable. Zodhiates is keen to note, however, that αἰδώς is not αἰσχύνη (ahee-skhoo'-nay) as used in 2 Cor 4:2 to indicate shame. There are distinctions here to note. Where αἰδώς is a moral reaction to the tangible acts of dishonor, αἰσχύνη is a feeling that accompanies the action of shunning that which is unworthy.[4] Where αἰδώς draws near, αἰσχύνη pushes away. Where αἰδώς is an action, αἰσχύνη is a feeling.

Therefore, αἰσχύνη is that feeling of having been replaced by a more honorable person (see Luke 14:9). The apostle Paul exhorts that we renounce αἰσχύνη as a kind of craftiness or dishonesty forged in secret (see 2 Cor 4:2). There are those enemies of the cross who glory in their αἰσχύνη whose end is destruction (see Phil 3:19). In this way, the Christian must resist not only the nature of αἰσχύνη, but certainly the glorification or reinforcement of αἰσχύνη in all of society. The one who is αἰσχύνη is also the one who minds or who hotly pursues worldly pleasures, ambition, power, and affluence. The pursuit ignores impropriety along the way. Indeed, it is the cross that despises αἰσχύνη (see Heb 12:2). In other words, the cross has overcome the αἰσχύνη of sin, guilt, and impropriety. Those who walk in αἰσχύνη are enemies of the cross because it is the cross that has destroyed αἰσχύνη.

---

3. Zodhiates defines αἰδώς with antithetical terms. That is, he begins with an inner quality that bemoans and perhaps speaks out against irreverence and dishonor. See Zodhiates and Baker, *Hebrew-Greek Key Word*, 1683.

4. See Zodhiates and Baker, *Hebrew-Greek Key Word*, 1684.

Jude does not mince words in describing αἰσχύνη as those who have gone in the way of Cain, having murderous intentions out of a coveting heart (Jude 1:11). Those with αἰσχύνη have traversed the same path of Ballam, seeking monetary gain with a heart intent on cursing (Jude 1:11). The slander and undermining nature of Korah is also an illustration of αἰσχύνη (Jude 1:11). Jude continues with the following description of αἰσχύνη when he writes,

> These are blots on your love feasts, while they feast with you without fear, feeding themselves. They are waterless clouds carried along by the winds; autumn trees without fruit, twice dead, uprooted; wild waves of the sea, casting up the foam of their own shame (αἰσχύνη); wandering stars, for whom the deepest darkness has been reserved forever. (Jude 1:12–13)

Thus, shame stains the agape feast, becomes a praxis of selfish ambition, and produces dead fruit. The shameful person is akin to a raging sea of fomenting waves, waves inevitably destined for self-destruction. Shame is antithetical to community, compelling the individual to wander from place to place without a home. Shame is darkness, blackness, a pitch-black state of despair where one gropes for some path, some familiarity, some herald to guide her.

Shame is a poorly estate described further as one who is wretched, miserable, blind, and naked (see Rev 3:17). Christ admonishes Laodicea in this way when he counsels the church, who is ironically wealthy, to purchase refined gold, white robes, and anointing salve for the eyes. These purchases lie in contrast to the purchasing of goods, buildings, luxuries of a prodigal nature, and hedonistic expenses. It is the shame, or αἰσχύνη, of nakedness that Christ counsels the church to cover, not in denial, but with the white robes of sanctification purchased by the blood of Christ (see Rev 3:18).

In summary, the elderly women have renounced the shameful acts that plague the soul and practice propriety and holiness with, yes, a sense of moralism, but a moralism that exudes compassion, mercy, love, forgiveness, and truth. The elderly woman speaks the truth while drawing the sinner to herself.

Next, we have another attribute illustrating elderly women in the Haustafel utilizing a negative sense. That is, elderly women are to refrain from false accusations of all sorts. The use of the Greek term διάβολος (dee-ab'-ol-os) stands to awaken us to the serious nature of such a description. It is where we derive the word diabolical and can infer demon possession in certain circumstances or contexts. It aptly describes a calumniator, one who utters maliciously false statements, charges, or imputations. It is one intent on destroying the reputation of another in the Haustafel. It is the witting, but more often unwitting, compliance with Satan himself to oppose the cause of God and bring down his servants by grinding them with salacious accusations to those with influence to sway them to join such an opposition.[5]

The word denotes one who casts through, throwing an accusation into the midst of community. The art of accusation and slander has its origin in the garden when Satan accused God in paradise. Paul refers to the term when qualifying deacons by the conduct of their wives. Their wives must be grave, not slanderers, sober, and faithful in all things (see 1 Tim 3:11). Paul likewise refers to διάβολος when describing humanity in the last days: they will be lovers of their own selves, covetous, boasters, proud, blasphemers, disobedient to parents, unthankful and unholy (2 Tim 3:2). Christ refers to Judas as διάβολος, as an evil spirit would influence Judas to accuse and betray Christ (John 6:70). Thus, the central notion of διάβολος is accusation, and in our case with Titus, false accusations.[6]

Pastor John was once blindsided when an elderly female staff member surprised him with an accusation. She stated that he was manipulating certain hires and was intent on destroying the church. The term at once incensed Pastor John and his anger escalated in defense of himself. Unfortunately, this rumor of manipulation and church destruction caught hold among the leadership of the church and those with influence, so that there came calls for his resignation and many staff members would no longer follow his leadership. This is the destructive power of διάβολος or false accusations. One elder of the church confronted Pastor John with this false accusation, stating that he ought to be sued for his apparent "manipulative hiring" practice. There was no defense Pastor John could offer. When he attempted to explain himself, he was verbally cut off and there was no openness to a contrary narrative or perspective. The rumor and accusation had become entrenched in the leadership and those who opposed Pastor John wore him down until he did finally resign from his post. Pastor John simply stated a preference in who he wanted to hire

---

5. Online Greek Bible, "Titus 2:3."
6. See Zodhiates and Baker, *Hebrew-Greek Key Word*, 1703.

(which is his prerogative and role as pastor); this was contorted to mean that he was manipulating the people and the process.

It is most tragic that both accusers of Pastor John in leadership were elderly females. One wonders, then, if διάβολος is a particular temptation for the elderly female in the Haustafel. Perhaps the tantalizing temptation of usurping over another, asserting one's opinion through gossip, amassing a gathering, and increasing one's influence can be a vulnerability for the elderly female where she may risk false accusations of blasphemy to accomplish it.

For example, Susanna Wesley describes false accusations in the following manner:

> This is like wounding a man in the dark, whereas a generous person should rather choose to confront his enemy and allow him fair play for his life. It always argues a base and cowardly temper to whisper secretly what we dare not speak to a man's face. Therefore, be careful to avoid all evil speaking and be ever sure to obey that command of our Saviour, in this case as well as others. "Whatsoever you would that man should do unto you, do you even as unto them."[7]

Next, Paul addresses perhaps another vulnerability for the elderly female, the temptation to placate with wine the stress or anxiety of living. The caveat "too much wine" appears to provide the sense that the temptation is toward drunkenness or intoxication rather than mere consumption of wine itself. Paul uses the Greek construction δουλεύω (dool-yoo'-o), which has a greater force of language than some English translations afford. It is typically used to convey the notion of slavery. As Rogers and Rogers note, the tense is in the perfect passive with the object being the one consuming wine, and the perfect tense to indicate one who is enslaved to wine.[8] The perfect tense also indicates a completed state or existence. The elderly woman in such a state gives herself completely over to wine—she is a slave to it.

Certainly the vice of an alcohol-use disorder would impede their function in the Haustafel to instruct younger women both by example and teaching. Where Paul qualifies the elderly women in the Haustafel with abstentions, he ends with a positive qualification. They are to teach the younger women. The elderly women both as a model and by verbal

---

7. Wesley, *Complete Writings*, 218.
8. Rogers and Rogers, *New Linguistic and Exegetical Key*, 509.

counsel, teach the younger women to be sober (and how can they do this, if they are not sober themselves?), to love their husbands, and to love their children. They teach the younger women about modesty, propriety, household management, goodness, and obedience. Thus, although this likely occurs organically in the Haustafel, churches would do well to revive such teaching relationships by instilling a virtuous curriculum where older women instruct the younger women in such manners.

We find that drinking among women is escalating as pressures also descend upon women who juggle work and home expectations. The following are just a few of the epidemiological forays into this phenomenon:

- 113.2 million females age twelve and older report drinking at some time in their lifetime.[9]
- 27.2 million women age eighteen and older report binge drinking in the past month.[10]
- According to the 2019 National Survey on Drug Use and Health (NSDUH), 85.6 percent of people age eighteen and older report that they drank alcohol at some point in their lifetime, 69.5 percent report that they drank in the past year, and 54.9 percent (59.1 percent of men in this age group and 51.0 percent of women in this age group) report that they drank in the past month.[11]
- An estimated 95,000 people (approximately 68,000 men and 27,000 women) die from alcohol-related causes annually, making alcohol the third-leading preventable cause of death in the United States.[12]

Thus, with such a great prevalence, it is no wonder that even in the first century, Paul is advising great caution concerning alcohol consumption. Moreover, we find ourselves in a culture where a joke about a glass of wine is the mode whereby one self-medicates her stress away. We hear very little warnings about the vice of alcohol, and particularly the easy transition to an alcohol-use disorder.

---

9. National Institute on Alcohol Abuse and Alcoholism, "Alcohol Use," para 1.
10. National Institute on Alcohol Abuse and Alcoholism, "Alcohol Use," para 1.
11. National Institute on Alcohol Abuse and Alcoholism, "Alcohol Use," para 7.
12. National Institute on Alcohol Abuse and Alcoholism, "Alcohol-Related Emergencies," para 1.

Setting in Order

SUSANNE WESLEY AND ELDERLY WOMEN

Now that these attributes have been etymologically explicated, I would like to explore the life and work of Susanna Wesley as further extrapolation of women in the Haustafel. I believe she may offer illustrations and reflections that accentuate the women's role in the Haustafel and bring much needed clarity.

Susanna Wesley was brought up in a Puritan Dissenting home during a time when there was fierce debate between the national Church of England and the Puritan resistance. Ironically, Wesley decided to join the church of England at odds with her family of origin. The decision, however, was weighty, and was made after calculating reflection at the tender age of thirteen years. However, this initial decision would be a coloring of Wesley's cunning ability and desire to think independently on a great many things theological and political.[13]

She married Samuel Wesley when she was just nineteen, after a relationship through letter exchanges. She immediately experienced financial hardship when Samuel transitioned on multiple occasions from curate to chaplain and then to literature to find steady work. At one time, she lodged in a boarding house and then had to stay with her parents before the birth of her first child.[14]

Wesley's life was punctuated by grief quite early on. Five of her children died soon after their births, some with preventable tragic causes. Her husband was quickly amassing debt that would plague the family for as long as he lived. It was out of this meager context that both John and Charles Wesley were born in 1703 and 1707. Their ministry would change the world, and one could claim their influence was first begun by the seed their mother planted within their minds and souls.[15]

Not only did Wesley suffer the grief of lost children, poverty, and multiple transitions, but what may have been a capstone to her grief, her husband, for curious reasons, abandoned the family. Perhaps he had despaired over not being more successful, perhaps he made an impulsive decision in the context of overwhelming depression, or perhaps there had been conflicts ensuing between he and his wife that preempted the escape. We are left to ponder the exact causes of his motivation, but

---

13. Metaxas, *Seven Women*, 31–33.
14. Metaxas, *Seven Women*, 34.
15. Metaxas, *Seven Women*, 34–35.

SETTING IN ORDER: THE ELDERLY WOMEN AND THE HAUSTAFEL

Wesley herself makes mention of a political divide that may have acted as a catalyst when she writes,

> You advise me to continue with my husband, and God knows how gladly I would do it, but there, there is my supreme affliction, he will not live with me.... I'm willing to let him quietly enjoy his opinions, he ought not to deprive me of my little liberty of conscience.[16]

And,

> My master will not be persuaded he has no power over the conscience of Wife.... He is now for referring the whole to the Archbishop of York and Bishop of Lincoln, and says if I will not be determined by them, he will do anything rather than live with a person that is the declared enemy of his country.[17]

Apparently, the entire debacle had begun by Wesley's omission of saying "amen" when her husband had prayed for the king of England, who she envisioned as an illegitimate monarch of Britain. Many are still puzzled over how seemingly little a conflict would lead to Samuel's elopement from his family. However, he would return one year later after Wesley's house burned down to assist in repairs.

It was at this time that Wesley turned to the education of her children. In this regard, she becomes a prototype and exemplary model for homeschooling. It is thought that her method of education was influenced by an amalgamation of both Puritan and Pietistic thought. She explored the writings of Danish missionaries to India, articles that were already conveniently located in her husband's library.[18]

WESLEY'S PEDAGOGY

It is to this method of education that we now turn as we explore Wesley's fulfillment of the Titus mandate to elder women to teach good things and the younger women to love their children (Titus 2:3–4).

Wesley began the formal education of her children on their fifth birthday and created a schedule that was firm and rigorous. That is, there was no play during the school day and each child enjoyed individual

---

16. Wesley, *Complete Writings*, 35–36.
17. Wesley, *Complete Writings*, 37.
18. Potter, "Influence of Danish Missionaries," 151–52.

Setting in Order

instruction with their mother through the week. It is thought that the Pietism of Danish missionaries to India became a seed that germinated in a certain emphasis on personal behavior embedded in Wesley's pedagogical method.[19]

She created a fixed method of education and can earnestly be considered the mother of methodism as John Wesley was indelibly influenced by his mother. The following is an account of her method:

> As soon as they knew the letters, they were first put to spell, and read one line, and then a verse; never leaving till perfect in their lesson, were it shorter or longer. So one or other continued reading at school time without any intermission; and before we left school, each child read what he had learnt that morning; and ere we parted in the afternoon, what they had learnt that day.[20]

We first find that repetition was a key element of Wesley's method, continuing in the said rehearsal until one achieves perfection. Now this perfection is left as an elusive component but likely created a standard of rhetorical excellence combined with an understanding of the text applied. Thus, the Scriptures became the bedrock and "pre-text" of all learning. Catechism was the primary course of learning, and all other disciplines became the offshoot of this catechistic system.

We again see Christian formation as the central tenet of Wesley's educational system in the following manner by which her children spent their day:

> When the house was rebuilt, and the children all brought home, we entered on a strict reform; and then was begun the custom of singing psalms at beginning and leaving school morning and evening. Then also that of a general retirement at five o'clock was entered upon, when the oldest took the youngest that could speak, and the second next, to whom they read the psalms for the day and a chapter in the New Testament: as in the morning they were directed to read the psalms and a chapter in the Old Testament, after which they went to their private prayers, before they got their breakfast or came into the family.[21]

---

19. Potter, "Influence of Danish Missionaries," 152.

20. Wesley to her son John, July 24, 1732, in Clarke, *Memoirs of the Wesley Family*, 257.

21. Wesley to her son John, July 24, 1732, in Clarke, *Memoirs of the Wesley Family*, 265.

SETTING IN ORDER: THE ELDERLY WOMEN AND THE HAUSTAFEL

Wesley indeed adhered to a method of education that integrated worship and the recruitment of older children in the process of catechism. It seems that the children were bumping into Scripture throughout their entire day while learning the value of singing the Psalms. Worship punctuated the beginning and ending of the school day and acted as an existential *inclusio*. Indeed, one would do well to include a Psalter in the education of children once more. The singing of Psalms provides both emotive expressions so common to human pathos while committing to memory the language sanctioned by God in such expression. The child can learn the depths of grief and agony, the godly sorrow of repentance, the joy of exultation and triumph, the fear of the Lord in judgment, and the war of the spirit with imprecation.

Private prayer was also included in Wesley's method which provided the student a sacred space for spiritual reflection while honing his or her spiritual ears to attune to the voice of God! The notion of the altar comes to mind where children can come, bow, and seek God for the benefit of his or her soul. The call to the prayer closet is yet another Scriptural paraenesis that the child can adopt by finding a secret place wherein he or she meets with the Lord.

Wesley comments on both the honor and challenge of educating her children with the following:

> Though the education of so many children must create abundance of trouble and will perpetually keep the mind employed, as well as the body, yet consider tis no small honour to be entrusted with the care of so many souls, and if that trust be but managed with prudence and integrity, the harvest will abundantly recompense the toil of the seed time, and it will be certainly no little accession to the future glory to stand forth at the last day and say, "Lord, here are the children which thou hast given me, of whom I have lost none by my ill example, nor by neglecting to instill into their mind in their early years the principles of thy true religion and virtue."[22]

Wesley envisions education as missional. That is, she is employed as a laborer in the harvest by means of educating her children. She sees this as toil, and yes, that it is—but also as honor to be entrusted with souls. She also assumes personal culpability if, by her own ill-tempered disposition, one would stray from the faith. Moreover, she also considers the neglect of instilling virtues at an early age as another possible

---

22. Wesley, *Complete Writings*, 208.

omission that may play a role in her children's digression. In this regard, her missional work as kingdom work is to also seek virtue and sanctification personally, so that she may serve her children by her example and instruct them in the virtues of the kingdom. I cannot help but wonder if she recapitulated her own statement when she met the Lord in eternity, "Lord, here are the children . . ." Who knows if there are mothers in the Haustafel right now who are raising the next John Wesley to endeavor yet another great awakening!

Moreover, Wesley encourages correction and discipline but also warns of incorrect motives when she asserts the following:

> Never correct your children to satisfy your passions but out of a sense of your duty to reclaim them from their errors and to preserve your authority. And then be exceeding careful to let the measure of correction be proportionate to the fault. Make great allowances for the weakness of their reason and immaturity of their judgments, but never spare them through foolish fondness when they sin against God. Instruct them in their duty and reason with them upon the several branches of it. Cherish the first dawnings of sense and reason and endeavor to tincture their minds in their early years with a sense of religion. "Train up a child in the way he should go, and when he is old he will not depart from it."[23]

Wesley of course calls for equitable admonishment that matches the fault. In this way, she warns against discipline out of a sense of satisfying our own carnal need for authority, or the exasperation of our children because we need to hear them acknowledge our own sense of authority because we are insecure or worse, craving power. However, one can also err on the opposite side and neglect correction because of a certain foolish fondness or improper affection for a child. That is, we can wrongly see our role as a parent to be a peer or attempt to "shelter" our children from correction when such "sheltering" can become injurious to the child's soul. Validate the dawn of reason and conviction while continuing to instruct them when the scales yet remain upon their eyes.

Of course, many monographs have been written on the life and work of Susanna Wesley, and I have provided a mere glimpse that I hope will spur many women to explore the treasury of Wesley's writings. This exploration may indeed benefit the woman's soul who endeavors to faithfully discharge her role as an elderly woman who instructs the younger

---

23. Wesley, *Complete Writings*, 238–39.

generation so that the tenets of the faith continue, "precept upon precept" (Isa 28:10).

Therefore, it is in this light that we now come to create a covenant statement for the elderly women in the Haustafel.

> I covenant to be holy, to be sacred—a priestess of my home (Titus 2:3). In this manner, I will conduct myself with a sense of modesty and propriety (1 Tim 2:9–10). I covenant to refrain from idle words, gossip, slander, and false accusations that are unbecoming to my home and the church. I covenant to abstain from the enslavement of alcohol—to model the taking of our cares to the Lord in prayer. I covenant to instruct younger women and my children in the ways of the kingdom. In so doing, I offer the Lord my services in hope of leaving a righteous posterity.

Chapter 20

Setting in Order:
The Young Women and the Haustafel

So that they may encourage the young women to love their husbands, to love their children, to be self-controlled, chaste, good managers of the household, kind, submissive to their husbands, so that the word of God may not be discredited.

TITUS 2:4–5

THE YOUNGER WOMEN IN the Haustafel are the ones being addressed as a legacy preserved and inherited from the instruction and conduct of the older women. Although it is implied that women of all ages are to behave in such a manner, we direct the following paraenetic material to younger women as instruments in the Haustafel to illustrate God's image in the following manner.

DISCRETION

The charge is again emphasized that the younger women are to be sober. Now this sobriety is in the immediate context of Paul's charge to older women that they refrain from drunkenness that can impair one's judgment. But we should also note that Paul's use of σωφρονίζω (so-fron-id'-zo) has greater nuance to convey one who is of a sound mind, disciplined, and one who is faithful to discharge one's duty. Discreet is how we often

SETTING IN ORDER: THE YOUNG WOMEN AND THE HAUSTAFEL

translate the word, but even this term typically falls short to convey the plethora of meanings conveyed by the Greek word. Zodhiates asserts that although sound mind is the literal rendering, this term also bears with it the intentional act of limiting one's own freedoms.[1]

It seems that this move to limit freedoms is a cognitive one. That is, young women are to engage in right thinking, and if this is done, then young women can behave in a way to limit certain liberties in the name of propriety. σωφρονίζω is juxtaposed with *hubristes*, which is to convey a kind of insolence and contempt that bursts forth in a temper of outrage.[2] Sophrosyne, a transliteration of σωφρονίζω, is an aspirational virtue in ancient Greece given much attention in their literature and culture. σωφρονίζω is designated the *virtus feminarum*, as feminine ways of being are underscored by this discipline of discretion and self-control. It is no wonder that Paul mentions it here, a virtue often lost in an impulsive and raging culture that compels one to pursue any hedonistic whim.

When Euripides's character Andromache is confronted with an accusation against her parents, she replies with sophrosyne, "The wise ought to shun the ways of evil parents."[3] Andromache, a slave in Euripides's play, does not erupt with an outburst at the preposterous accusation, but rather provides a wise proverb to defend her innocence. It is then that we emphasize the definition of sophrosyne as Antonelli does when he asserts, "Sophrosyne is the virtue of those who can exercise prudence and who are conscious of their own limits."[4]

The Greeks often distinguished knowledge/wisdom (sophia) from moderation (sophros) by illustrating this distinction with mythical fiction. In Homer's characters, the gods did not exact punitive measures for lack of wisdom (sophia) but for lack of self-control (sophrosyne).[5] Antonelli, admittedly borrowing somewhat from Aristotle, puts forth a theorem explicating sophrosyne in the following manner: "Paying attention in order to conveniently dwell in Being."[6] He goes on to tie this theorem into Girard's theory of mimesis and further integration into Christian ethics.

---

1. Zodhiates and Baker, *Hebrew-Greek Key Word*, 1761. Also, see Online Greek Bible, "Titus 2:5," para. 1.
2. Zodhiates and Baker, *Hebrew-Greek Key Word*, 1761.
3. Boulter, "'Sophia' and 'Sophrosyne' in Euripides' 'Andromache,'" 54.
4. Antonelli, "Mimesis and Attention," 260.
5. Antonelli, "Mimesis and Attention," 260.
6. Antonelli, "Mimesis and Attention," 261.

Setting in Order

Broadly, I am intrigued by the idea of why a simple and yet profound concept of discretion, limiting freedom, constraint, or whatever else we might call it, has drawn so much attention from our theologians and philosophers. Certainly, Paul mentions it in his litany of paraenesis concerning young women but does little else to explain the term. The paradox in Antonelli's definition involves the juxtaposition of action (giving one's attention) and inaction or perhaps less action (convenience). It is as if the giving of attention bears the fruit of presence. That is, the ability to be is perhaps a natural benefit of sophrosyne. And perhaps, if we truly recognize the moment we now encompass, our choice of words would be different. The uncanny ability to recognize the moment, dwell in the now, or discern the dynamics grants one a pause when considering action vs. inaction, words vs. silence, or perhaps even an integration of these seemingly contrasting states of being. To summarize, using Antonelli's language, "A wise person is someone who can judge the condition in which he needs to be, so the habitus or virtue he needs to possess in order to judge properly must be sophrosyne."[7]

Simone Weil helps us here as well when she writes on holy attention, framed quite conspicuously as the act of prayer that serves as a type of mediator for the creative production of judgment, discernment, or perhaps even our topic, sophrosyne. I feel it necessary to reproduce a lengthy citation for the sense of her thinking:

> There are some kinds of effort which defeat their own object (example: the soured disposition of certain pious females, false asceticism, certain sorts of self-devotion, etc.). Others are always useful, even if they do not meet with success. How are we to distinguish between them? Perhaps in this way: some efforts are always accompanied by the (false) negation of our inner wretchedness; with others the attention is continually concentrated on the distance there is between what we are and what we love.[8]

What we are is not necessarily what we love. In meditating on this quite contradistinctive existential irony, perhaps we encounter the chasm of these two disparate states conjuring up, in a sense, a type of sophrosyne, a better judgment, a discreet vicissitude that bears on the moment of now. Weil continues to unfold her polemic:

---

7. Antonelli, "Mimesis and Attention," 261.
8. Weil, *Gravity and Grace*, 118.

> Love is the teacher of gods and men, for no one learns without desiring to learn. Truth is sought not because it is truth but because it is good. Attention is bound up with desire. Not with the will but with desire—or more exactly, consent.[9]

Weil tackles foundational virtues in Christian ethics with the teleological aim being to further explicate sacred attention. Love teaches all, desire and love are bound up with each other. The pursuit of truth is envisaged not out of will, but out of desire. The desire for truth is not merely a pursuit of truth for truth's sake, but because truth is so good. It is the goodness of truth that spurns our desire, that invokes our love. Perhaps it is the beauty of truth that captures our imaginations to the extent that we long for it. And when it comes, we attend to it, and we better discern our moments. If we could, through our sheer will, place truth into our minds, it would be done as if we willed our hand to touch a table (a Weil aphorism).[10]

I want to believe that I can "will" truth into my life, but Weil quite convincingly argues for the contrary. I want to believe that I exercise discretion with a kind of cognitive fortitude that firmly grips principles that should be ubiquitous to every dilemma we face. Weil, however, in Augustinian fashion, recalls us to a different paradigm. She once again reminds us that right affections, desires, attention to beauty, goodness, and truth are the genesis of sophrosyne. If sophrosyne or discretion is a virtue, then it is procured as many, if not all, of the other virtues, as graces in relational encounters with God, moved along by holy desire, love, and affection in contemplative prayer and in meditation on God's revelation.

In this way, Weil reminds us again of kenosis, an epistemology for all who desire discretion. She claims that attention necessitates the dissolution of the *I* as the attention is directed to *Thou*. It is another reminder of the Buber *I-Thou* dialectic. Her words are worth reproducing here: "Attention alone—that attention which is so full that the 'I' disappears—is required of me. I have to deprive all that I call 'I' of the light of my attention and turn it on to that which cannot be conceived."[11]

Weil further asserts that discretion is an exercise in time not space. She states as much in the following manner: "In the inner life, time takes

---

9. Weil, *Gravity and Grace*, 118.
10. Weil, *Gravity and Grace*, 40–41, 45.
11. Weil, *Gravity and Grace*, 118.

the place of space. With time we are altered, and, if as we change, we keep our gaze directed toward the same thing, in the end illusions are scattered and the real becomes visible."[12]

But why then does Paul exhort young women to be discreet in our text? That is, if discretion is born out with time, should it be just out of reach for the young woman? We must not forget that Paul's primary audience here is the older women. It is the older women who are teaching and modelling sophrosyne. Perhaps, in this way, Paul implies that discretion is also teleologically culminated with time, not space as Weil further substantiates. Further, it seems to me that Weil also polemicizes that it is attention on the same thing (for our purposes, the divine) that provides further clarity between that which is real or authentic from that which is merely illusory. Perception is often the enemy of discretion, if indeed perception is wedded to the illusory. In prayerful attention, divine encounters, the enfolding of ourselves in the beauty of truth, perhaps we find ourselves, by and by, in the state of *video meliora* ("I see better"). And if we see better, then perhaps that can be an apt summary of sophrosyne, a discerning of the now moment with a now God.

CHASTITY

The apostle Paul will underscore ἀγνός (hag-nos), yet another attribute for older women to teach and younger women to aspire toward. The term is a corollary to the notion of sanctification, revealing such traits that are becoming to the kingdom such as consecration, holiness, and being set part. It is a partaking in God's purity with the contradistinction of renouncing or refraining from corporeal defilements. It is often envisaged as a young woman who remains a virgin. Indeed, if there is a illustration for this term, it would likely be that very image. A woman at the precipice of maturation, flowering and blooming, and chaste, having kept herself from sexual encounter—awaiting her groom.[13]

Thus, we must reckon with the Greek ἀγνός as a concept intimating sexual purity, one who refrains quite willingly from sinful sexual encounters as a means of setting herself apart for God's holiness. To illustrate further, we look at Joseph's conundrum, one of maintaining ἀγνός. He resists Potiphar's wife. The anecdote further substantiates the sexual

---

12. Weil, *Gravity and Grace*, 120.
13. Zodhiates and Baker, *Hebrew-Greek Key Word*, 1681.

indiscretion as not only a sin against Potipher, but against God himself (see Gen 39:9). Thus, sexual sin is both physical and metaphysical transgression affecting the body and spirit (1 Cor 6:18).

Chastity as virtue has long been personified by the feminine gender in antiquity, whereas it encapsulates both genders in Christian thought. But, as we are speaking to young women as is inherent in Paul's instruction, perhaps a lens from Shakespeare's Isabella may be helpful in elucidating this virtue more comprehensively, and of course its general influence upon society.

Shakespeare's lesser-known play *Measure for Measure* is essentially a drama that underscores the explicit and implicit laws of chastity in seventeenth-century England. It is a play on power and powerlessness. It is an exploration of the power of chastity and an implication that this feminine power of chastity influences the stability of an entire culture while also stabilizing the patriarchy of the times. And perhaps there are lessons to be learned from Isabella for the young women of today.

We begin with a young woman by the name of Isabella. She is otherwise known as Claudio's sister and a nun. As the play begins, the Duke of Vienna announces he is departing the city for a time and places his deputy Angelo in charge of the city's affairs. Angelo immediately enforces a law prohibiting sex outside of marriage. Angelo likewise immediately sentences Claudio to death for sleeping with Juliet, Claudio's now-pregnant fiancée.

Isabella appeals to Angelo to save her brother Claudio. But the hypocritical Angelo demands that Isabella prostitute herself to save Claudio's life. Isabella, clinging to chastity, refuses. The duke, who has remained in Vienna disguised as a friar, suggests to Isabella that Angelo's rejected fiancée, Mariana, could take Isabella's place. Although the cunning substitute succeeds, Angelo orders Claudio's death regardless of his own similar transgression. The duke saves Claudio, but he tells Isabella that Claudio is dead. The duke, resuming his identity, sentences Angelo to wed Mariana and then be put to death. But Mariana and Isabella remarkably plead for Angelo's life. Unveiling that Claudio is alive, the duke pardons Angelo and proposes to Isabella.

And why would Shakespeare take up this theme of chastity if it were not to extrapolate the society in which he lived? As Barbara Baines has contended, "A theologically prescribed virtue, chastity is appropriated as

SETTING IN ORDER

the standard upon which the economy of secular power is based."[14] Could this still be true? Is chastity the forgotten virtue of a secular society? Does chastity demonstrate economic influence? Is there something intuitive, and perhaps deeply embedded in our psyche, that portends valuing chastity as a stabilizer of society? And when we jettison this value, would not the inevitable be a society that disintegrates? Is this what Shakespeare is telling us in between the lines of his poetry?

Baines continues, "Chastity is the definitive virtue . . . because secular law prescribes it as a remedy for the diseased state."[15] Is it possible for a diseased society to find its healing balm in chastity? Does the young woman have this much sway, as to inspire politics of good fortune and peaceable lives? Baines is not timid to assert such, taking Shakespeare as an agreeable companion.

When Claudio is marching to his imprisonment, he answers an acquaintance who queries him concerning his charge. Claudio's answer is telling: "From too much liberty, my Lucio, liberty."[16] It is liberty or perhaps incontinence that was the seed of Claudio's demise. He indulged in sexual liberty, failed to restrain his impulse for love, and made the flower bloom before its time. And chastity is a restraint on unbridled liberty, and a restraint on unbridled liberty is necessary for the flourishing of a society. Otherwise, as Claudio further laments, "Our natures do pursue, / Like rats that raven down their proper bane, / A thirsty evil, and when we drink, we die."[17] Sexual indiscretion thus unravels a society as if consuming the full dregs of death itself. The sexual revolution of the 1960s was a revolution of death, a wage that still recompenses today.

Claudio himself has already pleaded with Angelo with no measure of success. He now implores his confidant, Lucio, to inform his sister and a nun, Isabella, of his demise. He implores her interpolation with a strange hope of her prowess to convince. He reveals that she has a rhetoric that is embedded in her character and perhaps we are not to overstate that her chastity is a key to her proverbial skill. He contends that Isabella "make friends / To the strict deputy; bid herself assay him."[18] Why would Claudio appropriate the term *assay* if he had not had a confidence that

---

14. Baines, "Assaying the Power of Chastity," 284.
15. Baines, "Assaying the Power of Chastity," 284.
16. Shakespeare, *Measure for Measure*, 1.2.122.
17. Shakespeare, *Measure for Measure*, 1.2.125–27.
18. Shakespeare, *Measure for Measure*, 1.2.178–79.

Isabella could engender a type of inspection of Angelo's character, and by doing so, lay bare a weakness of intellect?

The prowess Claudio speaks of, however, is not logic or rhetoric alone. For he makes further comment that his hope is in a rather unseen dynamic of power, a power of society birthed in the heart of a chaste young female. For he asserts, "I have great hope in that, for in her youth / There is a prone and speechless dialect / Such as move men."[19] Why is it that her youth is the essence to move men? What is it about her youth or speechless dialect, which is to say, her very embodiment that may be blessed with the influence to move a man's heart? Is it not her chastity? Is it not that she embodies a pure vision that appeals from an innocence that has the rather natural ability to sway the politics of power? Who can but resist a pure appeal, from a pure virgin, with a noble intent to save a life? I think, and perhaps I am naïve, that Shakespeare is awakening at least seventeenth-century England, that it is chastity which becomes the speechless dialect to move society. And as such, in a patriarchal society, it is chastity that acts as a stabilizing force of rhetoric, for it is rhetoric that is expressed bodily and incarnationally. It is a visceral argument for noble pursuits.

Lucio later confirms Isabella's seemingly unconscious rhetorical influence when he attempts to compel her to intercede for her brother's life: "When they [maidens] weep and kneel, / All their petitions are as freely theirs / As they themselves would owe them."[20] Maidens, of course referring to chaste virgins, who, when pleading through a posture of lamentation are often granted their petition. Or, at least, Lucio envisages that this is indeed a depiction of the day, and that Isabella is best positioned as Claudio's advocate given her status as a maiden. Indeed, if chastity is Isabella's power, the abrogation of chastity is her calamity as Baines further accentuates with the following: "Isabella's power, place, and value in society are so determined by her chastity that its forfeiture would constitute for her a form of social and psychological suicide."[21]

When Isabella first meets Angelo and thus begins her intercession, she gradually weakens his will for blood. Isabella employs the Christological argument that seems to send Angelo on a psychological journey and creates potential for acquiescing to her request. The Christological arguments are further extrapolated with Isabella's words as follows: "Go to

19. Shakespeare, *Measure for Measure*, 1.2.180–83.
20. Shakespeare, *Measure for Measure*, 1.4.89–91.
21. Baines, "Assaying the Power of Chastity," 288.

your bosom, / Knock there, and ask your heart what it doth know / That's like my brother's fault. If it confess / A natural guiltiness such as is his, / Let it not sound a thought upon your tongue / Against my brother's life."[22]

We might instantaneously recall Christ's "judgment," or rather acquittal, of the woman caught in adultery. Those thirsty for judgment were also thirsty for her death, longing for it in the name of justice. Or, more precisely, as Jesus knew very well, they longed for his blood and used the situation with the adulterous woman as a subterfuge for their true longing. And yet, Jesus, after mysteriously writing in the sand, so majestically handles the tension of condemnation not only with his silence but by turning the tables of the argument. In essence, he reveals the evil and tyranny of their own hearts and the wicked content therein that invokes a begrudged mercy (see John 8:1–11).

In a similar manner, Isabella invokes Angelo to peer into his own soul to consider whether he would likewise fall prey to sin's impulse when perhaps, in a vulnerable moment, his resolve is theretofore embittered. If Angelo has ever trespassed in similar fashion, even if not by exact disposition, mercy may indeed exude where harsh rigidity had thrived. In emulating the rhetoric of Christ, Isabella strikes a chord with Angelo and it is here where he speaks thus within himself: "She speaks, and 'tis such sense / That my sense breeds with it."[23] Whether by virtue of her chastity or prowess of rhetoric or whether by mere truth, Angelo's heart is being swayed by Isabella's plea for mercy and audacity to act as a lens for Angelo's own introspection of sinful accreditation.

Angelo himself points to virtue as the instrument of subjugation. For in Isabella's virtue, he feels caught under its authority, not as one who relinquishes his governance but one who has unwittingly loved her and by this love has lost his wits to resist her petition. And one of course could question whether it be love or lust, as Angelo does qualify his current dilemma as a temptation: "Never could the strumpet / With all her double vigor, art and nature, / Once stir my temper, but this virtuous maid / Subdues me quite."[24]

Angelo juxtaposes the strumpet with virtuous Isabella and precisely finds his conjuring of affection to be tied to Isabella's character. Her vociferous prayers for him, that he would be safe, that he would be honored, that heaven would smile upon him, are the gifts she offers in exchange for

---

22. Shakespeare, *Measure for Measure*, 2.2.166–71.
23. Shakespeare, *Measure for Measure*, 2.2.172–73.
24. Shakespeare, *Measure for Measure*, 2.2.220–23.

her brother's life. Isabella's virtue stands as a chalice of authority, subduing the strongest of governors, perhaps a Shakespearean allusion once more to the power of chastity. And moreover, the power is not wielded malevolently, but rather quite as an effort to liberate from death.

As Angelo and Isabella engage in a lexical duel, Isabella will not be outdone. She equates her chastity to her soteriology. If she were to sexually transgress, she reaps eternal death. She goes on to assert, "And 'twere the cheaper way. / Better it were a brother died at once / Than that a sister, by redeeming him, / Should die forever."[25] Isabella's alignment of her salvation with her chastity is a powerful argument which seemingly obliterates Angelo's argument that the transgression would be an act of charity. Ironically, Angelo's request for sexual impropriety is the very etiology of her brother's pending execution. Angelo displays a striking disregard for the law he has heretofore sworn to execute. He exits the scene with a rather calamitous confession, "Say what you can, my false o'erweighs your true."[26] It is the feigned power of political reputation on which he relies, no matter his corrupt motives.

Isabella, just prior to exiting scene four, contemplates her dilemma with an immense resolve, illustrating a determined faith in the necessity of chastity. Her adherence to purity is a spiritual commission that she cannot abrogate to the expelling of her soul. I do wonder if our contemporary society would as much as hint at the honor of a chastity that Isabella so cherishes. She does so to the extent of preserving it against her brother's mortality. She aptly sums up her fidelity with the following: "Then, Isabel, live chaste, and, brother, die. / More than our brother is our chastity."[27]

I heartily disagree with Baines who claims the following for Isabella: "Her language reveals a psychic construct that does not allow for a distinction between her body and her soul."[28] Rather, she does distinguish her body from soul as she is willing to part from her body. This parting would be sweet if it redeemed her brother's life. She is quite sure that her eternity would be secured if only this transaction were possible, for in it is an act of immeasurable love (see John 15:13). Therefore, Isabella can forfeit her body, but not her soul. She aligns the transgression of sexual impropriety with violation of her sacred vows to God. This poor use of

---

25. Shakespeare, *Measure for Measure*, 2.4.113–16.
26. Shakespeare, *Measure for Measure*, 2.4.184.
27. Shakespeare, *Measure for Measure*, 2.4.198–99.
28. Baines, "Assaying the Power of Chastity," 289.

her body jeopardizes her fidelity. For Isabella, the choice for her body is ignominy or nobility. The body is simply a vehicle for epistemology. Isabella models a kind of perseverance that is often missing in our hedonistic society, which refuses to envisage the body and the accompanying sexual appetites as conducting noble pursuits.

Shakespeare's thematic aperture returns with the Duke's remark, "Angelo had never the purpose to corrupt her; / only he hath made an assay of her virtue."[29] Is this not what our current dilemma conveys? Not only is there a constant assay of virtue, but perhaps worse is the sickness, for virtue is scorned in the mores of our schools and the conduct of Hollywood media models. There seems to always be an Angelo to assay the fortitude of virtue. Sexual propriety is no more, and the disastrous results have been a hearty embrace of sexual confusion and expression to the unraveling of our peaceful estate.

It should be noted that although Isabella is adamant about her chastity, she is willing to scheme with the friar (the disguised duke) to expose Angelo's incontinence vis-à-vis the use of his disaffected fiancée Mariana (see act 3, scene 1). We must therefore ask if this act does taint Isabella's virtue as she agrees to deceive Angelo to save her brother. We will see how Shakespeare handles this subtle assault on Isabella's virtue, and perhaps he does not have to as he may not envision this scheme as morally problematic but rather a device to expose the corrupt power of Angelo's proposal so that he may be "scaled."[30]

The scheme is indeed rationalized as proper conduct as Mariana was formerly betrothed to Angelo and wronged merely because her dowry perished with her brother at sea. Angelo therefore called off the wedding and scorned her affection. Let us hear the duke's moral reasoning: "Nor, gentle daughter, fear you not at all. / He is your husband on a precontract. / To bring you thus together 'tis no sin."[31] In essence, Mariana will consummate the broken contract with Angelo by deception. She is a proxy for Isabella. There is hope of both exposing Angelo as a villain and enforcing his own pledge to Mariana. Moreover, the scheme envisions the liberation of Claudio from the transgression that Angelo himself would be guilty of. It is an elaborate scheme indeed. The question remains, is it just a scheme? As a reader, there is some moral protestation, and yet Shakespeare does not shy from this kind of moral ambiguity.

29. Shakespeare, *Measure for Measure*, 3.1.182–83.
30. Shakespeare, *Measure for Measure*, 3.1.282.
31. Shakespeare, *Measure for Measure*, 4.1.78–80.

Once the duke reveals himself as the disguised friar, he sits as arbitrator and judge of the offenses committed by Angelo. The duke reckons Angelo to have committed two crimes: "Being criminal in double violation / Of sacred chastity and of promise-breach."[32] Although he commands marriage between Angelo and Mariana to remedy the latter, he adjudicates death as a "measure still for / measure."[33] Angelo's death is a penalty for Claudio's death, as of yet still conceived by the present company. Claudio as alive has yet to be revealed. It is the crime of ignoble violation of chastity that relates to our contemplative effort to reveal that this is a crime against body, society, soul, and legitimacy. We attach so little weight to this crime today, it is no wonder that we may be confounded as to the calamity we reap in the fragmentation of the family. The family, which, no less, is the fundamental unit of any society, has been tattered and torn by sexual impropriety and betrayal. Our wholesome good depends on the bonds of matrimony and this bond is strengthened by sexual fidelity. The chasteness of both parties leans into the strength of the marital bond and proceeds with a family-honoring fortitude as a virtue. Could it be, if chastity once again became a virtue, the spark of inviolable security would spread as a wildfire to consume the vice of unfettered lust? And perhaps, if recovered, we might also enjoy a more peaceable disposition, which we have currently forsaken.

The end of our story is first, justice; measure is forthwith exchanged for like measure. Angelo is exposed and convicted for the same measure that incarcerated Claudio. Angelo consummates his marriage to Mariana and Claudio is released to enjoy his marriage to Juliet. Second, Shakespeare concludes with the virtue of chastity and the assay of its power. This virtue draws the admiration of the duke so much so that he offers Isabel his heart and hand to be wedded. We have no words from Isabella in this last scene. Perhaps no more words are necessary. Her chastity speaks for itself. Her vow to God was kept in good faith and her reward is a marriage to a man who not only loves her but was also willing to save and pardon her brother. This has the appearance of restored life, and life restored is the fruit of chastity. Society indeed can reap the same benefit if chastity once again finds its place in the hearts of men and women.

In reading Shakespeare, an obvious question also emerges in the mind of the modern reader: Can chastity be assayed? Shakespeare

---

32. Shakespeare, *Measure for Measure*, 5.1.460–61.
33. Shakespeare, *Measure for Measure*, 5.1.467–68.

certainly affirms this notion in his play, and the result is life, joy, relational stability, and a peaceful state. One may conclude that it was truth and justice that restored such harmony with the duke and served as the catalyst for such action. And one would not be wrong, but one could also argue that it was Isabella's fidelity and chastity that inspired the duke to take such action. It is yet a potent illustration for a society to embrace chastity, not as a punitive enforcement but as a virtue worth pursuing out of affection for our Lord and for our neighbor. Pastors set churches in order by addressing with great affection the noble pursuit of chastity with each burgeoning generation. By doing so, families enjoy greater emotional stability, which in turn translates to churches who enjoy greater stability.

HOUSEKEEPING

When did housekeeping become an inferior call in our society? Was it a result of the feminist movement? Perhaps a repercussion of this movement indirectly has been to denigrate the traditional role of a woman who keeps her house as an archetype of oppression. What was once an expression of joy is now defined as one of bondage. To be liberated, women must also be liberated from housekeeping. And it is not to say that men also do not contribute to the glory of housekeeping, but that it is specifically addressed by Paul as an advantageous aspect of the Haustafel, a benefit conveyed by the young woman not only to her family, but to the church as a model (Titus 2:5). However, it seems to me that the church has implicitly adopted the cultural milieu where housekeeping is inferior to whatever else captures the attention of the church. Whether it be preaching, travelling, singing, or leadership, the role of housekeeping is lost in these implicitly elevated roles as determined by contemporary church culture. No wonder women find themselves exhausted under the weight of too many expectations. And no wonder the church continues to suffer loss as it promulgates an unreachable height for young women.

Imagine if we once again captured the glory and wonder of housekeeping in the church? Today, it would certainly be countercultural. What if we heard sermons about the theology of the home, theology of housekeeping, and finding the sacred in everyday tasks at home? By asking these rhetorical questions, I am attempting to contend that pastors are to do just that. We often think of setting a church in order by

SETTING IN ORDER: THE YOUNG WOMEN AND THE HAUSTAFEL

creating administrative structures and programs, and this is partly true. However, pastors often neglect the Haustafel in setting a church in order. The Haustafel is central to setting a church in order. One only needs to read the many Haustafel passages in Paul's Epistles to be awakened to the beauty of family and therein housekeeping.

In Jewish customs, housekeeping or οἰκουργούς was the honor of the matron of the home, who was accustomed to grinding flour, baking, laundering, cooking, nursing children, making beds, spinning wool, and hospitality toward guests.[34] This was both the matron's sacred duty and joy! And yet, as I write this, it seems like a foreign language in the culture we have molded. And it is hard to escape the notion that this image of the modern woman has largely influenced the church culture.

Carrie Gress and Noelle Mering have taken up the courageous task of reifying the sacredness of housekeeping to inspire yet another generation of women to God's work in the everyday. They begin with door of the home, citing John 10:9 and John 14:1–2 as premises of consideration for every domestic tranquility.[35] For example, Jesus as the door to heaven encapsulates a home metaphor for heaven as well (see John 10:9). Jesus preparing a place for us conjures the image of a groom preparing a home for his bride (see John 14:1–2). The door is the first exposure to any home and the initial approach to housekeeping. It is a metaphor of reception, a symbol of the heart. It is either open or closed and begins the journey of housekeeping.

Gress and Mering continue the emphasis on the door of the home by reminding us of the Epiphany Blessing, a centuries-old tradition originating in Europe.[36] The Epiphany Blessing is the marking of the upper door post of the home with chalk with the following inscription: 20+C+M+B+23. The numbers indicate the current year as bookends to the three letters. The letters indicate the following: *Christus mansionem benedicat* (Christ, bless our home).[37]

Imagine if every year at Epiphany, we revive this simple and yet profound tradition for every family to gather around the door, update the invocation upon the door post and pray for God's blessing. This inculcates in the child the notion that the home is sacred ground and is also our sanctuary where we live, eat, pray, work, and relate.

---

34. See Rogers and Rogers, *New Linguistic and Exegetical Key*, 510.
35. Gress and Mering, *Theology of Home*, 12.
36. Gress and Mering, *Theology of Home*, 14.
37. Gress and Mering, *Theology of Home*, 14.

Even so, O Lord, bless my home so that I envision its import in the discipleship of my children and reception of guests for the glory of God! If we think about it, we may engage in prayer more at home than we would ever do at church. And if this is the case, we reify the entrance into the interior castle where Teresa of Ávila has demonstrated that the "gate by which to enter this castle is prayer and meditation."[38] And as Ávila means to assert that prayer is the entrance into one's soul, then our homes can become the context where this soul work can take place.

Gress and Mering also envision a home to be a bastion of remembrance as a cosymbolic model to the church.[39] I would argue that it is the feasts we enjoy in our home and in which we invite others to dine that serve as a remembrance and as a foreshadow of things to come. And, when we include the Eucharist, it is indeed the remembrance of Christ's sacrifice and the foretaste of the marriage supper of the Lamb. The beauty of housekeeping includes meal preparation but can be seen as much more than a daily tedium. It has potential to create context for theophany as we remember Christ around the table.

Gress and Mering have invoked the Benedictine order when encapsulating housekeeping as a means for our sanctification baptized in prayer.[40] The Benedictine motto *Ora et labora* is translated as "order and prayer" by them, and has been translated as "work and prayer" by Geoffrey Wainright. For Gress and Mering, the daily laundry, sweeping of floors, making of the bed, removal of clutter, and every other chore in the household is a movement toward order.

The ordering of the home, like the Benedictine order, preserves a legacy for subsequent generations. Where the Benedictines are often attributed for saving Western civilization through conserving the great works, mothers and fathers can preserve a system of values, daily orchestrated to provide a legacy of ontology for their children and even their guests. Daily chores, prayerful order, and structure for the family are therefore translated as the way one may steward the world.

Wainright, in writing about the Wesleyan movement, affirms this notion of *ora et labora* with the following: "Prayer is our communion with God. Work is our stewardship of the earthly creation on God's behalf."[41] He also augments the phrase with the Wesleyan soteriological framework

---

38. Teresa of Ávila, *Interior Castle*, 278.
39. Gress and Mering, *Theology of Home*, 25–42.
40. Gress and Mering, *Theology of Home*, 118.
41. Wainright, "Ora et Labora," 97.

that all holiness is social holiness. In this way, he adds Dr. A. Watelet's assertion that the Benedictine order is only an order in the context of community. Therefore, to *ora et labora*, Watelet adds *in communione fraterna*.[42] And not only community as social acquaintance, but community as fraternal relating. We work and pray, setting our environment in order in the context of family relationships. We relate to one another as brother, as sister, as mother, as father, as grandmother, and grandfather, and so on.

St. Isidore of Seville, opining on Ps 28, integrates *ora et labora* in the following manner: "To pray without working is to lift up one's heart without lifting up one's hands; to work without praying is to lift up one's hands without lifting up one's heart; therefore it is necessary both to pray and to work."[43] John Wesley envisages prayerful work as a fulfillment of the commission to take dominion over the earth in the renewal of the imago Dei.[44]

Charles Wesley captures the copenetration of work and prayer in hymnody, a fusion of the "euchological and the ethical: prayer and work are subsumed in a single doxology."[45]

> Forth in thy name, Lord, I go,
> My daily labour to pursue,
> Thee, only thee, resolved to know
> In all I think, or speak, or do.
>
> The task thy wisdom hath assigned
> Oh, let me cheerfully fulfil,
> In all my works thy presence find,
> And prove thy acceptable will.
>
> Thee may I set at my right hand,
> Whose eyes my inmost substance see,
> And labour on at thy command,
> And offer all my works to thee.
>
> Give me to bear thy easy yoke,
> And every moment watch and pray,
> And still to things eternal look,
> And hasten to thy glorious day:

---

42. Wainwright, "Ora et Labora," 97.
43. Isidore of Seville, *Sententiae* 3.7.18.
44. Wainwright, "Ora et Labora," 97.
45. Wainwright, "Ora et Labora," 103.

> For thee delightfully employ
> Whate'er thy bounteous grace hath given,
> And run my course with even joy,
> And closely walk with thee to heaven.[46]

It was the Carthusians who set out to provide statutes for those working for God with a kind of trivium in the following: *Nunc lege, nunc ora, nunc cum fervore labora*, which can be translated as "Now read, now pray, now work hard."[47] And work can be joy, if we let it. Certainly it is not always joy, and there are days that we find labor as sorrow in a fallen world. The little fruit can be discouraging, and yet even the little fruit, when bathed in prayer, becomes the seedbed for determined joy. The housekeeping is transformed into hallowed ground as prayer invokes the divine in the washing of dishes.

Living can be praying. We can substantiate prayer as a lifestyle when mowing the lawn, caring for animals, planting a garden, picking up toys, and vacuuming the house. Domestic duties have unfortunately been overlooked in our world of media frenzy and sensationalism. We forget that to live simply is to find God amid everyday routines. The smoke and mirrors, lights and media, the production, these are not the only means of divine encounter, although we tend to craft our ecclesiology this way. Perhaps the Benedictine rule reminds us that God meets us with the pots and pans.

Gress and Mering posit what is likely their most confrontational chapter when addressing the work-life balance of the home. More than an address to the matron of the home, the message seems to find its audience in the men or fathers of the home, with whom I felt a soulful sting that I will reflect on after citing their content.

First, Gress and Mering assert that "if we cannot find Christ in our work where we are now, we will have a hard time finding him anywhere else."[48] At once I am confronted with my own imaginings, my own pie-in-the-sky dreams and ambitions that may not always include the elevation of home. I look inward and examine my own dissatisfaction with employment. Ironically, what I do now was once an imagination. But when reality does not encompass the fantasy, the wish dream, as Bonhoeffer puts it, this creates an ache in the soul that may never be satisfied.

---

46. Wesley, "Forth in Thy Name, O Lord, I Go."
47. Wainwright, "Ora et Labora," 104.
48. Gress and Mering, *Theology of Home*, 161.

> Every human wish dream that is injected into the Christian community is a hindrance to genuine community and must be banished if genuine community is to survive. He who loves his dream of a community more than the Christian community itself becomes a destroyer of the latter, even though his personal intentions may be ever so honest and earnest and sacrificial.[49]

I suppose this could also be said of community in the home. Our wish dreams can sometimes be mandated, and when we mandate our dreams upon our family without gratitude for what we already have, the result can be no community at all. Bonhoeffer continues to assert that this dreamer also has the potential to become an accuser: "He becomes first, an accuser of his brethren, then an accuser of God, and finally the despairing accuser of himself."[50]

I must confess that I am a dreamer. I am restless in my attempts to find Christ in my work as a physician. I often peruse job posts of churches needing pastors and although I dream of applying, I do not, as my dream is not the unifying dream of my family. My wife has found solace and, I would argue, Christ in our home, the schooling of our children, and homesteading. I, on the other hand, continue to look for Christ. My wife asks how I am unable to see Christ right in front of me. It is because I look for him solely in pastoring. My wife asks if that (finding Christ) is the only reason I seek pastoral ministry. A provoking question that I have put to reason and prayer.

Do I seek it for any other reason than love of God and neighbor? And, to echo Gress and Mering above, would I find Christ there if I am unable to find him now in my work as a physician? In the end, I become the "despairing accuser" of myself. For in not achieving this dream, I cognitively frame this as failure and the temptation is to loathe myself. It remains difficult for me to fathom that God may be deconstructing this dream in exchange for sincere and authentic community, beginning in my home.

And perhaps mothers at home, giving themselves to the domestic sacred call of housekeeping, may also sense the burden of a culture that continually denigrates such a call. Perhaps the church, unwittingly, has created a culture where housekeeping is an expectation but beneath the glamor of some other grandiose vision for the wife and mother. Have

---

49. Bonhoeffer, *Life Together*, 27.
50. Bonhoeffer, *Life Together*, 28.

we created unnecessary burdens that remain impossible for the wife and mother to carry?

Moreover, although Paul's exhortation is for older women to instruct younger women in housekeeping, does this abrogate men from any role at all? Gress and Mering acknowledge that women experience a "more palpable instinct," but also incorporate men in an emotional polemic that orders home as center of societal stability. However, if the home becomes a "burden getting in the way of his higher purpose; that is his career," then "the mother's mission is trivialized." The housekeeping or work of home is no longer "their common life's work but merely her burden to endure in service of a higher mission that is his alone,"[51] the result being a dissolution of united purpose. The domestic duties become "menial and heavy, and merely menial and heavy work will quickly feel suffocating and oppressive.... Resentment calcifies like a tumor as husband and wife become competitors rather than allies."[52]

My wife certainly envisions her home as the primary call and mission from God. Her creating a conducive environment for nurture and love is missionary work. The church is often a threat to this mission as it can compete with fostering home life in this way either through calling away from home through copious activities or emotionally defragmenting the family from the present moment.

When I look for pastoral opportunities, it seems as if I look for threats to the family. Thus, our vision for oneness looks very different and can be posited as competitive visions each with a desired goal of oneness but ironically causing divisiveness. On the one hand, I desire that we both experience oneness in pastoring a church together, but on the other hand she actualizes our oneness in keeping our home and raising our children. There are families who can integrate the two well; however, there may be others, and perhaps my family is one, where the integration is just beyond reach. Perhaps, if I engaged more fully in the work of the home, she would feel more secure in considering other missions. For pastors who are seeking to set the church in order, we must invest in setting our homes in order, and what better way to start than to love our wives as Christ loves the church (Eph 5:25)?

---

51. Gress and Mering, *Theology of Home*, 169.
52. Gress and Mering, *Theology of Home*, 170.

SETTING IN ORDER: THE YOUNG WOMEN AND THE HAUSTAFEL

Thus, rather than diminishing the role of home, mothers and fathers can envision the home as creating the future culture for society. It was Archbishop Fulton Sheen who gave the following remarks:

> Culture derives from woman—for had she not taught her children to talk, the great spiritual values of the world would not have passed from generation to generation. After nourishing the substance of the body to which she gave birth, she then nourished the child with the substance of her mind. As guardian of the values of the spirit, as protectress of the morality of the young, she preserves culture, which deals with the purposes and ends, while man upholds civilization, which deals only with means.[53]

One may then ask how does housekeeping contribute to societal formation? The home is the one and hopeful safe laboratory where discipline and order are learned. It is the one and hopeful peaceful laboratory for spiritual formation, habits, relational translation, and the development of a moral compass. Housekeeping communicates that the home is important, that unseen tasks are seen by God, that identity is relational, that family is honored, and that careers are meant to uphold and nourish the home, not to find ways out of home. Contrary to our postmodern myth, the home is not a competitive antagonist to our careers, but the apex of what our careers are meant to establish. The compensation for housekeeping is the relational capital of shalom.

SUBMISSION

The apostle Paul exhorts that a young woman is to be good (ἀγαθός, agath-os), as in wholesome (Titus 2:5). She is to be benevolent in benefiting others. She is to be profitable, as in seeking the welfare of her family (see Prov 31:13–19).[54] Afterward, we find what has become one of the more controversial paraenetic materials in Paul, the clauses for wives to submit to their husbands. This polemic is also found in the Petrine Haustafel where an allusion is made to Sarah honoring her husband by calling him lord. So we find, both in Paul and Peter, a domestic duty for wives to submit to their husbands.

---

53. Quoted in Gress and Mering, *Theology of Home*, 174.
54. See Zodhiates and Baker, *Hebrew-Greek Key Word*, 1680.

Setting in Order

Now it should be noted that an entire monograph could be dedicated to this duty of wives to their husbands. I have no room for such dedication and thus will only mention a few brief thoughts for reflection. My aim is to underscore that domestic dynamics and households are critical to setting in order the church. Without a household, ordered in right affections, it is unlikely that we will find a church with the same.

Peter's Haustafel is interesting as it connects certain attributes that may be correlative for wives to subsume the humility of submission. For example, chaste conversation, a pure word, a narrative of integrity and holiness, all have the potential to foster a nonbelieving husband's salvation (1 Pet 3:2). Rather than adorning oneself with exotic apparel, the donning of a meek and quiet spirit is the dress of an immaculate measure, sustaining a wise woman for ages and contributing, perhaps in part, to the notion of submission (1 Pet 3:4).

And then we have the allusion to Sarah as a exemplar or prima facie of submission (1 Pet 3:6). Peter cites Gen 18:12 where Sarah incredulously laughs at the notion of giving birth late in age and refers to her husband as "lord." Peter uses the term κύριος (koo'-ree-os), which intimates belonging. That is, Sarah belongs to another who possesses authority to decide her destiny. Moreover, κύριος has been used in New Testament thought to convey ownership and as such, one who can possess or dispossess. In reference to princes or chief rulers of a sovereign state, the term is used to convey honor and reverence and often uttered by a servant toward his or her master. The term is used to describe Christ, the Messiah, in the New Testament Greek cognates as well.[55] This is the same term found in the Septuagint of Gen 18:12, from which Peter draws his reference.

The Hebrew of Gen 18:12 uses the term *adon* to indicate proprietor, master, and lord. The Ugaritic and Akkadian cognates convey further nuance when terms such as lord, father, and mighty are used in translation. It was a term used to describe Abraham in our example above, Pharaoh (Gen 40:1), Joseph (Gen 42:10), Boaz by Ruth (Ruth 2:13), and Eli by Hannah (1 Sam 1:15). It is found to also describe God no less than 439 times in the Old Testament.[56] The dynamism between lord and Lord is one that may have contributed to a culture of patrilineage but without necessarily excluding the source and power of matriarchy.

---

55. Online Greek Bible, "1 Peter 3:6."
56. Zodhiates and Baker, *Hebrew-Greek Key Word*, 1594.

Indeed, Sarah is revered as she is considered "together with Rebekah, Leah, and Rachel . . . to be one of the four mothers of the chosen people."[57] She is also celebrated by the author of Hebrews as having conceived *pistei*, "in faith" (Heb 11:11). I would like to convey that submission is innately nuanced and expressed in relational dynamics that are not always intuitive. Indeed, the principle can be outright baffling as we will soon see with Abraham and Sarah's relationship.

If Peter so attaches a reward to women who model themselves after Sarah, it is worth explicating further how Sarah herself interacted with Abraham. The reward for women is that they become daughters of Sarah (1 Pet 3:6). But as we may soon discover, Sarah's example of submission is hardly monolithic, nor does it conform to what may be a traditional understanding of submission. Struggle as we may, the domestic codes from Paul and Peter include this notion of submission, but I find Peter's allusion to Sarah an interesting and perhaps thoroughly Jewish understanding of what is meant by submission. I do believe there may be irony in the discussion to follow. We may find that submission is not always the subordination that becomes the cliché of Christian culture, but a type of reverence and dyadic interplay that is contextually complex. And so, let us begin.

SARAH AND SUBMISSION

We find silence in our first example of Sarai and Abram (Gen 12:1–9). God calls Abram to leave his country for another and implicitly we understand Sarai to submit to her husband's call. Second, we find another implicit act of submission despite the possibility of sexual devastation. Abram entreats Sarai to cooperate with a deception for fear that Pharoah would murder him to attain Sarai as wife (Gen 12:10–20). Again, we hear nothing from Sarai but obedience is implied. She is taken into Pharoah's household presumably as a wife or concubine. Abram even benefits from the transaction, having received a multitude of cattle and slaves (Gen 12:16).

We know that God is angry with Abram's deception but ironically plagues Pharoah's house. Pharoah is apparently unaware of the etiology of God's wrath. However, he becomes acutely aware, whether intuitively or through some implicit disclosure, that Abram's wife Sarai is the source of God's wrath. Pharoah admonishes Abram and sends them both away.

---

57. Hillyer, *1 and 2 Peter, Jude*, 96.

Setting in Order

We arrive at a sense that Sarai's sexual fidelity was preserved as Pharoah mentions only the possibility of having taken her as a wife (Gen 12:19). Now, this pericope conjures up the ethical issues of a woman who is exposed to sexually ignoble or abusive acts at the hands of her husband. It is quite clear from this pericope that God censures such transgressions, and though we have no room here to extrapolate, Sarai's possibility of sexual ruin should not be envisaged as a polemic for wives to remain in a sexually or physically abusive relationship. Their safety is paramount. No marital work to repair the relationship can occur within the confines of abuse. One can only engage in emotional work when in a consistently safe environment.

Thus, we find two examples of Sarai's silence and implicit submission to Abram wherein we can draw certain comparisons to Peter's audience, the first-century church. Indeed, Michal Beth Dinkler does just that with the following:

> Just as Sarah entered dangerous situations by being taken as a ruler's wife, so Christian women entered potentially dangerous situations by converting without their husbands' consent. Just as Sarah discerned when to obey Abraham and when to speak her mind, so wives of unbelievers should be judicious about when to obey their husbands.[58]

Peter addresses wives married to unbelieving husbands so that by their chaste conduct they may win them to the faith (1 Pet 3:1). Although Peter does not himself draw this analogy, Dinkler expands Peter's analogy as above to include the precarious position Sarai was placed in within Pharoah's house to save her husband from possible harm. The Christian wife converts courageously, knowing she is in a foreign house, a house that remains unconverted as the paterfamilias has yet to consent to the faith. The Christian wife is silent, but her character and deeds speak loudly. Her conversation speaks of riches of heaven, the fruit of the Spirit, the character of God and thus becomes an overwhelming witness of God's goodness, grace, and mercy (1 Pet 3:1).

I resonate with the analogy Dinkler draws here, even if only implicit in Peter's writings. For in it we find that courage and submission are interwoven. On one hand, the Christian wife is somewhat subversive, for her conversion is without consent and could possibly draw the ire of her husband who remains pagan. On the other hand, she does not

---

58. Dinkler, "Sarah's Submission," 11.

protest against or rile her husband but quietly wins him over via holiness of conduct. She submits to loving him in his spiritual naïveté.

Now Dinkler addresses the culturally contested term ὑπακούω (hoop-ak-oo'-o), which is the verb to submit, attend to, or listen to. She links this verb with other uses in Peter as a form of synecdoche. That is, Sarai's obedience to Abram is one form of obedience in a series of other forms of submission that characterize the Christian life. For example, Peter first calls for ubiquitous submission to all authorities (1 Pet 2:13) with a polemic that we are mere pilgrims of this world. That is, we voluntarily submit to authorities for the sake of the gospel, knowing that we teleologically submit to Christ and await the establishment of his kingdom.[59]

Indeed, Dinkler notes that the grammatical sense of ὑπακούω is typically executed in the active rather than the passive sense inferring a volitional and voluntary submission on the part of the participant.[60] In this regard, wives voluntarily submit to their husband in contrast to coercion or brow beating. Moreover, Dinkler notes that the notion of submission is initially traced to 1 Pet 2:13 like Paul's Haustafel in Ephesians that begins with Eph 5:21—an injunction that we all submit to one another in the fear of God. Thus, the Christian way is one of submission, teleologically to Christ, practically manifested by our submission to one another. Indeed, our submission is characterized by our love. Love compels that we seek the benefit of the other. The Haustafel lines of authority are not to be oppressive but organic and divine ways of relating to one another with love, submission, respect, and honor. In such manner, we typify the kingdom of heaven and provide a polemic against the kingdoms of this age.

After a painful period of barrenness, Sarai requests that children be born to her through her servant Hagar (Gen 16:2). We find an ironic turning of the tables from the initial pieces we have just treated. Here, Abram attends to Sarai's request. The Hebrew *shama* is used to indicate one hearing with an intention to obey.[61] Now we should note here that submission is contextualized and complex within the marriage dyad. We should also note that Sarai's request is one that has the fruit of pain, division, and eventual exile. Nonetheless, God works his sovereignty within the confines of human misdeeds and blesses Hagar, revealing plans to create a nation from Ishmael. What we discover here is that despite the paterfamilias and patriarchal context of ancient Jewish families, Abram

59. Dinkler, "Sarah's Submission," 12.
60. Dinkler, "Sarah's Submission," 12.
61. Zodhiates and Baker, *Hebrew-Greek Key Word*, 1670.

obeys Sarai. But why? Why do we find such a heterogeneous example in Abram and Sarai? Could it be that submission is contingent on the dynamic of the relational context of the moment? Could it be that love at one time may compel the wife to submit to the husband and at other times for the husband to voluntarily submit to his wife? Perhaps the husband attending to his wife's cry sows the seed of future respect and submission by taking her petitions seriously.

Furthermore, something happens amid Abram and Sarai's sojourning in the covenant: God changes their names. As is often the case with the major Biblical figures, the changing of a name intimates a manifestation of God's covenant or mission with the individual. Moreover, the change illustrates quite tangibly the qualitative transformation, regeneration, or even sanctification of the individual (i.e., Jacob to Israel, Saul to Paul). Their names also stand as a prophetic sign of God's future work. For example, Abram becomes Abraham, or "father of a great multitude" (Gen 17:5). This, ironically, is conveyed at a time when Abraham had but one child in Ishmael. However, God's promises often have a touch of irony that acts as a catalyst for faith.

Second, Sarai becomes Sarah, or "princess" (Gen 17:15). This too indicates that kings will come from her womb (Gen 17:16). These tangible signs of God's covenant are parallel to yet another conspicuous sign of his covenant, for the entire transformation takes place within the context of God's command of circumcision. Circumcision would be a token of God's covenant between Abraham and himself (Gen 17:11). As such, every time a male child is circumcised, it is a corporeal reminder of God's everlasting covenant with Abraham and his people, a marker in the flesh to praise God for his everlasting fidelity (Gen 17:13).

Abraham's response to this transformation is again ironic. He laughs with incredulity. This parallels Sarah's laughter, which later also invokes an admonition from the mysterious visitors (see Gen 17:17 and 18:12). Later we will find that even this laughter is transformed from incredulity to marvel and is the basis for the son of promise, Isaac, whose very name means laughter (Gen 21:6). Indeed, I would like to assert a polemic that God is changing both Abraham and Sarah even in the context of submission or subversion in the narrative with laughter as the central motif manifesting this change. This change is from incredulity to wonder, from disbelief to faith, from despair to joy, from the ordinary to the extraordinary.

SETTING IN ORDER: THE YOUNG WOMEN AND THE HAUSTAFEL

Thus, the name changes indicate an office conferred upon Abraham and Sarah—they have become the patriarch and matriarch of God's covenant people and as such God honors this special consideration as Paul confirms in Rom 9–11. Circumcision also becomes the foreshadow of covenant and transformation as a parallel to Peter's assertion that new humanity has sprung on the scene because of Christ's atoning work on the cross. As Abram became Abraham and Sarai became Sarah, believers become the righteousness of Christ (1 Pet 2:24). We are to emulate the new creation illustrated by God's work with Abraham and Sarah by walking in the righteousness of Christ, the healing of the atonement, and the affectionate adherence to the Bishop of our souls (1 Pet 2:24–25).

Now, I must address the sentiment that Peter attempts to recapitulate the Hellenistic world view of the ideal wife by the utilization of the Abraham-Sarah narrative as a proof text. Van Rensburg, citing Aristotle, rightly asserts that the sociocultural context of Peter's day was likely one where women were denigrated and thought of as little more than the property of their husbands. Aristotle, in *Nicomachean Ethics*, asserts the following:

> But there is a different kind of friendship, which involves superiority of one party over the other, for example, the friendship between father and son, and generally between an older person and a younger and that between a husband and a wife and between any ruler and person ruled.[62]

Similarly, we have Philo and Josephus asserting synonymous claims concerning the Hellenistic view of the husband-wife dyad. Here is Philo in *Hypothetica*: "Wives must be in servitude to their husbands, a servitude not imposed by violent ill treatment but promoting obedience in all things." And here is Josephus in *Against Apion*: "The woman, says the law, is in all things inferior to the man. Let her accordingly be submissive, not for her humiliation, but that she may be directed, for the authority has been given by God to man."[63]

And although it is obvious that the culture in which Peter writes is Hellenistic with an emphasis on patriarchal authority, paterfamilias, and, unfortunately, where the abuse of the wife is legally and culturally legitimized, I do not concur that Peter's intent is to Hellenize the Abraham-Sarah narrative. Perhaps it is naïveté or mere simple trust, but I

---

62. Quoted in Van Rensburg, "Sarah's Submissiveness to Abraham," 254.
63. Quoted in Van Rensburg, "Sarah's Submissiveness to Abraham," 254.

do believe Peter's intent is to convey a marital pattern sanctioned by God and even subversive to the Hellenist culture. For example, it is doubtful that one would find paraenetic material instructing husbands to honor their wives in Hellenistic writings of the day (see 1 Pet 3:7). But this is what we find in Peter and Paul's Haustafel passages. Moreover, just as there is a promise to wives to become the children of Sarah, there is a promise to husbands who indeed honor their wives: "Their prayers will not be hindered" (1 Pet 3:6–7). Imagine answered prayers being contingent on the ways husbands treat their wives. This was likely unheard of in Hellenist contemporary writers of the day, and it seems that Peter means to subvert the abhorrent ways in which wives were treated in this sociocultural context.

I also disagree with Jeremy Punt and, by virtue of his citation, Magda Misset van de Weg, despite the clever use of Latin to assert the Hellenizing of Peter's reference to Sarah. In short, Punt cites Misset van de Weg in the following manner: "The author's hermeneutics of Scripture seems to be predominantly determined by social, political, and ideological concerns and objectives, which *mutatis mutandis*, mediated the actualization of the Abraham-Sarah cycle and resulted in his image of Sarah." Pun summarizes Misset van de Weg's polemic with the following: "In short, women's submissiveness needed to be grounded in sacred tradition."[64]

The Latin *mutatis mutandis* confers a literal rendering of "things being changed that have to be changed." Because of the sociocultural context of Hellenism, the Genesis narrative must take on new nuances to confirm the patriarchal ethos of the times. However, I would argue that the wife's submission to her husband predates Hellenism, and in part is a result of the fall of mankind in the garden (see Gen 3:16). Nonetheless, God can work his beauty in marriages despite the fall and by moving upon the husband to honor his wife and the wife to submit to her husband. Thus, I disagree that things being changed must change merely because culture dictates; quite the contrary, God often calls men and women to countercultural lives, and it appears to me that God is doing just this through the subversive means of husbands honoring their wives in a culture where this runs against the grain.

Moreover, if Peter desired to choose the model Hellenistic wife, Sarah would not be an ideal choice. Her relationship with Abraham is complicated by anecdotes of mutual submission. For example, Sarah

---

64. Punt, "Subverting Sarah in the New Testament," 459–60. See also Misset van de Weg, "Sarah Imagery in I Peter," 111–126.

implored Abraham to cast away Hagar and Ishmael after she conceived that Ishmael was mocking Isaac (Gen 21:8–10). Perhaps Sarah perceived a threat to Isaac, not only in status but also in potential gestures of future aggression. Abraham, grieved, appears to initially protest the idea, but God speaks and instructs Abraham to heed Sarah's counsel (Gen 21:12). God aligns with Sarah's counsel, or perhaps in actuality, Sarah unwittingly and perhaps even quite selfishly stumbles upon God's sovereign plan. For we find that the Ishmael-Isaac relationship will later become an allegory for slavery vs. freedom and law vs. promise (Gal 4:21–31). In many ways, Ishmael's exile foreshadows Christ's atoning work as superior and superseding the law or, rather, our inability to adhere to the law. Christians join in Isaac's status as the promised child when receiving the grace and righteousness of Christ whereas the Jews who remain in their obstinance to claim absolute adherence to the law (a rather futile notion), join Ishmael as the son of the flesh.

Thus, I do not agree that Peter utilized Sarah to ground Hellenism in sacred tradition. There are plenty of other less complicated examples that could have served this purpose. Rather, Peter's choice of Sarah from Gen 18:12, although appearing rather arbitrary, may have been more intentional than what we may initially perceive. For Peter attaches a promise to wives who follow Sarah's example of reverence and submission. Thus, I would argue that promise is central to Peter's choice of Sarah as the matriarch to emulate. Sarah was given a promise, and although she did not navigate the promise without mistakes and misdeeds, God was faithful to keep the promise. Likewise, wives are given the promise to be Sarah's daughters, and although they, too, may not navigate the promise without mistakes, God is faithful to keep such a promise to the heart whose longing is to honor God in their respective marriages.

I would like to argue that heretofore one endeavor of marital relations is to underscore God's promise. Perhaps *underscore* is a mild term; *realization of* God's promise may be more sufficient for the context. I do consider the Abraham-Sarah narrative to have as a center, God's disclosure, the promise of a multitude (in an eschatological sense), and the promise of a son (in an immediate sense). Likewise, I believe that Peter, and in some respects, Paul, emphasizes the Haustafel, and more specifically the relationships between husbands and wives, as a microcosm of Christ's relationship with the church in salvific terms. That is, husbands and wives engage in a perichoretic fashion, the promise of salvation and the eschatological relationship between the church and Christ. The often-complex relationship between Abraham and Sarah envisages a model of contextualized submission that is mutual and contingent upon the sociocultural context they find themselves navigating.

Moreover, the submission of either party (i.e., husband and wife) is not always holy and often appears to be the result of misdeeds if not acts of transgression. It is not always courteous or kind. It is not always honorable. And yet, it is an explicit and tangible illustration of the fidelity of God's sovereign intentions toward humanity as the promise is not jeopardized by human misdeeds. God's disclosure to Abraham as El Shaddai, the One who is Almighty, is a potent reminder that he can consummate the promise without human intervention and with Abraham and Sarah, despite their impatience (Gen 17:1).

Thus, I would like to accentuate the idea of promise. God uses marriage not only to fulfill his promise specifically to the husband and wife, and not only to use the husband-wife dyad to reflect a divine eschatological relationship, but to also bring the individual from the laughter of incredulity to the laughter of wonder and amazement.

LAUGHTER AND MARRIAGE

Now we often discredit Sarah for her incredulous laugh, but we should note that before Sarah's laugh came Abraham's laugh. "Can a child be born to a hundred-year-old man?" (Gen 17:17). This inquiry was posited after Abraham's incredulous laugh even though he "believed the Lord, and he credited it to him as righteousness" (Gen 15:6). On one hand Abraham believed, and yet on the other hand he laughs with disbelief, or perhaps rather a smidgeon of pragmatism. In either case, we are given a reflective lens into human frailty and likely resonate with Abraham's plight as one of human ubiquity. That is, how often have we doubted the promise of God? How often do we need reminders vis-à-vis divine encounter? Thus, we should not forget that Abraham laughs quite before Sarah.

Then, we have the moment that Peter cites in his Epistle, where Sarah laughs in disbelief at the announced promise (see Gen 18:12 and 1 Pet 3:6). Now, it certainly can be asserted that Peter performs a midrash on Gen 18:12, choosing to underscore Sarah's reference of "lord" for Abraham to underscore the notion that wives submit to their husbands. Many may gloss over this detail in the story as the center of Sarah's response is the laugh of incredulity. And although I am choosing not to necessarily emphasize Sarah's deference, though it remains present, I would like to propose that Sarah's metanarrative and several New Testament citations serve as an arc for marital relations in the church, from faith to belief, from barrenness to promise, from skepticism to confidence, from cynicism to certainty. This is evident from the chuckle that masks the pain of loss to authentic laughter that springs from the depth of amazement and wonder. Marriage becomes a potential vehicle for this transformation. Note that Issac's name is both symbolic of this dynamic and proleptic to communal laughter (Gen 21:6).

Everyone who hears the promise will also laugh, but we must understand that this is not a smirk, not a laughter of derision, but rather quite the opposite, it is a laugh of joy and wonder. Please see table 5 below, which summarizes what I intend to encapsulate concerning the Abraham-Sarah narrative, noting the parallels between 1 Peter and Genesis. One will note in the table that the parallels begin with the notion that we are strangers in this world who act as an impetus for other-worldly kinds of relationships. That is, the way husbands and wives relate reflects a heavenly paradigm that often subverts the current cultural ethos. Finally, promise and joyful laughter are the result of this kind of relating done well.

Genesis	1 Peter	Parallels
12:1 Out of your country	2:11 Strangers and pilgrims	Aliens of this world, citizens of heaven
12:15, 16:2, 18:6, 20:13, 21:12 Bidirectional submission	2:17 Honor all men	Mutual submission
17:5,15 Abram to Abraham, Sarai to Sarah	2:24 Dead to sins	New creation, transformation
21:12 Casting out the bondwoman	3:1–2 Winning unbelieving husbands	Evangelistic submission
18:12, 21:6 Laughter	3:6–7 Bidirectional honor	From incredulity to wonder

Table 5. The Genesis-1 Peter Parallels

"Laughter is like the rainbow which originates through a sort of contrast of sunshine with rain,"[65] is one of the opening polemics from Paul Carus as he explicates the philosophical underpinnings of laughter.

65. Carus, "On the Philosophy of Laughing," 250.

He cites Don Quixote and Aristophanes as substantive supportive works to his claim. Don Quixote, the mocked idealist, and Aristophanes, who notes the tragedy of Socrates's death and the destruction of the entire Athenian military—both are couched within the rubric of comedy. To add to Carus's example is the story of Abraham and Sarah, barren for decades only to receive laughter, a rainbow painted against the backdrop of dark clouds. The seriousness of life is not lost but rather contemplated through the medium of laughter.

Horace, writing a political treatise in his *Sermones* rather pithily provides the dictum *"ridentem dicere verum,"*[66] meaning "a man can speak the truth with a smile," intimating that sometimes truth is often powerfully communicated when humor is applied.

It is also notable that the ancients explored the origins of laughter. Cicero, a statesman and orator rightly accentuates the importance of laughter in the delivery of oration. We have a lengthy citation from him citing Caesar:

> But, to come to the third point, it certainly becomes the orator to excite laughter; either because mirth itself attracts favor to him by whom it is raised; or because all admire wit, which is often comprised in a single word, especially in him who replies and sometimes in him who attacks; or because it overthrows the adversary, or hampers him, or makes light of him, or discourages, or refutes him; or because it proves the orator himself to be a man of taste, or learning, or polish; but chiefly because it mitigates and relaxes gravity and severity, and often, by a joke or a laugh, breaks the force of offensive remarks, which cannot easily be overthrown by arguments.[67]

Laughter becomes the rhetorical weapon to mitigate the enemy's advancements. This conjures up the psalmist who writes in Ps 2 that the Lord himself laughs from the heavens at the nations who rage against him. Now certainly this is a scornful laugh, one of derision, and altogether a different laugh derived from motives of warfare or embattlement. However, I would be remiss not to include the philosophical or theological force accompanying laughter. Laughter can disarm one's opponents, entreat an offensive environment, and perhaps provide a medium whereby the offended are thus won over. We must acknowledge different forms of laughter with distinct purposes. There is the laughter

---

66. Quoted in Carus, "On the Philosophy of Laughing," 251.
67. Quoted in Carus, "On the Philosophy of Laughing," 253–54.

of incredulity, the laughter of derision, the laughter of amazement and wonder, and the laughter of dissolution. Please see table 6 below.

Context	Kind of Laughter	Potential
Grief	Laughter of incredulity	Despair
Conflict	Laughter of derision	Overthrow
Promise	Laughter of amazement and wonder	Faith
Offense	Laughter of dissolution	Disarm

Table 6. Theological-Emotive Potentials of Laughter

Now, we should note that this is not an exhaustive list of types of laughter but they should provoke us to think more deeply of our own episodes of laughter. I am presupposing that we, as a culture, do not quite think of laughter in these ways, for it is often spontaneous and physiological. Moreover, it is often reactionary to some substrate, quip, or comment that we digest. But if it is laughter that remains central to Abraham and Sarah, and if their example is one worth emulating in marriage, then should we not also investigate this phenomenon at least to some degree where we find its manifestation in our own marriage? For example, do we laugh together at the enemy as a means of scorn and overthrow? Do we laugh together in amazement and wonder at the promise of God? Do we emit the kind of laughter that dissolves offense when it rears its sinister purposes within the sacred halls of our hearts? Do we allow our laughter to transform us from incredulity to faith? Do we create an environment where our spouses participate in the transformation of our laughter? If a couple is not laughing together, perhaps one should ask why and then endeavor to restore the right kinds of laughter that precipitate wonder, amazement, and joy (I would also include the derisive laughter directed toward Satan).

Schopenhaur provides us with one definition of laughter, but we must note that he attempts to center his definition on the intuition of the ridiculous. That is, he limits the laughter to one particular zeitgeist and in so doing offers a rather narrow definition likely not generalizable to all forms of laughter. Indeed, we likely need several definitions to investigate the many etiologies of laughter. Nonetheless, his definition hits home concerning Abraham and Sarah's initial laughter of incredulity. Here is Schopenhaur's definition: "Laughing arises from a suddenly conceived incongruence between some real object and its idea, and that it is nothing but the expression of this incongruence."[68]

Abraham and Sarah's initial laugh is an expression of incongruence. God provides a metaphysical idea that seems to antagonize their lived reality. And not only that, Abraham and Sarah have an experience wherein the idea of conceiving at their age appears at face value quite a ridiculous idea altogether. Nonetheless, God introduces such a ridiculous idea to once again disclose to Abraham that natural laws or ways of things can be altered by his divine prompting, no matter how ridiculous it may seem. The idea here is that once God promises, nothing shall alter this promise, and God can complete the promise with the bending of nature. So, the incongruence of God's words with reality prompt a rather spontaneous and incredulous laugh.

Sarah's laugh, or *biqirbah* in Hebrew, seems to imply that it is an inward phenomenon. That is, her laugh is not a public and boisterous display where one surrenders to the sublimity of the moment. In contrast, this laughter is a mixture of incredulity and even pain. Thus the laugh is private. It is within herself, it is meant to further isolate from the public view given the shame of barrenness.[69] In this manner, there may be private laughter within a marriage. This is laughter that may be the result of bitterness, grief, pain, and unmet expectations, not unlike Sarah's laughter. The fact that God made public what was private is a lesson, I believe, for marriage. God reveals Sarah's private pain or laughter in part as an admonition to Sarah, but perhaps also so that Abraham can commiserate with Sarah's pain and become an agent of consolation and catalyst for faith. Thus, the incredulous laughter, often private, will likely need to be revealed whether in consortium as a couple, in therapy, or perhaps in a liturgical setting. It is in this regard that I would like to assert that the incredulous laughter is one God intends to unveil as a means of admonition, yes, but more so as an endeavor of transformation.

So, the next time that you laugh at the ridiculous, when at once it dawns upon your consciousness that whatever idea has prompted your laughter, and you have judged it incongruent with reality, ask yourself in the moment, Is God intending to transform my laughter by introducing the ridiculous? What is ridiculous to us is not to God. We laugh at what seems like a reflexive response to the ridiculous when perhaps the more

---

68. Quoted in Carus, "On the Philosophy of Laughing," 257.
69. Gift, "Sarah's Laughter as Her Lasting Legacy," 101.

accurate epistemology is that years of disappointment have cultivated the laugh long before it erupted. God knows this, calls it out, and then endeavors to transform the laughter. Our spouse can be the agent God uses for this kind of transformation.

"Laughing is not a matter of intellect but of character. It depends more on our disposition than our thoughts; and as we sometimes betray our feelings despite ourselves, so our laugh may frequently carry us away despite our trying to master and suppress it."[70] Think on this Beloved. Though it is the philosopher Paul Carus who introduces this thought, we must ask if there is resonance with our narrative of Abraham and Sarah. Did the laughter reveal their disposition and did the fulfillment of promise, in quite a miraculous manner, transform this disposition? If it is true that laughter can reveal character, let us pay attention to our laughter the next time we find it erupting quite spontaneously.

Let me share a personal anecdote as an illustration. A young man had an aspiration to one day pastor the largest church in the movement. This was the topic of conversation as I sat with a family and discussed our children. A spontaneous laugh erupted from me with a remark that this was magnanimously ambitious. However, why did the laughter erupt? In all honesty, I was surprised by it. In retrospect, the laughter was one of incredulity and originated from my own pain with church politics. I wonder if the laughter also revealed my character to some degree. A character that refuses to dream like this young man who obviously was dreaming with great joy. Or perhaps my character holds a hint of cynicism as the pain of long being forgotten continues to haunt my imagination. Perhaps my laugh was not necessarily at the young man but at myself, as if to say, The idea that I might pastor again is a ridiculous and ludicrous idea, which prompts a laughter of incredulity at a young man dreaming a dream. It appears that my laughter remains in need of transformation. The promise, whatever it may be for me personally, will consummate at some appointed time deciphered by God in his sovereignty. Will I wait with disbelief or maintain a disposition of merriment?

"The objective conditions that elicit a laugh are any such situation which bodes either the victory or defeat of someone—perhaps of ourselves. An absurdity, or an incongruity, or the contrast of the real and ideal are never in themselves ridiculous; they become ridiculous only if

---

70. Carus, "On the Philosophy of Laughing," 261.

they are somehow instrumental in defeating somebody, in worsting an adversary, or in conquering his cause."[71]

The more iterations from Carus, the more I seem to personally resonate with his epistemology and how it may resonate with Abraham and Sarah's laughter. Ironically, laughter can come from a paradox, either through victory or defeat. And the personal soul is the substrate of this paradox. That is, we may laugh at our own triumph as victor or, we may laugh at our defeat, perhaps scorning our own soul in derision as the laugh comes surreptitiously.

The juxtaposition herein is therefore subjective. The ideal and the real are contrasted and when the internal calculation has been performed, the distinction is so profound, signaling defeat or victory, prompting laughter. I was bested and conquered when a small group with influence secured my ousting as pastor. My family came under the fire of their formidable blows and we evacuated to preserve our emotional health. And yet, my emotional health continues to suffer and many of my laughs today erupt when I am once again confronted with the ideal (i.e., one day I may pastor in a faithful community) juxtaposed with the real (i.e., there is no path to pastoring either personally or vocationally).

And yet, God often calls us to hold to the ideal, the promise, to him over and against the real. I suppose that in so doing, the laughter is changed. The character of the laugh is not so much my suffering one defeat after another in my own mind. For I do rehearse the seeming contrast of the ideal and the real, and in so doing render my own self defeated. Perhaps God calls us higher to the ideal, clinging to his fidelity and not our own past defeat, and thus we surrender to triumph in Christ who then endeavors that we laugh at the enemy of our soul while also enjoying a laughter of sublimity. I find that my full surrender to this is lacking, perhaps because human nature is to nurse a wound and keep it from the Physician who has the antidote.

The good news here is that our Physician is a relentless One, pursuing the abscess, wooing our consent, and making us whole. Our Lord can use our marriages and our laughter as his prescriptions. And so, young women may typify promise through their submission to their husbands. This promise can also be anticipated or consummated by laughter, laughter that is joy and wonder. I also wonder, and I confess perhaps too extensively, if a wife's voluntary submission aids in the transformation of

---

71. Carus, "On the Philosophy of Laughing," 264.

her husband's laughter from incredulity to amazement. But maybe there is this potential and if so, then a young woman and wife has an amazing and uncanny ability to transform her husband's unbelief.

In conclusion, we arrive now at the covenant young women express for the body to hear and witness at the agape feast:

> I covenant to be sexually pure, knowing that this virtue, in part, may act to stabilize families, churches, and all of society. I covenant to keep my home and foster an environment for soul care (Titus 2:5). I covenant to open my home to guests as a ministry of hospitality. As Jesus prepares a home for me, I will prepare a home for others (John 14:1–2). I covenant to set my house in order, creating a context for prayerful labor and sanctification. I covenant to voluntarily limit my freedoms as a means of displaying discretion toward my family (Titus 2:5). I will be present in the moment so as to properly judge between action and inaction. I covenant to give myself to holy love and a pursuit of truth to learn discretion by attending to our moments as a family. I covenant to renounce and refrain from sexual impropriety. I will keep myself pure and undefiled. I await the covenant of love in the form of matrimony (Titus 2:5). I covenant to submit to my husband by discerning when and how to speak (1 Pet 3:1). I covenant to walk in the righteousness of Christ as a new creation, in part by displaying this righteousness by voluntary submission to my husband (1 Pet 2:24). I covenant to honor my husband both privately and publicly and as such, receive the promise of becoming Sarah's daughter (1 Pet 3:6).

Chapter 21

Setting in Order: The Young Men and the Haustafel

Likewise, urge the younger men to be self-controlled in all things, offering yourself as a model of good works and in your teaching offering integrity, gravity, and sound speech that cannot be censured.

Titus 2:6–8

Our final address in the Haustafel pericope is to young men and their covenant behaviors toward the household of God. The first charge is not so dissimilar to the charge given to young women, that of σωφρονεῖν, or temperance. For more discussion on this Greek term, please see the previous chapters for the elder and younger women in the Haustafel. In summary, young men are to voluntarily relinquish certain liberties in the name of discretion for the peace of the family, church, and society. Restraint may aptly sum up the pastoral request that is often impaired by the impulsivity of youth.

But, since we have already explored the notion of *sophrosyne* and temperance—a virtue ubiquitously encouraged to other members in the Haustafel—I would like to extrapolate two Greek terms distinctly charged to young men: ἀφθορίαν and σεμνότητα.

INTEGRITY VS. AVARICE

Integrity, or ἀφθορίαν in the Greek, signifies sincerity and pure character. It is character that refrains from mere lucrative gain or discrimination. It is a character wholly embracing pure doctrine not merely as an intellectual pursuit but as an epistemology, a way of being.[1] It is counsel to young men to resist the vice of avarice, so prominent in every age and the source of so many calamitous events in human history. And of course, Paul is neither discreet nor ambiguous about this vice, as he explains further in his Letter to Timothy that avarice or the love of money is the root of all evil (see 1 Tim 6:10). Indeed, avarice was given notoriety in the person of Judas, who betrayed the Lord for thirty pieces of silver (see Matt 26:15).

Jesus, in a display of ethical zeal, drives greed from the temple in exchange for the healing of the sick (see Matt 21:12–17). And of course, Jesus provides us a parable illustrating the utter calamity of avarice with the often-synonymous vice of prodigality (see the parable of the prodigal son, Luke 15:11–32). Indeed, the parable of the prodigal son is likely the parallel anecdote to Paul's paraenetic material to young men in his Epistle to Titus. The prodigal son, himself the younger brother, not having yet achieved full manhood, acts on his impulses to garner material wealth and likewise his intemperance to waste it all on luxuries. It is no wonder why young men are the audience as it may very well be that this population is vulnerable to the vices of avarice, prodigality, and intemperance.

It was Pope Gregory the Great who also asserted that avarice is the etiology of daughter vices, giving birth to such vices as "treachery, fraud, falsehood, perjury, restlessness, violence, and insensibility to mercy."[2] Avarice is sometimes summed up in the term *pleonexia*, or the desire to have more, an insatiable desire never quenched with acquisition but ensuing without satisfaction.[3] Avarice thus can become one's god, which is why our Lord juxtaposes the worship of wealth against the worship of God (see Matt 6:24) and why he employs the striking metaphor, "It is easier for a camel to go through the eye of a needle than for [the rich] to enter the kingdom of God" (Luke 18:25).

---

1. Rogers and Rogers, *New Linguistic and Exegetical Key*, 510.

2. See Pinsent, "Avarice and Liberality," 158, where he cites Gregory's consequential list of daughter vices from avarice.

3. Pinsent, "Avarice and Liberality," 158.

Setting in Order

It is to the great poet Dante Alighieri that we now turn to explicate the vice of avarice and, in so doing, hope to illustrate further how avarice is entirely antagonistic to integrity. To better comprehend Dante's description of avarice, it may behoove us to envision his circles of hell, encompassed in his writings in the *Inferno*. Dante writes of nine circles that act as degrees to the domain that descends into hell.

We find avarice and prodigality in circle four of the nine lamentable circles of hell. Other texts may define this circle as the hoarders and wasters. Dante is joined by a pagan poet Virgil, who initially resided in circle one, a state of limbo where the virtuous poets of antiquity were placed, quite ignorant of the greater revelation of Christ. Virgil is Dante's guide through the circles of hell and they arrive at circle four where there is an apparent war raging. The avaricious and the prodigals push two meaningless weights together and then separate the weights only to renew their efforts. This is to signify the fruitless efforts of amassing wealth or wasting it on luxuries in life.

The avaricious, while moving the formidable weight toward their enemy, would forever shout, "Why do you waste?" while the other camp, moving their weight, would shout to their adversary, "Why do you hoard?"[4] And so the fruitless bearing of weights and the constant rhetorical shouting persisted in this circle of hell.

Dante asks Virgil the identity of these suffering and implies that either one faction or both may have been the clergy.[5] Virgil confirms this conjecture with the following grievous indictment:

> These tonsured wraiths of greed were priests indeed,
> and popes and cardinals, for it is in these
> the weed of avarice sows it rankest seed.[6]

I suppose there is no human heart that this vice cannot touch. The religious guides were guilty of such excess, wantonness, power, and wealth. Like the Pharisees, Sadducees, and scribes of Jesus's day, wealth and power seemed to consume their very motives. I often wonder if some of these trappings suit my temptations as well. Perhaps it is to young men that this paraenetic material is given, for this form of integrity is instilled early and requires daily practice. Are religious leaders the rankest of members to be tempted with avarice? And if so, is this vice subtly

---

4. Dante, *Inferno*, 7:30.
5. Dante, *Inferno*, 7:39.
6. Dante, *Inferno*, 7:46–48.

leading our churches away from godliness as contentment? Bigger buildings, larger crowds, and bloated budgets appear to be the unspoken vision, perhaps influenced by the avarice that tugs and gnaws at our soul, persisting in the cause to make us stumble.

Avarice compels one to build that which is vain, tearing down all the virtues of a person in exchange for eternal mockery.[7] Such is the language that describes those who hoard and those who waste. No wealth of any stature could cause the futile exchange in this circle of hell from pausing. The weights move on, the souls must labor to set and reset the weights in an endless array of purposelessness. It seems to remind me also of the ponderous chain Marley is encumbered with because of his avarice in Dickens's *A Christmas Carol*. He was to carry the burden in death that he himself forged in life: pursuit of wealth at the expense of human business—charity and forbearance.[8]

Later, in purgatory, Dante envisions a looming and crowded cliff where so many avaricious make their lodging, creating a nearly impassable wall as Virgil leads on:

> I turned: my Guide set off along the space
> left clear next to the rock; for they who drain,
> slow tear by tear, the sin that east the race
>
> left little room along the edge.
> Thus, as one hugs the battlements in walking
> Atop a wall, we moved along the ledge.[9]

Dante asserts that avarice is a ubiquitous transgression, for the entire race is consumed by it. Perhaps this is why he illustrates a crowded cliff with weeping souls. It is a vice that remains restless, never satisfied until the individual or the whole of society is consumed.

Avarice is further personified as a She-Wolf, insatiable with hunger, ravenous, and mad. She feeds on her prey, the human souls who acquiesced to her vengeance upon humanity:

> Hell take you, She-Wolf, who in the sick feast
> of your ungluttable appetite have taken
> more prey on earth than any other beast![10]

---

7. Dante, *Inferno*, 7:61–63.
8. Dickens, *Christmas Carol*, 33.
9. Dante, *Purgatorio*, 20:4–9.
10. Dante, *Purgatorio*, 20:10–12.

Setting in Order

We are then introduced to an interpolator, who vocalizes a prayer in the form of praise for three individuals whose lives were a model of humility and charity. We later come to know the identity of the one whose praise utters a rectitude for mankind. He is Hugh Capet, the illustrious founder of the Capetian dynasty that he now repudiates. He is sickened by the greed and lust that has accompanied the succession of kings in France. Capet will state his penitentiary lament with the night but now lauds the three figures of history while it is day. He blesses Mary, Fabricius, and St. Nicholas for their humility and charity within the context of liturgical prayer for the purgation of his own soul:

> "How poor you were," the stricken voice went on,
> "is testified to all men by the stable
> In which you laid your sacred burden down."[11]

The humble birth of Christ in a stable antagonizes the avarice of the age that would rather inhabit golden palaces and fill life with pompous parades. We lust for wealth, recognition, and security, sometimes unaware that spiritual insecurity is the fruit of such pursuits. We forget that the love of money is the root of all evil. We spiritualize the pursuit by encasing the desire with fundraisers for the newest sound system, lighting apparatus, or online platform. But O, to return to the stable and know that great satisfaction for the soul is to be poor in spirit.

> And then: "O good Fabricius, you twice
> Refused great wealth that would have stained your honor,
> And chose to live in poverty, free of vice."[12]

Fabricius Caius Luscinus was Roman consul in 282 BC. He is honored here in Dante's litany and polemic against avarice as he disdained and refused bribes that not only had become acceptable for high political offices, but normative. In this regard, Fabricius became a voice for reform railing against the political corruption incessant in the form of bribery. And although his refusal of bribes was indeed costly,[13] his name lives on in honor for those who pick up the pages of Dante's epic poem. Perhaps we are indebted to Fabricius for the consideration of bribery as a high

---

11. Dante, *Purgatorio*, 20:22–24.
12. Dante, *Purgatorio*, 20:25–27.
13. Fabricius was so poor that the state had to purchase his burial plot and cover the expenses of the funeral. In addition, the state provided the dowry for his daughters as Fabricius was impoverished. See Dante, *Purgatorio*, 458.

SETTING IN ORDER: THE YOUNG MEN AND THE HAUSTAFEL

crime in our own country and one reason for the impeachment of one of the highest offices in the land.[14]

The final example and polemic against avarice is that of St. Nicholas. Listen to Dante's description:

> The voice was speaking now of the largesse
> St. Nicholas bestowed on the three virgins
> To guide their youth to virtuous steadiness.[15]

Saint Nicholas was informed of the poverty of a minor nobleman who was tempted to sell his daughters into sin as he could not provide proper dowries for them. On three successive nights St. Nicholas deposited a sack of gold for this family and with it the nobleman was able to purchase dowries, preventing a life of corruption for his daughters and securing one of virtue. It is said that St. Nicholas gave all his wealth to the poor.[16]

Capet then laments his own plight and that of his progeny. He identifies himself as the root of the "malignant tree which casts its shadow on all Christendom."[17] Capet is the founder of a dynasty riddled with corruption and oppression in the form of the Philips and Louises of France. This is further epitomized by his reference to the enslavement of a king's daughter; King Charles of France sold "his daughter, haggling like a pirate over a girl sold into slavery."[18] This anecdote moves Capet to a miserable lamentation and description of avarice as a cruel master. In this way avarice is further personified, given anthropomorphisms in the following expression:

> Avarice, what more harm can you do?
> You have taken such hold on my descendants
> They sell off their own flesh and blood for you![19]

Capet is furthermore loathe to recall the feud between Philip the Fair and Pope Boniface. Philip accused Boniface of heresy and Boniface,

---

14. See U.S. Const. art. II, § 4, para. 1, where the following is cited: "The President, Vice President and all civil Officers of the United States, shall be removed from Office on Impeachment for, and Conviction of, Treason, Bribery, or other high Crimes and Misdemeanors."
15. Dante, *Purgatorio*, 20:31–33.
16. Dante, *Purgatorio*, 458.
17. Dante, *Purgatorio*, 20:43–44.
18. Dante, *Purgatorio*, 20:80–81.
19. Dante, *Purgatorio*, 20:82–84.

in retribution, was prepared to excommunicate Philip. However, prior to the publication of the papal bull, the vicar and, in Dante's mind, "Christ himself was dragged in captivity."[20] Dante envisions avarice as the vice propagating such action. Philip's egregious action was unfortunately exponentiated when he seized papal land and treasures in 1314. In his animosity and wrath, he tortured his prisoners and compelled Pope Clement V to legalize the crime. "I see another Pilate," Capet laments, "so full of spite ... his swollen sails enter the very Temple without right."[21]

In canto 22, Virgil and Dante encounter Statius, who also has a deep regard for Virgil. While discussing Satius's earthly history, Virgil inquires as to whether avarice was a plague upon his soul and perhaps the cause of his time in purgatory. Statius replies that it was prodigality that conferred his necessary purgation: "I wept thousands of months for riotous expense."[22]

Indeed, Statius applauds Virgil's polemic against avarice in the *Aeneid* and credits this work as a precipitating factor to his own reform and decrying prodigality:

> Had I not turned from prodigality
> in pondering those lines in which you cry,
> as if you raged against humanity
> "To what do not you drive man's appetite
> O cursed gold lust"—I should now be straining
> In the grim jousts of the Infernal night.[23]

Dante envisions hoarding and wasting as two faces of avarice in allegorizing both hell and purgatory. I reference Dante not to legitimize purgatory in any way, but rather to accentuate the sermonizing of human vice to enact reform to the human soul. In many ways, if not all encompassing, this appears to be Dante's intent as well. He cites both historical and current figures to illustrate the vices of hell, the sifting of purgatory, and the blessings of heaven.

LESSONS FROM THE PRODIGAL SON AND SCROOGE

One can hardly neglect a discussion of Christ's parable in this regard as well. I cannot ignore it myself as it is a caricature of a young man who is

---

20. Dante, *Purgatorio*, 20:87.
21. Dante, *Purgatorio*, 20:91–93.
22. Dante, *Purgatorio*, 22:35–36.
23. Dante, *Purgatorio*, 22:37–42.

led astray by avarice. He sequesters an early inheritance, the first sign of avarice, and then wastes it on prodigal living, the second sign of avarice. And perhaps the fact that he was the younger brother may escape us, but it should not. For the Haustafel paraenetic material here employed by Paul concerning integrity is to young men. And perhaps it is avarice that confounds the blossoming of integrity in the infant heart of the young man.

Henri Nouwen explores this further when citing Kenneth Bailey's explication of the prodigal son. In essence, Bailey and Nouwen illuminate that the motive behind the request for an early inheritance is that the father would indeed die. "It is a heartless rejection of the home in which the son was born and nurtured and a break with the most precious tradition carefully upheld by the larger community of which he was a part."[24] Avarice destroys a home and untangles a legacy. Avarice has the potential to upend any kind of order in the family, tearing away the carefully constructed intimate relationships within the Haustafel. "He [Luke] speaks about a drastic cutting loose from the way of living, thinking, and acting that has been handed down to him from generation to generation as a sacred legacy."[25]

Or think of Charkes Dickens's miserly character Scrooge in the *Christmas Carol*. When asked for charitable contributions, he deplores such an act as impeding his hoarding of wealth and a waste of his time. Scrooge mentions poor houses as institutions that his taxes sustain. When there is further entreaty that defends the poor with the deplorable conditions of the poor houses that separate families so that these poor would rather die, Scrooge heartlessly responds, "Well if they would rather die, then they better do so and decrease the surplus population."[26]

Scrooge essentially wishes for the death of the poor as they threaten his hoarding of wealth. He is already disgruntled with his tax obligation and considers their very existence a perpetual threat to his avaricious intent. We then add to Dante's definition of avarice as being hoarding and wasting. With the assistance of Nouwen and Dickens, we must also conclude that avarice intends the death of another. This death is of anyone who opposes the accumulation of goods, power, or control. It is also the death of anyone who can potentially add to one's wealth in the form of an inheritance. The relationship is completely discarded and, quite before the death of the testator, there is a radical emotional departure

24. Nouwen, *Return of the Prodigal Son*, 41.
25. Nouwen, *Return of the Prodigal Son*, 41.
26. Dickens, *Christmas Carol*, 14.

from the heart of the Father. When we desire the death of our corporal father, (perhaps we could go further and not be accused of heterodoxy) we also desire the death of our heavenly Father. This desire for death acts quite unintentionally by slaying our own heart so that we live a life in the grave, predicting the hell that portends our future if those shadows do not change. Scrooge's disposition ends in the grave, and so is the destiny of the avaricious unless, like Scrooge, godly sorrow enters the soul and echoes the entreaty, "Assure me that I may change these shadows you have shown me, by an altered life!"[27]

DIGNITY

We have explored integrity as resistance to avarice. We must note, however, that this is one part of integrity and I do not intend for integrity to be reduced to a financial matter only. Nonetheless, resistance to avarice cannot be ignored by the young man desiring a pattern of good work, in doctrine, showing incorruption, gravity, and sincerity. Thus, we turn to our next term in exploring the young men in the Haustafel, σεμνότητα (sem-no-tes), signifying honor and dignity. It is a term also used by Paul when he implores that we intercede for kings so that we might live in σεμνότητα, or dignity (see 1 Tim 2:2). The term connotes decency as well.[28] A race colored by decency seeks the dignity of every human life. It is further denoted in 1 Tim 3:4 where a bishop is characterized by children who are in subjection with σεμνότητα, or dignity.

If there is a lesson to be learned from our ancient Greek predecessors, balance seems to be the paradigm preferred to be procured. For it was Aristotle, when defining σεμνότητα, who utilized two extremes as certain antitheses to σεμνότητα and the moderation or middle ground as a certain conceptualization of σεμνότητα. For example, on one hand, one acts contrary to σεμνότητα when one is arrogant for one is apathetic to the care and concerns of others. And, on the other hand, one also acts contrary to σεμνότητα when one is overly accommodating for in an ignoble pleasing of everybody, self-dignity cannot be preserved. Aristotle then envisions an expression of dignity as in between these two corresponding vices, arrogance and ignoble accommodation. The one who is dignified is neither arrogant nor overly accommodating, and will at the right time

---

27. Dickens, *Christmas Carol*, 151.
28. Zodhiates and Baker, *Hebrew-Greek Key Word*, 1756.

and moment assert him- or herself in contexts that call for such dignified acts. He refuses some entreaties discerning the context as to whether these requests promote dignity for the self and/or community.[29]

In contemplating Aristotle's definition of honor or dignity, I found the following citations rather compelling for reasons I will subsequently extrapolate:

> [Honor is] a scarce nonmaterial commodity, pursued mainly by men in small-scale, face-to-face communities in more or less aggressive forms of zero-sum competition.[30]

And,

> The point of honour is the basis of the ethic appropriate to an individual who always sees himself through the eyes of others, who has need of others in order to exist, because his self-image is inseparable from the image of himself that he receives back from others.[31]

Cairns and Bourdieu both embed Aristotelian ethics of dignity in the community. This is what I found compelling, for dignity, worth, or honor are appraisals of how we relate to one another. Now, I would not assume that one could not express dignity in solitude, but perhaps I would assert that the best kind of dignity and perhaps the more consummate expressions of dignity are manifest in relation to the other. This is the thought that grips me in reflecting on the citations above.

In contrast, I bristle at the possibility that dignity is somehow penetrated by competition that has no sum. Likewise, I find it difficult to accept that dignity is reduced to the perception others may have of us. However, if we were to offer a theological modification of dignity, we might assert that the purest kind of dignity is a rational and emotive conceptualization of self and others through how and what God has verbalized (logos) to us and how this was conspicuously modelled by Christ (Logos), so that *tine* (honor) and *axios* (worth), as Aristotle has written, are purely and wholly integrated when in relation to and with Christ (Logos). Thus, young men are to interact in community with a certain kind of dignity, discerning who to accommodate and where to assert one's courage, refusing to define oneself solely predicated on

---

29. See Zodhiates and Baker, *Hebrew-Greek Key Word*, 1756, for more discussion on Aristotle and the Greek term σεμνότητα.

30. Cairns, "Honour and Shame," 23.

31. Bourdieu, "Sense of Honour," 113.

perceptions of others, but surrendering to the one relation who perfectly defines dignity (namely, Christ), and expressing this divine relationship in temporal fashion while living. Christ, who was relatively young when his ministry was revealed, serves as the model in this regard.

For, if one is to give him- or herself completely to the perceptions of others, one will find despair to be the fruit. We cannot live upon the perceptions of others; that is, we cannot base human dignity merely on the whims or thoughts of others—although those thoughts may be important—we must also envision dignity as an imprint of the divine. We must see dignity as the imago Dei, every soul, every face, every person, made in God's image, walking as one in relation to God whether this is acknowledged or not. Every person bears the mark of God and thus has dignity in this manner. The young man is exhorted to see every maiden, every widow, every elder, every peer, every aristocrat, and every impoverished person as having this dignity.

KANT AND DIGNITY

What I have heretofore expressed, therefore, is dignity grounded in ontology. That is, dignity is a value conferred to every human being regardless of status. This contrasts with some of the ancient thinkers who base dignity on rank or status. Oliver Sensen, in explicating Kantian dignity, asserts that Kant himself draws his own thinking of dignity from this more traditional sense as well. Although, it should be noted that there are other authors who disagree and contend for a Kantian ethic grounded in universal human value as a form of dignity. Nonetheless, so that we can further reflect on Paul's use of dignity when exhorting young men in the Haustafel, let us explore this notion of a Kantian paradigm of dignity.

Sensen asserts that Kant expresses human dignity based on the following arguments:

> 1. Human beings are seen as elevated over the rest of nature in virtue of having freedom. 2. Dignity is a twofold nature that refers to the initial elevation of human beings, as well as the realized elevation of each individual. 3. One's initial dignity is said to be connected to a duty to make a proper use of one's freedom (to realize one's dignity). 4. The duty is in the first instance, a duty to oneself.[32]

32. Sensen, "Kant's Conception of Human Dignity," 316–17.

Kant's grounding dignity in freedom and this freedom as ontological and automatic raises interesting reflections. First, if freedom is the necessary bedrock of dignity, the converse is implied, so that the coercive removal of such freedom would be the loss of dignity. Thus, slavery in any form is undignified—a relational dynamic where the human is essentially dehumanized.

Second, Kant also places human agency as a component of realizing freedom. That is, although freedom is present by virtue of being human, this freedom must be realized by its proper use. So, in this sense, freedom can be ascertained or at least consummated in the sense where one emanates freedom via the use of reason, rationale, and virtue. The agency is the self. One must comprehend and work toward dignifying oneself by pursuing a realized freedom contingent upon one's internal schemas.

If Sensen is correct, and Kant envisions dignity as sublimity, then one must ascertain dignity vis-à-vis elevation. This elevation is the realization of freedom through its proper use. In this regard, Kant would be subscribing to a more ancient view of dignity. Moreover, and again if Sensen is correct, Kant's view of dignity is also contingent upon the human capacity of morality.

That is, humanity is sublime or elevated over the rest of creation by virtue of the human capacity to act with a moral compass. This contrasts with the rest of nature that acts purely upon instinct. Thus, in a type of summary, Kant seems to express an ontological human dignity embedded in freedom that is initially underrealized. This realization of freedom and dignity is consummated by human agency in making the proper use of freedom through thoughts and actions of morality.[33]

But this begs the question, To which moral law does Kant refer? That is, how is morality operationalized, and when would one know he or she is being moral? If freedom is realized vis-à-vis morality then this equation is the very expression of dignity. It might behoove us to know what morality is.

For the Christian, morality is grounded in Logos and logos. That is, the person of Christ—his works, words, and virtues—along with the Scriptures working in the human heart through the Spirit of God provide the framework for morality. And so, we turn to the Scriptures, more specifically the writings of Paul, for further explication of dignity and, as an extrapolation, the exploration of the dignity exhortation to young men.

---

33. Sensen, "Kant's Conception of Human Dignity," 319–20.

If we are to use Kant's freedom as the beginning of human dignity, then let us add theological concepts as elucidated by Paul, and we will refer to his Letter to Galatia as an illustrative example. For in it, we find a metaphorical or spiritualizing history of Hagar and Sarah concerning slavery and freedom. We might then modify Kant and perhaps argue a contrasting argument, at least in the way Sensen interprets Kant. And in this, I intend to convey that a theological model of dignity is always relational and that relations are always present so that dignity to some degree is always present.

DIGNITY AND FREEDOM

However, I do get ahead of myself. Let's explore Paul's use of freedom in the Letter to the Galatians. We were first introduced to the freedom-slave paradigm in Gal 2 when Judaizers deceitfully entered the church at Galatia, attempting to promote the necessary obligation to follow minute parts of the law as a means of justification. Specifically, this cohort was attempting to convince new converts that they needed to be circumcised according to the law of Moses. Titus was at the center of this controversy and Paul withstood this perceived obligation upon Titus with the following assertion: "But because of false brothers and sisters secretly brought in, who slipped in to spy on the freedom we have in Christ Jesus, so that they might enslave us." (Gal 2:4).

Paul then begins to work rhetorically while alluding to the Hagar-Sarah history to support his polemic. Faith is the conduit of the Spirit and the law is the conduit of the flesh (see Gal 3:2). Paul utilizes a *reductio ad absurdum* argument to nullify the notion that any kind of perfection can be consummated by the flesh or the works of the law. Teleological aims are navigated by faith in and through the Spirit of God.

Paul continues the juxtaposition by alluding to Old Testaments assertions such as "the just shall live by faith," and "cursed is every one that hangs on a tree" (Gal 3:11, 13). In doing so, the law and our inability to keep the law results in a curse and Christ having become a curse delivers us as we appropriate faith in him (see Gal 3:13). To strengthen his argument, Paul refers to the seed passage of Genesis while asserting that this promise emerged much before the law was ever conceived so that faith and promise are juxtaposed with law and works/flesh (see Gal 3:16–18

SETTING IN ORDER: THE YOUNG MEN AND THE HAUSTAFEL

and Gen 15:13-16). This is all quite important to Paul's view of dignity as it may inform or is informed by freedom as we shall soon see.

Freedom will become infused with faith, adoption, the work of the Spirit, and heirship. Paul emphasizes that a knowledge of God and being known by God are the hallmarks of true freedom. The beggarly elements of obligatory observations or works, and vain attempts to keep the law's ordinances that have already by this time been fulfilled by Christ, are bondage (see Gal 4:9). Of course, Paul does not seek to denigrate the law; rather, he envisions the law as a temporary holder blossoming in its maturity of faith when the promised Seed—namely, Christ—is revealed to destroy human bondage to sin. The law instructed or schooled us to consider that Christ and faith in him are the only way to freedom (see Gal 3:19-28).

We here receive a consummate thought and perhaps the epicenter of Paul's description of dignity: "There is no longer Jew or Greek; there is no longer slave or free; there is no longer male and female, for all of you are one in Christ Jesus" (Gal 3:28).

So, we return to Kant's view that there is no nonrelational component to human dignity, that worth and value imply some semblance of relational transaction that conveys status. This comports well with Paul's thought that theological dignity implies relationship, and status is not status as we would think in terms of human hierarchy but, rather, relational status that is metaphysical or epistemological. All corporeal status indicators are levelled in the person of Christ. These temporary designations are destroyed in the one consummate relational transaction with Christ. Believers are in Christ and this relationship conveys the status of child and heir. Thus, our status from slave to son and heir conveys a kind of dignity and, for the Christian, this dignity continues to be on display as we live by faith in Christ Jesus.

Now, I do not mean to convey that unbelievers are without dignity, for I intend to later add to Paul's thought here concerning the imago Dei that I will assert is a ubiquitous vestige and relational mark from God himself upon all humanity.

Finally, Paul will persuade his audience by bringing an allegory to the Hagar-Sarah narrative. Hagar was Sarah's servant or slave and embodies the law. Sarah is the free wife of Abraham and embodies promise. Hagar is the covenant of Mt. Sinai, namely the law which creates bondage as all are concluded sinners under the law. Sarah represents heavenly Jerusalem, a covenant enacted by Christ. Unto Hagar was born a son of the flesh, Ishmael. He was born from human anxiety and systems and therefore not born of promise. Rather, Isaac was born of promise, a decree from God himself. Paul will subsume believers under the promise by including them in his allegory. Freedom is promise, it is becoming children of promise, whereas slavery is human anxiety to make never-ceasing attempts to perfect ourselves that in the end will always be frustrated by our sinful nature. We have not been able, nor will we ever be able to arrive at teleological perfection by human endeavor. The humanists have erred, our own actualization and perfection is not within ourselves but outside of ourselves in the person of Christ who longs to dwell within.

So, to add to Kant's argument of freedom, we have Paul's allegory and rhetoric to qualify freedom. Freedom is not merely innate because we are creatures of reason. Freedom is rather theologically appropriated by faith, promise, sonship, and metaphysical relationship.

AUGUSTINE AND DIGNITY

It is to the imago Dei (image of God) that we now turn for further explication of human dignity, and particularly the Augustinian notion of imago Dei. For it is Augustine who was likely the singular influence on great thinkers such as Thomas Aquinas. Together, Augustine and Aquinas continue to generate debate on the confluence of human dignity and imago Dei today. Mathew Puffer envisions a progressive definition of imago Dei in Augustine from early to latter writings. For example, in Augustine's early writings, when exegeting Gen 1:26, Augustine emphasizes the preposition *ad* (to) so that human beings are made toward the image of God as an extrinsic teleological framework (*ad imaginem et similitudinem Dei*—to the image and likeness of God).[34]

This prepositional difference from *in* to *toward* is important for the entire theological thought of human vicissitude. Early Augustine envisions human nature as beginning with a disposition toward the image of God—namely, in the person of Christ—rather than being made in the image of God. And as such, it is proper love that thus mediates one ever closer to the image of God. Or as Puffer asserts concerning Augustine, "The image of God is an extrinsic telos toward which the human agent orients his or her love."[35]

---

34. Puffer, "Human Dignity," 69.
35. Puffer, "Human Dignity," 69.

SETTING IN ORDER: THE YOUNG MEN AND THE HAUSTAFEL

And of course, how can we not discuss properly ordered loves or orthopathy as central to Augustinian thought? Augustine appeals to progression toward the image of God as one who either ascends to the image vis-à-vis proper love or descends away vis-à-vis improper loves. These loves encompass both the higher and lower order in a sense of heavenly/spiritual and earthly/corporeal elements. For example, as Puffer asserts, "The weight of rightly ordered love of God and all things in God—including both higher goods (i.e., invisible, intelligible, eternal, immutable, incorporeal goods) as well as lower ones (i.e., visible, sensible, temporal, mutable, corporeal goods)—carries one toward God, an ascent, whereas the disordered love for lower goods carries one away from God, a descent."[36]

Later, when grappling with 1 Cor 11:7, Augustine will make a seismic shift in his conceptualization of the imago Dei. He finds that he cannot ignore the preposition (*est*) by Paul that is more direct and implies an intrinsic orientation in the imago Dei. Moreover, this imago Dei now encapsulates the Trinity rather than Christ only.[37] Now, the imago Dei, or at least, Augustine's conception of the imago Dei, moves from extrinsic telos to intrinsic imputation.

Moreover, Augustine revisions himself; whereas before he contended for a loss of the imago Dei at the fall, he later asserts that the image was rather veiled, in need of rightly ordered loves and God's glory to lift the veil (Augustine's exegesis of 2 Cor 3).[38] This is a critical conceptual difference, for it supposes an intrinsic dignity to human nature in the veiled imago Dei quite distinct from his earlier extrinsic paradigm. Every human is related to God by virtue of bearing his image and inherent in this is a form of dignity that appeals to respect, love, and honor.[39]

---

36. Puffer, "Human Dignity," 71.

37. See Puffer, "Human Dignity," 72, where he states the following concerning Augustine's evolution of thought: "Here, Augustine claims for the first time not that the human being is created toward the image of God (ad imaginem Dei), but rather that the human being is the image of God (est imago Dei)."

38. See Puffer, "Human Dignity," 74, where he states: "In the same year, in 413 CE, Sermon 362 and Letters 147 and 148 all return to this passage from Paul, arguing that the 'image transformed from glory to glory' (2 Cor 3:18) is not a recovery of what was lost but an uncovering of that which had been veiled."

39. See Puffer, "Human Dignity," 74, where he notes Augustine's transformation: "Thus, the old, unregenerate, *sub lege* human (of Col 3 and Eph 4) is just as much the image of God as is the new, regenerate, *sub gratia* human."

Thus, I would like to integrate Augustine's latter thought on the imago Dei as one informing the ethics of human dignity. That is, the imago Dei, veiled by the fall, is restorable by the regeneration of the human being in grace, faith, and love. However, even if grace and regeneration are rejected by human will, held in bondage to sin, the imago Dei in that person persists and his or her capacity for regeneration, contemplation, and rightly ordered loves also are present. Thus, every single human has intrinsic worth, value, and respect not merely as a form of social status, but because he or she is made in the imago Dei. It is a heavenly designation inherited through Adam and Eve on whom God gave the initial designation of imago Dei. We have the likeness, the vicissitude, the image within awaiting activation of regeneration by faith, love, and the work of the Holy Spirit. The image itself portends dignity, basic human rights, honor, and love for that person, no matter how vile or evil. The image also infers relationship to God whether one is the elect or whether one has chosen idolatry.

In contemporary Christian ethics, Stanley Hauerwas also argues for this kind of latter Augustinian thought, much like Aquinas before him, that the capacity for divine relationship withstands the lifespan and how we relate to one another also affords human dignity. For example, Hauerwas asserts a type of human euphemism that should also inform our way of thinking of personhood when he states, "It is only seldom that we have occasion to think of ourselves as 'persons'; when asked to identify myself, I do not think that I am a person, but I am Stanley Hauerwas, teacher, husband, father, or, ultimately, a Texan."[40]

Moreover, when opining on whether to promote life-sustaining procedures or withdrawal, Hauerwas continues to assert, "Rather, we care or do not care for him because he is Uncle Charlie, or my father, or a good friend."[41] In this regard, even if Uncle Charlie is vile, he remains an uncle, in relation to someone else. By this relationship he has dignity, but more than this, by his relationship with God by virtue of being made in his image, he has dignity.

In summary, the central attribute conferring dignity is the imago Dei, and I concur with latter Augustinian thought that this attribute of human existence is not lost but rather veiled or perhaps distorted by the fall. However, the capacity for regeneration remains and the imago

---

40. Hauerwas, "Must a Patient," 599.
41. Hauerwas, "Must a Patient," 600.

Christi acts as a catalyst for this regeneration as one places his or her faith and trust in Christ, his work, and the subsequent work of the Holy Spirit. Thus, one is born with dignity, and this dignity is perpetuated by relationship. One relates to God whether one wants to or not by bearing his image. One relates to others in the form of husband, wife, father, mother, friend, and so on.

Paul and Kant's use of freedom further qualifies human dignity, and if we consider freedom as distinct from nature, then again, the imago Dei is the starting point here as well. If freedom confers dignity, then freedom necessarily needs protection in civil society. Freedom is informed by promise. Promise is decreed by divine speech. If freedom is underrealized, it is so in the form of the veiled imago Dei. And, as Kant asserts, if freedom is realized by virtue of morality, it is revealed by faith in Christ who then enacts regeneration and morality through the Holy Spirit. Without the divine promise we have no true freedom. Laws and regulations for morality simply unveil our human propensity to sin and a dire need for a Savior. Please see table 7 below for a summary of these views.

Mode of Thought	Central Premise	Antagonist(s)	Telos
Aristotle	Status/rank	Ignoble accommodation/ arrogance	Balance
Kant	Freedom	Nonappropriation/ slavery	Actualization
Augustine	Imago Dei	The fall/wrongly ordered loves	Orthopathy
Paul	Promise	Works of the flesh/ unbelief	Sonship/heirship
Integrated	Relationship	Deconstruction	Restored Community

Table 7. Human Dignity

By placing relationships as the central premise of human dignity, one can integrate the few thinkers we have explored thus far. For Aristotle, dignity was based on the relationship that society conferred as rank but one that the individual maintained by navigating relationships with a balance between ignoble accommodation and arrogance. Kant bases his dignity on the notion of freedom but states that this freedom is first to oneself. He asserts an intrapersonal component to dignity—namely, how one relates to the self. Out of relating to the self, one then relates to others. Augustine's imago Dei is a physical demarcation of God upon the human that confers relationship between the Creator and the created. This imago Dei remains, withstanding the rejection of the created. Paul alludes to promise as the basis of freedom, but a promise intuits relationship. One makes a promise to another. My uncle Charlie may not be much of a person, but he is still a person deserving of honor and dignity because he is my uncle.

When a relationship deteriorates or, worse, is deconstructed, dignity suffers. It is here where we have seen emerge the most egregious forms of slavery, and indeed the slavery of human trafficking is the epidemic of this age. This is a result of deconstructed relationships with God and neighbor. To restore dignity, relationships must be restored. This is the teleological end of every human being. It is a consummate restored relationship first to God and then to neighbor. For the young man in the Haustafel, Paul exhorts the treatment of others with dignity. The young man must then act as an ambassador of reconciliation, becoming an ambassador of relationship. He moves to restore relationships in the home and in the church as a model for the greater society.

SOUND SPEECH

More will be said of a temperate tongue in the next chapter, but I do want to touch briefly on speech. The young man is also tasked with sound speech. Using the Greek ὑγιῆ (hugieh), meaning sound, whole, or healthy, Paul appeals to sound doctrine once again. This is the kind of speech that is above reproach. The young man in this instance cannot be condemned or accused as his speech is sound, accurate, careful, temperate, and holy.[42]

Language can divide as in Babel and unite as in Pentecost. Language is an essential means in how we relate, and language is the form in which God decided to incarnate himself (Logos, or Word becoming flesh.) Life comes from language and death comes from language (see Prov 18:21). Language can incite or dissipate reproach. And for Paul this is important as elsewhere he warns of outside reproach when asking young women to marry, bear children, guide the house, and thus give no occasion

---

42. See Rogers and Rogers, *New Linguistic and Exegetical Key*, 510.

SETTING IN ORDER: THE YOUNG MEN AND THE HAUSTAFEL

for the enemy to speak reproachfully (see 1 Tim 5:14). He exhorts the bishop, elder, or overseer to be above reproach as well, able to lead his own household.

When emphatic about sound doctrine he asserts that teaching be in alignment with the wholesome words of Christ and a doctrine of godliness (see 1 Tim 6:3). But the proud, those doting about words to engender strife, composing questions without answers, accusations, and political scheming are juxtaposed to those of sound speech (see 1 Tim6:4). Lust for power, corruption, and destitution with an eye on monetary or political gain also act as an antagonism to sound speech garnering reproach (1 Tim 6:5). Sound speech is essential to a character above reproach, which remains a duty of young men in the Haustafel.

Thus, we now complete the entirety of our address to the Haustafel by including our last covenant, the covenant young men make to the household of God:

> I covenant to behave with temperance, voluntarily restraining certain liberties for the greater peace of my home, church, and society (Titus 2:6). I covenant to act with integrity, resisting the vice of avarice in both forms of prodigality and hoarding, which act to compromise a life of integrity (Titus 2:7). I covenant to view every human soul with dignity, having intrinsic worth by virtue of being made in the image of God (Titus 2:7). I covenant to exercise sound speech and wise doctrine to refrain from bringing reproach upon the household of faith (Titus 2:8).

Chapter 22

Setting in Order and Submission

Remind them to be subject to rulers and authorities, to be obedient, to be ready for every good work.

TITUS 3:1

AS IS TYPICAL OF Paul's Epistles, he will end his letter with pragmatic exhortations that have to do with congregational living. In this conclusion to Titus, he offers a reflection and charge on submission (see Titus 3:1). This submission appears to go beyond submission to pastoral authority to encompass governmental agents as well. Paul is emphatic as he includes powers, principalities, and magistrates. We find in his message the resonance of Peter, who likewise urged the church to "honor everyone. Love the family of believers. Fear God. Honor the emperor" (1 Pet 2:17).

That is, not only ought the members of the church to honor ecclesiastical authority, but also societal leaders. At the time of Paul's writing, there was not one king, ruler, governor, or Caesar who espoused the Christian faith. Indeed, Paul was in and out of prison within Rome for his faith even as he wrote his Epistles. Nero was imminently edging closer to widespread persecution of the Christians to the martyrdom of many.

Submission is a Christian practice often spoken of, but with a praxis that is diminishing. I would argue that much of what we inherit as a cultural paradigm plays a role in our inherent inability to submit to authority. I believe Paul has provided a litany of dispositional virtues that accompany and enable one to submit to God's authority and likewise to ecclesiastical and societal authority. If submission was so easy, there would be less conflict. But as we have all experienced, conflict has penetrated all our lives to some extent, which is evidence that submission is truly a discipline that requires a work of the Holy Spirit to deposit temperamental virtues. It is the fruit of the Spirit that enables true submission. Therefore, I am writing in polemical fashion to assert that the dispositional virtues of temperance (a temperate tongue), peacemaking, and meekness are required for the genuine posture of submission. Furthermore, I argue that these virtues are only accessed through God's mercy unto salvation, washing through regeneration, and renewal by the Holy Spirit. The latter is a sovereign move of God upon the human soul through the agency of Christ's work upon the cross.

A TEMPERATE TONGUE

O how small a member, but what a fire can be kindled by the human tongue. With our words we curse and bless. With our words we inflame, and we bring peace. With our words we heal and injure. With our words we crush and restore.

I remember an incident during my pastorate when we (myself with the church and pastor's council) decided to reduce our personnel in a year where we projected a revenue loss of one hundred thousand dollars into the next year. This is a devastating cut no matter how one envisions where the cuts will be. For our church budget, this represented a nearly 10 percent cut in the entire budget, one that had already endured annual cuts to every ministry budget for the past ten years. As I began to sit with the employees we would be releasing, each encounter incurred a lamentation of some sort. But one encounter with an employee we were releasing will remain engrained in my memory, for it involved an unbridled tongue.

One employee had been informed of her termination prior to my conversation with her. I did not know how she was informed. She approached me with this information and continued to escalate the conversation after I requested that we speak of this during a scheduled appointment. She had chosen the wrong time and place to begin the discussion of her termination and the logistics of her severance. I was staffing the front office so that someone would be available for general phone calls or walk-ins. Thus, the conversation could have certainly

Setting in Order

impeded and offended a member or guest who could have arrived at the church offices.

As the conversation progressed, it was clear that emotions began to escalate. The employee at one point made a statement that did not bode well for my own patience. She stated that I had manipulated circumstances and people so that I could hire a children's pastor and family pastor who were a husband-and-wife team. She accused me of somehow doing something deceitful. This was a shameful remark concerning my character and integrity. I had made known to the leadership team all along my preference for the new hire. Is it not an appropriate use of authority for a lead pastor to state a preference and proceed with a hire?

However, I did not restrain my temper in the moment, raising my voice in admonishing this employee to temper her words and to refrain from personal slander. The content was necessary, but the tone of my voice was encompassed with anger, and I regret the outburst as I now reflect. The fire of her tongue had provoked a vulnerable place where there was a reservoir of anger. She had attacked my integrity. These kinds of attacks would continue later from a council member. Therefore, it appears that the intemperate tongue found its place among others with influence, so that they would believe my intentions to be deceitful. Pastors, when you near the threshold of an anger outburst, stop the conversation and delay it to another time where communication can be had without the potential for lashing anger to the one provoking the vulnerability of your heart. In a like manner, discipline and remove those from leadership who would falsely accuse you of wrongdoing. If he or she is willing to speak unashamedly to your face to injure your integrity, then the likelihood is that he or she is also speaking this way to others. True repentance would not only repair the injured relationship with you, but to those with whom he or she slandered your integrity.

The employee and I did meet later as was the original plan, and she did submit to a disciplinary process but also disdained the possibility that one ought to be terminated for such behavior. Looking back, this was yet another red flag that I ignored in the name of mercy. This employee was more concerned about her credentials of ministry than repair of the relationship and submission to authority. Pastors, true repentance invites mercy, but persistent disdain invites discipline. Do not ignore those who do not fully remediate the injury incurred but who rather incite a cohort to his or her cause. Or note one who denies the personal injury by not intentionally pursuing the parties to whom this slander was communicated.

Looking back, I would have apologized for my display of anger, but would have proceeded with a severance agreement. For there was not the comprehensive fruit of godly sorrow. The intemperate tongue persisted and if allowed to continue, future submission becomes untenable.

Perhaps this is why Paul addressed the tongue in Titus 3:2 as a means by which true submission can be performed. "Speak evil of no man," he states, even as he extends his instruction of submission with this virtue. Christians are to restrain the tongue, place a gate on the impulse to criticize, denigrate, disparage, and slander. The tongue can be a primary means by which the church fragments and disintegrates into an image so far from what God intends.

Paul uses the word βλασφημέω (blasphemeo) when addressing the need to circumcise the tongue for God's purposes. I have already explored this word when reflecting on 1 Timothy in *The Coming Winter*. As Paul intends to reiterate and emphasize the importance of sound speech, I will do so here as well. βλασφημέω can also be rendered in a way where one calumniates another. This is a transitive verb that is defined as one who utters maliciously false statements, charges, or imputations concerning another.[1]

MILTON AND THE INTEMPERATE TONGUE

For yet another trek into the concept of βλασφημέω, we turn to Milton's treatment of Gen 3 and the fall of humanity through the intemperate tongue to convince the intellect to accept a narrative that is a perversion of God's words and intent. In book 9 of John Milton's epic poem, *Paradise Lost*, he exposits a narrative that is all too familiar to us as we groan the retelling:

> Indeed, hath God then said that of the fruit
> Of all these garden trees ye shall not eat,
> Yet lords declared of all in earth or air?[2]

The serpent has appealed to the human sentiment of curiosity and thus misconstrued the pure desire of fellowship with the divine to

---

1. Vine, *Complete Expository Dictionary*, 69.
2. Milton, *Paradise Lost*, 9.656–58.

the perverted sentiment to be divine. Through flattery, the serpent has brought Eve now to the very suspicion of the divine command. The intemperate tongue begins with subtle questions, but inquiries that are leading. That is, the question is for the purpose of discrediting the divine injunction and, more than this, divine love.

And Eve, yet still sinless, adheres at first to the word, "Ye shall not eat / Thereof, nor shall ye touch it, lest ye die."[3] And the serpent, yet cunning and even the more emboldened "as when of old some orator renowned,"[4] doubles down and appeals to that nature of human wisdom that, if possible, can entertain a seed of an intemperate and βλασφημέω word—a βλασφημέω word that can find some way to eschew the vision and reputation of God himself.

> Queen of this universe, do not believe
> Those rigid threats of death; ye shall not die:
> How should ye? By the fruit? It gives you life
> To knowledge. By the Threat'ner? Look on me,
> Me who have touched and tasted, yet both live,
> And life more perfect have attained than fate
> Meant me, by vent'ring higher than my lot.
> Shall that be shut to man, which to the beast
> Is open? Or will God incense his ire
> For such a petty trespass, and not praise
> Rather your dauntless virtue, whom the pain
> Of death denounced, whatever thing death be,
> Deterred not from achieving what might lead
> To happier life, knowledge of good and evil;
> Of good, how just? Of evil, if what is evil
> Be real, why not known, since easier shunned?[5]

Milton performs a masterful work in illustrating the intemperate tongue of Satan. First, the tongue begins with flattery as a mechanism to incite rebellion. Coercion is better received when one is ingratiated. Pastors beware of the flattering tongue, there is usually an agenda associated with such pretentious words. "Queen of the universe" is a phrase appealing to a false sense of self as divine and with this divinity a preparation that there ought to be no limits set on such a queen.

---

3. Milton, *Paradise Lost*, 9.662–63.
4. Milton, *Paradise Lost*, 9.670.
5. Milton, *Paradise Lost*, 9.684–99.

Second, Milton ascribes to Satan the cunning of attributing perfection to that which was forbidden. Satan cites himself as a living but brutish example that one can taste of knowledge and attain a yet more perfect state. He does not disclose, however, that his taste for power left him with a bitter palate once cast from heaven. No, he rather seeks to pervert all with the same corruption he himself is plagued with.

Furthermore, Satan invites βλασφημέω of God by demeaning his intentions. This is the most harmful aspect of βλασφημέω, it moves to deceive others of someone's intentions by the mishandling of words. Satan attempts to convince Eve that God will rather praise her defiance as something virtuous. What a concoction of sophist nonsense covered in the wax of eloquence. βλασφημέω can have a flavor of wisdom, but with all the ingredients of overt rebellion.

Satan beguiles death as something of a fantasy, but the knowledge of good and evil . . . ah yes, this will engender all that is summed up in a happy life. A happy life indeed if you count sorrow, suffering, death, labor, and toil happy. Milton is not finished with the penultimate caricature of βλασφημέω through Satan's twisted words:

> God therefore cannot hurt ye, and be just;
> Not just, not God; not feared them, nor obeyed;
> Your fear itself of death removes the fear.
> Why then was this forbid? Why but to awe,
> Why but to keep you low and ignorant.[6]

Satan questions the very intentions of God toward humanity. If Satan can garner a suspiciousness of God's motives, then perhaps the βλασφημέω will have its final work in turning the heart to sin. Satan's sophism is therefore a movement toward atheism. For if God forbids knowledge of good and evil, he cannot be just. And if he is not just, he is not God. And if he is not God, then he need not be feared. βλασφημέω not only slanders the reputation and character of another but suspects their motives as something sinister. This is the consequence of an intemperate tongue, whether intentional or unintentional.

Satan begins to speculate that it is of malicious intent that God would forbid divine knowledge. Indeed, the knowledge is described by Satan as the means to divinity and if it is forbidden, it must be from an envious disposition.

---

6. Milton, *Paradise Lost*, 9.700–704.

> And wherein lies
> Th' Offense, than man should thus attain to know?
> What can your knowledge hurt him, or this tree
> Impart against his will of all be his?
> Or is it envy, and can envy dwell
> In heav'nly breasts?[7]

Wild speculation can also be a form of βλασφημέω, for it creates a nonreal state, an imagination that is projected onto reality that questions the intent of another without confirmation. As a pastor, so much speculation was circulated about my intent, my heart, and my motives. Speculation sought to paint a portrait of one who was manipulative, deceitful, rigid, and without care or compassion. Indeed, it was wildly speculated that I was prompting other community churches to inquire about purchasing our church building as an effort to destroy the church. Words and narratives had become so twisted and contorted that some came to believe a narrative founded upon βλασφημέω speculation. It is βλασφημέω when one seeks to injure one's reputation. It is βλασφημέω when one seeks to undermine godly authority. It is βλασφημέω when one seeks to slander one's character. It is βλασφημέω when one attributes sinister motives to the heart of another. It is βλασφημέω when one speculates envy, projecting the motive of Satan upon another. βλασφημέω is a false narrative with a premise substantiated on hearsay and wild speculation, and this, my brothers and sisters, destroys a church and impairs appropriate submission.

JAMES AND THE INTEMPERATE TONGUE

The intemperate tongue is likely not given such a comprehensive treatment in Scripture as it is in the Epistle of James. In Jas 3, the apostle likens the tongue to the rudder of ship that determines its destination (Jas 3:4). The tongue is described as set on fire by hell itself (Jas 3:6)! What a proclamation, that hell can somehow come to encompass our tongues, and that this small member of the body has the potential to defile the entire body (see Jas 3:6)! The tongue cannot be domesticated by human will. It cannot be tamed by our good efforts or intentions. As a wild stallion is broken by a persistent rider, so our tongues must be broken by the Holy Spirit (see Jas 3:8). We all make feeble attempts to tame our tongue but

---

7. Milton, *Paradise Lost*, 9.725–30.

commit to the impossible if we do not invite the bit of the Holy Spirit to take possession of our words.

We bless God with our tongue and in the same breath, curse men who are made in the image of God (Jas 3:9). And we find that James also correlates the virtue of meekness as a means by which the tongue can become temperate: "Who is wise and knowledgeable among you? Show by your good life that your works are done with gentleness born of wisdom" (Jas 3:13).

Good conduct can also be rendered good conversation. Meekness and gentleness, as we will learn later, are virtues that grant one the means of genuine and persistent submission to God and to godly authority. The temperate tongue, as we have now explored, is also a required virtue for submission as well.

Perhaps this is one of many reasons that Holy Spirit baptism involves language. It was the voice of idolatry spoken at the tower of Babel that caused confusion of language, and it was the fire of heavenly tongues vis-à-vis the Holy Spirit baptism that brought unity of language. The tongue is given over to the Lord in Holy Spirit baptism so that praises of God and concern for salvation become the content of our language. To blaspheme another's reputation or character even while one praises God is a paradox and is thus a return to the tower of Babel and the garden of Eden where the serpent has been allowed a stronghold upon the human tongue. If the Holy Spirit baptism was a solitary, sanctifying birth of the church, then we as individuals require ongoing infilling with the Spirit in desperate cries to God that we have a temperate tongue.

I have written concerning the intemperate tongue of a staff member as an illustration that one who behaves in this manner will have great difficulty with submission. I have returned to the garden of Eden to illustrate the first βλασφημέω committed by Satan himself, who cajoles all to do the same. Pastors, when hiring or when inspecting staff members, do not ignore an intemperate tongue; rather, confront it and, if it persists, remove this staff member from the church. In contrast, when hiring and perceiving one who has submitted entirely to the Holy Spirit, who has been given the grace of a temperate tongue, know that this person also has been given some capacity to submit to godly authority.

PEACEMAKING

Paul's second virtue is the antithesis of the negative attribution of "brawling": that of peacemaking. Pastors ought to know and practice peacemaking, but may find it easier to practice peacekeeping. Peacekeeping is passive and dangerous. Peacemaking is active and healthy. Paul correlates this attribute with submission when he describes the servant of the Lord to Timothy: "And the Lord's servant must not be quarrelsome but kindly to everyone, an apt teacher, patient" (2 Tim 2:24).

A servant is characterized as one who engenders and produces peace, not one who thrives on or longs for strife. If you find that you create conflict with those over you in the Lord, then reflect on your interpersonal dynamic. The one who is living an inner life that is tumultuous will also cause conflict within his or her relationships.

Jesus refers to peacemaking in his Sermon on the Mount and correlates sonship as a fruit of peacemaking (see Matt 5:9). Jesus uses the word εἰρηνοποιός (*eireno-poios*), which is rendered as peacemaking. It is used here and by Paul in Col 1:20 where we find an extrapolation of what peacemaking may entail: "And through him God was pleased to reconcile to himself all things, whether on earth or in heaven, by making peace through the blood of his cross" (Col 1:20).

So, we find two important theological implications of peacemaking. First, it is a result of a filial relationship with God (i.e., child of God). This is the existential fruit of peacemaking. Second, we find that peacemaking is a bloody process. How ironic that peace would be the result of death. For peace to be had, one must first die. For peace to exist, blood must be shed. Sin perpetuates unrest and the only overcoming factor to unrest, chaos, and violence is the relinquishing of our own blood. That is, our agenda, rigid accounts, proud purposes, and unrelenting grip must be sacrificed. Pastors, Jesus was a peacemaker by his shed blood. How much more will you need to give up your own dreams to make peace.

Peacemaking is reconciliation vis-à-vis self-sacrifice. It is the giving up of selfish ambition for the sake of restored relationship. Jesus sheds his blood, destroying the enmity between humanity and himself. Thus, the cosmic peacemaking and reconciling act was birthed through death. A seed must die in the ground before it can ever hope to live translated as wholly other after death (see John 12:24). Death translates the self into something glorious. And although it can be said that our literal death in Christ is the birth of a resurrection body, the abstract death of a dream, idea, existence, or purpose in Christ can result in a resurrected gestalt of divine proportions.

Die to live, give to receive, be a peacemaker who confronts the conflict but in the context of sacrifice. If blood is to be shed, then let it be yours. For more on peacemaking, we turn to one of America's greatest peacemakers in the era of civil rights, Martin Luther King Jr.

PEACEMAKING AND MARTIN LUTHER KING JR.

King writes from a jail cell for having participated in nonviolent demonstrations resisting racial discrimination. He writes to his fellow clergy in a letter simply titled "A Letter from a Birmingham Jail." In it, King explains the tenets of nonviolent resistance and defends this as a form of peacemaking. He calls one of the phases of preparing for demonstration the phase of self-purification where one honestly examines one's tenacity to resist retaliation: "'Are you able to accept the blows without retaliating?' and 'Are you able to endure the ordeals of jail?'"[8]

Peacemaking is thus the relentless resistance to retaliation. The temptation is to self-vindicate, defend, and act out in giving retribution for a hurtful word and slanderous tongue. However, the peacemaker overcomes this temptation. He or she does not provide a tit for tat, does not slander in return, and does not injure with his or her tongue. The servant under the fire of accusation, criticism, and slander must also examine his or her heart and ask the questions, Can you accept the blows of even those who are within? Can you endure the beatings of anger, ire, accusation, and emotional imprisonment and yet temper your tongue to resist evil without committing evil?

> We must see the need for nonviolent gadflies to create the kind of tension in society that will help men rise from the dark depths of prejudice and racism to the majestic heights of understanding and brotherhood.[9]

Peacemaking (εἰρηνοποιός) thus is not the absence of tension, but the engendering of a certain type of "creative tension" that leads men and women to critical analysis of their situation. Creative tension engenders a platform by which the human soul can engage in examination. Motives weigh in the balances. Intentions come under the scrutiny of the plumb

8. King, "Letter from a Birmingham Jail," 2.
9. King, "Letter from a Birmingham Jail," 2.

Setting in Order

line. Indeed, prophetic utterances can be the result of creative tension as a corporate sieve comes upon society to filter out the wickedness and bring justice to roll into a river of life (see Amos 5:24). Therefore, King gives us a perspective that peace is active and synergistic with tension, not a construct subject to passive evolution. Creative tension is at the center of εἰρηνοποιός, for it has an elevating quality, bringing a cognitive awareness to what familial relationships are meant to look and feel like.

This brings illumination to what Jesus said when he commented,

> Do not think that I have come to bring peace to the earth; I have not come to bring peace but a sword. For I have come to set a man against his father, and a daughter against her mother, and a daughter-in-law against her mother-in-law, and one's foes will be members of one's own household. (Matt 10:34–36)

Does Jesus espouse violence, even injury within one's own family? I think not! Rather, it is the violence that the sinful propagate in reaction to the person of Jesus and the kingdom that is obviously present in him. The citizens of this world's kingdom react with violence when the kingdom of heaven presents itself in radical juxtaposition. However, the peacemaker, the εἰρηνοποιός, relentlessly adheres to the other-worldly message and in nonviolence resists the gods of this age. This is the creative tension of the εἰρηνοποιός. The sword is the word of God, which is a purgation of the human soul, separating the soul and spirit (see Heb 4:12). The εἰρηνοποιός uses the tool of God's word to create tension for the human soul so that reconciliation is the fruit of a slain sinful nature. The εἰρηνοποιός therefore is not passive, but one with the sword of the Lord. He or she does not keep the peace by adhering to the status quo, but is doggedly determined to illuminate Christ, the kingdom, and his word amid human reaction.

The εἰρηνοποιός may break a law but does so "openly, lovingly, and with a willingness to accept the penalty."[10] King goes on to say,

> I submit that an individual who breaks a law that conscience tells him is unjust, and willingly accepts the penalty by staying in jail to arouse the conscience of the community over its injustice, is in reality expressing the very highest respect of the law.[11]

Respect is rendered through acceptance of consequence. The law, premise, status quo, and societal ill may be unjust and therefore resisted

---

10. King, "Letter from a Birmingham Jail," 5.
11. King, "Letter from a Birmingham Jail," 5.

SETTING IN ORDER AND SUBMISSION

but with full acknowledgment that there will be consequences and that we must submit ourselves to the fullness of these consequences. Jesus, under a sham trial, with false witnesses, and a political maneuvering of power submitted to the consequence of the farce verdict—a criminal's brutal death upon the cross. Certainly this act alone changed the consciousness of human musing for all generations, raising awareness of sin and subsequent dire need for repentance. For every soul, when coming to Christ, will inquire, How could one so pure and loving die for one so sinister and wicked? Love is violent toward the adversary of our soul through the εἰρηνοποιός of Christ wreaking havoc with his blood in the realms of hell itself. The εἰρηνοποιός of Christ took the keys of hell and liberated the captive. This is the εἰρηνοποιός who is victorious through death and resurrected because of submission to the dictums of the legal consequences of the Sanhedrin court to eliminate the threat to power, and ultimately the Roman circus that would rather keep the peace than make the peace.

As King continues his diatribe on peace and justice, he stumbles on an axiom that I believe helps with the understanding of peacemaking vs. peacekeeping. He is obviously quite frustrated and disappointed in the moderate white religious cohort that have advised waiting, inaction, and a cessation of demonstrations. He provides the following remarks when describing their disposition.

> I have almost reached the regrettable conclusion that the Negro's great stumbling block in the stride towards freedom is not the White Citizens Counselor or the Klu Klux Klanner but the white moderate who is more devoted to "order" than to justice; a negative peace which is the absence of tension to a positive peace which is the presence of justice.[12]

A negative peace would be a peacekeeper whose goal is simply the absence of conflict no matter the cost—even if it is the cost of another's true freedom. This kind of peace is not true peace, but an accommodation of those with influence. The peacekeeper enjoys the negative peace as an accomplishment of placation, but only for a time. The gadfly of creative tension will come again because the peacekeeper will be unable to please everyone with influence and will be unable to ignore those who are oppressed. In contrast, where negative peace is defined by absence, positive peace is defined by presence. With King, it is the presence of

---

12. King, "Letter from a Birmingham Jail," 3.

justice. Peacemaking seeks justice, but in a nonretaliatory way. Justice is sought openly, lovingly, persistently, and with words, not stones.

The peacemaker does not initiate conflict for the purpose of non-creative tension but stands within it as bold as a lion. The peacemakers of antiquity were not brawlers. The peacemakers of old were arrested for their testimony to which they persevered. They marched to their deaths at the stakes and at the mercy of wild beasts in the coliseums. The peacemakers of old, under tyrannical regimes, resisted the sinister ideology of murder, superiority, and Arianism. As much I would like to claim peacemakers as a zeitgeist void of conflict and "absent" of tension, I cannot look at Christ, the εἰρηνοποιός of emulation, and lay claim to this kind of peacemaking.

Rather, the εἰρηνοποιός and Christ as our examples defined peacemaking not in the "negative" sense, not as something omitted, but rather as something present. Indeed, I would argue that defining positive peace and peacemaking (vs. peacekeeping) is ultimately defined by *presence* and negative peace by *absence*. Or as Buber would say, peacemaking is an (I-Thou) relationship vs. peacekeeping which is an (I-it) relationship.[13] When God is present, there will be a sort of tension, for his kingdom is in tension with the kingdom of Satan, who has become the god of this age. Satan has so infiltrated this world that we cannot hope for an absence of all tension until the consummated kingdom and the creation of the new earth and the new heaven. If peacekeeping is our end, then we may find ourselves feverishly working toward absence. If peacemaking is our goal, then we may find ourselves enjoying the presence of God and fully becoming what God intends for us to become, a son or daughter. For a son and daughter bear the fruit of peacemaking!

A PASTORAL ANECDOTE

I must admit that I avoided conflict the final year I was pastoring to keep the peace. The spouse of a newly elected pastoral council member was criticizing one of our staff members openly for many months. There was a condescending approach that this spouse undertook, and I had designated the criticized staff member's supervisor to help arbitrate the conflict between the spouse and the staff member. Well, the absence of

---

13. King, "Letter from a Birmingham Jail," 3. King refers to Buber when he states that "segregation substitutes an 'I-it' relationship for an 'I-thou' relationship and ends up relegating persons to the status of things."

emails for a few short weeks was not a true reconciliation and this church member would not be placated but would go on to denigrate my wife to our state bishop.

In retrospect, this spouse's behavior had disqualified her husband from serving as a council member. He should have been dismissed from serving until true reconciliation could be ascertained. However, both this council member and his spouse would never submit to discipline or humble themselves to follow the authority over them in the Lord. Their fruit was one of inciting "brawling" for the sake of preeminence among the brethren and the assertion that somehow, they knew the better way for the church.

Pastors, confront this behavior, stand in the midst of creative tension. The tension is there for your training. It is creative, for it just might engender a new solution, a new way of being, and a bolder disposition. In many ways, I fell into my default approach that was learned as a child—withdrawal from the anger of others. This was my approach to my father's anger and became a snare to me when others were angry. I did not stand in the hour and vocalize my dissent to the sinful behaviors all around me but withdrew in the name of peacekeeping. I deferred to the state bishop to confront these behaviors.

Pastors, you must stand in the face of tension, knowing that somehow there is a redemptive quality at work in you and that the *presence of God* will guide you through the creative tension. At the same time, discern the noncreative tension—the conflict from dissension that seeks to undermine godly authority—and confront it! You may feel like this is a lonely venture, without the support of even those close to you, and thus be in a winter that fills your soul with a kind of solitude that causes you to shiver. But a fire is coming as you stand in the creative tension of gathering storm clouds. It is a fire that refines and warms the soul as you are ever forged into the peacemaker and child of God who submits to the Father entirely.

MEEKNESS

Meekness (πραΰτητα) is a cardinal virtue of the ancient near-eastern culture and a paradigm for those who live in and love their community and neighbors. Often it is a forgotten virtue in a modern culture of self-aggrandizement. We are immersed in a culture that is forever pulling us into postures that display a kind of strength opposed to gentleness. And although meekness may look like weakness, it produces fruit of great inner strength as the meek remains tame in a world that is spiraling into chaos.

Most modern definitions will render the term *meekness* with definitions that include gentleness or humility. In some ways, this helps us remove the connotation of weakness from the disposition of meekness. In other ways, our culture can adapt to gentleness and humility more readily than if we were to move toward a paradigm of weakness. At the same time, we should not always view meekness as the antithesis to might. Perhaps weakness is the very path to might when viewed through the lens of the kingdom.

πραΰτητα begins not as an outward display of interpersonal dynamics, but as an invisible work of divine grace wrought within the soul of a person. The primary object of meekness is first a disposition toward God than it is toward humanity. The Epistle of James brings clarity to the concept of the first action of meekness when he defines the context of primary meekness: "Therefore rid yourselves of all sordidness and rank growth of wickedness, and welcome with meekness the implanted word that has the power to save your souls" (Jas 1:21).

Therefore, we should conceptualize meekness in two manners. First, a primary meekness that is an inner disposition and posture toward God in that we come to him surrendered to a radical reliance on his grace. This will be termed *primary meekness*, as it is the first order relationship that provides a template for the second order relationship. The term *secondary meekness* will be used to define our interpersonal dynamic with others. The reference to James illustrates how we genuinely receive the word, with πραΰτητα. That is, we receive what is a mirror of our true selves, exposing both the sinful and righteous aspects of our nature. To receive the word with πραΰτητα is to surrender to the word's rendering of your soul.[14]

πραΰτητα is therefore a radical acceptance of God's dealing with us as being forever good. If we become the object upon which evil befalls, meekness accepts that God is working all things for our favor (see Rom 8:28). In meekness, we join Job in the refrain for the ages, "The Lord gives and the Lord takes away, blessed be the name of the Lord!" (Job 1:21). πραΰτητα does not resist, dispute, or curse the circumstances that are

---

14. See Gunton, "Using and Being Used," 248–59, where he explores more fully the hermeneutical premise, "The Bible reads us."

reforming his or her character.[15] Vices are expelled in adversity, resilience is refined in struggle, and perseverance is crafted in tribulation.

Aristotle has offered a definition of πραΰτητα in typical Greek philosophical fashion. He, as he does with many other Greek virtues, espouses a dialectical integration between two seemingly antithetical dispositions. For example, he states that πραΰτητα is an existential quality between excessive anger and excessive angerlessness. That is, it is being angry for the right cause, in the right measure, and at the right moment. Other forms, times, or amounts of anger are therefore restrained by the virtue of πραΰτητα.[16] In prototypical philosophical fashion, Aristotle relegates πραΰτητα to the paradigm of balance, medium, or ascertaining of some but not excessive humors when concerning temperament. And although this can be helpful when understanding πραΰτητα, Barclay goes somewhat further in contemplating a comprehensive definition when he comments on Matt 5:5:

> O the bliss of those who are always angry at the right time and never angry at the wrong time, who have every instinct, impulse and passion under control because they themselves are God-controlled, who have the humility to realize their own ignorance and their own weakness, for such people can rule the world![17]

In Barclay's definition, he incorporates Aristotle's concept but also gives πραΰτητα the nuance of radical reliance and surrender to the faculties of God. There is an accepted frailty with πραΰτητα to the extent that this submission is seen in the greater light of God's economy. To be gentle is to foster an environment for God's strength to be on display (2 Cor 12:9). The irony here is the greater the accepted frailty, the greater the bestowed authority.

There is likely no greater opportunity for πραΰτητα then when one is embroiled in conflict. Conflict is an inevitable human experience. Conflict colors our existence with opportunity and snare, pain and joy, triumph and failure. Conflict is the great luminary of our character. Our responses to conflict have the potential to transform our perspective in ways other experiences cannot. The meek have the uncanny ability to actively and deliberately accept the undesirable circumstances as a part of

---

15. Zodhiates and Baker, *Hebrew-Greek Key Word*, 1751.
16. See Barclay, *New Daily Study Bible*, 111, for more on a definition of πραΰτητα.
17. Barclay, *New Daily Study Bible*, 114.

a larger metanarrative God is writing concerning personal and corporate redemption.

My polemic is that the virtue of meekness, among others, is a dispositional requirement for submission. Paul's litany in Titus 3:2 includes this among other virtues in correlation with his first charge, "Be subject to rulers and authorities." But he also writes elsewhere on the topic, which may be helpful in the development of this polemic. He says,

> By contrast, the fruit of the Spirit is love, joy, peace, patience, kindness, generosity, faithfulness, gentleness, and self-control There is no law against such things. . . . Let us not become conceited, competing against one another, envying one another.
> (Gal 5:22–23, 26)

And,

> With all humility and gentleness, with patience, bearing with one another in love, making every effort to maintain the unity of the Spirit in the bond of peace. (Eph 4:2–3)

There is no law against meekness, for the meek uphold the law and submit to authorities God has placed in the land (Rom 13). But more than this, meekness is a catalyst for unity, peace, and perseverance. Meekness is not a passive resignation to fate, or a reluctant submission to events. Rather, meekness is the patient and hopeful endurance of trial, persecution, and difficulty where one may seem externally vulnerable and weak, but inwardly resilient and strong. Therefore, meekness is not weakness but altogether different—it is strength under fire.

Meekness is really a description of the strong who are placed in a position of weakness where they persevere without giving up. Think imprisonment for the sake of the gospel. We must never give up! If you find yourself in a position where you feel the most vulnerable and weak, without love, support, strength, or escape—persevere! Ask God for the meekness that he gave Moses: "Now the man Moses was very humble, more so than anyone else on the face of the earth" (Num 12:3).

Jesus continues to ask us to emulate his character, which by very nature is gentle and humble in heart, when he says, "Take my yoke upon you, and learn from me, for I am gentle and humble in heart, and you will find rest for your souls" (Matt 11:29).

To every pastor who is weary of striving, working, and anxious with activity, Jesus says to us all: Yoke yourself to me, Beloved. He is gentle, meek, and humble in heart—and in joining Christ in this way, we also become like him in character.

The definition of meekness is of course culminated in Jesus's total surrender to the cross and the laying down of his life for the sake of the world he so unceasingly loved. He entered this world in the condescension of a manger. He entered Jerusalem, gentle and riding on a donkey (Matt 21:5). He entered the garden of Gethsemane submitting to the cup his Father had prepared for him. He hung on the cross, asking forgiveness for those who were ignorant of their atrocity. He stood in the trial of accusation, and was silent before his accusers. He is the One who displays perfectly the meekness of heaven. A gentle Paschal Lamb that surrendered to death, which is the seed of his might.

The winter of your soul may feel like an open stable with you being vulnerable to the winter wind and shelter nowhere in sight. Perhaps the Lord places you there just as he placed Christ in an open stable, the most meek and humble of births for a lesson in discipleship. With every greater measure of meekness in your character comes a greater submission to God's authority. We would do well to offer a hymn to our Lord for the apprehension of spiritual fruit and virtue of meekness.

> Loving Jesus, gentle Lamb,
> In thy gracious hands I am;
> Make me, Saviour, what thou art,
> Live thyself within my heart.
> Lamb of God, I look to thee,
> Thou shalt my example be;
> Thou art gentle, meek and mild;
> Thou wast once a little child.
> Now I would be as thou art;
> Give me an obedient heart;
> Thou art pitiful and kind,
> Let me have thy loving mind.[18]

In conclusion, we have explored the components of submission, those being temperance, peacemaking, and meekness. As a pastor who is tasked with setting a church in order, he or she will find many obstacles to these attributes in the congregation and as such identify deterrents to godly submission. The pastor is to gently confront these deterrents while cultivating the attributes in his or her own character so as to model submission through a temperate tongue, creative tension for peacemaking,

---

18. Wesley, "Gentle Jesus, Meek and Mild," 793.

and perseverance through fiery trials. In so doing, a pastor begins the journey of setting a church in order that may be careening away from the kingdom as society lurches ever fiercely toward individual autonomy. The church is a family, the church has fathers, the church has appointed leaders, shepherds, and pastors to whom we submit with our own surrender to temperance, peacemaking, and meekness.

Chapter 23

Setting in Order and Heresy

After a first and second admonition, have nothing more to do with anyone who causes divisions, since you know that such a person is perverted and sinful, being self-condemned.

Titus 3:10–11

Oportet esse haereses, There must be heresies.[1]

Paul began Titus 3 with a call to submission. He provides dispositional virtues that we have already explored that accompany and are necessary in the act of submission itself. He then discusses the action of God upon the human soul; his kindness and mercy, his washing and renewing, the shed blood of Jesus, the justification by grace, and the becoming an heir of eternal life. This description of grace is still connected to Paul's initial thesis of submission. That is, a short summary would be that we submit to authorities out of the rich grace of God poured out upon us.

Paul then commends Titus to affirm the gospel of grace constantly among the congregation and to pick wisely the battles he ought to fight (Titus 3:8–9). One of these battles we will explore more fully in this

---

1. Fudge, "In Praise of Heresy," 25, where he explains the citation in the following manner: "The Latin Vulgate declared on the authority of St Paul that there must be heresies. Heresy has always been important in Christian history. Throughout the Middle Ages Christendom expected and anticipated the presence of heresy and heretics."

chapter is heresy. The battle of heresy is one that the pastor must engage with admonition. We have explored already that one of the tools of the pastor is admonition with the measuring rod of God's word. Paul is again prompting Titus, as he is all pastors, to admonish and even reject those who would persist in heresy (Titus 3:10–11).

DEFINITIONS

As is our custom in this work, we must understand definitions if we are to discern who a heretic might be. Paul uses the word αἱρετικός (hahee-ret-ee-kos), which is literally one who chooses or is capable of choice. However, "choice" here is quite nuanced. The choice is to take someone or something because of a certain suitability. This is contrasted with *eklegomai*, which is to choose because of love and the sincere desire to attach oneself to another. Heresy is, therefore, a choice, if you will, of a form of discipline, worship, or even an opinion on a certain matter because is it quite fitting or suitable.[2] This evokes a certain expediency with which we might be able to discern heresy. We should also note that choices from suitability and from love are not always mutually exclusive. For example, we find a combination of terms in Isaiah's prophecy as cited in Matthew's Gospel: "Here is my servant, whom I have chosen, my beloved, with whom my soul is well pleased. I will put my Spirit upon him, and he will proclaim justice to the gentiles" (Isa 42:1 and Matt 12:18).

The servant was chosen (αἱρετίζω) but was also beloved. God the Father chose Jesus (an etymological root of heresy, used only here in the New Testament) both because of his suitability and because he is the Beloved. Here we find the integration of both suitability and love in the choosing of Jesus to have the Spirit upon him and declare justice to the gentiles.

Therefore, I would like to contend that heresy (αἱρετικός) is the choosing of a person, system of worship, institution, or ideology from a moral compass of suitability rather than love. That is, the choice is from a motive of mere pragmatic suitability, institutional expediency, and cognitive fitting. In contrast, choices from a motive of love are not always concerned with suitability, but with the imago Dei. The choice born from love is concerned with the image of God in the person and how this image transfigures in the choices that ensue over time.

2. Zodhiates and Baker, *Hebrew-Greek Key Word*, 1684.

Unfortunately, the stinging remarks from a council member at the church I pastored continually plague me with the temptation to consider my worth and work before the Lord as unsuitable. She gave public remarks before the council and my state bishop that I was "not a good fit for the church." I would contend that her remarks were born from αἱρετικός (heresy) as the motive was purely suitability and not love. She had not taken the time to know me, she had not displayed the fruit of love for me or my family, she would later accuse me continually in an effort to have me removed. She had not considered the image of God in the person who was "not a good fit." Indeed, the entire counsel would ask that I resign as pastor or physician without ever inquiring into the needs of my family of eight with me as the sole provider.

Whenever suitability is the guiding principle of our decisions, we fall sometimes unexpectedly into αἱρετικός (heresy). Suitability is the ethos of this kingdom, of a world consumed with a corporate mentality, and a central tenet of evolution. It was Hebert Spencer who would make famous the phrase "The survival of the fittest."[3] We have made evolution our idol in a world that places power as king and humility and meekness as expendable virtues. In summary, αἱρετικός is choice without love.

Let us further explore the New Testament use of this word and concept to add to our definition above. We should first distinguish those who are αἱρετικός from those who cause division or schisms. Paul urges the congregation to mark those who cause διχοστασία (*dichostasia*), which is to say, mark those who cause division or sedition. "I urge you, brothers and sisters, to keep an eye on those who create dissensions and hindrances, in opposition to the teaching that you have learned; avoid them" (Rom 16:17).

We must be careful not to always assume that αἱρετικός are those who create διχοστασία. However, there is but a stone's throw from those who choose heresy, a choice of suitability, and those who cause division, urging others to follow a religious system of their own choosing. Certainly heresy can remain as an individual choice but is often unable to resist the temptation to undermine the pastor who casts a vision and preaches the word. It is the undermining and choosing of a different vision outside of the fidelity to God's word and God's appointed servants

---

3. See Spencer, *Principles of Biology*, 444–45, where he states the following: "The survival of the fittest, which I have here sought to express, in mechanical terms, is that which Mr. Darwin terms 'natural selection,' or the preservation of favoured races in the struggle for life."

that then transitions one from heresy to schism. Have we as the body of Christ ever paused to reflect that a pastor is one chosen by God? Or that those in authority in both ecclesiastical (bishops) and secular (mayors, governors, presidents) institutions are God's servants (see Rom 13)? If such a deep reflection stirred our spirit, we might be careful with our words and intentions when tempted to undermine this authority or create factions within the body of Christ convincing one to a coup. One can choose to disagree without creating dissension. One can choose a different path without becoming seditious. One can break with his or her leader without inciting others into rebellion. However, there is but a step between the two ways of being.

Pastors, we are to confront those who cause offenses and divisions and if they persist, avoid them. That is, the schismatics are to be disfellowshipped until the hopeful day that they repent with godly sorrow. Thus, the call is not that one should never disagree with their pastor, but that one in the end would respect the authority of the pastor by not undermining that authority. That is, one should not attempt to overthrow the appointment of a pastor by staging a rebellion within the church with those who have influence. The latter would be an example of διχοστασία, or schisms.

The difference between αἱρετικός and διχοστασία is further illustrated by Paul's presentation before Felix the governor when he himself was accused of heresy and sedition. "But this I admit to you, that according to the Way, which they call a sect, I worship the God of our ancestors, believing everything laid down according to the law or written in the prophets" (Acts 24:14).

Paul was accused of both heresy and sedition. The word *sect* in Acts 24:14 can be otherwise translated *heresy*. Paul clarifies that although he disagreed with the cohort of the Sanhedrin who opposed the resurrection, he was fully within theology proper to believe in the resurrection. Indeed, he illustrated this hope in the person of Jesus Christ wherever he went. So, though Paul was accused of heresy, he was indeed espousing an orthodox doctrine and more importantly, the summation of the Law and Prophets in the person of Christ. Second, even if he was a heretic of sorts, he was not schismatic. For we find this in his case he makes before Felix: "Now after some years I came to bring alms to my people and to offer sacrifices. While I was doing this, they found me in the temple completing the rite of purification, without any crowd or disturbance" (Acts 24:17–18).

Paul had not incited a rebellion, roused a mob, or created a tumult in order to overthrow the civil or ecclesiastical authorities. With great power but also great peace, he preached the gospel. He was not silent when it came to the death and resurrection of Christ, but nor did he attempt a coup of any sort. He was falsely accused of sedition and schism when he simply disagreed with some while illuminating the doctrine of the resurrection. Thus, Paul was neither a αἱρετικός or διχοστασία, but was rather a prophet to open the eyes of those who would see the kingdom of heaven breaking into this world in the person of Christ.

One of the less obvious travesties within the church is the propagation of heresy and sedition without a call to proper repentance. Paul is clear that both can represent a work of the flesh, for it is a choice birthed out of human rationale and not divine love.

> Now the works of the flesh are obvious: sexual immorality, impurity, debauchery, idolatry, sorcery, enmities, strife, jealousy, anger, quarrels, dissensions, factions, envy, drunkenness, carousing, and things like these. I am warning you, as I warned you before: those who do such things will not inherit the kingdom of God. (Gal 5:19–21)

Now the obvious works of the flesh are often given emphasis in Christian formation such as idolatry, witchcraft, and hatred. However, corporate instruction on dissension, sedition, and heresy is often neglected in admonishing the Christian on spiritual formation and maturation.

However, Paul could not be clearer, those who practice heresy and dissension, αἱρετικός and διχοστασία, will not inherit the kingdom of heaven. Repentance is the clarion call to those who stir up the body to dissent from God's appointments, godly authority, and petty arguments that have no eternal bearing. If a heretic or schismatic continues to bounce from one church to another, with the same fruit—undermine the pastor, create dissension, stir up rebellion, and create confusion through gnostic nonsense (the claim that he or she has some special revelation from God so that others are carried away into a whirlwind of false charisma)—then this person will not inherit the kingdom. For he or she has chosen perpetual sin without repentance, continued wickedness without confession, refused church discipline, and is under the influence of the accuser of the brethren. If you are reading this and are a church member and find that your tendency is to create dissension at every church you have attended, stop now and repent, for your soul is in jeopardy of hell!

If you are a pastor reading this now, confront the dissenter and call them to repent. Admonish once or twice, and if there is no repentance—reject! Those who sow in the flesh sow the wind and will reap the whirlwind.

Now I cannot call others to action without also examining my own motives under the rubric of choice without love. That is, did I make choices because of suitability rather than love? On one hand, my choice to resign as pastor was motivated by two factors. First, my love for my family. My wife was suffering, and I could not bear to see her suffer any longer or reinforce this by my continued role as pastor. Furthermore, I was becoming more and more emotionally distant from my children and if this continued, they would have had a father who was aloof. Moreover, my salary was diminishing with the church, and I was having an increasingly difficult time supporting my large family with a seventh child on the way. Finally, I was wounded beyond my own understanding. It became increasingly difficult to lead in my own brokenness. Therefore, by the time I committed to a choice, love for my family was indeed a primary motivation.

However, could I have made a more loving choice in the budget proposal I submitted that seemed to catalyze the calls for my resignation? In reflecting on this, I did attempt to explore the selling of our facility to preserve the staff. The council decided that this was not feasible after a subcommittee explored this idea. However, I do wonder if a more loving choice would have been to cut all salaries by 10 percent to refrain from having to terminate anyone's employment. Or, we could have continued to cut ministry budgets and have each department committed to fundraising. My contention with this was that many of our staff members were already receiving income below the standard cost of living and cutting their salary further would create more hardship on their respective families. If I am honest with myself, there is a part of me that proposed a budget based on suitability rather than love. And with that said, I am also my harshest critic. And to expose my heart all the more, my choices were somewhat birthed from my own grief. Why was the church declining? Why could we not turn the attendance and revenue around? Why was I now in this position of having to terminate employees? I entertained my own resignation because I was unable to lead the church out of a trajectory of decline. I recall sitting with our finance committee who was also reeling from the cuts that were required and the subsequent projected release of employees. The words, "I need to remain humble and realize that I may need to resign next year if this trend continues," emanated from my mouth and fell upon men without a response. So, I had already conceived the idea of resigning even before I was asked by the council. I never anticipated, however, the spiritual injury that would ensue. One year later, I am still struck with grief and have called into question my future in the ministry, or at least my conceptualization of my role in ministry. Spiritual injury can create cognitive distortions for the one navigating the valley of the shadow of death to believe false narratives about oneself.

Did I commit αἱρετικός by proposing a budget out of pragmatic suitability? I desire to answer in the negative, but the instinctive answer is "I don't know." The decisions were so nuanced, and motivations were manifold. I will say I never intended to be unloving in any budget proposal. My intention was to love the corporate body by stewarding resources within our means and ultimately desired to seek freedom from debt. My accusers who falsely surmised that I was somehow hiding financial details or presenting false revenue projections were quite erroneous and degraded our relationship, seeking to undermine my credibility. This was indeed an unloving posture birthed out of wild speculation and created διχοστασία (schisms) within the body. I am unaware of any repentance for these accusations, and I grieve for a council who remains unrepentant for lies, accusations, the undermining of God's appointments, and διχοστασία. Lord, please have mercy for it is your kindness that leads us to repentance.

CHURCH DISCIPLINE

We have heretofore explored the concept of heresy in relationship with schism. Now we move to the concept of church discipline that is the consequence of διχοστασία and αἱρετικός. The presiding elder (in this case Titus) and the church must "reject" such a one. For the αἱρετικός is one that is warped and sinning, being self-condemned (see Titus 3:11). The Greek term παραιτέομαι (par-ahee-teh'-om-ahee) has been used in New Testament writings to convey the following: to obtain by entreaty. Or to beg from or to ask for. It can also mean supplicate, to avert by entreaty, or seek to avert, and to deprecate. In the context of Titus, the meaning closely aligns with to refuse, decline, to shun, or avoid.[4]

Jesus illustrates this concept of refusing or rejecting a trespassing individual who refuses repentance when he states that "if that person

---

4. Online Greek Bible, "Titus 3:10."

refuses to listen to them, tell it to the church, and if the offender refuses to listen even to the church, let such a one be to you as a gentile and a tax collector" (Matt 18:17). Paul reiterates the definition of παραιτέομαι as "avoiding" when he writes, "I urge you, brothers and sisters, to keep an eye on those who create dissensions and hindrances, in opposition to the teaching that you have learned, avoid them" (Rom 16:17).

The term παραιτέομαι is further nuanced in the sense of actively withdrawing from the schismatic when he writes, "Now we command you, brothers and sisters, in the name of our Lord Jesus Christ, to keep away from every brother or sister living irresponsibly and not according to the tradition that they received from us" (2 Thess 3:6), and, "Take note of those who do not obey what we say in this letter; have nothing to do with them, so that they may be ashamed" (2 Thess 3:14).

Paul is clear here in terms of a protocol for church discipline. With a sinful, pervasive, and persistent schismatic, there is to be a public discourse that declares this individual as one who is disfellowshipped. The act is to stir conviction and a sense of shame for the sins committed by the schismatic. This is for the fruit of repentance to be born in the schismatic. Paul has already written earlier to Timothy that there will be those who have a form of godliness, but who deny the power of godliness; from such παραιτέομαι, turn away (see 2 Tim 3:5).

The apostle John will nuance παραιτέομαι with the following: those who do not reject one who dissents from the truth is to accept the dissenter while consorting and collaborating with the schismatic. "If anyone comes to you and does not bring this teaching, do not receive and welcome this person into your house, for to welcome is to participate in the evil deeds of such a person" (2 John 1:10–11).

Thus, παραιτέομαι is given some extrapolation as John warns not only that one not "receive" he who departs from the truth, but he extends yet another nuance in that those who accept him dissent from the truth. They partake in the wickedness of the schismatic. In the modern church, we do not exercise church discipline in this way. This is one reason why we have those who sin but never bear the marks of repentance. We suffer from those who are proud and, as such, are rewarded for their boasting with a lack of discipline. We groan from those who create factions and who are pitied. We suffer needless pain when we give preeminence to those with influence who slander. If we as the church and as pastors fail to "mark" these persons with public discipline, then we have indeed contributed to the division, not by intention but by omission.

One of my biggest errors was not to mark those who had transgressed with slander, schisms, lack of godly submission, and false accusation. Pastors must admonish these individuals once and then again, providing ample opportunity for repentance. However, after the second admonition, the instruction is clear. Disfellowship the individual, pray that he or she repents, and inform the congregation so that there is a corporate unity to withdraw from such an individual and pray for their repentance. This is New Testament correction and needs to be restored to the church with great veracity. Who will take up the challenge? Who will take up the difficult task of church discipline? Who will take up the mantle to reform an anemic system that seeks to privatize discipline in the name of civility? This was the cultural mantra that ensnared and paralyzed me from Biblical church discipline. And, as such, I now repent: Lord, forgive me for my passivity.

PARAHERESY

Now that we have defined heresy and discipline, we must now turn to paraheresy behavior, that of power and control. For this, we turn to Jan Hus, Martin Luther, and the Reformers. For in the history of ecclesiastical councils, determinations, and adjudications, there are likely no more renown "heretics" than those who instigated the medieval Reformation.

Thomas Fudge has given us a brief history of the Reformation while also exploring the notion of heresy. Fudge provides a statement of irony when he asserts that "in Hus we find the virtues of heresy and dissent."[5] Although tongue and cheek, and certainly we can gather that Fudge means to intentionally conflate terms, I must note the following: by attributing praise to heresy and dissent, Fudge fails to distinguish prophetic action against the tyranny of false authority and true heresy and dissent that splinter the church in the name of a false narrative.

The former continues to be motivated from a heart of love for God and neighbor vis-à-vis activism through prophetic speech. The latter creates dissent through accusation choosing from some other motivation such as power, scorn, woundedness, or misunderstanding. Therefore, I would not ascribe virtue to true heresy but would laud Hus as a voice crying out in the wilderness, not a heretic. Jan Hus defended the Scripture to his death and sought to bring the church to the rule and order of

---

5. Fudge, "In Praise of Heresy," 37.

divine inspiration. Fudge cites medieval canon law when defining heresy as the following: "Medieval canon law characterised heresy as holding views chosen by human will, contrary to Scripture, declared publicly, and defended stubbornly."[6]

In this light, Hus and Luther were not heretics, for their views were not contrary to Scripture, but rather in harmony with it. Now the fact that they persisted in their theological conviction even when held in contempt by ecclesiastical structures is where confusion can arise. The latter half of this definition would portend Hus and Luther to heresy, but without the former half of the definition, this would thus disqualify the attribution of heresy to Hus and Luther. As I have stated earlier, I would add to the definition of heresy above a decision by human will void of love for God or neighbor.

I do appreciate Fudge's insightful probe into the secondary gain of heresy. Accusations of such, if not carefully inspected by the one making such remarks, can come from a zeal for power rather than a zeal for love and truth. Fudge peels back the layer of many accusations of heresy when he says the following: "Accusations of heresy rarely relate to theology specifically, but rather are concerned principally with power and control."[7]

O how humanity seeks for power, authority, and renown. For those with true authority, there is given the formidable task of discerning whether opposition to authority is prophetic or seditious. Is the one resisting authority an agent of reformation or an emissary of Satan seeking to fragment the church? Is the person resisting pastoral authority bearing the fruit of the Spirit, appealing to and aligning with the Scripture, and accompanied by the Spirit of God in the community of faith? If not, then the one discerning ought to mark such a person as choosing a position not from love, but from power or recognition.

In my own situation, as I pastored a Pentecostal church, I noticed that in our community of faith, much abuse can come from labelling a word or action "prophetic." For example, as I have written earlier, the spouse of a council member wrote to the state bishop intimating that my wife and I were unfit for ministry, appealing to my wife's postpartum depression and my apparent busyness. Later, in council meetings, the council member whose wife decided to commit to such action called this

---

6. Fudge, "In Praise of Heresy," 25.
7. Fudge, "In Praise of Heresy," 38.

a "prophetic act." To give this action the construct of prophecy is to make it true. Often in Pentecostal/charismatic communities, if one would like to substantiate an action or word as "true" without any equivocation or argument, that one could claim that it is "prophecy." How could one argue with a prophecy?

However, a hermeneutic is required when these lofty claims are made. For example, does the action coincide with the general revelation of Scripture? Does the one performing the "prophetic" act bear the fruit of the Spirit as a substantive forerunner of the gift of the Spirit in prophecy? In this case, the person performing the "prophetic" act had countlessly criticized one of our staff members and refused to humble herself in submission to the staff member she criticized. Second, she refused to submit to pastoral authority, dodging every attempt to meet for the purpose of church discipline. Finally, the council member (husband), in this case, wildly claimed that I was invoking the demonic in my prayers. For these data points, I would discern as a leader that the claim to prophecy is untrue and heretical. The decision was not bathed in love or truth, but rather some other motivation. Perhaps the motive to act in the way she had may have originated from the grief that the church was declining and so, misguided, attributed this decline to the most obvious source, the pastor and his spouse.

Much of what heresy truly becomes is not necessarily love of God, love of neighbor, or zeal for truth, but rather grasping for power. It becomes about who is truly leading the church? Those who oppose each other would both appeal to Jesus Christ, that he is the one leading the church, but will eviscerate each other in the name that this or that person is the regent or agent of Jesus Christ. This is where Fudge is quite helpful, for he strips away the theological opacity of the heresy label, bringing to light the real struggle—authority.

This is where I appreciate Fudge's development of the power struggle. He provides a contrast between the Sermon on the Mount by Jesus (see Matt 5–7) and the Nicene Creed. In noting the contrast, he asserts that the Sermon is moral and behavioral in nature with very little to say about doctrine. However, the Creed is heavily doctrinal with the expectation that one assent to believe in this Creed without addressing specific morals. He goes on with the contrast:

> The Creed became ascendant. Doctrine replaced ethics. Theology superseded morality. Both Hus and Luther were aware of the unintended consequences of dissent and nonconformity but

neither were willing to stand down. Reformation is best exhibited when it equally values the Sermon and the Creed.[8]

Heresy thus can be misconstrued when forensics become the sole arbitrator. The soul must also come to bear in discerning heresy. Orthodoxy cannot stand on its own but requires orthopathy. Where the Creed develops orthodoxy, the Sermon evokes orthopathy. Both are needed for orthopraxy. O how we need a fusion of affection and faith by the Spirit of God in living together in God's economy. This is where the inspection of someone's fruit is so important when investigating their "prophetic" claims.

Discerning the prophet from the heretic is the task of the pastor with the elders bearing in mind the Augustinian statement and humble prayer, "*Ecclesia semper reformanda est* (the church must always be reformed)."[9] Thus, I would differ with Fudge in terms that dissent ought to be celebrated and encouraged for reasons that it is the medium of reformation within the church.[10] Rather, I would create a more nuanced rubric for celebration. Prophetic dissent to topple the kingdoms of tyranny ought to be celebrated. In contrast, true heresy—dissent void of love—requires church discipline and judgment. Again, in reading Fudge's article, I do gather that the spirit of the article is not to praise true heresy, but rather prophetic dissent as a vehicle for reformation. For example, he concludes the matter with the following:

> The ethos of heresy embodied by Hus and Luther that resisted the medieval church's effort to maintain conformity on major points of theology and religious practice is worth considering and a reminder that old-fashioned ideas like truth have never been determined by vote or even consensus.[11]

Truth is not always truth because there is a consensus or vote. This becomes a powerful statement when we think of the confidence we have placed in church councils who have voted on certain truth claims. Consensus sometimes requires the convulsions of the prophet who is the

---

8. Fudge, "In Praise of Heresy," 39–40.

9. Fudge, "In Praise of Heresy," 41.

10. Fudge, "In Praise of Heresy," 41. Fudge asserts the following: "In defying all the sage men of Christendom Hus bequeathed to the ages the principle that dissent and heresy should not simply be tolerated but practised and actively encouraged, following Abelard: 'By doubting we come to inquiry, by inquiry we perceive truth.'"

11. Fudge, "In Praise of Heresy," 44.

voice crying in the wilderness, alone, but preparing the way of the Lord. The church council voted by consensus that I ought to resign. The state bishop nullified this vote by stating that I ought to remain. Which is the way? Which is the choice of love? Which was the choice of suitability, and which was the choice of charity? Would I have prophetically dissented by remaining? Did I substantiate the council by departing? Did I acquiesce to consensus?

I must confess that my decisions were not as heavily guided by these inquiries of theological import, but rather the affections I experienced for my family. Perhaps this decision had to be made for my own personal soul. Perhaps my affections were all wrong. Perhaps my affections were contingent upon a certain dream of pastoring that unintentionally excluded my dream of husband and father. Considering this reflection, perhaps God is reordering my affections into orthopathy. Perhaps orthodoxy was my claim and way but could not result in orthopraxy until God ordered my affections. Love is the consummation of all things. When discerning and deciding, a simple filter can be applied to guide what may be an excruciatingly painful process. Is the choice from suitability or love? Is the choice for truth or power? These questions are not meant to undermine the complexity of heresy in the church but can provide a starting place for the pastor grappling with church dynamics.

Chapter 24

Setting in Order and the Pastor's Winter

When I send Artemas to you, or Tychicus, do your best to come to me at Nicopolis, for I have decided to spend the winter there.
TITUS 3:12

As Timothy before him, Titus is invited to Paul's winter. Artemas or Tychichus are to be sent to carry on the work in Crete while Titus joins Paul at Nicopolis, for Paul is determined to winter there. To determine a winter is to lodge at a place of one's own choosing. The winter is inevitable and will come to all who long to serve in the kingdom. But one can choose where and with whom one will endure the winter months. Paul chose Timothy and Titus. Paul chose Nicopolis.

A BRIEF HISTORY OF NICOPOLIS

The year was 31 BC and the triumvirate of Rome was disintegrating. Marc Antony, a renowned general to Julius Caesar, had fled from Rome to ally with Cleopatra of Egypt and claim her son in adoption and as legitimate heir to Caesar of Rome. For her son was believed to be the son of Julius Caesar himself. Octavian, on the other hand, an adopted son of Julius Caesar, demurred and began to consolidate his own allegiances in the west at Rome.

SETTING IN ORDER AND THE PASTOR'S WINTER

The Roman senate was initially split over who would be the rightful Caesar to ascend leadership in the vacuum left after Julius Caesar's death. As tensions mounted, fleets and armies grew. Alliances with other generals and nation-states in the Roman empire were made. Some allegiances came to side with Antony and Cleopatra while others aligned with Octavian. The battle came to a head in a naval conflict that would be called the decisive campaign to end the Roman Republic and birth the Roman Empire. Octavian dispatched Agrippa to lead his fleet and his general Titus to lead his armies. The two naval legions met in battle at the coast of Actium.[1]

As the battle raged on, for reasons that remain contested, Cleopatra abandoned the battle with her naval ships. Antony, again for reasons that continue to be debated, followed her. With both Cleopatra and Antony having fled, the ships fought on without their generals. Eventually Antony's fleet would surrender to Octavian, which ended the disputation over who would lead the Roman institution. Octavian had consolidated his power and would become known as Caesar Augustus. This transition also brought the Roman Republic to an end as Augustus was essentially deified not only as a Roman Caesar but as a Roman god.[2]

To memorialize his victory, Octavian built a city as a trophy to his victory. This city would be endeared to him as Nicopolis, which is rendered "city of victory." Within the confines of the city, Caesar Augustus would erect a temple to Apollos, his patron god, as homage to his victory. Antony and Cleopatra would eventually end their own lives as Augustus closed in on their whereabouts. Augustus would kill their son Caesarion, essentially eliminating any threat to his power and rule.[3]

I find the history of Nicopolis to be an illustration of the juxtaposition of two kingdoms. On one hand, we have the history of a city entrenched in conflict, blood, quests for power, and the legitimizing of a throne. In contrast, we have a renewed history of God's kingdom coming to Nicopolis in the form of the gospel, the quest to surrender power to Christ, and legitimizing of our eternal life through the death and resurrection. One kingdom sends a Titus as a general to defeat the armies of Antony, the other kingdom calls for a Titus to keep company with a man who is about to die for his faith. One kingdom erects a temple to Apollos, a false god who was given credit for Octavian's victory. The other

1. Shuckburgh, *History of Rome*, 780–84.
2. Shuckburgh, *History of Rome*, 780–84.
3. Seutonius, *Lives of the Twelve Caesars*, 71–191.

SETTING IN ORDER

kingdom calls for Apollos to come for preparations to send the gospel into far reaching territories (see Titus 3:13). One kingdom calls for a son of Caesar to be the king of the kings, another kingdom reveals the true King of kings in the person of Jesus Christ.[4] One kingdom boasts of the defeat and death of the armies of Antony and Cleopatra. The other kingdom boasts on the sacrificial death of Jesus in the name of divine love.

Therefore, could it be that Paul was sent to Nicopolis to redeem its history? To redeem the city? Does God redeem the history of cities? Paul is now the general of Nicopolis, sent there to winter. He calls his generals to the city in preparation for a war against the deceit of Satan in territories where the good news has not yet come. The city of victory may have been Paul's last city as he prepares for his own personal victory, his entrance to the kingdom of heaven. For Paul, he has fought the good fight, he has kept the faith, and there is a crown of everlasting life awaiting him (see 2 Tim 4:7).

Williams Shakespeare has dedicated an entire play to the narrative of Antony and Cleopatra and their demise propagated by misinformation and despair. In act 2, Menas makes a remark that has embedded wisdom for those who seek after corporeal glory:

> We, ignorant of ourselves,
> Beg often our own harms, which the wise powers
> Deny us for our good; so find we profit
> By losing of our prayers.[5]

Whether knowingly or not, Shakespeare illustrates for us the redemptive guard of God to keep us from our own demise. The wisdom of James says likewise: "You ask and do not receive because you ask wrongly, in order to spend what you get on your pleasures" (Jas 4:3).

Perhaps the ambitious desires of Antony and Cleopatra were not fulfilled for if granted would have produced a greater calamity. It is difficult to find palatable that either Octavian or Antony would ascend the leadership of Rome, both with ambitions to murder any opposition and grasp for totalitarian authority. Nonetheless, God is always working even in the vices of humanity. He is redeeming Nicopolis, translating it from a city of victory through vestiges of sinful ambition, pride, and idolatry to a

---

4. Reinhold, *Studies in Classical History and Society*, 58. Octavian and Cleopatra render this title to Cleopatra's eldest son who was believed to also be the son of Julius Caesar. This title was more of a political token utilized to claim the leadership of Rome based on dynastic lineage.

5. Shakespeare, *Tragedy of Antony and Cleopatra*, 2.1.7–10.

kingdom headquarters where missionaries are dispatched with the everlasting gospel. It also becomes the city of Paul's winter, his time and place of fellowship and companionship before the spring of his martyrdom.

REDEEMING A PASTOR

Therefore, I would like to propose perhaps something remarkable. Setting a church in order aids in setting a city in order. Moreover, choosing to lodge in a city in a season of winter has a transformative quality for the individual and the city. The ambitions of Octavian and Antony are being crucified in the pastor who winters at Nicopolis. A new way is formed in the desolation of the snow and ice. It is the winter that can forge new dreams for the pastor, which impacts his or her city. There is a reordering of affections. Prayers that went unanswered are answered in ways we would never have imagined.

Instead of a Titus to squash those who oppose you, a Titus is sent to bring comfort. Instead of declarations identifying who really is in control, there is a stepping back and a surrender to the Lord who is in control. In the winter at Nicopolis, God is undoing the human desire to fashion a Caesarion as a god. Rather, God undoes us! It is the winter where you are the caraway seed beaten as an aromatic for the world to taste (see Isaiah 28:27).

In the winter, God takes your flight from trouble and transforms it into a mission for his kingdom. In the winter, the temple to Apollos, built within the human heart on the bloodshed grounds of hubris, is being torn asunder by God who is sending a different Apollos altogether, "an eloquent man, well-versed in the scriptures" (Acts 18:24).

In Martin Luther's winter, he spent many months locked away in a lonely castle, away from the noise of a burgeoning reformation. But it was there where he wrestled with his own physical infirmity. It was there where he began his monumental work, the translation of the New Testament into the vernacular for all of Germany to read. Rather than being present to argue for the reforms he was calling for in the public square, he remained hidden in a winter where he was cut off from all the seminal voices of his time. And yet, he was completing a kingdom assignment that would reform the church in a way that he could hardly imagine—the word was prevailing!

Setting in Order

JOY IN WINTER

In the winter Zenas is sent, a lawyer, not as a prosecutor but as an advocate who is sent to lift the weary arms of a pastor and intercede. In the winter, a pastor may be surprised by who it is that reaches out. The surprise is like the phrase C. S. Lewis coined, the phenomenon of being "surprised by joy." In his book with the same title he attempts to define what joy is, stating, "The inherent dialectic of desire itself had in a way already shown me this; for all images and sensations, if idolatrously mistaken for Joy itself, soon honestly confessed themselves inadequate."[6]

Simply put, joy can be subtly replaced with desire. But this is a mistaken definition for joy. Indeed, Lewis goes so far as to claim that this is an idolatrous fallacy. It is erroneous to disgrace joy with the pauper notion of desire. Desire is altogether inadequate for the human soul who longs for true joy. Desire is insufficient to produce joy that is more like unspeakable rapture (see 1 Pet 1:8).

Furthermore, Lewis seeks to identify joy by also suggesting the right location for joy. That is, the locus of joy is not within but without. Joy is not an event, but a person.

> Joy itself, considered simply as an event in my own mind, turned out to be of no value at all. All the value lay in that of which Joy was the desiring. And that object, quite clearly, was no state of my own mind or body at all.[7]

Indeed, the object of all joy is the person of Jesus Christ, and this joy surprises the pastor in winter. Why is it a surprise? Well, you find joy quite unexpectedly in the most chilling of circumstances. The metrics of quantity become the metrics of quality. Your worth is no longer in the numbers on a Sunday morning or the affirmation from your peers that your church is growing. Your joy is not in the building programs and the exterior veneer of titles and adulations. Rather, in the winter, in Nicopolis, the pastor is stripped of these trappings to become surprised with a soteriological joy located in holding the hand of Christ as he says to you, "You are mine." One's worth is in knowing that you are a son and daughter of the Lord.

For many, we preach this but do not believe this about ourselves. The worth of so many pastors is in the number of naval ships sailing near

---

6. Lewis, *Surprised by Joy*, 212.
7. Lewis, *Surprised by Joy*, 213.

Actium and the building of a Nicopolis to pay homage to the name of self-aggrandizement. I do wonder if winter is necessary in all of our lives so that we come to the end of ourselves and find that we are surprised by a joy that is divine. Perhaps we find a new way of "working out our salvation" in a trembling that is a response to the winds of winter. Lewis was surprised by joy when he turned from atheism to faith.[8] Perhaps a pastor is surprised by joy when, stripped of all things, he or she finds all things. And this is where all things consist, were created by, and are substantiated by Jesus Christ.

As I write it is November and the leaves are falling from the trees and I awoke to frost on the ground. I will not fear the cold. I will not disdain what must be. Rather, I will embrace the season as a necessary reformation in my soteriological journey. I will find that there is joy in the new way of being, in the smile of my wife, in the hugs from my children, in my daily talks with God, in the warming of my hands near the fire, in the bearing of my soul in the fellowship with Timothy and Titus. Apollos is there as well. Zenas is coming. And as we all know, Jesus is coming and in his coming, all winter melts in the flame of his parousia. It is here where all things will be set in order. It is here where all things will be set right. It is here where the great Overseer of our souls will set the cosmos in order forever. Maranatha, Lord, come quickly!

---

8. Indeed, Lewis's work *Surprised by Joy* chronicles his journey from atheism to faith.

Appendix A
Spiritual Dynamics Inventory

Spiritual Dynamics Inventory

A tool designed to help pastors understand the spiritual dynamics of the church family.

Please answer all questions which seem most intuitively and prayerfully honest to your experience. Please note that this tool is not intended to replace direction received in prayer.

Is Scriptural truth regularly expressed and discussed in the church family?

☐ 1 ☐ 2 ☐ 3 ☐ 4 ☐ 5

None Some Several Most All

Is mercy (i.e. lovingkindness) regularly on display in the church family?

☐ 1 ☐ 2 ☐ 3 ☐ 4 ☐ 5

None Some Several Most All

Is there an emphasis on righteousness, holiness as God's standard of living, practiced in the church family?

☐ 1 ☐ 2 ☐ 3 ☐ 4 ☐ 5

None Some Several Most All

Is false doctrine confronted, and its adherents admonished on a consistent basis?

☐ 1 ☐ 2 ☐ 3 ☐ 4 ☐ 5

None Some Several Most All

Is grace on display, salvation being worked out, and new converts coming to the faith?

☐ 1 ☐ 2 ☐ 3 ☐ 4 ☐ 5

None Some Several Most All

Is there an emphasis on the coming of Christ on how we talk and live our lives?

☐ 1 ☐ 2 ☐ 3 ☐ 4 ☐ 5

All Most Several Some None

APPENDIX A

Spiritual Dynamics Inventory

Is church discipline being implemented and are those who refuse discipline being disfellowshipped?

☐ 1   ☐ 2   ☐ 3   ☐ 4   ☐ 5

None   Some   Most   All
Several

Are there multiple generations engaged in the church?

☐ 1   ☐ 2   ☐ 3   ☐ 4   ☐ 5

None   Some   Most   All
Several

Is there evidence of regeneration, changed lives, transformation evident in the body?

☐ 1   ☐ 2   ☐ 3   ☐ 4   ☐ 5

None   Some   Most   All
Several

A score of 36 or higher places a church at a low risk of unhealthy dynamics. A score of 26 to 36 places at a church at moderate risk of unhealthy dynamics. A score of 25 or lower places a church at high risk of unhealthy dynamics.

Appendix B
Mark Driscoll Resignation Letter[1]

October 14, 2014
Michael Van Skaik
Chairman, Board of Advisors and Accountability
Mars Hill Church

Dear Michael:

By God's grace I have pastored Mars Hill Church for 18 years. Today, also by God's grace, and with the full support of my wife Grace, I resign my position as a pastor and elder of Mars Hill. I do so with profound sadness, but also with complete peace.

On August 24th I announced to our Mars Hill family of churches that I had requested a leave of absence from the pulpit and the office for a minimum of six weeks while a committee of elders conducted a formal review of charges made against me by various people in recent times. Last week our Board of Overseers met for an extended period of time with Grace and me, thereby concluding the formal review of charges against me. I want to thank you for assuring Grace and me that last Saturday that I had not disqualified myself from ministry.

You have shared with us that this committee spent more than 1,000 hours reviewing documents and interviewing some of those who had presented charges against me. You have also shared with me that many of those making charges against me declined to meet with you or participate in the review process at all. Consequently, those conducting the review of charges against me began to interview people who had not even been a party to the charges.

---

1. Bailey, "Mark Driscoll's Resignation Letter."

APPENDIX B

I readily acknowledge I am an imperfect messenger of the gospel of Jesus Christ. There are many things I have confessed and repented of, privately and publicly, as you are well aware. Specifically, I have confessed to past pride, anger and a domineering spirit. As I shared with our church in August, "God has broken me many times in recent years by showing me where I have fallen short, and while my journey, at age 43, is far from over, I believe He has brought me a long way from some days I am not very proud of, and is making me more like Him every day."

Prior to and during this process there have been no charges of criminal activity, immorality or heresy, any of which could clearly be grounds for disqualification from pastoral ministry. Other issues, such as aspects of my personality and leadership style, have proven to be divisive within the Mars Hill context, and I do not want to be the source of anything that might detract from our church's mission to lead people to a personal and growing relationship with Jesus Christ.

That is why, after seeking the face and will of God, and seeking godly counsel from men and women across the country, we have concluded it would be best for the health of our family, and for the Mars Hill family, that we step aside from further ministry at the church we helped launch in 1996. I will gladly work with you in the coming days on any details related to our separation.

Recent months have proven unhealthy for our family—even physically unsafe at times—and we believe the time has now come for the elders to choose new pastoral leadership for Mars Hill. Grace and I pledge our full support in this process and will join you in praying for God's best for this, His church, in the days and years ahead. Grace and I would also covet your prayers for us as we seek God's will for the next chapter of our lives. Therefore, consider this written notice of my voluntary termination of employment.

Finally, it would be my hope to convey to the wonderful members of the Mars Hill family how deeply my family and I love them, thank them, and point them to their Senior Pastor Jesus Christ who has always been only good to us.

Sincerely,
Pastor Mark Driscoll

Appendix C
Liturgy for the Ordination of Elders

- Responsive Reading: Acts 14:23

    Call: So, when they had appointed elders in every church, and prayed with fasting,
    Response: they commended them to the Lord in whom they had believed.

- Rationale: The office of an elder is a noble office to which one may aspire and to one to whom the Lord may call. It is given to one who is a faithful follower, emulating the pattern of our Lord Jesus Christ. It is an office of authority, but must also illustrate submission first to our Lord, but also to the presiding elder, the church pastor and to his or her pastors, the regional and state overseers. An elder must in open forum now be examined with public affirmation of the qualities necessary in character to esteem to the office of an elder. The elder candidates now set before you have fasted and prayed in preparation for this most holy occasion in true desire to pursue the will of God.

- Qualifying Affirmations:

    Pastor: Have you in your walk in the community of faith submitted to the authority of Jesus and the authority of those over you in the Lord? Have you submitted to the Word of God and church discipline? And do you now commit to submit to godly authority and to those who the Lord may appoint to lead you (1 Timothy 3:2, Titus 1:6)?

APPENDIX C

Candidate: I have, and I do commit to submit first to our Lord Jesus Christ and second to godly authority and church discipline.

Pastor: Have you honored your spouse, prayed for and with your spouse, affirmed your spouse in public, and served your spouse as Christ would serve the church? Have you remained faithful to your spouse, forsaking all others until death do you part? Do you commit to honoring, serving, loving, remaining in fidelity, and respecting your spouse as you fulfill your role as an elder (1 Timothy 3:2, Titus 1:6)?

Candidate: I have remained faithful and commit to honoring my spouse for as long as I shall live.

Pastor: Are your children committed to serving the Lord Jesus Christ? Do they know and follow Jesus Christ? Do your children submit to godly authority and to the discipline of the church? Do your children honor God and those in authority? And do you commit to serving your children, commending them to the Lord as a first fruits ministry prior to serving the church (1 Timothy 3:4–5, Titus 1:6)?

Candidate: My children serve the Lord with all of their hearts and submit to our Lord and to godly authority. I commit this day to serve my children as a primary ministry, ensuring the Word is therefore deposited within their hearts.

Pastor: Do you publicly confess that you remain free from any addictive or harmful substances that would impair your judgment? Do you remain sober and watchful in all things material and spiritual (1 Timothy 3:2)?

Candidate: By God's grace, I am free from all addictive and harmful substances. I commit to maintaining sobriety and will be watchful in all things material and spiritual.

Pastor: Do you publicly renounce the pursuit of this office for selfish gain, either in public renown or in pursuit of wealth? Are you longsuffering, patient, not given to anger outbursts? Do you now commit to be a steward of God's grace through the bearing of the cross given to you (Titus 1:7)?

Candidate: I lay down and crucify any motive that would be selfish in nature. I affirm to honor God's grace by stewarding this office in humble reverence to our Savior and contrition of soul. I now pray for the fruit of the Spirit to be evident within me. I publicly confess to take up my cross daily by God's help.

Pastor: Do you affirm the spiritual gift of teaching given to you by the Holy Spirit as this is a gift required of the office of an elder? This gift is thus required so that you may exhort the church with sound doctrine and convince those in opposition of the truth (1 Timothy 3:2, Titus 1:9).

Candidate: I commit to teaching God's Word by God's help. I affirm the desire to teach and pray God cultivate the gift to teach through His Spirit. I am committed to teach all of Scripture, holding to the promise that all Scripture is inspired of God. I commit to both exhorting the church in sound doctrine and admonishing those who oppose the truth.

Pastor: Do you now affirm that you have walked with the Lord for a long season, having disciplined yourself to the pattern of our Lord Jesus Christ? Have you illustrated your commitment through faithful service to the church and mission over several years (1 Timothy 3:6)?

Candidate: I have walked with the Lord by God's grace over several seasons and years throughout my life and commit to serving the Lord in perpetuity, advancing His cause and mission.

Pastor: Do you have a good reputation in the community? Are you free from any genuine accusations either through litigation or media that would bring a reproach to the Name of Christ (1 Timothy 3:7)?

Candidate: I affirm today that I have not willingly brought shame to the name of Christ in our community. By God's grace, I have and will serve my community to bring honor to the name of Christ.

- Hymn of Consecration: Take my Life by Francis Havergal
- Responsive Reading: Acts 20:28-35

    Call: Therefore take heed to yourselves and to all the flock, among which the Holy Spirit has made you overseers, to shepherd the church of God which He purchased with His own blood.

    Response: For I know this, that after my departure savage wolves will come in among you, not sparing the flock. Also from among yourselves men will rise up, speaking perverse things, to draw away the disciples after themselves.

    Call: Therefore, watch and remember that for three years I did not cease to warn everyone night and day with tears.

APPENDIX C

Response: So now, brethren, I commend you to God and to the word of His grace, which is able to build you up and give you an inheritance among all those who are sanctified.

Call: I have coveted no one's silver or gold or apparel. Yes, you yourselves know that these hands have provided for my necessities, and for those who were with me. I have shown you in every way, by laboring like this, that you must support the weak.

Response: And remember the words of the Lord Jesus, that He said, "It is more blessed to give than to receive."

- Commissioning Charges:

    Pastor: Do you unreservedly commit to being watchful over the congregation to discern the adversary's movements and emissaries within or against the congregation and provide adequate warning and discipline (Acts 20, 1 Peter 5:8)?

    Candidate: I do now commit myself to be watchful and discerning. I commit to warning and providing discipline when necessary.

    Pastor: Do you unreservedly commit to preaching and teaching the Word of God as the Spirit should enable you (1 Timothy 3:2)?

    Candidate: By God's grace, I commit to teaching and preaching the entire Word of God in exhorting and admonishing the church.

    Pastor: Do you unreservedly commit to leading the flock into the purposes God intends in submission to and in cooperation with the church pastor?

    Candidate: By God's grace, I will support the pastor's vision and commit to leading the flock into the purpose God's reveals for the church.

    Pastor: Do you unreservedly commit to presiding over the deacons, staff, and other leaders of the church in submission to and cooperation with the pastor in order to help the pastor cultivate the development of these leaders in the faith?

    Candidate: By God's grace, I commit to leading our servant leaders in the faith.

    Pastor: Do you unreservedly commit to guard the flock from the devices of the enemy?

Candidate: I commit to guard the flock by preventing and exposing demonic strongholds that would attempt to gain access to the flock.

Pastor: Do you unreservedly commit to inspecting the flock for wounds, sins, wickedness, and unrepentance? Do you also commit to engaging the healing and disciplinary processes that may be required of you?

Candidate: By God's grace, I commit to inspect the flock and discern the need for church discipline. I also commit to be a vessel for healing and church discipline where needed.

Pastor: Do you unreservedly commit to implement and maintain healthy boundaries in the flock through supporting those in authority and operating within the framework of conspicuous roles of authority? Do you commit to communicating these roles of authority to the flock?

Candidate: By God's grace, I commit to implementing and maintaining clear boundaries within the congregation. I commit to communicating these roles, boundaries, and support for godly authority where needed.

- Hymn of Ordination: O for a Thousand Tongues to Sing by Charles Wesley
- Anointing with Oil:

    Posture of Submission: The elders all fall prostrate before the Lord and in one accord worship the Lord with the following utterance: You are worthy, O Lord, To receive glory and honor and power; For You created all things, And by Your will they exist and were created (Revelation 4:11)."

    Anointing: The candidates then stand for the anointing service. The Pastor anoints each candidate with oil as existing elders lay hands on the candidate for service.

- Credal Confession (said by all)

    God was manifested in the flesh, Justified in the Spirit, Seen by angels, Preached among the gentiles, Believed on in the world, Received up in glory (1 Timothy 3:16). And we all say, Amen!

Appendix D
Church Discipline, Restoration, and Reconciliation[1]

THE PURPOSE OF CHURCH DISCIPLINE

"Brethren, if a man is overtaken in any trespass, you who are spiritual restore such a one in a spirit of gentleness, considering yourself lest you also be tempted. Bear one another's burdens and so fulfill the law of Christ" (Gal 6:1–2 NKJV).

IN THE EVENT THAT biblical disciplinary actions become necessary and appropriate, it is important to keep in focus that the purpose of church discipline is restoration and reconciliation. When initiated, biblical discipline is for a person's spiritual growth through repentance and restorative discipleship. The church leadership who oversees the rebuilding process needs to invest in the appropriate plan and accountable nurture that aligns best with this goal.

A clear distinction is to be affirmed as to the difference between *discipline* and *punishment*. Discipline is designed to encourage the restoration of the one involved in wrongdoing. It is to be instructive and corrective with the biblical goal to engage restorative grace and personal transformation. Punishment generally focuses on retribution for the wrong done as it seeks primarily to assert justice.

---

1. Adapted from Rock Church, "Church Discipline, Restoration and Reconciliation."

BIBLICAL FOUNDATIONS FOR CHURCH DISCIPLINE

- Discipline should move through appropriate steps toward restoration (Matt 18:15–20).
- Sin and disobedience should be taken very seriously as God desires the church to reflect his character and holiness (Acts 5:1–11).
- Unrepentant sin is to be grieved by the church and addressed deliberately (1 Cor 5:1–5).
- When a church leader sins, discipline is to involve appropriate authentication and suitable public rebuke that others may take warning (1 Tim 5:17–22).
- Discipline is to be corrective in nature for the purpose of growth (Heb 3:12–13; 12:5–17).

THE PRACTICAL PROCESS FOR STAFF, LEADERSHIP, AND CONGREGATION

If church discipline is warranted, the following actions will become a part of the restoration process:

- An identified pastor will oversee the specific restoration process for the individual(s) involved.
- If the conflict involved any legal violations, PR/Legal will be consulted for approval to review any legal entanglements before engaging the process.
- The pastoral team coordinator will be consulted with in relation to the incident and restoration plan. *(The pastoral team coordinator will notify the Executive Leadership Team regarding the person, plan, and process if it involves a church member, the lead pastor will inform the Administrative Council/Elders if the conflict involves a staff member.)*
- The offending individual(s) will be given the opportunity to submit to the restoration plan and process.
- Documentation of the incident and the restoration plan will be recorded on the attached document and will be filed.

- A documented restoration process will be formally agreed upon with appropriate boundaries and actions identified for the individual in relation to their sin or offense.
- As part of the restoration plan an accountable leader will be identified to be the point person for follow-up growth and transformation. This individual will report to the overseeing pastor for ongoing responsibility to the plan for discipline, discipleship, and/or counseling.
- The offending individual may be released from all ministry responsibilities until the pastoral leadership and mentor agree on the time to reengage ministry. A specific boundary of time will be recommended before ministry involvement is approved.
- If the biblical authority of the pastoral leadership and restoration plan is not agreed upon or is defied by the offending person, then the individual will be given appropriate private and/or public communication that biblically aligns with the consequences of an unrepentant person.
- Also, a member that feels that discipline is unwarranted can appeal to the conflict committee comprised of elder members for further mediation.

CHURCH DISCIPLINE, RESTORATION, AND RECONCILIATION

THE BIBLICAL PROCESS OF CHURCH DISCIPLINE

Scripture addresses a number of specific areas of unrepentant sin/offense that may require an accountable discipline process (e.g., immorality, blasphemy, divisiveness, false teaching, and unresolved personal conflicts).

Examples of biblical church discipline:

Offense	Biblical Reference	Actions	Purpose
Various Sins	1 Cor 5:1–13	Corporate grief Private reproof/discussion Public announcement	Restoration Purification
Laziness	2 Thess 3:6–15	Private reproof Removal from congregation	Conviction Restoration
Divisiveness	Rom 16:17–18	Warnings provided Reject from fellowship	Protection of church's unity
False Teaching	Gal 1:8–9 1 Tim 1:20; 6:3–5 2 John 9–11; Rev 2:14–16	Need 2–3 witnesses If sin continues, rebuke publicly	Restoration Purification
Unresolved personal conflicts	Matt 18:15–20	Private reproof Private discussion Public announcement Removal, no association	Restoration Reconciliation

APPENDIX D

CHURCH DISCIPLINE, RESTORATION, AND RECONCILIATION

Today's Date _____/_____/_____

Name:_____ DOB____/____/____

Address _____
City_____ State_____ Zip_____

Primary phone (____)_____ Secondary (____)_____

Email: _____

If no permanent address, where are you staying? _____
_____

Specific history and narrative of the incident (include dates where relevant):

The following statements were made concerning those in leadership that merit more reflection, action, and reconciliation:

- First, the accusation was made that the lead pastor had "maneuvered" certain staff members into place, which implies that there was a sense of manipulation and untoward exercise of pastoral authority.
  - i. The lead pastor had made known his hiring preference to the ELT and advocated such, which is/was not manipulative but an appropriate exercise of pastoral authority when choosing who to hire.
  - ii. Second, the preference was made public to the entire ELT and not in secret and thus done in transparency.
  - iii. Thus, this comment is inappropriate and attacks the integrity and personal character of the lead pastor.
- Second, certain judgments were made regarding the hiring of the campus pastor from inaccurate information.

i. The staff member making such judgments did not attend this meeting when the decision was made and thus had come to a conclusion based on hearsay from a member of the council.

ii. It is an inappropriate boundary violation for council members to be consorting with staff members on critical financial decisions which include hiring and firing. Thus, the staff member will abide by appropriate boundaries. All communication of this sort should be between the lead pastor and the staff member. The council simply advises the pastor in confidentiality.

iii. Thus, the staff member is to come to the lead pastor prior to making conclusions and again accusing the pastor of operating in some sinister way. This is inaccurate and untrue.

- Third, there was a comment that needs more clarity. The comment was that I would be given more trouble or grief from the church because of making what truly have been painful decisions.

    i. This had a threatening tone that could be interpreted as the staff member herself would engender strife and division among the church.

    ii. Of course, this would do more harm to the church, who will already be reeling with the grief of our current financial situation.

As part of my personal plan, I acknowledge the following actions, requirements, and decisions regarding my involvement at any of the facilities, ministries, and / or events:

- I agree to refrain from attacks on the lead pastor's integrity and character. I will seek understanding from the pastor prior to coming to conclusions about the pastor.

- I agree to refrain from any further discussion with council members regarding the decisions that are still being made regarding the financial situation of the church. I recognize that this is not my role or place.

- I agree to hold in confidence the information I already know and will not disclose to any members of the church including staff members of the church as this could exacerbate an already grievous situation.

APPENDIX D

- I will trust the pastor to make systematic disclosures to the staff involved, then to the entire staff, and then to the congregation.
- I am repentant and deeply apologetic of my accusation toward the pastor. I acknowledge that any decision for next year is a difficult one and I entrust the church unto the Lord.
- I will meet with the lead pastor weekly until my questions are sufficiently answered at which time the lead pastor and myself will conclude our weekly meetings.
- I agree to pray for the church and encourage its leadership not to tear down or disrespect the leadership with personal attacks.
- I agree to refrain from personally creating division within the church as a result of these decisions. I can disagree respectfully without creating an environment of personal injury, attack, and division.

I agree with this plan: _____
(Initial if applicable)

I do not agree with this plan: _____
(Initial if applicable)

I understand that violating this agreement may subject me to further consequences. _____
(Initial)

These consequences will be determined by other pastoral leadership in consultation with the conflict committee.

I acknowledge and understand that I have been advised: _____
(Initial if applicable)

In person _____
Via telephone _____
Via email _____

I understand that I may reapply for consideration for reconciliation with the church after: _____

Signed by:
Printed Name _____
Signed_____ Date_____

CHURCH DISCIPLINE, RESTORATION, AND RECONCILIATION

Witnessed by:
Printed Name _____
Signed_____ Date_____
(A staff member or volunteer leader representing the church)

Printed Name _____
Signed_____ Date_____
(A staff member or volunteer leader representing the church)

Appendix E
A Polity for Local Church Elders

> Keep watch over yourselves and over all the flock, of which the Holy Spirit has made you overseers, to shepherd the church of God that he obtained with the blood of his own Son.
> Acts 20:28

A LOCAL CHURCH SHALL have a body of elders with the presiding elder being the local church pastor. The elders will be appointed by the local church pastor and the number that comprises this body will be determined also by the local church pastor (1 Tim 3). Each elder compensation is determined by the local church pastor in council with the Finance Committee of which is brought before the local congregation for affirmation (1 Tim 5:17; Acts 28; and 1 Cor 9:14). The Finance Committee also determines the pastor's total compensation which is to be no less than what is iterated by the minutes of the Church of God and affirmed by the congregation in an annual business meeting. Please see the form and function of the Finance Committee in the polity of the Church of God. The duties of this body of elders are one of governance and spiritual direction and are as follows:

- Cooperate with the pastor as he or she shepherds the flock (1 Pet 5:2).
- Be watchful of the adversary's movements and emissaries (Acts 20).
- Teach and preach the word of God (2 Tim 4:2; 1 Pet 5).
- Lead the congregation as priest in worship, hymns, and the offering of prayers (Rev 5:8).
- Lead the flock into self-emptying of the will, servanthood, and victorious witness to Christ (Rev 4:4, 10).

- Assist the pastor in leading the flock into the purposes God intends (1 Pet 5:2).
- Preside over a local expression of the church in cooperation with the local church pastor. This also includes an oversight of lay leaders and paid/volunteer staff members in the church (Acts 20).
- Guard the flock from the devices of the enemy (Acts 20; 1 Pet 5:8).
- Discern with the pastor sin and wickedness within the body and to call for repentance when necessary (1 Pet 5:2).
- Assist the pastor in the folding of the flock of God vis-à-vis healthy boundaries, clear roles, and conspicuous lines of authority (1 Pet 5:2).
- Assist in mediating conflict and arbitrate as judges in the church between conflicted members (Acts 15). The pastor will begin mediation but may need to call upon two to three elders for further mediation. If conflict is not resolved in this manner, the individual is brought before the entire body of elders. If the individual is determined to require disfellowship as a form of discipline, this is to be made public to the church in a called business meeting presided by the pastor having obtained consent from the state overseer (Matt 18:15–20; Rev 20:4).
- Confirm the financial direction of the church in cooperation with the pastor. The final direction becomes ratified after the church confirms the budget in a called annual business meeting.
- Work toward creating accountability and financial transparency through the utilization of outside and independent audits. One such organization, the Evangelical Council for Financial Accountability (www.ecfa.org), is such a tool for elders to consider.

The elders do not, however, evaluate the pastor's ministry. Evaluation and encouragement of the pastor can be done by the state overseer in an annual meeting where ministry goals and accomplishments are discussed and a written evaluation provided to the pastor.

The elders do not act independently of the local pastor; they do not meet without the pastor. The church pastor is the presiding elder and chair of the elder board. The sole exception to this is when the pastor recuses him or herself for the Finance Committee to determine his or her compensation. The Finance Committee recommends a personnel budget

APPENDIX E

to the elders for consideration. The elders then present the budget to the congregation in an annual conference for a vote of affirmation.

The role of the elder is critical to the operations, vision, financial integrity, and future vision of the church. Thus, each one must meet biblical qualifications prior to being considered for appointment by the local church pastor. The elder must have the following qualifications (1 Tim 3:1–7; Titus 1:5–9):

- They have accomplished ordination in the church.
- They are blameless and above reproach.
- They are a faithful husband or wife. Although a divorced individual is not altogether precluded from service, the local pastor must inquire regarding the circumstance of this divorce and it must meet the acceptable reasons already specified in the minutes of the Church of God (Matt 5:31–32).
- They are vigilant, discerning of the times.
- They are sober, not given to drinking or to the lusts of this age. Again, the local pastor should inquire as to whether the candidate for elder meets the behavioral expressions already specified in the minutes of the Church of God in accordance with the practical commitments.
- They exhibit good behavior, wholesome conduct, are quick to listen, and slow to speak (Jas 1:19).
- They refrain from disputations and do not easily quarrel. They do not stir up dissension in the church.
- They are given to hospitality. The elder does not necessarily require the spiritual gift of hospitality but must have the temperament and heart of hospitality.
- They have an aptitude to teach. This is an essential and necessary qualification. The elder must have the spiritual gift of teaching as this is the primary role of an elder.
- They do not seek fame or fortune. They do not covet another's possessions, qualities, gifts, or talents.
- They have a home that is characterized by respect, peace, and harmony. That is, the elder is ruling his or her own house well. The

local pastor is to interview both the candidate and his or her spouse when determining this qualification.

- They are seasoned and mature in the faith as evidenced by the baptism of the Holy Spirit, consistent in tithing, and have undergone church membership. The local pastor has latitude in determining this qualification further based on the fruit and duration of time the candidate has served the Lord.
- They have a good reputation in the community. The local pastor can interview the candidate's suggested references or the ministry leaders where the candidate has served to discern this attribute.
- They are either already ordained as a minister of the Church of God or working toward ordination for ministry (Acts 14:23; Titus 1:5).

A local church pastor is to create an application for eldership based on the principles above that candidates are to complete and submit to the pastor. The pastor can appoint unilaterally or consult with an existing board of elders to determine the candidacy of the applying elder.

If one or more elders is in conflict with the local pastor, then the state overseer will mediate this conflict. The state overseer provides the final jurisdiction in determining a verdict in the matter and will determine the course of action.

There is no appeal after the final determination is made. If an elder seeks to be restored to the fellowship, he or she must submit a request in writing and present him or herself with the fruit of repentance before the state overseer. A restoration plan will be determined by the state overseer. Any unbecoming conduct by an elder will be treated as is already specified in the minutes of the Church of God concerning unbecoming conduct of a church member.

Appendix F
Martin Luther's Table of Duties[1]

CERTAIN PASSAGES OF SCRIPTURE for various holy orders and positions, admonishing them about their duties and responsibilities.

    A bishop must be blameless, the husband of one wife, vigilant, sober, of good behavior, given to hospitality, apt to teach; not given to wine, no striker, not greedy of filthy lucre; but patient, not a brawler, not covetous; one that ruleth well his own house, having his children in subjection with all gravity; not a novice; holding fast the faithful Word as he hath been taught, that he may be able by sound doctrine both to exhort and to convince the gainsayers. 1 Tim 3:2ff; Titus 1:6.

WHAT THE HEARERS OWE TO THEIR PASTORS.

Even so hath the Lord ordained that they which preach the Gospel should live of the Gospel. 1 Cor 9:14. Let him that is taught in the Word communicate unto him that teacheth in all good things. Gal 6:6. Let the elders that rule well be counted worthy of double honor, especially they who labor in the Word and doctrine. For the Scripture saith, Thou shalt not muzzle the ox that treadeth out the corn; and the laborer is worthy of his reward. 1 Tim 5:17–18. Obey them that have the rule over you, and submit yourselves; for they watch for your souls as they that must give account, that they may do it with joy and not with grief; for that is unprofitable for you. Heb 13:17.

---

1. Book of Concord, "Table of Duties."

CONCERNING CIVIL GOVERNMENT.

Let every soul be subject unto the higher powers. For the power which exists anywhere is ordained of God. Whosoever resisteth the power resisteth the ordinance of God; and they that resist shall receive to themselves damnation. For he beareth not the sword in vain; for he is the minister of God, a revenger to execute wrath upon him that doeth evil. Rom 13:1–4.

WHAT SUBJECTS OWE TO THE MAGISTRATES.

Render unto Caesar the things which are Caesar's. Matt 22:21. Let every soul be subject unto the higher powers, etc. Wherefore ye must needs be subject, not only for wrath, but also for conscience' sake. For, for this cause pay ye tribute also; for they are God's ministers, attending continually upon this very thing. Render therefore to all their dues: tribute to whom tribute is due; custom, to whom custom; fear, to whom fear; honor, to whom honor. Rom 13:1, 5. I exhort, therefore, that, first of all, supplications, prayers, intercessions, and giving of thanks be made for all men; for kings and for all that are in authority, that we may lead a quiet and peaceable life in all godliness and honesty. 1 Tim 2:1. Put them in mind to be subject to principalities and powers, etc. Titus 3:1. Submit yourselves to every ordinance of man for the Lord's sake, whether it be to the king as supreme, or unto governors as unto them that are sent by him, etc. 1 Pet 2;13.

FOR HUSBANDS.

Ye husbands, dwell with your wives according to knowledge, giving honor unto the wife, as unto the weaker vessel, and as being heirs together of the grace of life, that your prayers be not hindered. 1 Pet 3:7. And be not bitter against them. Col 3:9.

FOR WIVES.

Wives, submit yourselves unto your own husbands, as unto the Lord, even as Sarah obeyed Abraham, calling him lord; whose daughters ye are, as long as ye do well, and are not afraid with any amazement. 1 Pet 3:6; Eph 5:22.

FOR PARENTS.

Ye fathers, provoke not your children to wrath, but bring them up in the nurture and admonition of the Lord. Eph 6:4.

FOR CHILDREN.

Children, obey your parents in the Lord; for this is right. Honor thy father and mother; which is the first commandment with promise: that it may be well with thee, and thou mayest live long on the earth. Eph 6:1–3.

FOR MALE AND FEMALE SERVANTS, HIRED MEN, AND LABORERS.

Servants, be obedient to them that are your masters according to the flesh, with fear and trembling, in singleness of your heart, as unto Christ; not with eye-service, as men-pleasers, but as the servants of Christ, doing the will of God from the heart; with good will doing service as to the Lord, and not to men; knowing that whatsoever good thing any man doeth, the same shall he receive of the Lord, whether he be bond or free. Eph 6:5ff; Col 3:22.

FOR MASTERS AND MISTRESSES.

Ye masters, do the same things unto them, forbearing threatening, knowing that your Master also is in heaven; neither is there respect of persons with Him. Eph 6:9; Col 4:1.

FOR YOUNG PERSONS IN GENERAL.

Likewise, ye younger, submit yourselves unto the elder. Yea, all of you be subject one to another, and be clothed with humility; for God resisteth the proud, and giveth grace to the humble. Humble yourselves, therefore, under the mighty hand of God that He may exalt you in due time. 1 Pet 5:5–6.

FOR WIDOWS.

She that is a widow indeed, and desolate, trusteth in God, and continueth in supplications and prayers night and day. But she that liveth in pleasure is dead while she liveth. 1 Tim 5:5–6.

FOR ALL IN COMMON.

Thou shalt love thy neighbor as thyself. Herein are comprehended all the commandments. Rom 13:8. And persevere in prayer for all men.

1 Tim 2:1–2.
Let each his lesson learn with care,
And all the household well shall fare.

Appendix G
My Genogram

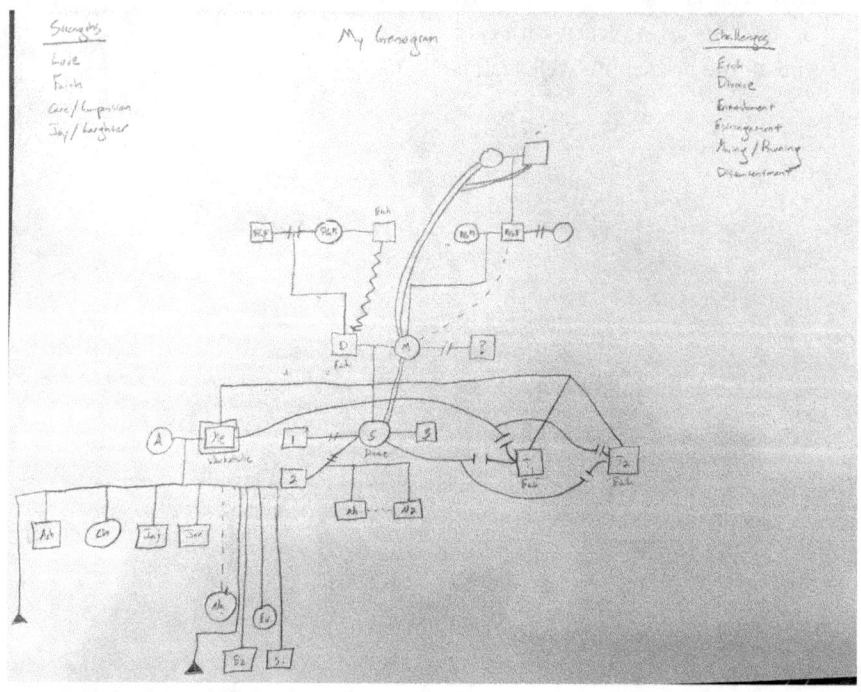

Appendix H
Erik Erikson's Stages of Psychosocial Development[2]

Erikson's Stages of Psychosocial Development

Approximate Age	Psychosocial Crisis/Task	Virtue Developed
Infant - 18 months	Trust vs Mistrust	Hope
18 months - 3 years	Autonomy vs Shame/Doubt	Will
3 - 5 years	Initiative vs Guilt	Purpose
5 - 13 years	Industry vs Inferiority	Competency
13 - 21 years	Identity vs Confusion	Fidelity
21 - 39 years	Intimacy vs Isolation	Love
40 - 65 years	Generativity vs Stagnation	Care
65 and older	Integrity vs Despair	Wisdom

(C) The Psychology Notes Headquarters - https://www.PsychologyNotesHQ.com

2. Psychology Notes HQ, "Erik Erikson's Stages."

Appendix I
The Haustafel: Covenantal Relating in the Church

PATHOS

Any behavior or interpersonal relatedness has a pathos or motive by which such behaviors are expressed. The church thus has the following virtues that motivate faithful interrelatedness in the body of Christ, which become the components of any table of fellowship that seeks to relate to one another in a way that honors the Lord.

- Parallel subordination: As noted in Eph 5:21, this pathos or virtue colors the manner of relating to one another in Christian fellowship. This is expressed sacramentally through the act of foot washing (see Gen 18, John 13).

- Filled with the Spirit: Any effort to mutually submit to one another is contingent upon being filled with the Spirit to accomplish this otherworldly phenomenon (see Eph 5:18). Thus, the Haustafel is only accomplished teleologically in a community filled with the Spirit.

- Eucharist: Gratitude is a virtue that plays a role in enabling behaviors of interrelatedness as it integrates our inclusion in the metanarrative of the *passio Dei*. This is sacramentally expressed through the Lord's Communion (see Gen 18, Col 3:17).

- Pilgrimage: The people of God are sojourners, foreigners, and pilgrims in this world. As citizens of heaven, we formulate an ethical manner of relating that comes from above. Moreover, as strangers, we welcome the stranger, oppressed, marginalized, and outcast to the table to feast, pray, love, and mutually submit to one another in

Christ. When we gather at the table, let us always remember that we are strangers in a foreign land (see 1 Pet 2:11).

- New humanity: The table duties are meant to be a manifesto of new humanity. It is the way the people of God show their love for one another. The world will know that we are the disciples of Christ by the way we love one another. Paul exhorts in both the Ephesian and Colossian Haustafels that the premise of such practices is based on putting on the new person in Christ, reflecting the imago Dei vis-à-vis interpersonal relation (see Eph 4:24 and Col 3:10–11).

- Love: In order to submit to one another, we must have a heart filled with love. Love seeks the welfare and fortune of another. Love covenants to be with in time of great peril. Paul prefaces the Haustafel with the virtue of love and a motive that enables the behaviors that follow (see Col 3:14 and Eph 5:2). Peter addresses the Haustafel with "dearly beloved" (see 1 Pet 2:11). Thus, the table of duties is first the table of love which enables us to covenant with another to honor and subordinate ourselves in the nuanced Christian duties that follow.

PRAXIS

- Sound doctrine: Sound doctrine is a prominent theme in the Haustafel practice in Titus (see Titus 2:1). Thus, as living epistles, we live out sound doctrine in the way we relate to God and others. We not only teach mutual submission and honor, but we also model it in our interpersonal interactions in the family and in the church.

- Prayer: The church must recover and perpetuate the practice of prayer for the pathos and praxis of the Haustafel to become a reality in the community. Paul prefaces his exposition of the Haustafel in 1 Timothy with prayer (see 1 Tim 2). Therefore, the practice of Eucharist, agape feast, and foot washing will benefit also from the practice of prayer for the ethos of Christian table duties to find expression.

- Worship: The Haustafel in Colossians is predicated upon worship (see Col 3:17). That is, whatever is done, is done in the name of the Lord Jesus. By predicating praxis with worship, a context for being filled with the Spirit is perpetuated as one seeks to honor God in word and deed and the Spirit responds with the help, counsel, and power to live in the light of holy interpersonal relatedness.

- Foot washing: Washing the saints' feet is a kingdom praxis of hospitality, subordination, humility, and sanctification. It is a most appropriate practice for the Haustafel as a recurrent inculcation of the Haustafel pathos of mutual subordination, teleological love, and pilgrimage (see John 13).

- Hospitality: Hospitality is an extension of love, one that is unafraid to love the stranger. It may seem odd that the Haustafel, a table of duties, a fellowship of meals should also include consideration of the stranger. But indeed, this is not odd if we consider the human race as image bearers of God and by virtue of this, family for every Christian with a table to share a meal. Radical hospitality opens our doors, hearts, and families for the grace of God to be evident in our table fellowship (see Gen 18:1–15; Ps 68:5–6).

- Agape feast: Nothing quite measures a community more than how they feast together. This is a natural human rhythm and fosters conversations about story, heart, dream, and destination. The feast, when incorporating the Lord's Supper, also reminds us of the Paschal Lamb, both the past sacrifice and the anticipated glory and reign. Christ waits to share a feast with all who belong to him in the eschaton. We rejoice in this anticipated feast when we gather around the table in Christian community. It is in this context where the people are reminded of their respective covenants in the Haustafel and reiterate these covenants so that the home will be healthy and, by extension, the church will likewise be healthy.

THE TABLE FELLOWSHIP COVENANTS

What husbands covenant to their wives:

I covenant to love my wife as Christ loves the church (Eph5:25). I covenant to act as a conduit where she is sanctified by speaking the word of God over her (Eph 5:26). I covenant to love my wife as Christ loves the church, by sacrificially laying down selfish ambition for the sake of her welfare (Eph 5:27). I covenant to treat my wife with the same respect, love, and provision that I provide my own body (Eph 5:28). I covenant to live with my wife as one in agreement, intimacy, and unity (Eph 5:31). I covenant to refrain from bitterness toward or against my wife (Col 3:19). I covenant to honor my wife in both private and public domains while treating her as one who is an heir of grace in eternity (1 Pet 3:7).

What wives covenant to their husbands.

I covenant to submit to my husband as unto the Lord (Eph 5:22). I covenant to engage in purity and reverence with my speech (1 Pet 3:2). I covenant to adorn my heart and spirit with meekness and a quiet spirit more than external luxuries (1 Pet 3:3–4). I covenant to love my husband and children (Titus 2:4). I covenant to be self-controlled, pure, a steward of my home, and obedient to my husband that the word of God would not be blasphemed (Titus 2:5). I covenant to feed my family, invest wisely, help the poor, and practice radical hospitality (Prov 31:15, 20–21). If married to an unbelieving husband, I covenant to be in subjection to him that he may be won to Christ according to my conduct (1 Pet 3:1). This covenant, however, is subordinate to my covenant to Christ, so that, if my unbelieving husband requires that I engage in sin, I must graciously dissent (1 Pet 2:1–12, 19–20). Moreover, as an agent and recipient of peace, I covenant to submit myself to Christ and depart from a physically or sexually abusive husband for the sake of my and my children's welfare, being released from bondage and being called to freedom (1 Cor 7:15).

What fathers covenant to their children.

I covenant to refrain from attitudes, words, and actions which would drive my child to angry exasperation or resentment via excessively severe discipline, unreasonable harsh demands, abuse of authority, arbitrariness, unfairness, constant nagging, and condemnation. I covenant to refrain from subjecting a child to humiliation, and all forms of gross insensitivity to a child's needs and sensibilities (Eph 6:4). I covenant to bring up my child in the nurture and admonition of the Lord by means of moral, cognitive, physical, and spiritual training (Eph 6:4).

APPENDIX I

What mothers covenant to their children.

I covenant to love my children, to be discreet, chaste, keepers of the home, good, and obedient to my husband so that the word of God will not be blasphemed (Titus 2:5). I covenant to guide the house by managing my home affairs in wisdom so that I give no occasion for the adversary to speak reproachfully (1 Tim 5:14). I covenant to work willingly with my hands for the nurturance of my family (Prov 31:13). I covenant to feed my family, invest wisely, help the poor, clothe my children, and practice radical hospitality (Prov 31:15, 20–21). I covenant to clothe myself with strength and honor so that I may speak wisdom with the law of kindness (Prov 31:25–26). If working outside the home, I covenant to implement healthy boundaries so that I do not neglect my domestic duties of the home (Prov 31:24, Acts 16:14).

What children covenant to their parents.

I covenant to obey my parents in the Lord, as this is right (Eph 6:1). That is, it is my right to preserve my relationship with God and my parents, and obedience mediates the formation of this righteousness as an internal virtue. I covenant to honor my father and mother, which is the first command, and one with an associated promise (Eph 6:2). I am grateful that the fruit of honor is well-being and long life (Eph 6:2). I covenant to not only hear the encouragement and admonition of my parents but will attune my soul to listen to their instruction (John 8:43). I covenant to not only obey in practice, but also with a pure intent.

What servants covenant to their leaders.

I covenant to be faithful to the Lord so that my superior and all with whom I work may know that God is with me (Gen 39:2–3). I covenant to diligently work to advance a conduct of pure character and integrity (Gen 39:4). I covenant to serve others as if I am serving the Lord, worshipping Christ through my service (Gen 39:5). I covenant to obey those in both ecclesial and secular leadership with sincere solicitude concerning my performance of duties (Eph 6:5). I covenant to serve with immense devotion and singleness of heart (Eph 6:5). I covenant to serve with excellence, not to be seen by others, but in knowledge that God sees all (Eph

6:6). I covenant to order my soul unto service as I realize that God is ordering my role in creation—*ora et labora*, "for prayer and work" (Gen 2:15). I covenant to submit to the sanctification that service can create in my discipleship and walk with the Lord. I covenant to obey those in leadership over me, knowing that a promise of inheritance awaits me and that by doing so, I adorn the doctrine of God (Col 3:24 and 1 Tim 6:1). I covenant to refrain from despising those in leadership (Titus 2:9). I covenant to steward the tasks and money of those in leadership over me, refraining from all forms of embezzlement (Titus 2:10). I covenant to obey leaders who may have an austere nature and prepare for suffering injustice for the glory of God (1 Pet 2:19–20).

What leaders covenant to their servants.

I covenant to refrain from threatening those under my leadership (Eph 6:9). I covenant to render just judgment and discipline when necessary (Rom 13:1–4). I covenant to engage in self-reflection, counsel, time, Scriptural meditation, prayer, and, if necessary, repentance prior to rendering judgment or discipline upon anyone else (Matt 7:1–7). I covenant to lead by searching the heart of God and executing his will (being a deacon of God) within my sphere of leadership (Rom 13:4). I covenant to view subordinates with a new kind of profitability that encapsulates them as servants of the Lord first and servants of the task second (Phlm 1:11). I covenant to receive those under my leadership with intentional hospitality and interact with them in a way that confers eternal relationships; that is, how we relate in heaven acts as a dictum to how we relate here upon the earth (Phlm 1:15). I covenant to care for those under my leadership as if he was my brother and she was my sister (Phlm 1:16). I covenant to condescend to voluntary servitude, ministering to those under my care (Matt 23:5–12).

What elderly men covenant to younger men.

I covenant to live a life of restraint, deferring immediate satisfaction of impulsive desires until a more prayerful consideration can be made (Titus 2:2). I covenant to live a life of dignity and honor by immersing myself in the sacred (Titus 2:2). I covenant to be temperate, voluntarily placing restrictions on my freedom for the sake of the next generation

(Titus 2:2). I covenant to be sound in faith by practicing sound doctrine (Titus 2:2). I covenant to integrate all the admonitions over my life as a way of passing a legacy of sound faith. I covenant to be sound in sacrificial love by living with and in sacred community (Titus 2:2). I covenant to endure in the faith by being trustworthy through manifold trials with a determined hope that Christ is all in all (Titus 2:2). I covenant to hold to the faith as a child holds to his beloved Father (Matt 18:3). I covenant to integrate faith, hope, and love in my old age as a means of passing a sound legacy to younger men (1 Cor 13:13).

What elderly women covenant to younger women.

I covenant to be holy, to be sacred—a priestess of my home (Titus 2:3). In this manner, I will conduct myself with a sense of modesty and propriety (1 Tim 2:9–10). I covenant to refrain from idle words, gossip, slander, and false accusations that are unbecoming to my home and the church. I covenant to abstain from the enslavement of alcohol—to model the taking of our cares to the Lord in prayer. I covenant to instruct younger women and my children in the ways of the kingdom. In so doing, I offer the Lord my services in hope of leaving a righteous posterity.

What young women covenant to the household of God.

I covenant to be sexually pure, knowing that this virtue, in part, may act to stabilize families, churches, and all of society. I covenant to keep my home and foster an environment for soul care (Titus 2:5). I covenant to open my home to guests as a ministry of hospitality. As Jesus prepares a home for me, I will prepare a home for others (John 14:1–2). I covenant to set my house in order, creating a context for prayerful labor and sanctification. I covenant to voluntarily limit my freedoms as a means of displaying discretion toward my family (Titus 2:5). I will be present in the moment so as to properly judge between action and inaction. I covenant to give myself to holy love and a pursuit of truth to learn discretion by attending to our moments as a family. I covenant to renounce and refrain from sexual impropriety. I will keep myself pure and undefiled. I await the covenant of love in the form of matrimony (Titus 2:5). I covenant to submit to my husband by discerning when and how to speak (1 Pet 3:1). I covenant to walk in the righteousness of Christ as a new creation, in part by displaying this righteousness by voluntary submission to my husband (1 Pet 2:24). I covenant to honor my husband both privately and publicly and as such, receive the promise of becoming Sarah's daughter (1 Pet 3:6).

What young men covenant to the household of God.

I covenant to behave with temperance, voluntarily restraining certain liberties for the greater peace of my home, church, and society (Titus 2:6). I covenant to act with integrity, resisting the vice of avarice in both forms of prodigality and hoarding, which act to compromise a life of integrity (Titus 2:7). I covenant to view every human soul with dignity, having intrinsic worth by virtue of being made in the image of God (Titus 2:7). I covenant to exercise sound speech and wise doctrine to refrain from bringing reproach upon the household of faith (Titus 2:8).

Bibliography

Antonelli, Emanuele. "Mimesis and Attention: On Christian Sophrosyne." *Forum Philosophicum* 23 (2018) 259–74. https://www.academia.edu/41586703/Mimesis_and_Attention_On_Christian_Sophrosyne.
Bailey, Sarah Pulliam. "Exclusive: Mark Driscoll's Resignation Letter to Mars Hill Church." RNS, Oct. 15, 2014. https://religionnews.com/2014/10/15/exclusive-mark-driscolls-resignation-letter-to-mars-hill-church/.
Baines, Barbara J. "Assaying the Power of Chastity in *Measure for Measure*." *Studies in English Literature, 1500–1900* 30 (1990) 283–301. https://doi.org/10.2307/450518.
Barclay, John. "The Family as the Bearer of Religion in Judaism and Early Christianity." In *Constructing Early Christian Families: Family as Social Reality and Metaphor*, edited by Halvor Moxnes, 66–80. London: Routledge, 1997.
Barclay, William. *The New Daily Study Bible: The Gospel of Matthew.* Vol. 1. 3rd ed. Edinburgh: Saint Andrews, 2001.
Barrett, C. K. *The Epistle to the Romans.* Harper's New Testament Commentaries. New York: Harper & Brothers, 1957.
Bauman-Martin, Betsy J. "Women on the Edge: New Perspectives on Women in the Petrine *Haustafel*." *Journal of Biblical Literature* 123 (2004) 253–79. https://doi.org/10.2307/3267945.
Bayer, Oswald. "Nature and Institution: Luther's Doctrine of the Three Orders." *Lutheran Quarterly* 12 (1998) 125–59. https://gudribassakums.wordpress.com/wp-content/uploads/2012/10/1998-three-orders-bayer.pdf.
Bonhoeffer, Diedrich. *Life Together.* Translated by R. H. Fuller, revised by Irmgard Booth. San Francisco: Harper Collins, 1954.
Book of Concord. "Table of Duties." https://thebookofconcord.org/small-catechism/appendix-ii/.
Boulter, Patricia Neils. "'Sophia' and 'Sophrosyne' in Euripides' 'Andromache.'" *Phoenix* 20 (1966) 51–58. https://doi.org/10.2307/1086315.
Bourdieu, Pierre. "The Sense of Honour." In *Algeria 1960*, 95–132. Cambridge: Cambridge University press, 1979. https://www.amherst.edu/media/view/292931/original/bourdieu_the%2Bsense%2Bof%2Bhonour_1979.pdf.
Bowen, Murray. *Family Therapy in Clinical Practice.* Lanham, MD: Rowman & Littlefield, 1985.
Bradley, Keith. "The Roman Family at Dinner." In *Meals in a Social Context: Aspects of the Communal Meal in the Hellenistic and Roman World*, edited by Inge Nielsen and Hanne Sigismund Nielsen, 36–55. Aarhus Studies in Mediterranean Antiquity 1. Oakville, CT: Aarhus University Press, 1998.

Brown, Michael L. *The Real Kosher Jesus*. Lake Mary, FL: FrontLine, 2012.

Brueggemann, Walter. *The Prophetic Imagination*. 2nd ed. Minneapolis: Fortress, 2001.

Butterfield, Rosaria Champagne. *The Gospel Comes with a House Key: Practicing Radically Ordinary Hospitality in Our Post-Christian World*. Wheaton, IL: Crossway, 2018.

Cairns, Douglas. "Honour and Shame: Modern Controversies and Ancient Values." *Critical Quarterly* 53 (2011) 23–41. https://doi.org/10.1111/j.1467-8705.2011.01974.x.

Calvin, John. *Commentaries on the Epistles to Timothy, Titus, and Philemon*. Translated by William Pringle. Edinburgh: Calvin Translation Society, 1856.

Campbell, Jim. *Madoff Talks: Uncovering the Untold Story Behind the Most Notorious Ponzi Scheme in History*. New York: McGraw Hill, 2021.

Cappeau, Placide. "O Holy Night." 1847. Translated by John S. Dwight, music by Adolphe Adam. In *The Celebration Hymnal*, 285. Franklin, TN: Word Music/Integrity Music, 1997. https://hymnary.org/hymn/CEL1997/285.

Carus, Paul. "On the Philosophy of Laughing." *Monist* 8 (1898) 250–72. https://www.jstor.org/stable/27897482.

Chrysostom, John. "An Address On Vainglory and the Right Way for Parents to Bring up Their Children." In *Christianity and Pagan Culture in the Later Roman Empire*, translated by Max L. W. Laistner, 85–122. Ithaca, NY: Cornell University Press, 1951.

———. "Homily on Philemon." In *Biblical Sermons to Savonarola, A.D. 27–1498*. Vol. 1 of *20 Centuries of Great Preaching*, edited by Clyde E. Fant Jr. and William M. Pinson Jr., 101–7. Waco, TX: Word, 1971.

———. "Treatise on the Priesthood." In *Chrysostom: On the Priesthood; Ascetic Treatises; Select Homilies and Letters; Homilies on the Statutes*, edited by Philip Schaff, translated by W. R. W. Stephens, 51–147. Vol. 9 of *The Nicene and Post-Nicene Fathers*, Series 1. New York: Christian Literature, 1886.

Clarke, Adam. *Memoirs of the Wesley Family: Collected Principally from Original Documents*. London: Kershaw, 1823.

Cowper, William. "There Is a Fountain." 1772. In *The African American Heritage Hymnal*, 257. Chicago: GIA, 2001. https://hymnary.org/hymn/AAHH2001/257.

Dante Alighieri. *The Divine Comedy: The Inferno, the Purgatorio, and the Paradiso*. Translated by John Ciardi. New York: American Library, 2003.

Dickens, Charles. *A Christmas Carol, In Prose: Being a Ghost Story of Christmas*. 1843. Facsimile of the original edition with an introduction by G. K. Chesterton. London: Palmer, 1922. https://archive.org/details/christmascarolinoodickuoft/mode.

Dinkler, Michal Beth. "Sarah's Submission: Peter's Analogy in 1 Peter 3:5–6." *Priscilla Papers* 21 (2007) 9–15. https://www.academia.edu/35174528/Sarahs_Submission_Peters_Analogy_in_1_Peter_3_5_6.

Dreher, Rod. *The Benedict Option: A Strategy for Christians in a Post-Christian Nation*. New York: Sentinel, 2017.

Ellicott, Charles J. *Ellicott's Commentaries on the Epistles of St. Paul*. Boston: Halladay, 1868.

Erikson, Erik. *The Life Cycle Completed*. New York: Norton, 1982.

Faber, Reimer A. "'Evil Beasts, Lazy Gluttons': A Neglected Theme in the Epistle to Titus." *Westminster Theological Journal* 67 (2005) 135–45. https://www.academia.

edu/5165084/_Evil_Beasts_Lazy_Gluttons_A_Neglected_Theme_in_the_ Epistle_to_Titus.

Fleming, Jody B. "Spiritual Generosity: Biblical Hospitality in the Story of Lydia (Acts 16:14–16, 40)." *Missiology: An International Review* 47 (2018) 51–63. https://doi.org/10.1177/0091829618794942.

Foster, Richard J. *Celebration of Discipline: The Path to Spiritual Growth*. New York: Harper Collins, 1978.

Friedman, Edwin H. *Generation to Generation: Family Process in Church and Synagogue*. New York: Guilford, 1985.

Frilingos, Chris. "'For My Child, Onesimus': Paul and Domestic Power in Philemon." *Journal of Biblical Literature* 119 (2000) 91–104. https://doi.org/10.2307/3267970.

Fudge, Thomas A. "In Praise of Heresy: Hus, Luther, and the Ethos of Reformation." *Journal of Religious History* 43 (2019) 25–44. https://doi.org/10.1111/1467-9809.12571.

Gause, R. Hollis. *Revelation: God's Stamp of Sovereignty on History*. Cleveland, TN: Pathway, 1983.

Gift, Kristine. "Sarah's Laughter as Her Lasting Legacy: An Interpretation of Genesis 18:9–15." *Midwest Journal of Undergraduate Research* (2012) 99–110. https://research.monm.edu/mjur/files/2019/02/MJUR-i02-2012-7-Gift.pdf.

Glancy, Jennifer A. *Slavery in Early Christianity*. New York: Oxford University Press, 2002.

Gombis, Timothy G. "A Radically New Humanity: The Function of the *Haustafel* in Ephesians." *Journal of the Evangelical Society* 48 (2005) 317–30. https://etsjets.org/wp-content/uploads/2010/06/files_JETS-PDFs_48_48-2_48-2-pp317-330_JETS.pdf.

Gray, Patrick. "The Liar Paradox and the Letter to Titus." *Catholic Biblical Quarterly* 69 (2007) 302–14. https://www.jstor.org/stable/43725968.

Gress, Carrie, and Noelle Mering. *Theology of Home: Finding the Eternal in the Everyday*. Charlotte, NC: TAN, 2019.

Gunton, Colin. "Using and Being Used: Scripture and Systematic Theology." *Theology Today* 47 (1990) 248–59. https://doi.org/10.1177/004057369004700303.

Hauerwas, Stanley. "Must a Patient Be a Person to Be a Patient? Or, My Uncle Charlie Is Not Much of a Person, But He Is Still My Uncle Charlie." In *The Hauerwas Reader*, edited by John Berkman and Michael Cartwright, 596–602. Durham, NC: Duke University Press, 2001.

Havelock, E. A. "'Dikaiosune': An Essay in Greek Intellectual History (In Tribute to George Grube, the Distinguished Author of *Plato's Thought*)." *Phoenix* 23 (1969) 49–70. https://doi.org/10.2307/1086568.

Hillyer, Norman. *1 and 2 Peter, Jude*. New International Biblical Commentary. Peabody, MA: Hendrickson, 1992.

Isidore of Seville. *Sententiae*. Translated by Thomas L. Knoebel. Ancient Christian Writers 73. Westminster, MD: Newman, 2018.

Jakimowicz, Samantha, et al. "Bowen Family Systems Theory: Mapping a Framework to Support Critical Care Nurses' Well-Being and Care Quality." *Nursing Philosophy* 22 (2021) e12320. https://doi.org/10.1111/nup.12320.

Jensen, T. Patrick. *The Coming Winter: Pastoral Reflections on 1 Timothy*. Bloomington, IN: WestBow, 2021.

———. *Legacy: Pastoral Praxis in 2 Timothy*. Eugene, OR: Wipf & Stock, 2024.

Jouen, Anne-Lise, et al. "Common ERP Responses to Narrative Incoherence in Sentence and Picture Pair Comprehension." *Brain and Cognition* 153 (2021) 105775. https://doi.org/10.1016/j.bandc.2021.105775.

King, Martin Luther, Jr. "Letter from a Birmingham Jail." Originally in *The Christian Century: An Ecumenical Weekly* (1963) 767–73. PDF 1–11. https://minio.la.utexas.edu/webeditor-files/coretexts/pdf/1963_mlk_letter.pdf.

———. "Shattered Dreams." In *Marshall to King, 1902–*. Vol. 12 of *20 Centuries of Great Preaching*, edited by Clyde E. Fant Jr. and William M. Pinson Jr., 384–91. Waco, TX: Word, 1971.

Klever, Phillip. "The Multigenerational Transmission of Family Unit Functioning." *American Journal of Family Therapy* 33 (2005) 253–64. https://doi.org/10.1080/01926180590952436.

Krauth, Charles P., trans. *Augsburg Confession*. Philadelphia: Tract and Book Society of St. John's Evangelical Lutheran Church, 1868.

Larkin, Clarence. *The Book of Revelation*. Philadelphia: Moyer, 1919.

Lewis, C. S. *Surprised by Joy*. New York: Harcourt Brace, 1955.

Louw, Daniel J. "The Infiniscience of the Hospitable God of Abraham, Isaac and Jacob: Re-interpreting Trinity in the Light of the Rublev Icon." *HTS Theological Studies* 75 (2019) 1–10. https://hts.org.za/index.php/hts/article/view/5347/14097.

Lovik, Erik G. "A Look at the Ancient House Codes and Their Contributions to Understanding 1 Peter 3:1–7." *Calvary Baptist Theological Journal* 11 (1995) 49–63. https://biblicalstudies.gospelstudies.org.uk/pdf/cbtj/11-2_049.pdf.

MacDonald, James. "Pastor James' Statements of Repentance." James MacDonald Ministries. https://jamesmacdonaldministries.org/2019-repentance/.

Martin, Lee Roy. *Fasting: A Centre for Pentecostal Theology Short Introduction*. Cleveland, TN: CPT, 2014.

Mason, C. H. "The Whole Truth." *Church of God Evangel* 6 (1915) 3.

Metaxas, Eric. *Seven Women: And the Secret of Their Greatness*. Nashville: Nelson, 2015.

Miller, Alexander Blaze. "Chrysostom's Pedagogy of Christian Fatherhood: Reorienting the Christian Family in a Non-Christian Society." In *Love, Marriage and Family in Eastern Orthodox Perspective*, edited by Theodore Grey Dedon and Sergey Trostyanskiy, 160–78. Piscataway, NJ: Gorgias, 2016. https://doi.org/10.31826/9781463237028-013.

Milton, John. *Paradise Lost*. In *The Norton Anthology of English Literature*, edited by M. H. Abrams and Stephen Greenblatt, 1815–2044. Vol. 1. 7th ed. New York: Norton, 2000.

Misset van de Weg, Magda. "The Sarah Imagery in I Peter." In *The Use of Sacred Books in the Ancient World*, edited by L. V. Rutgers et al., 111–126. Contributions to Biblical Exegesis and Theology 22. Leuven, Belg.: Peeters, 1998.

Moody Church. "Meet Our Senior Pastor." July 2020. https://www.moodychurch.org/new-pastor/#1584647325022-0f23753c-ee9f.

Muris, P., et al. "The Emotional Reasoning Heuristic in Children." *Behaviour Research and Therapy* 41 (2003) 261–72. https://doi.org/10.1016/S0005-7967(02)00005-0.

National Center for Fathering. "The Extent of Fatherlessness." Fathers.com. https://fathers.com/the-extent-of-fatherlessness/.

National Institute on Alcohol Abuse and Alcoholism. "Alcohol-Related Emergencies and Deaths in the United States." Updated November 2024. https://www.niaaa.

nih.gov/alcohols-effects-health/alcohol-topics-z/alcohol-facts-and-statistics/ alcohol-related-emergencies-and-deaths-united-states.

———. "Alcohol Use in the United States: Age Groups and Demographic Characteristics." Updated February 2025. https://www.niaaa.nih.gov/alcohols-effects-health/alcohol-topics-z/alcohol-facts-and-statistics/alcohol-use-united-states-age-groups-and-demographic-characteristics.

Nouwen, Henri J. M. *In the Name of Jesus: Reflections on Christian Leadership*. New York: Crossroad, 1989.

———. *The Return of the Prodigal Son*. Anniv. omnibus ed. with *Home Tonight*. New York: Convergent, 2016.

The Online Greek Bible. "1 Corinthians 7:15." https://www.greekbible.com/1-corinthians/7/15.

———. "1 Peter 2:11." https://www.greekbible.com/1-peter/2/11.

———. "1 Peter 3:6." https://www.greekbible.com/1-peter/3/6.

———. "1 Timothy 5:14." https://www.greekbible.com/1-timothy/5/14.

———. "Ephesians 6:1." https://www.greekbible.com/ephesians/6/1.

———. "Philemon 1:2." https://www.greekbible.com/philemon/1/12.

———. "Titus 2:3." https://www.greekbible.com/titus/2/3.

———. "Titus 2:5." https://www.greekbible.com/titus/2/5.

———. "Titus 2:9." https://www.greekbible.com/titus/2/9.

———. "Titus 3:10." https://www.greekbible.com/titus/3/10.

Parker, Joseph. *The Epistle to the Ephesians*. Grand Rapids: Baker, 1956.

Parsons, Michael. "Slavery and the New Testament: Equality and Submissiveness." *Vox Evangelica* 18 (1988) 90–96. https://biblicalstudies.org.uk/pdf/vox/vol18/slavery_parsons.pdf.

Pinsent, Andrew. "Avarice and Liberality." In *Virtues and Their Vices*, edited by Kevin Timpe and Craig A. Boyd, 156–75. Oxford: Oxford University Press, 2014.

Potter, Claire. "The Influence of Danish Missionaries to India on Susanna Wesley's Methods of Education and Its Subsequent Influence on John Wesley." *Methodist History* 52 (2014) 148–67. https://archives.gcah.org/server/api/core/bitstreams/9bf1b9df-8f3e-4284-ae2b-78999ebdab25/content.

Psychology Notes HQ. "Erik Erikson's Stages of Psychosocial Development." Apr. 11, 2021. https://www.psychologynoteshq.com/erikson-stages/.

Puffer, Matthew. "Human Dignity After Augustine's Imago Dei: On the Sources and Uses of Two Ethical Terms." *Journal of the Society of Christian Ethics* 37 (2017) 65–82. https://scholar.valpo.edu/cgi/viewcontent.cgi?article=1047&context=cc_fac_pub.

Punt, Jeremy. "Subverting Sarah in the New Testament: Galatians 4 and 1 Peter 3." *Scriptura* 96 (2007) 453–68. https://journals.co.za/doi/pdf/10.10520/EJC100843.

Reinhold, Meyer. *Studies in Classical History and Society*. Oxford: Oxford University Press, 2002.

Rogers, Cleon L., Jr., and Cleon L. Rogers III. *The New Linguistic and Exegetical Key to the Greek New Testament*. Grand Rapids: Zondervan, 1998.

Rublev, Andrei. *The Trinity*. [1425–1427?]. Icon, tempera on panel, 55.7 x 44.8" (141.5 x 114 cm). Tretyakov Gallery, Moscow. https://commons.wikimedia.org/w/index.php?title=File:Angelsatmamre-trinity-rublev-1410.jpg&oldid=515614343.

Schaff, Philip. "Prolegomena: The Life and Work of St. John Chrysostom." In *Chrysostom: On the Priesthood; Ascetic Treatises; Select Homilies and Letters;*

Homilies on the Statutes, edited by Philip Schaff, 7-40. Vol. 9 of *The Nicene and Post-Nicene Fathers*, Series 1. New York: Christian Literature, 1886.

Sensen, Oliver. "Kant's Conception of Human Dignity." *Kant-Studien* 100 (2009) 309-31. https://doi.org/10.1515/KANT.2009.018.

Shakespeare, William. *Measure for Measure: With the "Historie of Promos and Cassandra."* United Kingdom: Huge Print, 1899.

———. *The Tragedy of Antony and Cleopatra*. Edited by R. H. Case. 4th ed. London: Methuen, 1920.

Shortt, Joann Wu, et al. "Emotion Socialization in the Context of Risk and Psychopathology: Mother and Father Socialization of Anger and Sadness in Adolescents with Depressive Disorder." *Social Development* 25 (2016) 27-46. https://doi.org/10.1111/sode.12138.

Shuckburgh, Evelyn Shirley. *A History of Rome to the Battle of Actium*. New York: Macmillan, 1917.

Simpson, A. B. "A Personal Testimony." *Alliance Weekly* 45 (1915) 11.

Son, Angella. "Anxiety as a Main Cause of Church Conflicts Based on Bowen Family Systems Theory." *Journal of Pastoral Care & Counseling* 73 (2019) 9-18. https://doi.org/10.1177/1542305018822959.

Spencer, Herbert. *The Principles of Biology*. Vol. 1. London: William and Norgate, 1864.

Stein, Robert H. "The Argument of Romans 13:1-7." *Novum Testamentum* 31 (1989) 325-43. https://doi.org/10.1163/156853689X00270.

Seutonius. *The Lives of the Twelve Ceasars*. Translated by Alexander Thomson, revised by T. Forester. London: Bell & Sons, 1923.

Teresa of Ávila. *The Interior Castle*. In *Wellsprings of Faith*, 251-518. New York: Barnes and Noble, 2005.

Thomas, John Christopher. *The Apocalypse: A Literary and Theological Commentary*. Cleveland, TN: CPT, 2012.

Thompson, Steven. "Was Ancient Rome a Dead Wives Society? What Did the Roman Paterfamilias Get Away With?" *Journal of Family History* 31 (2006) 3-27. https://doi.org/10.1177/0363199005283010.

Trahman, C. R. "Odysseus' Lies (*Odyssey*, Books 13-19)." *Phoenix* 6 (1952) 31-43. https://doi.org/10.2307/1086270.

United Methodist Church. *The United Methodist Hymnal of 1989*. Nashville: United Methodist, 1989.

United States Census Bureau. "Parent/Child Family Groups with Children Under 18." Nov. 14, 2023, last updated Oct. 25, 2024. https://www.census.gov/library/visualizations/interactive/parent-child-family-groups.html.

———. "Parents' Living Arrangements." Nov. 14, 2023, last updated Oct. 25, 2024. https://www.census.gov/library/visualizations/interactive/parents-living-arrangements.html.

U.S. Const. art. II, § 4. https://constitution.congress.gov/browse/essay/artII-S4-4-1/ALDE_00000690/.

Van Rensburg, Fika J. "Sarah's Submissiveness to Abraham: A Socio-Historic Interpretation of the Exhortation to Wives in 1 Peter 3:5-6 to Take Sarah as Example of Submissiveness." *HTS Theological Studies* 60 (2004) 249-60. https://doi.org/10.4102/hts.v60i1/2.499.

Vespa, Jonathan, et al. *America's Families and Living Arrangements: 2012; Population Characteristics*. Washington, DC: United States Census Bureau, 2013. https://

www.census.gov/content/dam/Census/library/publications/2013/demo/p20-570.pdf.

Vine, W. E. *Vine's Complete Expository Dictionary of Old and New Testament Words*. Nashville: Thomas Nelson, 1996.

Wainwright, Geoffrey. "Ora et Labora: Benedictines and Wesleyans at Prayer and at Work." *Asbury Theological Journal* 50 (1995) 95–113. https://place.asburyseminary.edu/cgi/viewcontent.cgi?article=1367&context=asburyjournal.

Wallis, Arthur. *In the Day of Thy Power: The Scriptural Principles of Revival*. Fort Washington, PA: CLC, 2010.

Weil, Simone. *Gravity and Grace*. Translated by Emma Crawford. London: Routledge, 1986. https://cominsitu.wordpress.com/wp-content/uploads/2021/09/simone-weil-gravity-and-grace-2.pdf.

Wesley, Charles. "Forth in Thy Name, O Lord, I Go." 1749. In *Church Hymnary*, 529. 4th ed. Norwich, UK: Canterbury, 2005. https://hymnary.org/hymn/CH4/529.

———. "Gentle Jesus, Meek and Mild." 1767. In *The Songbook of the Salvation Army*, 793. St. Albans, UK: Salvation Army, 1986. https://hymnary.org/hymn/SBSA1986/793.

Wesley, Susanna. *The Complete Writings*. Edited by Charles Wallace Jr. Oxford: Oxford University Press, 1997.

Willems, Roel M., et al. "Seeing and Hearing Meaning: ERP and fMRI Evidence of Word Versus Picture Integration into a Sentence Context." *Journal of Cognitive Neuroscience* 20 (2008) 1235–49. https://doi.org/10.1162/jocn.2008.20085.

Witherington, Ben, III. *Letters and Homilies for Hellenized Christians*. Vol. 1. Downers Grove, IL: IVP Academic, 2006.

Zodhiates, Spiros, and Warren Baker, eds. *The Hebrew-Greek Key Word Study Bible: King James Version*. Chattanooga, TN: AMG, 1991.

Scripture Index

HEBREW BIBLE/ OLD TESTAMENT

Genesis

1:26	280
2:15	176, 188, 357
3:16	256
4:21–31	257
12:1–9	251
12:1	259
12:10–20	251
12:15	259
12:16	251
12:19	252
15:6	258
15:13–16	279
16:2	253, 259
17:1	258
17:4	170
17:5	254, 259
17:6	170
17:7	170
17:11	170, 254
17:13	254
17:15	254
17:16	254
17:17	254, 258
18	110, 111, 145, 352
18:1–15	354
18:2	106
18:4–5	138
18:4	109
18:6	259
18:12	250, 257, 258, 259
18:13	106
19:2–3	137
20:13	259
21:6	254, 258, 259
21:8–10	257
21:12	257, 259
39	171
39:2–3	187, 356
39:2	171
39:3	171
39:4	171, 188
39:5	172, 188, 356
39:9	235
40:1	250
42:10	250
45:7	199
45:8	199
50:7	67

Exodus

3:16–18	67
20:12	149
20:17	173
29:30	171
32:32	38

Leviticus

19:34	113

SCRIPTURE INDEX

Numbers
11:17	67
12:3	302

Deuteronomy
23:15–16	195

Judges
19:19–20	138
19:20–21	138

Ruth
2:13	250

1 Samuel
1:15	250
2:1–4	141
2:11	171
3:1	171
13:17	171

2 Samuel
15:31	86

1 Kings
1:15	171
8:1–3	67
19:21	171

2 Kings
4:10	138
4:16	138
4:35–37	138

1 Chronicles
24:4–6	72

Esther
2:2	171

Job
1:21	300
2:10	211

Psalms
2	260
28	245
56:8	74
68	111
68:1	140
68:5–6	140, 354
68:6	140, 142, 143
124	59
141:2	73

Proverbs
9:10	81
15:1	47
18:21	284
22:28	97
23:22	147
31	136
31:13–19	249
31:13	145, 356
31:15	126, 145, 355, 356
31:20–21	126, 145, 355, 356
31:24	145, 356
31:25–26	145, 356

Ecclesiastes
3:20	213

Isaiah
28:10	229
28:27	321
42:1	306

Jeremiah
5:5	30
30:12	215

Ezekiel
33:1–7	58

Daniel
5:27	207

SCRIPTURE INDEX

7:9   69

Amos
5:24   296

Malachi
3:2   78

NEW TESTAMENT

Matthew
1:21   17
1:23   17
1:25   17
5:5   301
5–7   315
5:9   294
5:11   183
5:22   44
5:31–32   344
6:24   267
7:1–7   207, 357
7:1–5   192
10:34–36   296
10:42   6
11:29–30   32
11:29   302
12:18   306
12:50   200
15:2   67
18:3   212, 217, 358
18:15–20   335, 343
18:17   312
18:18   34
19:28   77
20:16   9
21:5   303
21:12–17   267
22:21   347
23:5–12   201, 207, 357
26:3   67
26:15   267
28:18   29

Mark
1:12   105
3:5   95
6:8   206
10:29–30   200

Luke
1:31   17
2:7   17
6:35   183
14:9   219
15:11–32   267
17:33   80
18:7   10
18:25   267
22:66–71   67
24:29–31   138

John
2:19   3
5:22   34
6:70   221
8:1–11   238
8:43   151, 152, 169, 356
10:9   243
12:24   294
13   111, 352, 354
14:1–2   243, 265, 358
15:13   78, 239
20:23   34
21:17   33
21:18   205

Acts
2   105
3:6   95
4:7   95
5:1–11   335
5:29   101
6   68
6:7   146
8:20–24   82
9:36   137
9:39   137
11:30   68
12:25   68

Acts (continued)

13:49	20
13:50	19
14	83
14:23	65, 68, 329, 345
15	343
16:6–10	1
16:12–14	137
16:14	137, 145, 356
16:40	138
17:28	88
18:24	321
20	332, 342, 343
20:17	68
20:28–35	331
20:28	342
20:34–35	207
24:14	308
24:17–18	308
28	342

Romans

2:4	193
3:10	148
5:1	125
5:13	204
5:19	64
6:17	146
8:28	300
9:3	38
9–11	255
10:3	148
10:16	146
12:17–21	191
12:17	191
12:18	191
12:19	191
13	191–194, 302, 308
13:1–7	191
13:1–6	191
13:1–4	207, 347, 357
13:1	190, 347
13:2	190
13:4	190, 191, 193, 207, 357
13:5	183, 347
13:7–8	191
13:7	191
13:8	191, 349
13:9–10	191
13:10	191
13:17	193
16:17	307, 312

1 Corinthians

5:1–5	335
5:3	35
6:15–20	218
6:18	235
7	123
7:6	125
7:12–13	124
7:15	124, 126, 355
9:14	342, 346
11:7	281
13:13	214, 217, 358
15:32	91
16:17	198

2 Corinthians

2:13	12
3	281
3:18	281
4:2	219
7	12
7:5–7	12
7:13–16	13
8:6	13
8:16	13
12:9	301
12:14–15	36
12:18	16
13:10	86, 92

Galatians

2:1–5	2
2:3	1, 17
2:4	278
3:2	278
3:11	278
3:13	278
3:16–18	278
3:19–28	279

3:28	279	**Colossians**	
4:9	279	1:20	294
5:19–21	309	3	111
5:22–23	106, 302	3:9	347
5:26	302	3:10–11	353
6:1–3	82	3:10	114
6:1–2	334	3:14	114, 353
6:6	346	3:17	112, 352, 353
		3:19	115, 355
Ephesians		3:20	147
1:13	106	3:21	128
2:16–17	125	3:22	348
3:14–15	131	3:24	177, 188, 357
4	111	4:1	190, 348
4:2–3	302		
4:24	114, 353	**1 Thessalonians**	
5	111	1:3–4	212
5:2	114, 353	1:3	214
5:18–21	105		
5:18	106, 352	**2 Thessalonians**	
5:21	105, 253, 352	1:8	146
5:22	125, 348, 355	2:6	193
5:25	115, 248, 354	3:6	312
5:26	115, 354	3:14	146, 312
5:27	115, 354		
5:28	115, 355	**1 Timothy**	
5:31	115, 355	1:20	33
6:1–3	146, 348	2	112, 353
6:1	169, 356	2:1–2	349
6:2	169, 356	2:1	347
6:4	115, 127, 133, 348, 355	2:2	274
6:5	172, 188, 348, 356	2:8	80, 128
6:6	175, 188, 357	2:9–10	219, 229, 358
6:8	177	2:9	179
6:9	189, 207, 348, 357	2:10	179
		2:11	181
Philippians		2:12	181
2:12	173	2:13	181
2:15	96	3	342
2:17	39	3:1–7	344
2:25	198	3:2	104, 105, 209, 329, 330, 331, 332, 346
2:30	198	3:4–5	330
3:10	3	3:4	274
3:19	219	3:6	331
		3:7	331

1 Timothy (continued)

3:8–16	68
3:11	221
3:15	130
3:16	333
4:12	96
5:5–6	349
5:8	131
5:13	134
5:14	134, 136, 145, 285, 356
5:17–22	335
5:17–18	346
5:17	68, 342
6:1	177, 188, 357
6:3	285
6:4	285
6:5	285
6:9	206
6:10	206

2 Timothy

1:2	17
1:7	210
2:21	196
2:22–23	196
2:24	294
2:25	82
3:2	209, 221
3:5	312
4:2	87, 342
4:7	320
4:8	77
4:11	196

Titus

1	83
1:1–9	91
1:1–4	6
1:1–3	7
1:1	8
1:2	10, 90
1:4	1, 7, 9, 14, 17, 19–20
1:5–16	6
1:5–9	6, 7, 344
1:5	6, 27–32, 62–63, 68, 345
1:6	104, 329, 330, 346
1:7	38–44, 50–52, 67, 330
1:9	71–77, 331
1:10–16	6, 8
1:10–11	84
1:10	5, 11, 84, 86, 90
1:11	8, 87, 91
1:13	8, 84–88, 86, 92, 96, 210
1:16	87, 90
2	111
2:1–15	6
2:1–10	91, 95, 97, 104
2:1–2	6, 7
2:1	90, 95–96, 353
2:2	92, 96, 104, 189, 208, 214, 216, 217, 357, 358
2:3–4	225
2:3	6, 7, 104, 210, 218, 229, 358
2:4–5	6, 7, 120, 134, 230
2:4	125, 127, 210, 355
2:5	104, 126, 136, 145, 209, 231, 242, 249, 265, 355, 356, 358
2:6–8	6, 7, 266
2:6	146, 209, 285, 359
2:7	96, 104, 285, 359
2:8	285, 359
2:9–10	6, 7, 170
2:9	177, 188, 357
2:10	96, 104, 188, 357
2:11–15	6, 91
2:11–14	112
2:11	8
2:12	8, 88
2:13	8
3:1–11	6
3:1–7	6
3:1–2	192
3:1	286, 347
3:2	289, 302
3:5	8
3:8–11	6

3:8–9	305	3:9	293
3:9	5	3:13	293
3:10–11	8, 305, 306	3:18	125
3:10	8	4:3	320
3:11	311	5:16	82
3:12–15	6		
3:12	5, 6, 10, 318		
3:13	320		

Philemon

1:2	195
1:8–11	194
1:10	194, 195
1:11	194, 198, 207, 357
1:12–14	194
1:12	196, 197
1:13	194, 197
1:15–17	194
1:15	198, 199, 207, 357
1:16	195, 207, 357
1:18–19	194
1:18	195, 198

Hebrews

3:12–13	335
3:19	2
4:12	296
5:8	186
5:9	146
9:10	62
11:8	146
11:11	251
12:2	219
12:5–17	335
13:2	138
13:15	74
13:17	346

James

1:19	344
1:21	300
3	292
3:1	203
3:4	292
3:6	292
3:8	292

1 Peter

1:3–12	121
1:8	322
2	111
2:1–12	126, 355
2:11–12	113
2:11	113, 114, 259, 353
2:13	113, 253, 347
2:17	259, 286
2:18	182
2:19–20	126, 188, 355, 357
2:19	182
2:20	183
2:21	185
2:23	185
2:24–25	255
2:24	255, 259, 265, 359
3:1–2	259
3:1	126, 252, 265, 355, 358
3:2	125, 250, 355
3:3–4	125, 355
3:4	250
3:6–7	256, 259
3:6	123, 250, 251, 258, 265, 348, 359
3:7	115, 256, 347, 355
3:14	184
3:17	184
4:12–14	187
4:14–15	184
5	342
5:1	68
5:2–4	77
5:2–3	203
5:2	342, 343
5:5–6	348
5:8	332, 343

2 Peter

3:1	120–121

2 John

1:10–11	312

Jude

1:11	220
1:12–13	220

Revelation

1	83
1:2	70
1:9	70
2:10	77
3:4	71
3:5	72
3:12	193
3:16	193
3:17	220
3:18	220
3:21	69, 77
4:4	71, 342
4:10	79, 342
4:11	333
4:13	79
5:5	80
5:8	72, 73, 342
5:9–10	82
5:10	82
6:9	74, 78
6:11	74, 78
7	83
7:11	71, 72
7:13–14	78
7:14	72, 73
7:15	73
8:3	74
8:5	74
11	83
11:17–18	80
12:17	70
14:2	73
15:2	73
19:10	70
19:14	79
20:4	69, 77, 343
21:12–14	72

www.ingramcontent.com/pod-product-compliance
Lightning Source LLC
Chambersburg PA
CBHW070009010526
44117CB00011B/1473